# MICKEY NEWBURY

## CRYSTAL & STONE

By

**Joe Ziemer**

ISBN: 1-4140-7808-0 (e-book)
ISBN: 1-4184-2794-2 (Paperback)
ISBN: 1-4184-2793-4 (Dust Jacket)

First published by AuthorHouse 04/30/04

Library of Congress Control Number: 2004091291

This book is printed on acid free paper.

Printed in the United States of America
Bloomington, IN

# Table of Contents

# Preface

In 1966 we lived in Maracaibo, where Dad operated an exploration-logging firm to service offshore drilling rigs. Tom Jones was immensely popular then and there, and his *Funny Familiar Forgotten Feelings* dominated the airwaves. My Venezuelan buddies enjoyed "La Voz," and the structure of his hit seemed similar to the dramatic style of Latin ballads. Nevertheless, our rock and roll band - Los Hippies - did not perform the song, reserving it instead for soft guitars and four-string cuatros at midnight beach parties on moonlit Lake Maracaibo.

March of '68 found me in the Army at Fort Polk, Louisiana, mastering the mud-pit low-crawl. Guess you could say I had *Just Dropped In To See What Condition My Condition Was In.* Though the rocker moved me, black groups from my unit congregated on barracks steps to harmonize Temptations material. That was fine with me. Great music.

Fast forward to 1974... University of California at Davis... a church social... my friend Jerry Freeman takes the stage. Jerry played great guitar, possessed a nice tenor voice and is one of the most talented performers I've known. On that warm summer evening, he sang of "1912 in New York" and "Paris in the twenties" and "War is hell to live with." In the midst of the trilogy, a simple chorus - repeated twice - hit me like a sledgehammer, knocking me out of my chair: "We're all building walls / They should be bridges." The song surrounded me, lassoed me, and I am sure I turned a whiter shade of pale. As Jerry stepped from the stage, I stammered, "Wha... what in the world was that!" "A Mickey Newbury number," he smiled. *Heaven Help The Child."*

Though a starving student with family to feed, the following day found me in a local record shop, on a quest for anything Newbury. Rummaging through alphabetical LPs, executing the drill Newbury fans know well: Willie Nelson... New Christy Minstrels... There it was! Mickey Newbury. I grabbed them all; bought every Newbury album in the store. Paying quickly, I ran outside, jumped on my old ten-speed and went straight home. Cueing up *"Heaven,"* I sat back and closed my eyes. I have never recovered.

Something drew me to Newbury... an immediate, inexplicable connection. His musical style runs the gamut from country to folk to blues to bluegrass to easy listening to rock. He mixes genres in the same song, sometimes flavoring the tune with a dash of jazz or chamber music. Just as we use different tones of voice to communicate different feelings, so he varies genus to match subject, often of epic or operatic proportion. His melodies

v

carry simple words, easily remembered rhyme patterns with as many meanings as would be listeners. Riding the melody to deliver the lyric is that incredible voice... a haunting angelic tenor, boyishly young yet wise with wisdom. On that California evening in 1974, I realized the man's ability to transcend musical spheres made him great. But something else drew me to Newbury. He sounded familiar plus the poetry made it clear he knew where I lived. I was simultaneously shocked and hooked.

A few Newbury releases materialized in record bins during the late seventies and I snatched them up. His material disappeared for almost a decade, and many fans thought he had departed the industry, perhaps the world. Then, in a new age - in the late eighties - I stumbled on his first CD. Pictured on the cover was an older Newbury, but glory hallelujah, the man was still here. After that... another hiatus until the mid nineties.

Meanwhile, my wife Roxanne and I had started a company that supplied broadcast equipment to worldwide radio and TV stations. We promptly hired a firm to set up our online computer network. After the installation was completed, a technician began teaching us how to navigate the worldwide web. Starting on a search page, he asked, "Anything you'd like to search for?" "Yes," I said, and typed in "Mickey Newbury."

A few keystrokes and voilà, we were on Newbury's website. I could not believe that a cyber-gathering place existed with so many Newbury friends. In a few days, I was corresponding with him. In a few weeks, he telephoned. We talked many times for many hours, and we became friends. Though I tried, he would not let me hold him in awe. Then we met and I caught his final public performance at the Songwriter's Festival in Gulf Shores.

Concurrently, I began to research Mickey Newbury, and that early study yielded positive results. First, I compiled a list of songs written by him, which had been covered by other artists. Initially containing 126 covers, the living list has eclipsed the 670 mark. Second, while hunting for the recordings, I came across a mountain of intriguing information. Added to correspondence and conversations with Mickey, the total experience motivated me to write a 6,000-word <u>Goldmine</u> article in June of 2000.

We continued to talk on the phone... for hours... about everything. We would see each other at a reunion in Oregon. A year later, I would visit him in his Springfield home. And then all too quickly, he was gone. But oh the legacy...

Knowing Mickey and many of his friends inspired me to write this book, though some folks may not appreciate it. His good friend, Larry Jon Wilson, wrote, "What Mickey was as a song crafter now belongs to the world of

Chroniclers. I wish them a tiny fraction of his eloquence when they try to describe him." Larry Jon is right. Newbury is so loved... stripping away the myth... explaining the myth... is difficult and dangerous. Mickey was tough, loyal, funny, friendly, fragile, fearless, stubborn, obliging, intelligent, opinionated, sophisticated, well-read, open-minded, tender-hearted, spiritually perceptive, a country boy, a family man, a rambler at heart and perhaps bipolar. He was Complex.

Distinguishing truth from fiction is often easier said than done. Personal agendas, individual bias and the aberration of time can shroud the subject in a Halloween costume. Every attempt has been made to unveil the subject. In some instances, three sources were established to triangulate the truth. Interpolation - estimating a value that *lies* between known values - was minimally and cautiously employed. Perceived balance was not automatically a goal, nor should it be.

Due to the complexity of the subject, several others were recruited to speak here. More than 200 friends, critics, peers and family members are quoted, and each person presents his or her truths about the man. In the end, oak, maple and pine become a forest, and we are left with a broader view. In consideration of what has been amassed and amalgamated, the <u>Goldmine</u> piece was shabbily written.

Mickey entered into a contract in the mid nineties to have his biography written by another writer. Though that book is undelivered, the agreement remains in place; and therefore, as Mick was a man of his word, this work must be labeled "unauthorized." Research methodology, content and context were unaffected. The Herculean project was strengthened by our mega conversations, and his support is the book's foundation.

A world of thanks is due Mickey's family, especially wife Susan and mother Mamie, two lovely ladies who answered all my questions and repeatedly reviewed the manuscript for accuracy. We must tip our hats appreciatively to cousin Doug Byrd for providing detailed genealogical information. We are indebted to my friends Martin (Marty) Hall, Ron Lyons and Roy Stamps. For indispensable counsel, I am grateful to Mike Lopresti, Senior Writer for Gannett News Service. And Jerry Freeman, God bless you for turning me on to Mickey's music in the first place. I owe you a champagne dinner.

Nietzsche said, "Without music, life would be a mistake." I'm not so sure about that. I believe, however, that music is unequaled in painting human emotions, and nobody has pulled that off better than Mickey Newbury. Initially he wanted to be a painter. Well... Mickey... you succeeded way beyond your Texas teenage dreams.

How does the da Vinci of music grab you?

*To my children - Donovan, Jamie, Kristopher, Joey and Megan:*
*Please don't ever give up.*

# Foreword by Martin Hall

I can conceive a no more impossibly difficult challenge than to attempt to capture in writing the life of Mickey Newbury. For those of us blessed to have known him, to have been touched by him, even attempting to capture our feelings about him and his music, is, in its essence, impossible.

<u>Mickey Newbury: Crystal & Stone</u> comprehensively chronicles Mickey's life, his work and his humanity. There is no easy way to tell the story, as author Joe Ziemer is first to attest. Yet he beautifully tells the story, interweaving time, experience, music and poetry, both in his words and in the in the words of Mickey and those who knew him.

Mickey Newbury was a singer and songwriter of uncommon and timeless quality. He had a career of considerable accomplishment, and he was recognized by peers as being among the very best of the very best. Yet the sheer weight, rewards and pressures of his career did not deter him from holding most closely what he most valued: his family, his craft and his friends.

His life was a fine, multi-faceted gem. Some facets were brilliant and clear, some were dark and obscure, and each was an ever-changing miracle unto itself. It is impossible to listen to his music and not be affected, moved to and by those parts of our experiences both in the sunshine and in the darkness of our life journeys. It is not simply that he wrote of those places in our hearts; it is that he wrote *from* those places in our hearts. Somehow in listening to his music, our joys and our sorrows and Mickey's joys and sorrows become joined in spirit, and if only for a few moments, Mickey and we are not alone.

Mickey Newbury was thoroughly, genuinely decent. Humble, inclusive and kind, Mickey did not seek to diminish anyone. It is fair to say that only his decency as a human being stands above his musical mastery. And that is a fine, fine comment about any man.

For those who knew him, reading his story will be a coming home of sorts, a time to commune with the experience it was to be in his presence. For those who never had the privilege of knowing him, <u>Mickey Newbury: Crystal & Stone</u> offers a glimpse of a true American treasure, and a very fine man.

# Prologue

They came to Gulf Shores from 27 states and from as far away as England and Australia. Waiting for the Flora-Bama to open its doors, an eclectic clan impatiently stood in line: a banker, a biker, a farmer, a lawyer, a homebuilder, a photographer, a missionary, a defense contractor, a music box maker, a drunk. What homing signal drew these birds of a different feather thousands of miles to a honky-tonk lounge? The first 154 would be rewarded with catbird seats to a venerable venue. Mickey Newbury was appearing on center stage.

Meanwhile, line mates talked about Newbury. They spoke of how four of his songs simultaneously conquered different record charts... how his compositions were interpreted by scores of disparate artists... how he helped launch careers for Kenny Rogers, Kris Kristofferson and Townes Van Zandt... how his groundbreaking albums were instrumental in expanding musical boundaries and changing Nashville's Old Guard... how he refused to sell out... how most people in line knew him and many knew him well. How sadly... the farmer mentioned... he was ill.

On that balmy evening in late 1999, Newbury's last public performance would not disappoint. While taking oxygen, the man sang his heart out, and throughout the two-hour marathon, there was not a dry eye. As usual, the warm tenor delivered simple words seamlessly wrapped in emotional packages, and when he was done - when he couldn't go any more - the village people reacted. They stood and cheered and screamed and cried for 10 minutes. He reached everyone... the missionary and the defense contractor and the drunk. They were all Newbury'd.

Peers say he possessed exceptional skill, talent bordering on the uncanny. Newbury is frequently called a songwriter's songwriter **and** a singer's singer, highest possible accolades, mutually exclusive 99.999 percent of the time. Strange as it may seem, little is known of this extraordinary person. He was, to quote Kristofferson, "One of the most confoundingly complex bundles of contradictions..."

Bulls-eye. Newbury was uncategorizable. He was deep and many chroniclers failed to get a bead on him. His story is an intricate account of ups and downs, an emotional roller coaster. Like most rides, it starts at the beginning, in Newbury's case, at his roots. Retracing the tracks of his ancestors, then, is the first step to getting a handle on the Legendary Mickey Newbury. The "L" word, though, made him awfully uncomfortable. He preferred just *Newbury*.

# Chapter I: *Nary A Newbury*
## 1600 - 1939

The early 1600's saw the beginning of a great tide of emigration from Europe to North America. Spanning more than three centuries, this movement grew from a trickle of a few hundred English colonists to a flood of millions of newcomers. Most European emigrants left their homelands to escape political oppression, to seek the freedom to practice their religion, or for adventure and opportunities denied them at home. Impelled by these powerful and diverse motivations, they built a new civilization on the northern part of the continent.

The first English immigrants to what is now the United States crossed the Atlantic long after thriving Spanish colonies had been established in Mexico, the West Indies and South America. Like all early travelers to the New World, they came in small, overcrowded ships. During their eight-week voyages, they lived on meager rations. Many died of disease; ships were often battered by storms and some were lost at sea.

> *The ship went down the captain drowned*
> *Do no good to cry*
> *THE SAILOR*

Few people could afford the cost of the trip to make a start in the new land. In return for passage, several colonists agreed to work under contract as indentured servants for four to seven years. Free after this term, they would be given freedom dues, sometimes including a small tract of land. It has been estimated that half the settlers living in the colonies south of New England came to America under this system of semi bondage. The arrangement carried no social stigma.

Throughout the 1600's and 1700's, Newburys sailed to America from England, Ireland and Scotland; accompanied by shipmates with surnames such as Gandy, Woollums and McAloon. A few Newburys came as indentured servants and worked diligently for freedom dues. Seeking a land where they might shape their destinies, Newburys settled in Virginia, North Carolina, Connecticut, Massachusetts, Rhode Island, New York and New Jersey.

*Let me be a shelter from this cold and angry world*
*A bridge that will not burn a tree that will not sway*
*A ship that rides the morning wind*
*With all its cloth unfurled*
*But one that will not take you where you cannot stay*
*SAIL AWAY*

The name Newbury comes from the Old English words for new (nēowe) and borough (burg). A borough is a town that has been formed into a legal corporation and is self-governing. So "Newbury" signifies a new (fresh, original or innovative) town or community that governs or directs itself.

Striking self-determination is a common thread throughout Newbury history. In 1706, Henry Newbury and family were registered as Quakers with the Newport Society of Friends. Founded in England in the 17th century, the Society is a Christian denomination that is committed to pacifism and rejects formal sacraments, ministry, and creed. Other Newbury men worked as lawyers, carpenters, physicians and a few served as Christian ministers.

Before long, the early settlers would be requested to fight for the precious independence that had brought them to America. Taxation without representation - or paying the king's piper without having creative control - played against a basic reason why many immigrants had left their homelands. The infuriating issue eventually escalated to a general call-to-arms.

The revolutionary government swiftly seized upon the generous supply of land to accomplish recruitment goals. Bounty lands were a propaganda technique for enrolling support for the war among the citizenry and preventing them from lapsing into the British fold when the tide of battle ebbed. All were aware that to the victor belonged the spoils and that defeat brought no reward.

Certain of victory, the British soldiers were more than cocky. Even as they mocked the New Country bumpkins with endless rounds of *Yankee Doodle*, the settlers stole the tune, adopting it as a fight song. Armed with the infectious melody, a righteous cause and the prospect of winning their own addresses, an astonishing number of male colonists - two-thirds - fought in the Revolutionary War. Britain just did not believe so many colonists would battle so long and hard. The Redcoats also didn't know how to combat wilderness fighting... the unsophisticated hide, hit and run tactics. In the end, unyielding determination - held together by a dream, a song and a prayer - won the seven-year war for the new Americans.

Many Newburys participated and were rewarded. Eight years after Paul Revere's freezing ride, Andrew Newbury, a Continental soldier, was awarded bounty land in Tennessee; and Samuel Newbury was granted property in Virginia.

Contributing to America's population of 3.9 million, Mickey's **Great-Great Grandfather**, Thomas Newbury was born in 1790 in Wilkes County, North Carolina. Located 30 miles west of Winston-Salem, the region was home to a large number of Native Americans. Several Cherokee tribes in the area and the U.S. government had recently come to terms through The Treaty of 1785. Article XIII of that accord reads, "The hatchet shall be forever buried and the peace given by the United States, and friendship reestablished between the said states on the one part, and all the Cherokees on the other..." Thirty-seven Cherokee chiefs signed the document with "X" marks...

Newbury's locale, Wilkes County, also was home to Tom Dula pronounced Dooley. Known far and wide for the ballad, *Tom Dooley*, Tom Dula was a bona fide person with a sweet tooth for the ladies and vice versa. Handsome and gifted with the fiddle, he was hanged for allegedly stabbing his lover in the heart.

Meanwhile, Thomas left North Carolina and ventured 300 miles west. In 1815, he married Polly Payton in Knoxville, and they settled on Indian Lands in the hills of northern Tennessee. (The word "Tennessee" may come from a Creek or Cherokee word meaning, "meeting place.") Now called Overton County, the pristine wilderness area was named after pioneer Nashville attorney, John Overton. In 1819, Overton co-founded Memphis with James Winchester and fellow Nashville resident, Andrew Jackson. The latter - "Old Hickory" - became the seventh President of the United States and is reportedly Mickey Newbury's distant cousin.

Like many Southern landowners of the era, Thomas and Polly owned several slaves. Together they worked their Overton plantation near the mighty Cumberland River that had delivered the earliest settlers to Nashville. But what about entertainment? Perhaps they made music. Men of different classes, from the wealthy to indentured servants and slaves, played violins or fiddles. So maybe Thomas was a fiddler. Instruments of choice for women included harps, guitars and harpsichords. English and Baroque ten-string guitars were replaced in America about 1820 with the introduction of the standard six-string. Perhaps Polly strummed the guitar while Thomas fiddled around. Maybe they sang about Tom Dula while the Cumberland River rolled on by.

Another voice was added to the Newbury band on September 30,1823, when Polly gave birth to Stephen C. Newbury, Mickey's **Great-Grandfather**. In 1832, Thomas and son Stephen traveled to Georgia to participate in a gold-land lottery. They were successful, walking away with a parcel of Georgia farmland. It was through these lotteries that land belonging to Creek and Cherokee Indians was distributed to the white man. The 1832 lottery gave the Cherokee Nation to Georgia settlers, and sparked the 1838 Trail of Tears, endorsed by President Jackson. Almost three-fourths of the land in present-day Georgia was distributed in this way.

When Thomas and Stephen first arrived in Georgia, an economic boom was spurring growth throughout much of the state. Railroads were beginning to move cargo in the area, and this forever changed the face of Georgia. From its beginning as a rowdy town of rail-hands and prostitutes, Atlanta, at a crossroads of rail systems, grew quickly to become a major producer of many manufactured goods. Times were good. Apparently too good.

Wild speculation in land, canals, roads and rails began a hyped ascension in 1833. It was far too easy to borrow too much money to purchase over-priced property. The balloon collapsed on economic expansion though, as euphoria turned to fear. At the onset of the Panic of 1837, American banks abruptly called in loans. Out of 850 banks, 343 closed entirely and 62 failed partially. The paranoid lack of confidence brought on one of the worst economic depressions in the nation's history. Lasting five years, Georgia suffered terribly until the mid 1840's. Nevertheless, in 1843, twenty-year-old Stephen married his nineteen-year-old sweetheart, Eliza Christian, and together they worked their forty acres of free and clear Georgia farmland.

> *Lord his daddy was an honest man*
> *Just a red-dirt Georgia farmer…*
> SAN FRANCISCO MABEL JOY

After a patient four years of marriage, Stephen and Eliza's first child, Rebecca arrived in 1847; and about that time, Stephen Foster wrote *Oh! Susannah*. Rebecca was followed by Noel Mathis in 1853, and Polly Ann in 1855. Another daughter, Tennessee, was born in Indiana in 1860 - one year before the Civil War began. The fifth child, a girl they named Texas was born in Tennessee in 1866 - one year after the war ended. One century later, Mickey Newbury's first child Joe would be born in Texas - while he was living in his car in Tennessee.

While Mickey's ancestors were building the family, railroad workers were busy laying tracks to support Georgia's burgeoning manufacturing and enormous cotton-textile industry. An Atlanta - formerly Marthasville - to Chattanooga interstate railroad link was completed in 1850; and by 1860,

Georgia had 1200 miles of track and the best rail system in the Deep South. The Newburys survived the Civil War by staying on the move... far away from skirmishes and battles. The Georgia train system probably saved their lives.

*Movin' like a midnight train through rainy Georgia*
*WISH I WAS*

Although the railroad may have saved their hides, the music lifted their spirits. Thousands of songs flooded the sheet-music market then, commemorating events, such as *The Flag of Fort Sumter*, and simple longing, such as *When Johnny Comes Marching Home*. "It was the beginning of the American songwriting industry," wrote Jan Swafford, author of Charles Ives: A Life With Music; "the country needed music to express their feelings."

The passions of the war created some of the nation's most enduring tunes. American slaves of the era adopted a Jamaican spiritual, a lament aptly titled, *All My Sorrows*. Yankees and Rebels claimed their own music, too, even if fathered by the other side. A Northern minstrel singer penned the South's beloved anthem - *Dixie*, and a Southerner scored the music for the North's New Testament prayer - *Battle Hymn of the Republic*. As a first step towards emotional unification, President Lincoln requested *Dixie* to be performed on the White House steps the day the war ended. He would be murdered three days later by a racist. One century later as an emotional encore, Mickey Newbury would unite the three pieces into one healing song of redemption.

Imagine living in the South following the devastation of the Civil War. Family belongings had been stolen or destroyed, and even family graves were dug up for treasure. Many wives and slaves were raped and killed. Everything dear had disappeared or been burned down. The apocalyptic destruction is graphically described in the Paul Kennerley song *They Laid Waste To Our Land* from the album, "White Mansions": "On November 15, 1864, General Sherman cut out the back of Atlanta with 68,000 hard-worn Yankees. He drove them down through Georgia to the sea. With hate in their hearts, they moved in a line, cutting a scar through God's blessed country, 50 miles wide; burning, looting gutting our land like vultures. They tore up the railroad tracks. They burnt the cotton and the gins. Lord, they made everybody suffer."

*She left me with ten acres of grow nothin' Georgia ground*
*BUGGER RED BLUES (THE TRUCK SONG)*

Property was gone and people in the Southland were starving. In 1866, Kentucky sent 100,000 bushels of corn to the famished Georgia populace. In neighboring Tennessee, ex Rebels formed an underground, reactionary organization as the Ku Klux Klan was born 75 miles from Nashville.

Under military government and Army enforcement, the Newburys tried to return to some semblance of their former lifestyle... but it was not possible. And so for good reason, Stephen and Eliza decided to leave their chaotic, burned-out state. By October of '69, one year after Georgia was readmitted to The Union, they had realized sufficient gain from farming and the sale of their property to load up the kids and move on. They headed west by covered wagon, singin' songs, whistlin' *Dixie* and dreamin' of a new land with good people and fair opportunity. They were tough folks, these western travelers, intent on beating the odds. They crossed Georgia, Alabama, Mississippi and Louisiana, cutting a pass through piney woods, searching for solid ground over treacherous swamplands; and finally they made it... into the heart of Texas, a state which had been annexed by the United States just 25 years earlier.

After 1,500 miles of prayer and 35 days on a wagon train, they arrived at a location 44 miles east of Austin, the state capital. Compared to Georgia, Texas was in great shape. The Civil War had the curious effect of rejuvenating the economy of Texas, mainly due to increased demand for the state's hardy longhorn cattle. On January 13, 1870, Stephen paid gold for 1,142-½ acres of prime cotton farmland in an unincorporated area of Texas, on the Old Spanish Road. About two months later, Congress readmitted the largest state into the Union. Stephen's land investment paid off in 1872 when the area was incorporated, and a new town was established; Paige was located at the site of a railroad water tower on the recently built Houston and Texas Central Railway.

Stephen and Eliza started selling land parcels, primarily to relatives and in-laws, and the piecemeal distribution continued for several years. Perhaps Georgia, Tennessee and North Carolina broods had pooled their funds so Stephen could front the initial land transaction. Or maybe they needed money.

Stephen and Eliza's sixth child, Stephen Jr., was born in 1874, three years before Thomas Edison patented the cylinder-playing phonograph. Tragedy struck the Newburys in 1881 when Eliza died unexpectedly. After 40 years of marriage, Stephen had lost his beloved wife. Two of six children were still at home, fifteen-year-old-Texas and seven-year-old Stephen Jr.

Needing a break, Stephen Sr. went to Illinois to visit his Uncle Joseph; and while there, he met Sarah Hawkins - Mickey's **Great Grandmother**.

6

Stephen was smitten by the lovely but tough, 100 pound, 4'11" blue-eyed brunette with beautiful dark complexion. Sarah was similarly impressed by the well-established, sixty-year-old Southerner. They shared stories, quickly discovering how much they had in common.

Stephen talked of Tennessee, Georgia and Texas, and Sarah told him about her life. She had been born in 1848 in Jefferson County, Field Township, Illinois - near Mt. Vernon. The area was rich in timber and good soil, and populated by a fair class of farmers. When she turned 16, she had married Levi Sims Howard. Three years later they had a son, John, followed by Alvira in 1871 and Elias in 1874. Their fourth child, Sims, a boy, was born in 1875, and Louise came in 1879. Tragedy struck in 1880 when Sarah's husband Levi died suddenly. Widowed at thirty-two, she desired a decent life for herself and five kids.

And so in 1882, Southerner and Northerner - Stephen and Sarah - were united in matrimony at her father's home in Illinois. Sarah and children subsequently packed up their pasts and headed west to Stephen's farm in Texas. About this time, Paige's population reached 500, and the town became a railroad-shipping center for cotton, cattle, hogs and produce. Times were good.

Stephen and Sarah - He nicknamed her "Sally" - began having children. The first child Mark came the year after they were married. Alonzo Brown - Mickey's **Grandfather** - was born in 1888, one year before the invention of the coin-operated phonograph. A third son, Write Stiles would follow in 1890. Sadly, Stephen and Sarah would have just 10 years together. He made his Last Will and Testament on October 24, 1891 and died about two months later, on January 12, 1892. Stephen was survived by many children.

> *HEAVEN HELP THE CHILD*
> *Heaven help the children to find their way*

Sarah remained behind as stepmother to Stephen and Eliza's six perhaps unfriendly children (ages 18 to 45); five had married, promptly adding several youngsters to the count. From her marriage to Levi, three of Sarah's kids were at hand (ages 13 to 18). What's more, Stephen and Sarah's three boys were just getting started; Mark was seven, Alonzo was four and little Write was a toddler of two. If that were not enough, she also had a farm to run.

> *His mama lived her short life havin' kids and balin' hay...*
> *SAN FRANCISCO MABEL JOY*

Soon afterwards, Sarah started seeing shadows or her accusers said she did, and she was admitted to the state hospital's senile annex on August 24, 1894. Senility can be defined as forgetful, confused, or otherwise mentally less acute behavior in later life. Sarah was 46, young for classic senility, though at this point she surely had memories better left alone. Losing two spouses, haggling with an army of demanding kids, slaving over acres of impatient cotton - such torment - would cause most souls to become "mentally less acute."

And so, "Sarah spent a good deal of her later life in the San Antonio and Austin State Hospitals (for the insane)... But I've heard stories that she wasn't really crazy at all. That she was committed by the children of Stephen's first wife (Eliza) so they could get their hands on her land... That sort of shenanigan was common practice back in those days. Relatives who visited her said she acted sane... and she made these wonderful quilts with tiny perfect stitching." Wherever the truth lies, Sarah spent the last half of her life institutionalized. On September 15, 1941, at age 93, Sarah Sally Howard Hawkins Newbury departed this world. Seventy-seven years earlier - on that exact date - she had married her first husband Levi. In other words, she died on her wedding anniversary.

A special thank you is extended to Doug Byrd, Mickey's first cousin (Catherine Louise's son - see below), for providing genealogical information and quotations used in this chapter. Doug wrote, "I visited the Ridgeway Cemetery (in Paige, Bastrop County) where so many (of our ancestors) are buried: Eliza (Stephen's first wife) with the tallest Newbury grave, Stephen in a very small one with a carving of two hands clasped in friendship, and that lonely unmarked grave down at the end of the line where rest the bones of (Great Grandmother) Sarah. I had passed through a torrential downpour to get there, but then the sun came out... But there were no flowers. On other people's graves yes, but nary a Newbury, 'cause nobody I spoke to in town remembered them."

The land "just dribbled away bit by bit. I don't think Stephen and Sarah's three boys wanted to be farmers anyway. They wanted to go where the money was. I don't think they had much luck." The youngest, Write Stiles, became a barber who enjoyed chewing tobacco and a game of poker. He married Olga Viola Valenta, a Bohemian. "Aunt Olga would take me with her to the Elk's club and set me up in front of a one-armed bandit with a handful of nickels."

Stephen and Sarah's firstborn, Mark, married Dora and moved to Brown County. Mickey's Grandfather Alonzo worked for the railroad and in later years, in the oilfield. In 1909, Alonzo married Lettie Bell Boyett of Louisiana *(LA)* and promptly moved to the Cajun state. Lettie Bell is reported to have

8

been a beautiful woman; "She appears to have been something of a fox." When they married, she was underage; but more appreciably, "It has been said that Old Man Bill Boyett and wife Mary Jane sold her to Alonzo, like an indentured servant."

*Destitution's child born of an LA street called shame*
*SAN FRANCISCO MABEL JOY*

Alonzo and Lettie Bell's first child, Leonard Sidney - "Skeet" - arrived in 1910, the year *My Old Kentucky Home* was a popular hit. He was followed by Milton Sims, Mickey's **Father**, on August 10, 1913, in Dido, Vernon Parish, Louisiana, 100 miles southeast of Shreveport. Five more children would be born in the next thirteen years: John Tom (JT), Darrell Leslie, Catherine Louise and Fred Hamilton.

During Milton's early years, the Santa Fe Railway operated a scheduled shelter stop in tiny Dido, where the coming and going of trains was the area's lone activity. Townsfolk could hear the iron horse whistle for miles, an incredible and unforgettable sound something of a cross between a dinosaur's yell and a chorus of pan pipes. They listened for the whistle, and it told them there was a way out, that freedom was just around the bend.

*Nothin' like a freight train*
*Get you to the city*
*HEAVEN HELP THE CHILD*

Milton spent his boyhood and teenage years in De Ridder and Leesville... tough west Louisiana lumber towns. At one point there were 11 sawmills in the Leesville area, including the second largest sawmill in the world. The KCS - Kansas City Southern - Railroad's arrival had helped to increase clear cutting of the remaining virgin pine... and helped to increase the area's hard labor workers. A boy growing up in such a redneck environment would need to become a tough guy... just to survive.

*Who growled, "Your Georgia neck is red but sonny, you're still green"*
*SAN FRANCISCO MABEL JOY*

Following the birth of their last child in the late twenties, Lettie Bell walked out on Alonzo and ran away with Red Hall the Bootlegger. Alonzo experienced his share of pain. His dad died when he was four; his mom was locked away incommunicado in a mental hospital, and the Mrs. had vanished with a high roller. The living nightmares must have taken their toll. "Alonzo was not the nicest guy in the world... until he got to be a sweet sad old man who rescued toys from garbage dumps and repaired them for little children. God, such stories... the poverty, all that, makes you want to

9

weep." If Milton's mother, Lettie Bell, found happiness with Red Hall, it was short lived. She was diagnosed with cancer and died a few years later.

In 1930, Lettie Bell resurfaced a few years before succumbing to her malignancy. She immediately moved five of the children - Milton, Darrell, JT, Fred and Catherine - to Kilgore, Texas. Oil had been discovered and there was money to be made. Kilgore had been established in the late 1800's with the arrival of the Great Northern railroad. A quiet farming community of a few hundred, it was forced into the media spotlight in 1930 with the discovery of a subterranean ocean of oil. In two weeks, the town's population exploded as 10,000 opportunists swarmed Kilgore from all over the world. By the late thirties, a forest of 1,200 oil derricks crowded together within the city limits, concentrated within one square block, The World's Richest Acre. Though Kilgore made millionaires of many men... not one was a Newbury. The family was however back in Texas.

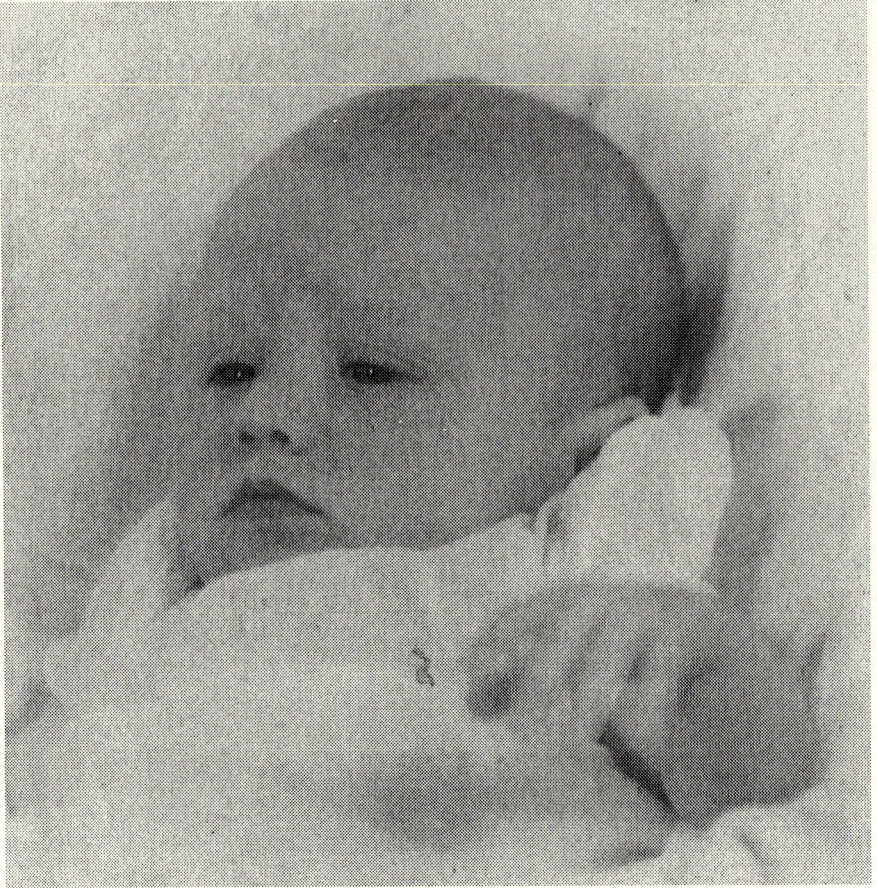

**Mickey at four months**

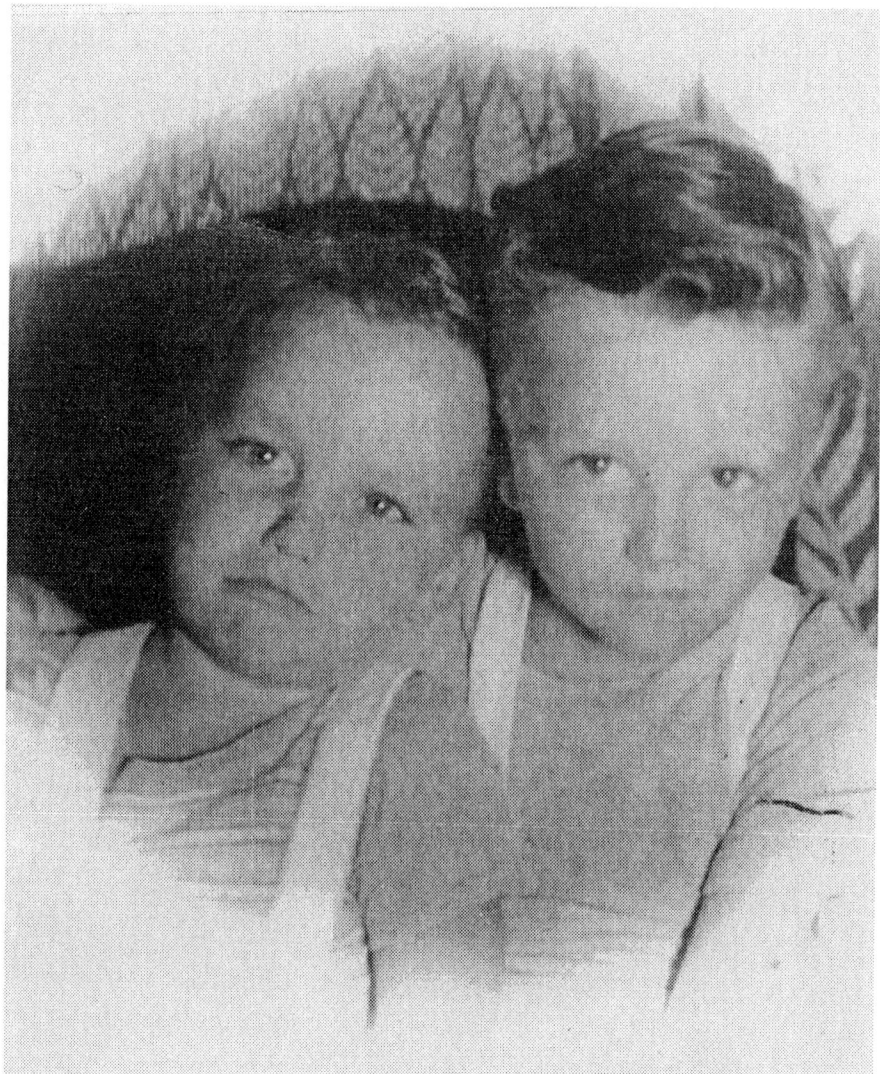

**Mickey at six (r) with brother Jerry at four**

**Mickey at six**

14

# Chapter II: *116 Westfield Street*
## 1917 - 1954

In 1917, a black military policeman stationed at Camp Logan in northwest Houston, complained to white policemen about their use of force in arresting a black woman. He was promptly pistolwhipped and thrown into the patrol wagon with the woman. When a second black MP tried to find out what happened, he was also beaten and jailed. Black troops from Logan learned of the incident, marched on the police station in Houston and an all night battle broke out. Eventually - after many people were killed - the National Guard restored order. Sixty-five black soldiers from Logan were sentenced to jail, some for life. State Congressmen used the disaster to demand removal of black troops from Texas, and Secretary of War Newton Baker ordered no more blacks to be inducted into the Army.

Along with racial discrimination, Houston's population roared into the twenties, reaching 138, 276, a jump of 75 percent since 1910. Blacks numbered 33,960 or one quarter of the total. Evocative of the Logan debacle, a local chapter of the Klu Klux Klan was formed. And then in one incredible ceremony, 2,051 Houstonians were inducted, meaning one of every twenty white men belonged to the Klan. Since the organization figures time by counting from its Tennessee inception (1866), the year 1921 would have been expressed as 55 AK (Anno Klan).

Reflecting the surge in population, the city was on the move. Building permits passed the $10 million mark, inaugurating an eight-year construction boom that created a new skyline in Houston. Local AM radio station WEV began broadcasting music and speeches for a few hundred receivers. The first radio station to endure, KPRC (Houston Post Dispatch), went on the air. Texas - then the biggest state - became the nation's greatest oil producer, with Houston as the world headquarters of petroleum commerce.

At the onset of the commercial activity, Mickey's **Mother**, Mamie Ellen Taylor, was born on December 11, 1920 in Chappell Hill, Texas. Born breach at 1-½ pounds, she was not expected to live. Refusing to let her die, Mamie's resourceful grandmother wet-nursed the tiny baby and placed her in a shoebox on the oven door, an incubator of sorts. Miraculously the child survived.

Chappell Hill - the place of Mamie's birth - was blessed with natural resources. The fertile land of the Brazos River with its abundant stands of

15

native cedar had drawn prominent families of the Old South to the beautiful pastoral landscapes. Located 57 miles northwest of Houston, the community boasted several sawmills, productive cotton fields, a railroad line and five churches. About 800 people lived in Chappell Hill when Mamie was born, and her father worked on the pipeline.

*Headed south to work a pipeline*
*Make some gage, Lord, in the meantime...*
*MOBILE BLUE*

During the twenties, blues and country music were incubating, too. In 1920, another Mamie - a Mamie Smith - made the first blues record by a black singer, and Westinghouse launched the age of commercial radio with the inauguration of Pittsburgh station KDKA. And then in 1924, the Singing Brakeman - Jimmie Rodgers - was diagnosed with tuberculosis. The irony of this development was bittersweet for the twenty-seven-year-old hard drinking, hard-living womanizer. The disease temporarily ended his railroad career, but gave him a chance to get back to his first love, making music. Negro railroad workers had taught Rodgers how to pick and sing, and in the process, country music married the blues. America's Blue Yodeler was on his way.

Country music was given a prominent stage in 1925 when Nashville became well known for its live radio broadcast, Barn Dance, later sarcastically nicknamed the Grand Ole Opry. Beginning as a business platform for National Life and Accident Insurance Company to hawk its services (hence WSM - "We Shield Millions"), the program provided entertainment from the local pool of white Christian folk singers and fiddlers.

While the Opry was being created, Christian fundamentalists and Darwinian evolutionists squared off just down the tracks in tiny Dayton, where public school teacher J.T. Scopes was charged with violating Tennessee House Bill No. 185, teaching evolutionary theory. The peaceful Cumberland Mountains community was transformed overnight into a circus of caged apes, hotdog stands, Holy Rollers, colorful banners and hawkers of biology texts. Tempers boiled over for two hot weeks in July, as the Scopes Monkey Trial reached daily fever pitches. The upshot? Scopes was found guilty and fined $100; but more importantly, the Southern cannon would stand for four decades.

Another tiny Tennessee town would make history in 1927, when Bristol was visited by talent scout Ralph Peer. After negotiating an alliance with the Victor Talking Machine Company of New York, Peer went to the Appalachian community to find and sign hillbilly artists. Setting up state-of-the-art equipment in an empty furniture store, Peer hung old quilts on the walls as acoustic baffles. He then ran a line from a microphone to a steel needle, to cut the sound into a thick wax disk (thus the phrase "cutting a record"). Perhaps his most brilliant move was convincing the local newspaper to place a "notice" on the front page. "This worked like dynamite," Peer wrote, "and the very next day I was deluged with long-distance calls... Groups of singers who had not visited Bristol during their entire lifetime arrived by bus, horse and buggy, train, or on foot." He spent the next two weeks recording 76 songs by 19 different hillbilly, string band and gospel groups. Often called the Big Bang of country music, two recordings featured the Carter Family and Jimmie Rodgers.

When the 78's featuring Rodgers, the Carter Family and other Bristol session performers were released that fall by Victor, the buying public went wild, and soon the label was selling hundreds of thousands of records. Targeted to rural audiences, the music was marketed through mail order catalogues such as Sears and Roebuck. It was the first national distribution and the first major commercial success for old-time tunes, also called hillbilly and, later on, country - those sentimental heartfelt songs about the things rural folks had in common, such as love or suffering.

Whatever the genre might be called, it had its first superstars, and the country music industry was launched. Many new stars appeared on the Opry and the show's popularity soared. Jimmie Rodgers and his trademark twelve-bar blues quickly became a mainstay for many Southerners; and though he never appeared on the Opry, he would be hailed as the Father of Country Music. Nashville would be proclaimed Country Music Capital of the World, and recording studios would soon establish themselves along Music Row just west of downtown.

On September 29, 1929, the American stock market collapsed. In a single day, on Black Tuesday, 16 million shares were traded - a record - and $30 billion vanished into thin air. While despondent businessmen were leaping out high-rise windows, Houston continued to expand. It became the largest city in Texas in 1930 with a population of 292,352, a rise of 111 percent over 1920. Blacks remained the largest minority, numbering 63,337. Throughout the depressed thirties, 780 people per month came to Houston seeking employment. All discovered the same thing... a new significance for the word home.

Some migrated to Houston to escape the Dust Bowl. Extensive farming and prolonged drought caused the soil to be blown away by the wind, forming huge dense clouds of dust. In 1935, the drought and dust that had destroyed 35 million acres swept the Texas panhandle. It was the worst dust storm of the era. Some referred to it as "the end of the world."

Many impoverished farming families made their way west along Route 66 - The Dustbowl Highway - to the oil and crop fields of California. Woody Guthrie was with them, the half-million Okies, and sang of their plight: "The police at the port of entry say / You're 15,000 for today / If you ain't got the do-re-mi... You better go back to beautiful Texas / Oklahoma, Kansas, Georgia, Tennessee." John Steinbeck wrote of their travails in the great American novel, The Grapes of Wrath. But not all refugees went west. Many headed south to Houston.

Mamie's family, the Taylors, had long since relocated to Wellborn. The Texas town of 200 inhabitants was originally a construction camp of the Houston and Texas Central Railroad. As Roy Acuff was polishing his fiddling and singing skills in a traveling medicine show, the Taylor's joined the southern migration. In 1932, they moved from Wellborn 100 miles to the northern outskirts of Houston, settling close to Camp Logan. Mamie was 12. Thousands of country folks were moving into the city then. "There were lots of people like my family," Mickey explained, "who couldn't make it in farming so they moved to the city." They were simply trying to stay alive.

Hunger often outweighs obedience of the law, and the Newburys were not an exception. Attempting to put food on the table, Milton was arrested one evening for allegedly stealing tires. The rest of the story though... he took a fall for his cousin and was promptly sentenced to three years imprisonment.

> *He turned twenty-one in a grey rock federal prison*
> *The old judge had no mercy on that Waycross Georgia boy*
> *SAN FRANCISCO MABEL JOY*

Milton was sent to Eastham Prison Farm, an over-crowded model of Texas Justice, where inmates were subjected to grueling physical labor for up to 16 hours a day, and it was common practice to beat inmates to death with baseball bats. Eastham had gained infamy when Texan Clyde Barrow - of Bonnie and Clyde fame - was sentenced there in 1930. Time in The Bloody Ham "changed Clyde from a schoolboy to a rattlesnake." Located on 13,040 acres in north Houston County, roughly 50 percent of The Ham's prisoners were white, 40 percent were black and 10 percent were Mexican American.

> *I'm spendin' time on the EASTHAM PRISON FARM*
> *I'm spendin' time on the EASTHAM PRISON FARM*
> *My clothes are ragged, my shoes are worn*
> *I cuss the day I was ever born*

*Spendin' time on the EASTHAM PRISON FARM*

*Workin' those fields from five in the mornin' till nine*
*Workin' those fields from five in the mornin' till nine*
*Workin' those fields from five till nine*
*Pickin' that cotton, got a long, long time*
*Spendin' time on the EASTHAM PRISON FARM*

*Pickin' that cotton, white cotton all day long*
*Pickin' that cotton, white cotton all day long*
*Puttin' that cotton in a seven foot sack*
*Got a twelve-gauge shotgun at my back*
*Spendin' time on the EASTHAM PRISON FARM*

Folks in these depressed days needed emotional relief. The popularity of country music increased then when many Southerners were leaving rural homes and migrating to the big city. The music was everywhere, spurred on by the popularity of the Grand Ole Opry and fueled by a need to lighten up. Just a generation or two off the farm, the new urbanites were full of nostalgia for hoedowns, fishin' ponds and other aspects of the life they'd left behind, including the songs they'd grown up with. About this time, Bill Monroe formed The Blue Grass Boys and soon introduced a foot stompin' get-with-it sub-genre of country music - bluegrass.

After what seemed an eternity in the Eastham hellhole, Milton was released in 1938 and headed south to Houston, where he found work as a truck driver. That was not all he found. While *Over The Rainbow* was dominating the airwaves in 1939, he met Mamie at a friend's house in Houston. Drawn to each other at once, they enjoyed music of country artists, such as honky-tonk star, Ernest Tubb and King of the Hillbillies, Roy Acuff. Above all, Milton loved the heart-wrenching songs of Jimmie Rodgers.

After Mamie graduated from Jeff Davis High School, Milton asked her for her hand. She accepted, and they were married in Houston on August 12 after knowing each other for seven months. Two weeks later - on September 1 - Germany invaded Poland, and then France and Australia declared war on Germany.

On May 19, 1940 - a Sunday - Milton Sims Newbury Jr. was born at Herman Hospital in Houston to parents Milton and Mamie. "He was a dry birth," Mamie advised, "and was born after 13 hours. Because it was a dry birth, I was rendered unconscious from all the medication. So I don't remember any of it. He was short and beautiful, with not blond, but gold curls. He weighed in at 6 pounds, 11-½ ounces. He was climbing at six months and talking at ten months."

Grandfather Alonzo, by then a railroad section chief, nicknamed the child. "I was born a junior," Mickey explained. "My Grandmother (Lettie Bell) named my Father and my Grandfather never cared for the name. The day I was born he named me 'Mickey' and no one in the family has ever known me by any other name." A few years later, Mickey would nickname Alonzo, "Pappydad." Mickey's middle name, Sims, had come down from Great Grandmother Sarah; it had been the middle name of her first husband, Levi. The Newburys resided then at 115 Wisenberger, seven blocks north of the railroad.

> *I was born in a shotgun shack that leaned against a railroad track*
> *I could hear a whistle blow all the way to Del Rio*
> *IN '59*

During the time of Mickey's birth, Winston Churchill became the British Prime Minister, and Holland surrendered to Germany. "Gone With The Wind" was in theaters, and Woody Guthrie was making his first recordings in New York. Bandleader Bob Wills was breaking concert attendance records with his brand of Western swing, spurred on by his signature song, *New San Antonio Rose*. Frank Sinatra launched his career with Tommy Dorsey's big band. *Star Dust* by Glenn Miller, *You are My Sunshine* and *When You Wish Upon A Star* were top hits. Minimum wage for an American worker was 43 cents per hour; average annual income was $1,925, and one gallon of gas cost 17 cents.

Houston continued to swell during these terribly depressed years. It ranked 21st in the nation with 384,514 people, a 31 percent increase over 1930. Cotton and oil remained the city's primary industries. Houston served as a location for 1,205 oil companies, which employed 40,000 workers - more than 10 percent of the city's population.

About the time Mickey started climbing, Lone Star native Ernest Tubb's *Walking The Floor Over You* became the earliest country hit to cross over to pop. Even Bing Crosby covered it. That was fine with Milton and Mamie, as they loved Tubb's music. Then two weeks before Mickey's second Christmas, the Japanese bombed Pearl Harbor, and the next day; President Franklin D. Roosevelt declared war on Japan.

A special playmate arrived for Mickey when his brother, Jerry Lynn Newbury, was born in Houston on April 18, 1942, while the Newburys were living at 8720 East Montgomery Road. Mickey easily summed up his relationship with Jerry, "Always was close to my brother. He's my best friend." To celebrate Jerry's arrival, Great Uncle Write Stiles - "Uncle Lucky" - gave Mickey his first haircut, and Mickey would "remember it as though it was yesterday." The number one song at the time? *Deep In The Heart Of Texas*. Also that year, RCA Victor sprayed gold over Glenn Miller's million-copy-seller *Chattanooga Choo Choo*, creating the first gold record.

On the day before Halloween, Roy Acuff, the Opry star soon to be anointed King of Country, and Fred Rose, the Tin Pan Alley writer (who would soon write *Blue Eyes Cryin' In The Rain*) formalized a partnership with a simple handshake. The accord created Acuff-Rose, Nashville's first music publishing house. Shortly thereafter, Bing Crosby released the song that would become the top holiday ballad, *White Christmas*. Needing more room, the Newburys moved to a bigger house on Basswood Street in early 1943.

> *I think I will sit in the shade today*
> *In this rockin chair my Daddy made*
> *When I was a little baby sittin' on his knee*
> *Shades of '43*
> *SHADES OF '63*

Meanwhile in Nashville, The Grand Ole Opry moved to the more spacious Ryman Auditorium, formerly the Union Gospel Tabernacle. Perhaps to commemorate the Opry's move, Mickey sang publicly for the first time in Houston. "He sang his first song at three years of age at church," Mamie explained. "When the Sunday school teacher asked him if he could sing *Jesus Loves Me*, his answer was, no, but he could sing, *Take Me Back And Try Me One More Time*. The teacher smiled and said 'that would be fine.' She told me about it and thought it was funny."

On the day of rest, Mamie, Mickey and Jerry donned their Sunday best to attend services at Airline Baptist Church, in Houston. Milton chose not to participate in the family's church-going activities. Mickey wrote, "I would hear the preacher tell how Sampson slaughtered thousands with the jaw bone of an ass... and I got the strangest little picture... in my mind... and I am quite sure... an equally confused look in my eyes." Though amusing through the eyes of a child, these early lessons provided a rock-solid Christian foundation on which Mickey would develop a profound spirituality.

> *LEAD ON your words are like a fire*
> *Although my body may be cold*
> *If I reached out in time and touched eternity*
> *I would find no other fire to warm my soul*

As Houston was hot as hell, the youngsters craved cool, sweet treats such as ice-cold soda pop and Blue Bell ice cream. "But," as Mamie explained, "money was tight. When Mickey was four, the ice cream truck used to drive down the street, ringing its bell, and Mickey would come running in the house, saying he wanted an ice cream. When I would tell him Mama couldn't buy him an ice cream, because I was broke, he would say, 'Well, fix yourself; I want an ice cream!'"

Milton and Mamie were trying to fix things. They were willing to try just about anything. Since truck driving paid poorly, Milton began rebuilding water heaters. Because of the war, it was almost impossible to buy a new one. In 1945, he entered a training program to become a licensed plumber. Eddy Arnold's *Cattle Call* and Bill Monroe's *Blue Moon of Kentucky* were riding the airwaves at the time. Little could Milton imagine that these celebrated and well-to-do singers would one day record his son's songs... and one of the songs would rise to become a Number One Hit. The Newburys could have used the money then.

*I can hear my Mama pray... prayin' for a better day.*
*I can hear my daddy say, 'Honey, I will find a way.'*
*He worked his fingers to the bone to make that shotgun shack a home...*
*IN '59*

Atomic bombs were dropped on Hiroshima and Nagasaki in August of 1945, bringing World War II to an end. Across America people celebrated and danced in the streets. For the first time in 15 years, optimism swept the nation, paving the way for enormous urban growth and prosperity. The year 1945 saw 43,280 freight trains move in and out of Houston, an average of 146 trains daily, or one every 10 minutes. If each train blew its whistle twice on arrival and departure, then every 2-½ minutes, a train would have sung out. The Singing Brakeman indeed.

A polio outbreak terrorized Houston in 1946, so to remove the kids from danger, Mamie took them to Mobile Bay, Alabama. They stayed six weeks with Mamie's brother-in-law and sister, Dean and Marie - Uncle Dean and Aunt "Ree." Mickey referred to the adventure as a vacation and fondly spoke of a sweet memory. When Dean's younger sister Laura returned home from work, she brought the boys a tasty treat, yummy candy red apples. This, and witnessing the chain gang working the road under shotgun supervision, left a lasting impression on young Mickey.

*Rich man, poor man, beggar or thief*
*First one gets you down the road*
*The others get you grief*
*Last one gets you ninety days of cotton pickin' peas*
*On the captain's farm*
*APPLES DIPPED IN CANDY, sweet potato wine*
*One is for your belly; the other's for your mind...*

Milton completed the licensed plumber course, and his income increased immediately. Soon afterwards, the Newburys were able to afford a nicer place. They moved into a pale green house with light colored brick wainscot at 116 Westfield Street. "We had this house in Houston just a few blocks from Mickey's school, Roosevelt Elementary," Mamie said. "The house had two bedrooms, so Mickey and Jerry shared a bedroom until they became teens. Our house had a huge, great big living room. When we first moved there, we didn't have television, so we use to listen to the radio. We had this big ol' screen porch on the front... Was about a 14 x 20... and we spent hours and hours out there... All of our friends came over."

*Here, on this street, is the house that once sheltered us all.*
*Oh, I can still hear the laughter that once followed me down the hall.*
*116 WESTFIELD STREET*

Six-year-old Mickey was exposed to the Tex-Mex culture in the new neighborhood. "There was a Mexican family down the street from us," explained Mamie. "They had eight girls and one boy, and our kids and their kids all played together, and we mothers babysat for each other. The mother's name was Renalda Martinez and the oldest girl's name was Rena May."

Mickey's future wife, Susan Pack, was born in Hollywood, California on July 13, 1947. Her mother worked as a professional entertainer. Mickey's uncles were also entertainers, or at any rate, amateur musicians. "My uncles," he explained, "all played and one of them had a band. I grew up humming and singing just like anybody else that likes music." Mamie recalled, "When he was about seven, he wanted to take violin lessons at school, so I went and bought him this little ol' junior-size one. And his daddy whistled all the time, you know, so he'd started tryin' to do that thing. His daddy would just almost go bonkers." Mickey remembered, "I got as far as *Twinkle, Twinkle, Little Star*, which I haven't played since age seven!"

"We lived in North Houston," Mickey continued, "a short distance from the railroad tracks. I remember Dad sitting on the front porch whistling the blues when he would get the blues... a poor man's harmonica. It seems his whistle was as lonesome as a train rollin' at midnight when you longed to be at another place." Milton enjoyed whistling the tunes of his hero, the Singing Brakeman.

*Would you pick another sad song for me Jim?*
*HEAVEN HELP THE CHILD*

"I grew up near the tracks," Mickey continued, "and there are many reasons why I fell in love with trains. The track could make a penny larger than a silver dollar so... I assumed it should be worth more! Like so many others... it was symbolic of a way out of town. Adventure... all those names of places I had seen only in the picture shows... That Whiiisssssstle that could be heard for 50 miles... comin' and goin' and the way it would tear at your heart... the world's largest harmonica! Last but not least... when you were able to... at last... board one; it was all you hoped it would be... and more." Good for the heart and soul, trains offered North Houstonians the dream and opportunity to leave the flatlands, hence Newbury's observation: "Only a flatlander can truly understand a train song."

Many Houstonians wanted to leave the flatlands - and for good reason. When Louis Armstrong was forming the All-Stars in 1947, establishing himself as America's jazz ambassador, North Houston's tough neighborhoods consisted of poor white, black and Mexican families. Though the FBI recommended 2.2 patrolmen for every 1,000 people, Houston had .93 per 1,000, and the city's official homicide rate reached 24.4 per 100,000 residents. Perhaps the expression "Houston we have a problem" originated during these perilous times.

Although documented as an extremely dangerous area, North Houston's tri-ethnicity exposed Mickey to country, R&B, jazz and Mexican music at an early age. The music that helped shape his writing reflects the diversity of his precarious birthplace, in the largest and only state to serve under six colorful flags.

Houston had doubled its size by 1948 to almost 75 square miles through annexation of neighboring areas, and it ranked as the fastest growing city in the United States. Houston Port became number two in the nation in tonnage handled, ranking only behind New York. The LP (long-playing record) was introduced, and the first TV station - KLEE - was on the air in Houston. Since the Newburys could not afford a TV, Mickey said, "We'd all go to the movies every Saturday and I dug those western movies with the cowboy songs. Roy Rogers and Gene Autry stuff."

Rogers influenced Mickey and a nation of youngsters. He gave society the Code of the West and the Cowboy, a Good Guy in a white hat when times were bleak. There were more than 2000 Roy Rogers Riders Clubs globally. Every member received a membership card with 10 rules to live by, such as be clean, love God and always obey your parents.

Mamie's "Firstborn" loved to please Mama, and she recalled a special memory. "Once, when Mickey was about eight, he attempted to sell magazines. If he could sell a certain amount, he would receive a juice

24

pitcher with serving glasses that he intended to give to me. Well, he came up a little short, and didn't win the juice set, and he cried. I told him that it didn't matter. That he was what mattered to me. And you know he always cried the biggest tears I ever saw. Five teardrops would about fill a teacup half full."

*Remember Mama when I was just a little boy*
*How sometimes late at night I would cry*
*You would take my hand and tell me stories*
*Until at last I would close my sleepy eyes*
*Well Mama TELL ME A STORY*

*TELL ME A STORY*
*You always seem to know the right things to say*
*Tell Me I'm dreamin'*
*Tell me I'm dreamin'*
*Mama make the hurt go away*

Yet when Mickey visited country relatives, he felt like a millionaire. "I grew up in the city, but when I visited all my kinfolks in Kountze, 90 miles from Houston, we're talking outhouse and no electricity... They lived on land that didn't belong to anybody... So I was exposed to two different worlds." The kinfolks in Kountze consisted of Aunt Jhonnie and Uncle Albert, on Milton's side; and they had eight children, three boys and five girls. Kountze, originally established as a Texas railroad town in 1881, is 28 miles north of Beaumont on US 69. The hot, piney area is home to the uninhabitable Big Thicket National Preserve, humorously discussed by Mickey in *Booger Red Rap*.

"We were real close growin' up, especially my cousins over in Kountze. I was really close to them, my aunts over there... I mean because that was some of the fondest times in my childhood, the times over there in the woods with them... I mean it was all very, very primitive, even when they finally got the well dug. I mean it was still pump. All of us would bathe in a damn washtub. You just hoped you weren't the 15th kid bathing, you know... And there was no electricity... All kerosene lamps and wood stove. It was a log house. I'd go back to the primitive if it was like that everywhere. I don't like the modern world. I think that it's not nearly as good." "Texas," observed John Steinbeck, "is a state of mind." Kountze is one reason why.

*Those heart-breaking, aching, eggs and bacon country songs*
*They take me back to hardwood floors, outdoor johns and mason jars...*
*HOW I LOVE THEM OLD SONGS*

25

*How I long to be in those East Texas woods.*
*I would be in those old piney woods if I could.*
*A LONG ROAD HOME*

To visit Milton's Aunt Nenee - shortened from Eúganie as it was easier to say - the Newburys drove to Shreveport, Louisiana. They listened to AM radio throughout the trip, that is, once they agreed on a station. "The boys always argued over which kind of music we were goin' to listen to," Mamie remembered. "Mickey wanted to listen to country music and Jerry wanted to listen to pop... Of course there was a real difference between music then..."

Like most school-age children, the boys came down with measles. Mickey's case was extreme, leading to encephalitis, an inflammation of the brain tissue usually brought on by stress and viral or bacterial infection. As the encephalitis worsened and he fell into a deep coma, Mamie prayed her firstborn would survive. After an eternity of four days, Mickey came out of it partially paralyzed, as is often the case. Miraculously he overcame the paralysis. Once immediate symptoms disappear, though, the long-term effects vary by individual. In Mickey's case, nine years would pass before the dragon emerged.

Two decades following the Big Bang, Hiram Hank Williams opened the golden age for honky-tonk with a string of seven hits. Concurrently but not coincidentally, RCA began producing the seven inch 45 rpm record. Mickey listened to Hank's debut performance on the Opry that year. He sang *Lovesick Blues* and sang and sang... to the tune of six encores. Like Jimmie Rodgers, a poor Negro had taught Williams how to play the guitar and sing.

Mickey probably turned on the radio in '49 to hear Margaret Whiting and Jimmy Wakely sing, *Slippin' Around*, Country & Western's first entry into the Top 10. Penned by Texan Floyd Tillman, the song helped usher in the social realism era of country songwriting. In short, it was the first cheating song to top the charts.

About this time, Mickey's pet raccoon that he had raised from a baby viciously turned on his Mom, biting her foot to the bone. "The raccoon wouldn't let go," Mamie recalled, "and blood was everywhere... and I was screaming!" After considerable effort, Milton wrestled the critter off Mamie and threw him into his cage. When Milton returned with his shotgun, Mickey begged him not to shoot it. After Mickey's pleading and Mamie's intervention, the raccoon was spared, a miracle as, "Mom cooked everything that moved: coons, blackbirds, possums, squirrels, catfish, armadillos..."

Houston continued to swell in 1950, to 596,163 people, a jump of 55 percent over 1940. Almost one quarter of the inhabitants were blacks, who lived as third-class citizens. More by custom than by law, blacks were barred from white establishments such as hotels, theaters, restaurants, public schools, colleges and hospitals. An ambulance designated for white patients would not transport an injured black citizen, even if he were bleeding to death. One sign that the Mexican American community had come of age was the inauguration of KLVL, Houston's first Spanish-language AM radio station. La Voz Latina quickly became the broadcasting voice of the local Mexican-American community. In June, the station announced, "Ha empezado la guerra con Corea." (The Korean War has begun.)

Mickey performed for the second time at age 10, and the producer's decision opened his eyes. "I took violin lessons as a child," he explained, "but I played so badly I was asked to sing instead at a Christmas show." Disappointed in his lack of progress, he told Mamie, "I don't believe I want to learn to play the violin anymore. Mama will you teach me how to play the guitar?" Mamie answered, "Son, I don't know enough. All I know how to do is just the major chords, you know, and accompany myself while I sing, but I'm not that good. (Mamie played guitar and harmonized with a blind man at gatherings, performing Roy Rogers and Bob Wills material.) But we bought Mickey a guitar. He learned himself. Shut himself up in his room, and he learned all his licks right by himself."

"Mickey was a real loving but temperamental child, and his dog 'Ducky' provided him with a great deal of comfort," Mamie explained. "He was easily led off, you know. Someone could talk him into almost anything... except for the fact that he knew he'd have to answer to Mama when he got home. So he was careful not to be led too far in the wrong direction." To ensure he was not led too far astray, Mamie made sure that Mickey and Jerry attended church every Sunday, where Mickey sang in the choir.

But Mickey was mischievous. "When I was 10," he swore, "I brought the great horned toad frog from Muskogee, Oklahoma to Texas. Now they're all over Texas!" Whether or not cause and effect can be determined, this is amusing, and perhaps when Texans hear the horned toad sing his eerie song, they'll think of Newbury.

Also when he was 10, something happened to tell of times to come. "They gave Mickey a tuberculosis test at school," Mamie explained, "and it was positive. I took him to a private doctor, and the doctor said it was not TB, but the respiratory problem that he had... He always had respiratory problems..." About the time Mickey was being examined, the parents of his future wife, Susan Pack, moved the family from Hollywood, California to Eugene, Oregon. Susan was three.

27

In 1951, Jackie Brenston's *Rocket 88*, often tagged as the first rock 'n' roll record, was released by Sam Phillips' Sun Studio. It would soon be covered by Rock 'n' Roll pioneer Bill Haley. Over the next two decades, artists and studios would deliver music with sweeping variations in structure and rhythm, while lyrical expression would radically change to reflect the era. Methods of delivery were changing also, with television soon to be in most every American's home.

"After we finally got television," Mamie said, "everybody in the country came over to watch wrestlin' on Friday nights." Twelve-year-old Mickey also watched the NBC program, "Ted Mack's Original Amateur Hour," the first top-rated TV show. Perhaps he fantasized about performing and winning as had a skinny, good-looking kid named Pat Boone. At the opposite end of the spectrum, when he preached to 60,000 people in Rice Institute Stadium, Billy Graham prophesized on live TV in 1952, "Most Houstonians will spend an eternity in hell."

While Graham was preaching, Mickey entered the seventh grade at North Houston's Burbank Junior High School. There he met classmate Martin Talmage Bell, and the two boys became friends. "I was a new boy in school and a country boy," Talmage explained. "Mickey took me under his wing and helped me. He was a very loyal friend. Mickey was overweight at this time, but he would soon outgrow it." The boys would remain lifelong friends.

A few months later, on January 1, 1953, television and radio covered a tragic story. At age 29, Hank Williams had been found dead in his car from alcohol and drug overdose. The Hillbilly Shakespeare tallied 11 Number One singles, 16 Top Five's and nine Top Ten's in a brief career; and after his death, his record sales soared. Mickey was stunned by Williams' death. Little did the twelve-year-old know how much these events would affect his future.

Reflecting the conservative early fifties, petticoats, pillbox hats, classic two-inch pumps and mind-numbing gray flannel suits were in fashion. Teenage boys sported clean crew cuts, while the girls arranged buns or ponytails, depending on the occasion. As for music, radio's offering of innocuous American pop - Kay Starr, Doris Day, Perry Como, Mario Lanza and Rosemary Clooney - was at best a schmaltz fest guaranteed to induce drowsiness. White teenagers were without a music or a cause they could call their own.

On the political front, former General Eisenhower - who was born in Texas and married a lady named Mamie - was inaugurated as the 34th President on January 20, 1953. Six months later, the signing of a truce brought an armed peace along the border of South Korea. The death of Joseph Stalin the same year caused shifts in relations with Russia. Meanwhile, Russia and the United States had developed hydrogen bombs. The cold war was beginning. KPRC made Houston's first color TV broadcast in early 1954, and about then, Senator Joseph McCarthy began televised hearings into communists in the Army. This was an adult's world, and these were their concerns.

But like many American teenagers, Mickey was restless. The winds of change were starting to stir.

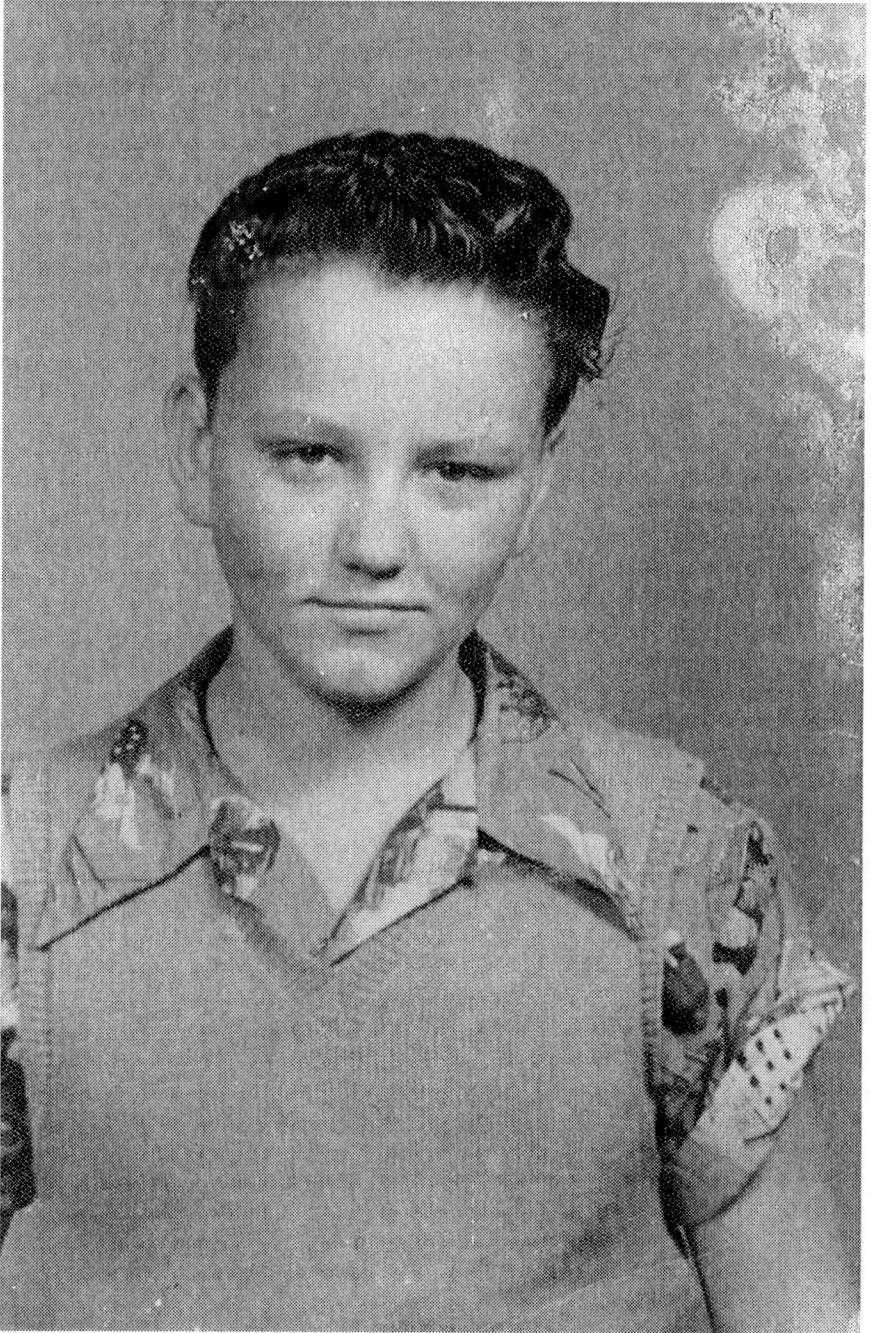

**Mickey - 8<sup>th</sup> grade**

SCHOOL DAYS 1956-57
SAM HOUSTON H.S.

**The Embers with Julian Barnett front and center**

# Chapter III: *The Embers*
## 1954 - 1958

On Mickey's 14th birthday, the U.S. Supreme Court ruled that segregated public schools violated the Constitution. While blacks were rejoicing, Texas Attorney General John Shepperd requested that his state be allowed to desegregate "gradually," explaining he feared immediate desegregation would lead to violence. In a poll, four of five white Texans opposed integration. One year later, the Supreme Court ruled that Southern schools should proceed with "all deliberate speed" to desegregate. Many people felt that Southern school districts, including the Houston school district, proceeded with deliberately slow speed. Houston schools were still segregated in 1960; and consequently, Mickey's schools - kindergarten through grade 12 - excluded black students from enrolling. Also akin to public school systems throughout the South, the Theory of Evolution was not taught.

But life went on. "Mickey and Jerry were getting older," Mamie said, "so we sold our dining room furniture, and we (Milton and I) moved into the dining room at 116 Westfield, so they could each have a room." She treated her boys evenly. "I suppose the most upset I ever was with Mickey, was one time after he was a teen, he accused me of being partial to Jerry, because I allowed Jerry to do something that Mickey was not allowed to do at that age. I explained to him that I had to learn with him, and there never would be a day that I wouldn't love them equally."

The timing was right for Mickey to have his own bedroom, as he needed privacy. "I'm gonna write songs," he announced, and Mamie replied, "Good for you, I tried that too." He asked, "What do you think, Mom?" Mamie answered, "Stick your chin out there, honey, and say, 'here I come' and don't stop until you get what you want." With this spirit, Mamie explained, "I went through a lot of bad times and good times, and I managed to get over the hurdles, and I raised him where he could do the same thing."

Mickey was a teenager, an American term which had not existed until the fifties. The sudden identification of adolescents in this way was society's recognition that they were a separate economic group. Establishing a micro economy at 14, Mickey picked up his first part-time job at Hardees Food Market, just around the corner from his house on Westfield. He worked as a stock clerk and helped customers with carryout. It was vital to have a paying job, as Mickey had taken notice of the opposite sex and had started collecting records. The two pursuits required substantial amounts of money.

One of his first 45s, *(We're Gonna) Rock Around the Clock* by Bill Haley and the Comets, was a reworking of a raunchy old R&B number entitled *My Daddy Rocks Me With A Steady Roll.* (Rockin' and rollin' and reelin' were terms used in the black community to describe sex.) Haley became the Father of Rock, and his song became history's most successful rock single, selling more than 25 million copies. By blending country and western influences with soulful R&B, Haley and his Comets pioneered the rock 'n' roll standard. He was, to put it briefly, the first artist to bring rock and roll to the mainstream.

On July 8, 1954, Dewey Phillips of WDIA in Memphis became the first DJ to play an Elvis Presley song on the air. Broadcast at 9:30 PM, *That's Alright Mama*, made the station's phone board light up like a Christmas tree. When Phillips interviewed the "Hillbilly Cat" later that evening, station listeners were shocked to hear Elvis say he had graduated from Humes High School. Only white students went to Humes. Memphis and Houston had much in common. A few months later - on November 25 - Elvis performed in Houston for the first time at the Houston Hoedown. Like thousands of teenagers, Mickey listened to the performance, broadcast live by local radio station KNUZ. Rock 'n' Roll the baby was in labor.

As the first enormously successful white performer to dress, sing and shake like his black counterparts (especially like handsome Wynonie Harris - a raucous R&B shouter from Omaha), Elvis opened the doors on crossover opportunity between hillbilly, country, blues and rock artists. He was the first white boy to sing hillbilly in R&B time. As Newbury told Jim Delehant of <u>Hit Parader</u>, "Rock and roll isn't anything but country music. Elvis had the blues influence. This music was always there. It's just that there wasn't a hit until Elvis came along."

> *Rock 'n' roll ain't nothin' but the blues with a beat*
> *DIZZY LIZZY*

Elvis asserted the point during a '56 interview with the <u>Charlotte Observer</u>. "The colored folks been singing it and playing it just like I'm doin' now, man, for more years than I know. They played it like that in the shanties and in their juke joints, and nobody paid it no mind 'til I goosed it up. I got it from them. Down in Tupelo, Mississippi, I used to hear old Arthur Crudup bang his box the way I do now, and I said if I ever got to the place where I could feel all old Arthur felt, I'd be a music man like nobody ever saw."

Mickey experienced the same influences. "My music was country music... but I also use to listen to what they called 'race' stations because in those days there was no chance to hear a black artist on a white station. I liked all the music I heard then. There was a lot of good jazz music happening too; Brubeck was really big... I discovered the rhythm and blues radio stations with groups like the Penguins, the Clovers and the Flamingoes... I'm sure most of us went through the rhythm and blues thing before Elvis hit. In Houston it happened real big."

The forms of music riding the airwaves of Mickey's youth - blues, jazz, white gospel, black spirituals, R&B, the Grand Ole Opry's country sounds - were parts of a common Southern culture. As a teenager, he listened mainly to R&B radio stations. Houston's KYOK with deejays Daddy Deep Throat and Dizzy Lizzy was very popular. Mickey and Talmage tuned in to Dizzy Lizzy just about every evening. Unregulated superpowers XERB and XERF - just across the border from Del Rio, Texas - hit Houston like a bomb, especially at night. And late in the evening, WLAC from Gallatin, Tennessee was a Newbury favorite.

During the fifties, WLAC on 1510 KHz was the nation's most influential R&B outlet. After dark, the station's clear-channel signal boomed the voices of jive-talking deejays Gene Nobles, Hoss Allen and John Richbourg - John R - to thousands of listeners across the country. "We all listened to John R from Nashville," Mick said. Accompanied by ads for Royal Crown hairdressing, "He came on the radio late at night with an all rhythm and blues show."

"I was listening to Ray Charles in '54 when he first got started, and all he did was pure blues. But that country blues thing is at the root of the music I like. I can remember my father singing all those old Jimmie Rodgers songs. The only country artist I liked at this time was Hank Williams."

During this period, Milton occasionally drove the family to visit Aunt Nenee in Shreveport. While they negotiated radio stations throughout the six-hour ride, Mickey lobbied for R&B. They also tuned in to KCIJ, hosted by top-country DJ, T. Tommy Cutrer, who would later announce the Opry. T. Tommy played the traditional country music that Milton and Mamie loved. Perhaps his name influenced Mickey's song, T. *Total Tommy*.

Moreover, they enjoyed Shreveport's Louisiana Hayride, broadcast by local radio station KWKH, by Little Rock's KTHS with 50,000 watts and by affiliates of the CBS Radio Network. Appearing on the Hayride in late '54 and all '55 was a young rising star, actually a constellation. Elvis and his rockabilly music got credit for making the Hayride even more famous, and then for killing it when rock and roll was making money and country wasn't.

Mickey entered the ninth grade at Sam Houston High in September of 1954. "I would love to say he was a genius," Mamie said, "but that would be a falsehood. He just got average grades. His favorite classes were acting (drama) and music. He hated math. He also hated timed tests, as they made him nervous and he always drew a blank." Schoolmate Mike Henley remembered, Mickey "had a really nice DA - coif à la duck ass - and wore his collar turned up. His big problem, though, was that boyish face, too cute to be tough." Baby blue eyes and a dimpled chin did not help matters either.

Mickey's friend Talmage entered Sam Houston then and remembered, "I was driving in '54, as I had my license at 14. Mick's folks would drop him off to go roller-skating. We enjoyed eyeballing cute chicks in skimpy skating outfits. Sometimes, I'd have my car there and we'd sneak off to go to Playland Park, an amusement park in South Houston. We even went to Galveston a few times!"

"Mickey dated more than I did in high school. He was a good-looking guy. Mick would set me up with his date's sister. We'd go to drive-ins, and if we were low on money, Mick and his date would hide in the trunk. Our favorite was the Princess Drive-In on Humble Road in North Houston."

"We were really close," Talmage continued. "Once at Mickey's house, we decided to become blood brothers. We went into the kitchen looking for a sharp knife to do the deed. Well, we couldn't get up the courage to use a knife, so we went into the bathroom and used the end of a comb. We cut our hands 'till they bled and then we joined hands... brothers for life."

Mickey attended a school sock hop a few months after starting high school, where a local group, The Sharps, was performing. A sixteen-year-old Houston native, Kenneth Donald Rogers - Kenny Rogers - sang tenor for The Sharps at the time. About a year later, Rogers would sing in another Houston group called The Scholars. Mickey asked the lead singer, Don Angelo, if he knew anyone who would like to start a singing group. Angelo replied, "Sure, my neighbor" and introduced him to Chuck Augustus Gengler - CAG. Don Angelo and CAG lived next door to each other; Kenneth's house was a few blocks away. The three boys went to Jefferson Davis High School, and Mickey attended Sam Houston High.

"Mickey and I auditioned each other," CAG affirmed. "I don't believe we impressed each other all that much. Mickey was trying to sound like the lead singer of The Hilltoppers, Jimmy Sacca, singing *If I Didn't Care*. Anyway, we became real close friends, like brothers. We would walk the streets doing two-part harmony. Mamie referred to us as 'Mutt and Jeff,' as I'm 6'4" and Mickey was about 5'7" then..." Mick finished painting the picture: "On a warm night in 1954... two young guys were slipslidin' down the sidewalk on the north side of Houston. Our dreams in our hands and a few nickels in our pockets. We had decided to start a doo-wop group...

become rich and famous and see a world outside the limited one we had known..."

"We needed someone who could play an instrument," CAG continued, "and we soon found James Walker, who played guitar. It was then that we named ourselves, 'The Embers.' Believe the name was my idea. I was always the spokesman and organizer for the group. I handled the business stuff."

They (Newbury, Gengler and Walker) sang as a trio for several months. "It was too dangerous to sing on the street corners," Mickey advised, "because Houston was very tough back then. There were lots of gangs around from the transit population." And in a 1972 interview with <u>Disc</u>, Mickey stated, "The whole of my childhood seemed so transitory - the areas we lived in were full of young kids hooked on narcotics, and the crime rate was as high as the kids were young." For this reason, CAG said, "Mamie was very protective of Mickey. He had to report in. She was really strict. I got my license at 14 and was driving. I said to Mamie, 'Mrs. Newbury, I don't drink. I'm a good driver. I don't even smoke. Can Mickey ride with me in my Dad's car?'" Mamie gave permission but always wanted to know where her boy was and when he'd be home.

CAG introduced Mickey to Kenneth Rogers. The fourth child of eight, Kenneth was raised in a Houston federal housing project. Whenever CAG and he spotted one another, they performed the same ritualistic greeting, drawing knives to see who could whip it out and flick it open first. Kenneth carried a Gambler's Special (!) with a five-inch blade, while CAG preferred a standard issue switchblade. CAG laughed and said, "The one problem Kenneth had was that he used his pant leg to push open the knife. A pair of khaki pants would only last him about a week! They would be in shreds!" Little did sixteen-year-old Kenneth realize that his career would be launched into the stratosphere with a Newbury song.

Mickey remembered the khaki pants. "Mexican kids had a big influence on us young people. We wore tailored khaki pants... with belt loops and baggy shirts. We all wore these Cadillac shoes. They were long with points on the end and white strings on the side. There were lots of Mexicans in high school. They didn't have too much influence on the music but I learned to dig Mexican people. The Mexican kids I knew were into the vocal group thing just like we were. They were into rhythm & blues."

Influenced by Beat Poets such as Lawrence Ferlinghetti and Jack Kerouac, Mickey began reading poetry in beatnik coffeehouses to guitar accompaniment. (A representative Ferlinghetti quotation, "Keep an open mind but not so open that your brains fall out." A representative Kerouac line, "My witness is the empty sky.") Mickey described the style as "Abstract lyrics like Edgar Allan Poe... 70 years later." He enjoyed hanging out in local beatnik joints, such as The Purple Onion. "It was when everybody was wearing tennis shoes and tee-shirts with a hole in them... They'd sit and talk about books and write poetry. Then it just eased into the music thing, and the poets started picking up guitars, trying to write songs with their poetry." Mickey began dating Mary Jane, also the name of his Great Grandmother - Lettie Belle's mother. He and Don Gant would co-write a song about her in the mid sixties.

> *Mary Jane, Mary Jane, Mary gonna take a trip with me*
> *Acapulco here I come*
> *Gonna cool my dreams in the golden sun*
> *Cause Mary Jane, Mary Jane, MARY WANNA MARRY ME*

American teenagers were defined as a separate generation for the first time in the mid-fifties, and were represented by James Dean who wore blue jeans in "Rebel Without a Cause," creating a fashion and attitude sensation. The "separate generation" claimed its own music, too. While rock 'n' roll was just beginning, doo-wop was already popular with teens, especially in the larger cities.

Doo-wop features close-harmony singing, frequently at slower tempos. Most of the early groups lacked the financial means to buy instruments; and therefore, the harmonized lyrics are often carried by a beat of low-tone, nonsensical syllables, thus the term doo-wop. (The style is akin to skat singing of jazz artists such as Louis Armstrong and Ella Fitzerald.) Doo-wop was developed on the street corner or building stoop of the inner cities, for instance New York and Philadelphia and Houston. As an indication of the genre's popularity, a few thousand doo-wop groups recorded at least one record. Popular artists such as the Coasters and the Drifters sang songs with lyrical themes that voiced concerns of American teenagers.

Mickey's doo-wop ensemble was completed when lead singer Don Angelo left Kenny Rogers' group - The Sharps - and joined Mickey's trio, which then became a singing foursome, The Embers. Dark-complexioned Angelo was of Syrian descent, Mickey explained, so he "could almost pass... We looked like a mixed group, you know, back when it was not real popular to be mixed, but it didn't matter in those days. Not in the black community anyway. It mattered in the white community."

"I spent half my time over in the black community in after-hours places listenin' to good blues music. The best blues music in the world. Texas blues music was really poppin' then, you know. Bobby Blue Bland, B B King, Gatemouth Brown, Guitar Slim... A different kind of blues music from the blues music down in the Delta or in Chicago, but it was really valid... Lightning Hopkins... Lightning lived out in Conroe, Texas (40 miles north of Houston). Just broker 'n hell. Be thrilled to see you when you had a bottle of wine. Fingernails clear out to here. Don't know how he ever played the guitar, but he sure did. Not very well, but what was comin' out of his brain was wonderful."

The "mixed" Embers recorded one single on the Herald and two singles on the Mercury labels and sounded like black doo-wop groups of that era, the Penguins and the Drifters. "My group did songs like *Earth Angel, Speedo, Annie Had A Baby...* By the time I was 15, I was in a group, playing Army bases and places like that at night and going to school in the day." The Embers also performed at several school sock hops, including Davis, Bellaire and Sam Houston High.

> *Are the villains in black hats are the heroes in white*
> *Are there sock-hoppin rock and rollin' Saturday nights*
> *Would a '49 Mercury still be out'a sight*
> *THAT WAS THE WAY IT WAS THEN*
>
> *You were like Natalie I was James Dean*
> *Slow walkin' soft talkin' silently mean*
> *Surely the rebel in me lives again*
> *But without a cause to be all caught up in*
>
> *It's a quarter to ten and I am lyin' in bed*
> *Spinnin' that old memory thing in my head*
> *The times were so good; the times were so sad*
> *It was a game we would play feelin' good feelin bad*

The Embers consisted of Newbury - tenor, Angelo - lead, Gengler - bass, and Walker - guitar and baritone. Mickey did not play guitar in The Embers and did not sing lead. "I think I always knew I could sing. The problem was... I was always so introverted. I never sang lead with our group. I was the tenor singer. I was so shy that I could not even look at the audience. Every picture of us performing... I was always a profile shot... I was lookin' straight at Chuck... I didn't start singin' until I started writin' my own songs... Singin' my own words never ever made me uncomfortable... But when I was with the group, I was terrified before every show." About this time, he wrote his first song, *The Sea of Life*. "I was sure I has seen enough of life to write about it... and you know what... I had."

Mickey and CAG would "remain friends forever," Mickey explained. "In fact his Mother and Dad were just like another Mother and Dad for me... CAG's home became my home away from home. His mother, a lady with enough love for two dreamers... his little sister, always around with a sandwich, a coke or just a little hug. His father, Charles Sr., in time my second father..."

Mick spent considerable time with the Genglers, and CAG remembered, "Mickey just about lived with us one summer. His dad was a tough guy. But Mickey was not full of himself at all. Actually he had very little self-confidence. The Embers gave us a sense of strength... of identity. We were teenagers and we wanted to be popular."

Mickey also wanted to impress his Mom. "A local radio station made broadcasts every Saturday from the Variety Boys Club," CAG recalled, "and The Embers were regulars on the program. Well, one Saturday Mickey said, 'If I don't get to sing like I told my Mom, then I'm gonna quit the group.' We let him sing."

The Embers hit the road, performing at black R&B clubs across Texas, where Mickey was nicknamed "The Little White Wolf" by Gatesmouth Brown and B B King. "We really didn't have a problem with being white and playing in black clubs," CAG explained. "We also hung out at black radio stations."

Mickey explained the orientation to <u>Country Song Roundup</u>: "Well, my family's from the country and I've always heard country music as a kid. I just dug it. All the music I do, even the way out stuff has country roots in it... Basic lyrics. Three chord progressions. Any kind of music that goes back to the fields in its feeling whether it's country or blues. You know, Negro blues and country music are a lot alike. Country music came from the cats working in the fields. So did blues. One came from the Negro, the other from the white. The chords are just about the same and the stories are usually hurtin' stories." Mickey had an inherent understanding of "cats working in the fields." It was in his blood. "Nobody can play rhythm and blues but black people... that's bullshit," he advised Peter O'Brien. "Rhythm and blues is not uniquely black, anymore than country is uniquely white."

When Mickey was 15, a neighborhood gang purposely broke a window in the Newbury house. An angry Mick stormed down the street to challenge the gang leader to a fight. Accepting the challenge, the fight began and "went on for at least an hour. We rolled and tumbled for five blocks. I knocked the kid into a ditch a few times, and then would wait for him to climb out and pick the briers off his clothes and body before continuing! Ha Ha Ha Ha!" Mick won the fight, and they never again had a problem with the gang. Mickey said, "That was the first time my Dad showed me some respect by saying, 'I'm proud of you.'"

"My Dad was not a nurturing father. Was a disciplinarian... I kiss my six-foot son every night... I don't want him to get all that macho shit wrapped up around his brain like I had it around my brain... Mom would sit in the car and finish her cigarette while I would finish kicking some kid's ass... The only time my Daddy ever smiled at me, when I was growing up, was when he was drunk or when I whipped somebody... I saw my Daddy whip six men one night... His arms were as big around as my leg... All his self worth was that... He was still fist fighting in his fifties... When he had the second stroke, he lost all that."

> *Now when I was a boy I was wild I was lazy*
> *I was the shame of my dad*
> *A WEED IS A WEED*
>
> *We're all building walls; they should be bridges...*
> *HEAVEN HELP THE CHILD*
>
> *Who would have thought it could ever have come tumbling down?*
> *That is my childhood...*
> *116 WESTFIELD STREET*

"Milton was a very insecure man, and an introvert," Mamie explained. "You know how that fits with an extrovert like me. Not too well. When we were alone was when he was happiest. He was a very hard working person, but he let people beat him every time he did a job. Birthdays and Christmases meant a lot to him, but he wasn't too much on New Years Eve. He just didn't fit in with crowds. He was a good man to me though."


During 1956, Elvis' *Hound Dog* and *Heartbreak Hotel* became the first songs to simultaneously top the (white) country, (black) R&B and (white) pop charts. On Mickey's 16th birthday, a Newbury favorite, *The Magic Touch* by The Platters peaked at number four on the pop singles chart. Irrespective of Southern canons and white hoods, blacks and whites were communicating through music. That struck a harmonious chord with Mickey, and he learned a vital lesson then that he would voice simply: "Music has the greatest opportunity as a bridge between cultures."

He was head over heels in love with music at this point. "I got an old Gibson guitar and learned chords. There was this old boy, Julian Barnett that played in a popular Houston group, and he got me going on guitar. I played like him. He played chords like I never heard, with a lot of bass and real creative. He reached across two strings with one finger. I didn't learn country guitar. He showed me how to use a drone but mostly I learned all the conventional stuff. I play real simple, mostly four chord stuff. I love open chords. It's not blues or country. It's just an extension of what I learned from Julian. I didn't learn things off records because I couldn't pick fast enough." Julian would temporarily join The Embers, filling in for lead singer Don Angelo.

A few months later, in September of '56, The University of Texas became the first major university in the South to admit blacks as undergraduates. Meanwhile at a black club in Houston, the white Embers opened for America's number one doo-wop group, the black Coasters. The Embers did package shows with Sam Cooke, Paul Anka, Jackie Wilson, Laverne Baker, T-Bone Walker, Buddy Holly, Johnny Cash, Frankie Avalon, the Everly Brothers and many others. Mickey remembered when "You'd get on the bus with 10 or 12 other acts and go out and do one song. Oh yeah man, it was fun!" Music in those days was "just havin' a good time and meetin' girls."

"We performed at the Incarnate Word, an all-girls Catholic high school in Houston," CAG recalled. "The nuns and sisters were charging the girls 15 cents for each of our autographs. We were in hog heaven, smiling, signing autographs and getting telephone numbers for our little black books..." As they had become a popular singing group, an Embers Fan Club was formed, and members - mostly teenage girls - wore special shirts with fancy red stripes.

Mickey earned a little spending money in The Embers, though erratically and never enough. Seemed like he was constantly broke. In late '56, he obtained part time employment in the Record Department at Foley's Department Store. He liked the job at first because he could listen to music at work and the pay supported his expensive habit - filterless Camels. But young Newbury was restless and fed up with the humdrum routine of school and work. So he quit his job, dropped out of school and went to Galveston.

*I was turnin' seventeen when I packed up my hopes and dreams,*
*Loaded up my old beat up car, turned the key and burned the tar...*
*IN '59*

*Lord, when you're chained there's nothin' you cherish like freedom*
*FRISCO DEPOT*

Located two miles off the Texas mainland on the Gulf of Mexico, Galveston occupies a 30-mile long island of beautiful white beaches. An easy one-hour drive southeast from Houston, the Queen City of the Gulf was a breath of fresh air for Mickey. The island offered roulette, slot machines, great dining and big name entertainment. In the fifties, bathhouses and lavish hotels such as the Tremont and Galvez along the waterfront made Galveston a playground for the wealthy. In short, the place was Paradise Island - providing one could afford the tab.

"I was workin' in Galveston, and I had two jobs at one time. One of the jobs was workin' in a cocktail lounge... I was workin' as a lounge lizard in a little piano bar... Didn't play guitar. Just sang songs like *Mood Indigo* and *The Nearness of You* and those kind of songs... The sound was terrible in the fifties. The mics were awful. Every bar had carpet four inches thick. The walls were padded with velvet material... and I mean it was just like singin' in a casket, a big large casket. There was a group called the Quarter Notes and they had all these silk suits and alligator shoes... Well I am vertically disadvantaged so the shoes were hung too big and the coat was hung down to here and the collars were all (way too big)... But it was okay because they were silk coats and alligator shoes. I was in fine shape as long as I walked in and sat at the piano bar and nobody knew. All they could see was the shiny silk."

"So I would go through my little lounge lizard act and then I would go to this gamblin' casino called the Balinese Room... (One of Sam Maceo's most famous nightclubs, the Balinese Room had hosted such performers as Guy Lombardo and Duke Ellington.) My manager was a guy named Jack O'Too, and Jack said, 'Mickey, do you do Latin music'? Well whatever they asked me... yeah I did it! I needed the work and so the only thing I knew how to play was *Malagueña*... So I worked as a stroller with these big puffy sleeves you know and a big cummerbund... I could speak no Latin language, but as I had grown up in a basically black and Chicano neighborhood, I said, well hell I can get away with it. I would walk between the tables... Nobody's payin' any attention anyway... It's like workin' in a strip joint which I did a lot of that too... It was a lot of fun... Ahhhh... But I'd go (strumming flamingo style while singing): 'Pras mi render che le vive jal'... And I'd just make up stuff you know... And once a week someone would say, 'What language is that'? And I'd say... I'd say... 'Portuguese... Portuguese folk songs.' Deadpan serious... And I worked there for about four or five months... Never got called... Jack was very, very satisfied."

Though he had a great time, the two Galveston gigs did not provide Mick with enough money, so he packed up his few belongings and headed 300 miles northeast to Shreveport. He stayed with Great Aunt Nenee's son, his cousin Herman Boyette, who was married to Mamie's foster sister. (During the late sixties, Herman's brother, Jay Boyette, would briefly manage Mickey in Nashville.) Mickey found scant success in Shreveport. The area's blue-collar unemployment rate was high, and it was next to impossible to find a decent job. He was however able to land a job singing... in a strip club.

No, he did not sing, *Itsy Bitsy Teenie Weenie Yellow Polka Dot Bikini*. True to form, though, he found a way to reach the audience with material he wanted to perform. "I started singin' this song - *Danny Boy* - when I worked in strip joints back when I was a kid. They were not there to see me obviously. So I would pick what appeared to be an Irishman... if he had red hair, blond hair, if he was big... And I would sing *Danny Boy*. And I would sing it straight to his table. And about the first five bars he had everybody in there shut up. If I didn't see an Irishman and I saw an Italian, I would sing *O My Papa*. The ol' man who ran the strip joint asked me about it one time, he said, 'You're the only singer I've ever had who can get an audience quiet.' I told him about that (the Irish - Italian strategy) and I thought I was gonna have to bury him right there he laughed so hard... It's not so much WHAT you do but HOW you do it, and it's not how the crowd treats YOU but how YOU treat the crowd..."

Though the position increased his anatomical and sociological knowledge, the pay was lousy. Since he had not graduated from high school, Mickey could neither find a good-paying job, nor join the Marines... which he tried. And so he returned home from Shreveport and Paradise Island, tail between his legs.

> *As little feet grew to be restless feet*
> *Feet that carried me through meadows with fruit so sweet*
> *But fruit that was not for me, oh no, not for me*
> *BETWEEN THE BITTER AND THE SWEET*

When Mickey arrived at home in Houston, his parents told him he would need an education, but he replied, "I don't need a diploma to write songs." Mamie recalled, "So then Milton - a very tough boss - put him to work on a plumbing job. After three weeks, he decided plumbin' was not for him, so he returned to school."

Throughout the ordeal of dropping out, quitting his job, running away, returning to Houston, working with his dad as a plumber's assistant and returning to school... one important person stood by him. "His high school assistant principal," Mamie continued, "Mr. Elrod, understood and supported him. That was as near to a favorite teacher as he had. He supported Mickey right down the wire until he received his diploma." Back in the routine at school, Mickey met a pretty girl, Sharon, who became his first serious girlfriend.

> *You are the one that I think of most often*
> *You were the first woman I came to know*
> *But I was so young*
> *And the young have no wisdom*

*But Sharon I loved you so long ago*
*WINTER WINDS BLOW*

Sharon and Mickey swooned to Sam Cooke's romantic *You Send Me*, which sold two million copies in 1957. The song made Cooke the first gospel star to achieve major crossover success. About this time, Chester "Chet" Burton Atkins became head of RCA Nashville, championing a smooth, commercial sound that would birth singers such as Patsy Cline. Romantic music was just a turn of the radio dial away. Mickey and Sharon also watched Dick Clark's "American Bandstand," which launched a successful debut that year.

Although the media continued to predict rock 'n' roll's demise throughout 1957, the fad had grown into a monster, powerfully charged by the Japanese transistor radio introduced that year. As it turned out, 18 of the top 30 records of 1957 were rock 'n' rollers. Major hits that year made up an eclectic bag: *Marrianne* - Hilltoppers, *Diana* - Paul Anka, *Butterfly* - Andy Williams, *Party Doll* - Buddy Knox, *School Day* - Chuck Berry, *Little Darlin'* - The Diamonds, *Blue Monday* - Fats Domino, *You Send Me* - Sam Cooke, *Love Letters In The Sand* - Pat Boone, *Searchin'* and *Young Blood* - The Coasters, *Lucille* and *Jenny Jenny* - Little Richard, *That'll Be The Day* and *Peggy Sue* - Buddy Holly, *Bye Bye Love* and *Wake Up Little Susie* - Everly Brothers; and *Whole Lotta Shakin' Goin' On* and *Great Balls Of Fire* - Jerry Lee Lewis. Elvis led the pack with *Don't*, *Teddy Bear*, *Jailhouse Rock* and *All Shook Up*.

Mickey listened intently to the music and to the language of these artists. He was in school and this was his best subject. He memorized lyrics, melodies and rhythm. He studied emotive phrasing and varied styles, mimicking favorites. Perhaps he was searching for a common thread or an underlying emotion. Ultimately he would find it, as artists of pop, rock, country, polka, reggae, metal, rumba and R&B would one day line up to record his songs.

One of those artists would be Jerry Lee Lewis, the fiery piano player from Ferriday, Louisiana, who followed the footsteps of Elvis to Sun Records in Memphis. There he scored the first success of his killer career with the primal boogie, *Whole Lotta Shakin' Goin' On*, banned in many states for sexual innuendo. Little did Jerry Lee know that in a decade he would cover Newbury's songs... as would Elvis, Carl Perkins, Johnny Cash (These four rockabillies would become "The Million Dollar Quartet"), Pat Boone, Andy Williams, the Everly Brothers and about 500 artists representing most every genre of American music.

In 1957, though, the old record-chart divisions segregating pop, rhythm and blues and country releases were not making much sense. Not only were white artists such as Elvis, Jerry Lee Lewis and the Everly Brothers selling big in black markets, but black stars such as Chuck Berry, Little Richard and Fats Domino were achieving unprecedented success in the white pop market. These cultural border crossings contributed more to desegregation than any legislation to date, and the two-way communication made a lasting impression on Newbury.

CAG recalled his most lasting memory with The Embers. "In 1957, The Scholars with Kenneth Rogers and several groups performed at the Miss Texas Pageant at the coliseum in Houston. Jerry Lewis - the comedian who had just broken up with partner, Dean Martin - was the emcee. Our group, The Embers, was the only group he complimented. 'Great!' he said... 'Fresh sound... Terrific!' As a result of his praise we were given a huge write-up in the local newspaper. Meant a lot to us as we were so competitive." "And then," Mickey added, "promoters started booking us as 'Just Off The Jerry Lewis Tour.'"

CAG also remembered how rough North Houston was in the late fifties. "We walked a tightrope... Too good - the guys would kick your ass... Too bad - the law would get you. We were in some really tough neighborhoods. One of my classmates was shot dead through his bedroom window." And Mickey stated, "I had a half-dozen friends who were killed before they were 20 years old."

"One night in late '57," recalled Talmage, "Mickey and I were out with two sisters and two carloads of guys jumped us. Evidently we were dating their girlfriends. They beat us up bad and Mick got hit in the head with a tire iron. I drove him to the hospital, but the doctor wouldn't treat him without calling the police first. Mickey would not permit it. He did not want to turn them in."

> He was not unlike this ofay ember
> When they want blood someone's got to bleed...
> But it's all right with me
> If it's all right with you
> Cause I'm just a kid of seventeen
> DIZZY LIZZY

("Ofay" is a black African word for white man.)

Mickey would inform Martin Neil in an interview, "I turned to writing poetry, after a savage attack by a gang from a rival district. They worked me over real bad... I decided that I didn't want any part of that environment. I didn't want to leave school so I became a recluse. Apart from school I just stayed at home all the time... writing, listening to country blues and classics ... and learning to play the guitar." Escaping North Houston's mean streets, he spent one year - "One," according to Mamie, "not two!" as has been misreported - in his bedroom painting, playing the guitar, writing deep morbid things and reading the works of the Beat Poets and Poe.

Shades of Kerouac... the boy was scared to death... the color of his seventeen-year-old world was Terrified. A psychologist friend analyzed the isolation as a nervous breakdown. In a <u>Rolling Stone</u> (May 1975) article, Mickey explained, "I grew up in a knot 'cause I hated to fight... I hated violence, yet it came automatic. If I hadn't dropped out I might of killed somebody. I was so paranoid that I had gotten a pistol... I became my own psychiatrist."

> *I got the news from home today*
> *My old friend AL had died*
> *He fought the war in Vietnam*
> *He came home; his mother cried*
> *But a bullet didn't get him Lord*
> *It was just a switchblade knife*
> *In some ungodly men's room*
> *In some North-side dive.*
>
> *I'll be dead asleep in back of Richard's North Side Lounge*
> *IF YOU EVER GET TO HOUSTON LOOK ME DOWN*
>
> *Sitting in the dark, in the darkness of my room*
> *I wonder why I look the sky look the sky*
> *Begins to softly cry...*
> *WRITE A SONG SONG*
>
> *Take me back to where I've never been...*
> *HEAVEN HELP THE CHILD*

While hula-hoops and 3D movies were the craze, Mickey spent a stressed-out year holed up in his bedroom fighting inner demons. His defensive weapons included painting, poetry, songwriting, the guitar and self-analysis. But most North Houston teenagers experienced the same mean streets. Many strolled the same frightening sidewalks, yet few boarded up in seclusion for 12 months. Why was Newbury's response so extreme?

When he was eight, the encephalitis - inflammation of the brain - may have triggered manic-depressive or bipolar moods in later life. This is a documented psychiatric symptom often expressed through frustration, intensive mood swings, risk-taking behavior, difficulties with memory, aggressiveness and at the extreme end, destructiveness. Mickey would say years later he should take medication, but he refused, as he feared it would stifle his creativity. He stated many times he did not write when happy, but drew from unhappiness or "insanity" to create music. Depression is more indicative and more specific than insanity.

"This world is as close to hell as we'll get," Newbury explained, "though we do get a taste of heaven here now and then. Insanity though is nothing more than an alternative reality. I have fought pain all my life, and everything I have done in my life has been out of fear... Music has never been anything but an escape from depression for me... A person may be bipolar and go through life without anybody ever knowin' it, because they do somethin' that releases those chemicals and takes care of it in a natural way... by painting or by singing or by writin' a song or whatever." He referred to the plunder as "Robbing the Dragon."

Robbing the Dragon - a courageous healing process - produced a dark thread throughout Newbury's many Poe-like writings. "I learned from Edgar Allan Poe," Mick would say, "how words have their own music... their own rhythm."

> *Pleasure is a thread of pain when it is undone*
> *Moments of insanity are never like a chain*
> *I only know I am not free the nights when I am sane*
> *LET'S HAVE A PARTY (and) NIGHTS WHEN I AM SANE*
>
> *I put my dangerous feelings under lock and chain*
> *Killed my violent nature with a smile*
> *Though the demons danced and sing their songs*
> *Within my fevered brain*
> *All my God-like thoughts are not defiled*
> *THE THIRTY-THIRD OF AUGUST*
>
> *I was born no good, girl, until my dying day*
> *The DEVIL ON MY SHOULDERS got the man*
> *I wish I could change, girl, but I know there's just no way*
> *The DEVIL ON MY SHOULDERS got the man.*
>
> *My world is like a river, as dark as it is deep...*
> *SWEET MEMORIES*
>
> *God knows I'm tryin' to deal with my sadness*
> *Although at times I swear I do not know*
> *When I am happy or when it is madness*
> *Do you understand why the WINTER WINDS BLOW...*

"When Mickey locked himself up in his room," CAG recalled, "he taught himself to write poetry, play the guitar and paint. I'd go over to visit him, and he'd play some new song for me. When Mickey finally came out of his room, he was committed to writing songs." Kenneth Rogers exclaimed when Mickey returned from sabbatical, "I have never seen such a transformation of talent in anyone in my life! He came out incredibly accomplished..."

About the time Mickey emerged from the gloom in 1958, The Country Music Association was founded, and Wesley Rose, of Acuff-Rose Publishing, began serving as its first Chairman. Later that year after completing a summer make-up session, Mickey graduated from Sam Houston High. He had a Mexican-American girlfriend then, a pretty girl named Ruth Martinez. They communicated in English, as Mick never learned to speak Spanish. Riding the airwaves was a sing-along song claimed by many to usher in the folk movement of the sixties: *Tom Dooley*.

Meanwhile, The Embers had several close encounters with Kenneth Rogers. He performed *Crazy Feelings* at a show in Houston, backed up by The Embers less Don Angelo. Also Rogers' brother, Leland, booked a few gigs for them. And once, Kenneth played with The Embers. CAG explained, "We often recorded and booked clubs and military bases under a different group name. In late '58, we released a Mercury single (# 71580) titled, *I'm Sorry Dear*, under the name, 'Don Angelo,' who sang lead on it. We took cash dollars up front and released future rights. Kenneth plays stand-up bass on that record."

The Embers took their final bows in late '58 at Club Unique in Austin, the city where Great Grandma Sarah had been institutionalized. A highfalutin promoter - "The General" - had arranged to be there to audition two successive shows. This was an important gig for the group, as it could lead to better bookings and bigger bucks. "Unfortunately," CAG recalled, "we flopped on the first show, just had an off performance. The club manager came runnin' in and yelled, 'You guys really blew it!'"

"We were so down and out. We decided that after our second performance, we would just quit as a group. Then we went out and did the second show. We were terrific! Got a standing ovation! We knew The General would love us. The club manager came running up and yelled, 'Why the hell didn't you do that when The General was here?'"

"What? You mean he's not here?"

"That's right!" the manager growled. "He was so disgusted with the first show, he left early."

51

**On leave with brother Jerry**

# Chapter IV: *Swiss Cottage Place*
## 1959 - 1963

1959 was the Year the Music Died. Out of the blue, three major rockers were killed in a plane crash on February 3rd. Texas teens were in a state of shock, as the tragedy took two of their own: Buddy Holly of Lubbock and the Big Bopper of Beaumont. Also on board the ill-fated craft was a gifted seventeen-year-old Chicano from Southern California, Ritchie Valens. The deaths left a vacuum in rock 'n' roll that has never been filled.

Nor was the leader of the pack around to help fill the void... He was stationed in West Germany, entrenched in the Army for another year. When Elvis was finally let loose... when The King did return to his homeland to reclaim the throne... his music would be less spontaneous and more "mature." By this point, many fans felt abandoned.

Another dagger fell in late Fall, as Alan Freed, the man who coined the phrase "rock and roll" and the country's most famous DJ, was charged with taking bribes in exchange for radio airplay. To convey the common practice of record companies payin' the piper, Variety magazine fashioned the curt term, "payola," a contraction of the words "pay" and "Victrola." On Mick's 20th birthday, Freed would be arrested and charged with 26 counts of payola. A second celebrated DJ was implicated, though Dick Clark would receive only a mild warning. As the fifties came to an end, the purity and innocence of rock 'n' roll was history.

Mickey's world was in a state of disarray, too. While The Embers were a smoldering memory, music buddy CAG was glowing from newfound life as a newlywed. Though Mickey served as best man at the wedding, circumstances did not make him feel like the best man. "I sold my guitar and everything at that time, just got disgusted with music I guess. I had no plans on getting back into it either."

Needing to go somewhere, Mickey went to Shreveport and stayed with Talmage and his uncle for a few months. Since he could not get anything going, he returned to Houston... alone. Mickey felt isolated, completely cut off from the possibility of a positive future. Boredom put him on the North-side streets, where he "had incredible fights with other kids. Had a fight every day, and then when I was 19, I went into the Air Force... I knew it was the only way to get out of the rut I was in. Split Texas and see the world."

*I hate to leave the old man all alone to work the cotton*
*But the country never seems to bother him*
*HEAVEN HELP THE CHILD*

For opportunity, Mickey enlisted in the Air Force in October. He wanted the opportunity to work, desired the opportunity to travel and desperately needed the opportunity to escape Houston's sadistic streets. The scared kid was simply trying to stay alive. "Everything I have done in my life," Mickey explained, "I have done out of fear." And so he signed up to a four-year hitch.

He was ordered to boot camp at Lackland Air Force Base in San Antonio. On the way there, the military bus made a pit stop so the boys could grab a sandwich and soft drink. A lone black enlistee was asked to sit outside on a bench while the whites dined inside. This disturbed Mickey, so he lagged behind to keep the man company.

Mick spent the first day in the Air Force like all new recruits... in fraternal initiation. On arrival, they were lined up so the drill sergeant could welcome them with the standard military greeting: "You are the sorriest looking bunch of..." Mick's perfect DA soon fell to the barbershop floor. Sporting a regulation GI haircut - quarter-inch on top, white-walled on the sides - he marched in mustered unison and waited in endless lines for shots, uniform, bedding and chow. Grits, java, S.O.S. (shit on a shingle) and okra (he hated okra!) most likely graced the mess hall menu. A communal shower was taken in the evening, and barracks lights disappeared at 10 PM. Lying in the darkness, the boys listened to the loneliest tune in the world, *Taps*. Blinding lights returned at a rude 5 AM, as the sergeant growled, "Git yer lazy asses up!"

Mickey spent the first four weeks in the military completing basic training. He learned how to shoot, salute and spit-shine boots. After mastering the mud pit low-crawl and obtaining M-1 rifle certification, Newbury passed the Radio Operator's Test, which required simultaneous translation and transmission of five code words per minute. He was then transferred to the Advanced Electronics School at Keesler Air Force Base in Biloxi, Mississippi. Mickey completed radio training there with good friend, 6' 5" Keith "Chaz" Chastain.

"We were in the same flight, class and barracks," Chaz explained. "They packed us in four to a room, and Mick and I were in adjoining rooms. The two of us picked up code faster than anybody, and that turned into a friendly competition. I guess we were drawn to each other as class leaders. We liked each other immediately. I called him 'Newbury' and he nicknamed me 'Chaz' (a name since carried)."

"Mickey was a little older than me, and I saw him as more worldly. He could do one-hand pushups and tear a phone book in half. He was a tough guy. He's always had the charisma, but when I met him, he was 19 and pretty unsure of himself. Actually we had that in common. On the outside we looked self-confident and poised. But on the inside we were driven to perform because of feelings of inadequacy. We were both afraid of failure... so sometimes... we wouldn't even try."

"We would sing together in march formation coming back from class... cadence count songs such as *I Got A Home In Glory Land.* The first time I heard him sing outside of formation, I knew he was an extraordinary talent. What a voice! We'd walk and whistle together a few miles at a time. I'd sing harmony and he'd sing lead. Just this high, sweet, pure tenor... An amazing voice! *Misty* was one of our walk and sing songs. We also sang some doo-wop."

"Our group of six would gather 'round the piano at the Airman's Club. Four white and two black guys were in our singing group, and one guy had a Smokey Robinson voice. Each had parts to sing, like lead or tenor or baritone. We'd buy two quarts of beer at a time, so as time went on, more frequent bathroom visits became necessary. So what happened... when a singer's part came up, he'd be missing in action... in the john relieving himself. We got tired of singers missing parts, so we moved the group into the bathroom. The acoustics were great and we could continue singing regardless of second-hand activities. Girls visiting the base and servicemen would gather outside the bathroom door to listen to our concert. We'd hear this applause... That hallway became the hangout."

"We snuck off base a few times by climbing an eight foot chain-link fence. We'd sneak into town, but that was risky, so we only did it when we had money, which wasn't often. Once, Mickey wanted to go to a family reunion in Houston but couldn't get a pass. So he snuck into the guardroom and signed himself out! Then he called a cab and hid in the trunk, so it appeared like an empty taxi was leaving base. In town (Biloxi) Mick caught a Greyhound to New Orleans, and from there, he took a train to Houston. After the weekend, I believe Mamie brought him back to Biloxi, dropping him at an off-base club."

"Later, Mickey got a job at the swanky Tidewater Beach Hotel singing and playing guitar. He did this for two or three months and made about $25 per weekend." Mick remembered another gig, a much less formal venue. "Some of my fondest memories are floating 'round in Gulfport. I used to burn that highway down between Biloxi and Gulfport (10 miles distance) when I was there in the military in 1960. Mrs. Brown at the Basewater Hotel set aside a room there for me... and all I had to do was sing, *You're Nobody 'Till Somebody Loves You* for her when she was in."

"He was also dating an officer's daughter," Chaz continued, "and got to use her car, a light blue Chevy convertible. She'd pull up in front of the barracks and toot the horn and Mick would come running out." Veterans will understand the paramount social status in this event. For those with a nonmilitary past... in the eyes of fellow troops, Newbury was a General.

Like many servicemen of the era, Mick got tattooed... his, on the right forearm. Susan Newbury filled in the details: "He had a commanding officer who retired as a Marine, became bored, and re-enlisted in the Air Force. He constantly told the company they were not men because they were not Marines. One night Mickey found himself - or lost himself - in a tattoo parlor and decided to get an eagle tattoo with a banner on the bottom that said 'Marines.' The tattoo artiste finished the eagle and completed the 'M' when he realized that Mick was wearing an Air Force uniform. He told Mick that he was going to get killed when he walked back on his base with a tattoo that said 'Marines.' Mick thought he could convince his commanding officer that he too, had been in the Marines, but that the Air Force was better. By this time his senses were getting a little clearer, and so he had the man change it to 'Mom&Dad.' In later years, he hated the bold tattoo and wore long sleeves most of the time in public."

Seven months after signing up, Mickey was assigned to England, land of his ancestors and "the first civilized place I'd been to in my life." He worked as an Air Traffic Controller, based at RAF Croughton near Banbury, Oxfordshire. Meanwhile Chaz would be sent to Guam and Mickey's future wife, Susan Pack, started singing with a band in Portland, Oregon. She was 12.

> *I burned that highway down IN '59*
> *Yes, I burned that two-lane highway down in 1959.*
> *I never did look back; I did not see that railroad track*
> *But I burned that highway down IN '59.*

The sixties were the age of youth, as 70 million children from the post-war baby boom became teenagers and young adults. The movement away from the conservative fifties continued and eventually resulted in revolutionary ways of thinking and change in the cultural fabric of American life. No longer content to be images of the generation ahead of them, young people wanted change. The changes affected values, lifestyles, laws, and entertainment.

A major voice of the sixties generation, Bob Dylan (nè Robert Zimmerman) dropped out of college in 1960 to seek out his idol, Woody Guthrie in New York City. As beehive hairdos became the rave, Berry Gordy founded Hitsville USA, the forerunner of Motown Records. Meanwhile, three days on and three days off from the Air Force job found Mick gallivantin' around London so much that he "kept a flat with some guys" in Swiss Cottage Place. It became in his words "a party that lasted for three years."

*In a room full of mem'ries, in a house built for love*
*On a street down in SWISS COTTAGE PLACE...*

If London were a country, its population and economy would make it Europe's sixth largest. London is the capital of the United Kingdom, which consists of England, Wales, Scotland, and Northern Ireland. The city's Victorian architecture notably Buckingham Palace, Westminster Cathedral, Big Ben and Tower Bridge - must have been stunning sights to Newbury. He could relax in the safe city, where policemen called "bobbies" carried truncheons and whistles rather than guns and brass knuckles. Matter of fact, in 1829 the non-military police force was invented by British subject, Sir Robert - hence "Bobby" - Peel.

Mickey fell in love with London Town, and his modus operandi changed at once. No longer having to slug it out on mean streets, he found refuge in 200 art museums. The Tate Gallery became a favorite hangout. He also enjoyed the city's 1,700 green parks and mild temperature, normally 20 degrees cooler than hot-as-hell Houston.

The "proper" British manner of speaking the English language would have grabbed Mick's attention. It is a safe bet he never heard a North Houstonian ask, "Have you no peaches?" An East Texas boy could get his ass kicked for makin' queries like that! As George Bernard Shaw remarked, "England and America (especially the South) are two countries separated by the same language."

Mick heard several strange expressions such as: bird (girl), pub (bar), mate (friend), loo (bathroom), garden (yard), tele (television), flat (apartment), way out (exit) and spot of (small amount). An English buddy might have remarked, "Right mate, the bird in the pub watched a bit of tele, had a spot of tea, went looking for the way out, and ended up in the loo!"

Double-decker red public buses caught his eye. He would have boarded one, climbed the stairs and rode up top. Automobile driving seemed an alternate universe experience here, as the steering wheel was located on the right-hand side of the car, and cars were driven on the left side of the street. This is unsettling to an American - particularly while making left turns or negotiating 40 mph roundabouts. Driving could be left to the cabbies though, as British taxis are safe, clean, spacious and inexpensive. Plus the courteous driver wears a shirt and tie. Imagine.

On liberty weekends, Newbury enjoyed wandering the historic garden city of York. The charming community was a breath of fresh air. Mick also hung out at a music club in Coventry - to listen to a jazz saxophonist named Tubby Hayes. "He was a mean son of a... He was my sergeant." Mick went to nearby Oxford too - a great party town - where Rhodes Scholar Kris Kristofferson was studying the works of Shakespeare and Blake and boxing on the side. The men did not know each other then as has been misreported.

Mick also traveled to Wales off the northwest coast of France. A railroad depot with the world's longest name is there: Llanfairpwllgwyngyllgogery-chwyrndrobwyll-llantisiliogogogoch, which means "the Church of Mary in a white hollow by a hazel tree near a rapid whirlpool by the church of St. Tisilio by a red cave." The affable Welsh would have enjoyed the East Texas boy's accent, particularly his pronunciation of their train station, and most amusingly, following the third round of drinks.

In place of the macho nightspots of Texas and Louisiana, Mr. Newbury now frequented civilized pubs and participated in a few calm games of intellectual darts. He did not just order "beer." Oh no. He requested light ale, bitter ale, brown ale, mild ale, stout ale or lager. Connoisseurs or "pint pros" specify a mixture, such as light and bitter or brown and mild. He downed a few pints in century-old pubs such as the Bell and Crown on the north bank of the Thames at Strand on the Green, near Chiswick. And eating? In place of Mamie's fresh catfish, red beans, cornbread and bread pudding, Mickey dined on whitebait - deep-fried whole minnows - and Yorkshire pudding. Houston was a gazillion miles away.

Though Mickey missed his family, telephoning home was a problem. Overseas calls were expensive, and obtaining a circuit was difficult. So pretending to be an officer, Airman 1st Class Newbury would radiotelephone home under codename "Nan Yoke." He was able to do this by using a multi-hop phone patch carried by single sideband.

And music? "I learned to play a little bit of piano while I was there (taught himself), but not much else musically. I listened to a lot of music. That was when I first listened to Bob Dylan and Peter, Paul and Mary and Peggy Lee... and Roy Orbison. I personally dig Dylan the best of anybody." From Dylan's first self-titled album, Mickey listened to songs such as *Freight Train Blues, Talking New York* and *House of the Rising Sun.* Dylan's early music sounded like a beatnik-coffeehouse version of Woody Guthrie... only better, much better. And when "The Frewheelin' Bob Dylan" followed in May of '63, two songs - *Blowin' In The Wind* and *Don't Think Twice It's All Right* - forever changed the musical landscape. Winds of social change were stirring, and Britain's conservative powers were concerned.

Because Britain controlled information and music disseminated by the media in this era, external broadcasts gained enormous popularity with the country's youth. After 11 PM, pop music could be heard from a tiny neighboring country; Radio Luxembourg's AM transmitter boomed a powerful signal throughout Continental Europe. And Radio Caroline, the infamous pirate ship anchored off the Isle of Man in international waters, was regularly broadcasting a northern service of censored music - R&B and pop - into the UK.

Newbury was also introduced to classical music aired by BBC Radio. As he mentioned during a '77 Country Music People interview, "I think probably if I could put my finger on one influence in Britain, it was something very subtle because of all the classical music I listened to - I was never exposed to classical music 'til I came here." Hmmnn... polite policemen... art museums... taxi drivers with ties... Amadeus Mozart... Houston must have seemed like the Wild, Wild West compared to this cultural utopia.

On January 20, 1961, John Fitzgerald Kennedy was inaugurated as the 35th President of the United States. Shortly thereafter, an Air Force top-secret assignment sent Radioman Newbury to the Belgian Congo to monitor the Mercury Space Shot. The race to space was under way. After spending a few weeks in French-speaking Africa and completing the mission, Mick took authorized leave and went to Spain for vacation and vino. "At that time," he said, "some good Spanish bread and a bottle of wine would get you down the road and out in the beautiful countryside."

Returning to England, he began joining in at musical gatherings, singing and playing informally with a few Air Force buddies. "I had to get my hands on something that made music. I generally would borrow a guitar from a guy who had one... When you're making the kind of money you make in the Air Force, you can't afford to buy one."

Back in America, a struggling songwriter nicknamed Booger Red lay in the middle of a Nashville street - Broadway - before dawn, saying he hoped a car would run over him. "I got so drunk and discouraged," Willie Nelson said, "that I laid down in the street in the snow and waited for a car to come along." That didn't work, though: no traffic. "Eventually, I got up and bought another round of drinks... It was just drunken stupidity." Willie wouldn't be down on Broadway too much longer. Patsy Cline would soon take his *Crazy* to number two on the country chart, and Faron Young would score a huge hit with *Hello Walls*.

But as Booger Red was lying in the street, Mick was listening to his music. "It was the first time I heard Willie," Mick remarked. Released on the Liberty label, Willie's first LP, "And Then I Wrote," became his auspicious debut as a singer. Mick said he loved the album, especially *Funny How Time Slips Away*, "a great blending of country and jazz... and the very best of Willie's music."

In early 1962 at the pinnacle of Chubby Checker's twist craze, Ray Charles released his classic genre-crossing album, "Modern Sounds In Country & Western Music." Blinded by glaucoma at age seven, Charles developed his music - a melting pot of styles - by merging soul with R&B, gospel, jazz and country. These white-man's country standards - institutionalized by Hank Williams and his ilk - translated by a black man to orchestrated blues and jazzy swing tunes, influenced Mick enduringly. Stunned and shaken by the striking originality and beauty of the work, Mick would say, "Ray Charles did more for contemporary music than anyone else alive."

As Mickey celebrated his 22$^{nd}$ birthday, Marilyn Monroe sashayed to the microphone to purr *Happy Birthday* to President Kennedy at Madison Square Garden, while wearing a dress described as "skin and beads." On the same day, Ray Charles released *I Can't Stop Loving You* as a single. Meanwhile, NASA opened an office in Houston as the Cuban missile crisis rocked the world. Then on March 5, a Piper Comanche crashed in Camden, Tennessee, 100 miles west of Nashville. The tragedy claimed the life of thirty-year-old Patsy Cline, indisputably acknowledged as poster girl for the sophisticated new Nashville Sound. The country music community was devastated.

In England, Rock and Rollers were boppin' to a fresh, new sound from Liverpool. Just before detonation of global Beatlemania, Mick had an opportunity to see The Fab Four in concert. "In '62 or '63 I saw The Beatles perform in Dambury Cross in a 300 seat auditorium. Ringo was not with them then. Everybody was standin' up, and they were great! After the concert, I talked with John Lennon for a while. Told him that 'they could be a hit in America, but they would have to change their hairstyle (bowl cut, mop-top) and lose the pointed boots.' Lennon just looked at me kind of funny and smiled. Now that's another example of my great advice!"

While "Bye Bye Birdie" was rocking British and American theaters in October, Buck Sergeant Newbury received an Honorable Discharge from the Air Force. Though he considered re-upping, he was ready to return to civilian life. Four years earlier a scared but tough kid had enlisted. The military provided the terrified teenager with a responsible job, steady income, camaraderie and opportunity to travel. Houston's mean streets were replaced by the kinder, more polite cobblestone ways of London Town, where inteligencia outranked machismo.

And Newbury milked the experience. He absorbed the classics of printed word, song and canvas, turning on to Poe, Dylan, Charles, Mozart, Chopin, Monet, da Vinci and The Beatles. Visiting a few countries, he tasted the vinos, savoring Spanish reds and Portuguese whites. He went most everywhere by on-time train and came to love a civilized European culture. Now 23 years of age, he walked with more confidence and sophistication. The tough guy still had wild oats to sow, but the scared Houston teenager had become a man of culture.

# Chapter V: *Oh That Road Hits Back*
## October 1963 - 1965

Being discharged from military service is akin to being released from indentured servitude. Mickey was filled with joy and anticipation when the day arrived. After four years, he was free to pursue horizons of choice. For starters, exchanging the uniform - monkey suit - for civilian threads makes one feel fresh, aesthetically rejuvenated. The metamorphosis was important to Mickey. He developed a taste for fine suits in England, and while there, he ordered several custom made. The man of culture returned to North Houston as a man of élan, dressed to the nines. What a difference four years can make.

Though elated to see family and friends, the old haunts had little to offer. Trading places - London for Houston - was like traveling back in time, cultural shock in reverse. Mick knew he needed to move on. Remembering the great times enjoyed in late '56 as a Lounge Lizard and strolling Portuguese folk singer, he went back to the happy-go-lucky coast. But this time he went down to South East Texas to work on the shrimp boats in Galveston.

Mickey had great passion for boats, rivers, lakes and oceans. He loved warm Gulf breezes and the serenity of gliding over cool water into the open horizon. Shrimping, then, provided him with a paid vacation of sorts plus a spicy dose of excitement and camaraderie. And the work was exhilarating.

Most shrimping is done after the sun goes down, and 16-hour workdays are typical. Usually 50 to 65 feet long, shrimp boats are rigged to tow two trawl nets. As the boat races along at top speed at night, the wench operator releases steel cables connected to 60-foot nets. This is kind of scary and makes a thunderous noise. Skill is required to do it just right so the nets rake the bottom. If too much cable is released, the nets dig in creating a potentially disastrous situation. If not enough cable is released, the nets ride above the ocean floor and catch no shrimp. The men learn quickly to depend on each other.

The experience was poetry in motion for young Newbury. After work was done, as waves rocked them up and down and back and forth, the men joked and passed the bottle. Celebrating the moment, Mickey would make up a song. The shrimpers laughed and cheered; the seagulls cried and Mickey would sing again. As the sun set off the ship's stern, bottlenose dolphins danced to the beat of the boat. Meanwhile the ocean - always the same, always different and always powerful - provided majestic rhythm and transition to Newbury's music.

A shrimp boat has no room for a prima donna, and this is one reason Mick enjoyed the experience. "The cabin consisted of the wheelhouse, bunk beds and the galley," shrimper Charles Johnson wrote. "There were no bathrooms on the shrimp boats. You just did your business over the rail. You did not take a shower 'till you returned to port, sometimes 10 to 15 days. You could wash off in seawater, or jump over the side and swim if you wanted to. I did that until, I had an encounter with what seemed to be a large barracuda. I used buckets to wash with after that close encounter. You usually had only one or two changes of clothes for the trip. By the time you returned to port, your jeans could stand up by themselves..."

Irrespective of hygienic considerations, Mick found his sea legs and had a blast. "I liked the ocean," he explained, "and I liked the free style of living the shrimpers and fishermen had. They were doing what they enjoyed, which I liked. Good people to be around. A lot of fun. It gave me time to write. That was a real good time for me. I guess when I went down in the Gulf was when I really started writing. When I was working on the boats. I'd write songs about the shrimpers. They got a kick out of that. About tearing their nets up, the sort of problems they had..."

"I'd go to Louisiana a lot too, and work on the shrimp boats for a while. (Many shrimpers in Louisiana come from a French-speaking Creole background.) There's a little joint down there where the shrimpers go and I sing there sometimes and they all pass the hat and give me money. It's never been hard for me."

The primary driving route from Galveston to southern Louisiana is Interstate 10, the loneliest highway in the world. I-10 goes for 279 miles across Louisiana and 879 miles across Texas, half of which is without a spur route - a 110, 210, 310 and so on. Not much for Mick to do on a trip like this except listen to the radio and write songs in his head.

> *Out on this long stretch of Interstate 10,*
> *that ol' Del Rio station just keeps rollin' right in*
> *Many the night it was my only friend*
> *Just me and the radio...*
> *A LONG ROAD HOME*

"I'd slowly been putting together my poems with my music," he explained to Disc magazine, "And I dug the country idiom, so I just thought I'd try some songwriting." About then, his dad asked, "Have you figured out what you're gonna do with your life, son?" Mick answered, "Yep, I'm gonna write songs." Milton cautioned, "It's awful hard," and Mick agreed, "I know it." "Well son how long are you gonna give it?" Mickey thought for a second and replied firmly, "For the rest of my life. I mean I don't have no intentions of failing."

"Dad never made more than about $75 a week in his whole life. It was awful hard for him to... You see, out of my family of about 300, I was the first one with a high school education. They expected more from me than they did anybody else. I was educated. You know... you gotta understand... to them that was almost like a doctorate degree... I had written about 40 songs, and a guy in Houston named Ray Rush (not Ray <u>B</u>ush, as has been misreported) took 15 of them to Wesley Rose (of Acuff-Rose, the publisher) in Nashville. Wesley called me and asked if I'd come sign as a staff writer," which he would do in about a year.

For the moment, restless Mick wanted to travel. He covered Texas and Louisiana in his '54 Pontiac, performing here and there for food and cash, playing his new songs and others he cared about, such as *"Blowin' In the Wind.*" He recounted a humorous gig. "I was playing in this bar in a bowling alley in Shreveport, Louisiana. Was in the middle of my performance when this beautiful woman came in. I wanna tell ya... she was drop dead gorgeous." As Mickey was vertically challenged, they had put him up on a bar stool on top of a grand piano. "While singin' and eyeballin' her, I began to lean back on the barstool. Well, I got lost in the song or in her eyes and leaned back just a little bit too far. I fell backwards off the barstool, bounced off the piano, and landed on the ground on my head. I didn't feel so bad though, 'cause I was dressed up in one of my fine hand-tailored English suits. Anyway, we went clubbin' for a week and had a blast... Our relationship was strictly platonic. Just really good friends. Her name was Billie Jean Jones. She was Hank Williams and Johnny Horton's widow."

Ironically, Billie Jean's husbands had given their final performances at the same venue, The Skyline in Austin, Texas. Afterwards, Williams was found dead in his car on New Year's Day, 1953; and Horton was killed in a car accident in 1960. Billie Jean would be one of several links in a chain connecting Newbury to Hank Williams.

After singing in the bowling alley and partying with Billie Jean for a week, Mickey returned to Houston. On November 22nd, racist Lee Harvey Oswald gunned down President Kennedy in nearby Dallas. "I watched him give a speech that morning, Mickey said. "Later when the traumatic news came, it tore me up." Vice President Lyndon Baines Johnson from central Texas was promptly sworn in and would remain in the Presidency for five years. November 22nd is also the day of St. Cecilia, Patron Saint of Music.

*Do you think about me every now and then*
*Do I ever cross your mind*
*Sounds like old man winter threw his fiddle in the wind*
*Oh I need a good friend here tonight*
SAINT CECILIA

Following the assassination, Mickey went to Dallas. Since he was living in the Pontiac, the car served as a bedroom and closet. Thieves broke into the automobile and stole 15 tailor-made English suits. "They left me one pair of blue jeans and a sweater a girl in England had knitted me." During that winter, Mickey nearly froze to death.

*The cold nights had no pity on that Waycross Georgia farm boy*
*Most days he went hungry; then the summer came*
SAN FRANCISCO MABEL JOY

What was playing on the radio in these days? In February of '64, The Beatles accounted for 60 percent of records sold in North America, and in March, the group pulled off an unprecedented music industry coup, simultaneously holding the top five slots on the <u>Billboard</u> singles chart. Beatlemania was sweeping the nation just as Elvis had in the fifties - even though Lennon didn't "lose the pointed boots." Meanwhile, another British invasion of sorts drew moviegoers to the theater to watch James Bond match wits with "Goldfinger."

Desiring a change of pace and perhaps music, Mickey went to Nashville still living in the Pontiac clunker. The state capital of Tennessee, Nashville had a genuine small town feel with cosmopolitan diversity. Names reflecting the city's many personalities include: Jackson Town, Music City, Printing Capital, Protestant Vatican, City of Parks, Athens of the South, Hog and Hominy State, Hollywood of Country Music, Wall Street of the South and Buckle of the Bible Belt. Each of these names reveals a different side to Nashville's personality; Gnashville and Nash-Vegas are nicknames the city had yet to acquire.

Mick relied on his guitar for company, and when he was too tired or too broke to drive, he parked. "I slept in the back of the car with my clothes piled all on top of me. Or in laundromats, or wherever else I could find to sleep." Nashville's average low temperature in winter is 30 degrees F, while wind-chill brings the temperature down to shiver state. On cold evenings, the local laundromat must have felt like the Waldorf Astoria.

*When you're cold there's nothin' as welcome as sunshine*
FRISCO DEPOT

"I'd drive from Nashville to Memphis to Shreveport to Houston and back to Nashville. I didn't stay in one place more than six weeks for years." Alone, Mickey made this 1,640-mile loop many times. He loved to drive and wander, but more significantly, he "was searching for something. Not sure what." Mick would say years later, "If anybody wants to understand my songs, then they should go to Texas and drive the back roads for about a week."

> *Just cruisin' the back roads with nothin' but time*
> *Miles from the highway with no hills left to climb*
> *Me and the whispering pines*
> *LONG ROAD HOME*

Rambling around Texas, Tennessee and Louisiana, Mickey retraced the footsteps, wagon wheels and train tracks of his ancestors. Great-Great Grandparents Thomas and Polly had settled in the Hills of Tennessee, by the mighty Cumberland River. Great-Grandfather Stephen covered common ground 100 years earlier, when he delivered the family to Paige, Texas. Grandfather Alonzo traveled the route many times while working for the railroad and during his courtship of Lettie Bell in the Cajun State. And to visit relatives, Miton and Mamie frequently drove the youngsters from Houston to Shreveport. It is no surprise that a nomadic Newbury revisited family paths of the past.

> *You find yourself searchin' your past for the links to the chain*
> *FRISCO DEPOT*

What Mickey was looking for is difficult to articulate, but what he was seeking to escape was perfectly clear: the absence of something worthwhile.

> *I hear a freight train off in the distance*
> *Goin' where I do not know*
> *I just know it is going somewhere*
> *That is where I want to go*
> *THE SILVER MOON CAFE*

The trips were productive. "I do most of my writing in the car while I'm travellin'," Mick explained. "The car is a good place to write because there aren't any distractions. Your other mind seems to be free... If you really write a good song, you write that song from a level below conscience and that level is where you have years and years of set up rhyme patterns."

Speaking of traveling and good song writing, as Mickey turned 24, Roger Miller's autobiographical song *King of the Road* was awarded a gold record.

Miller, a Texan raised in Oklahoma, caused a stir in Nashville by writing smash hits such as *Chug-a-Lug* and *Dang Me*. Filled with slant rhymes, irregular rhythm and nonsense phrases, the songs were unique and capricious. Their paths had not yet crossed, but the men would soon meet and become friends.

Mick arranged to perform at the King Edward Hotel in Beaumont on "The Right Side Of Texas." Formerly called The LaSalle, the hotel was a swanky twelve-floor high-rise, which attracted oil businessmen and high rollers from Houston and New Orleans. Mick considered the King Edward a great place to play, since comfy room and tasty board were included, plus the Kountze clan was just 30 miles away. Tips were decent too.

Since the car was broken down and Mick was just plain broke, he hopped - "nailed" in hobo lingo - a freight train to get there. Mick nailed trains as an "Airedale" - one who travels alone, and learned quickly to watch out for the "bull" - the railroad security guard. He enjoyed riding in semi-open boxcars so long as the door did not slam shut, and he remained warm and dry. Sometimes he brought along a cheap wine - "Sneaky Pete" - to kill the chill. Mick loved riding the rails and listening to whistle and wheels sing their powerful song as the train rocketed ahead.

> *WISH I WAS an old guitar*
> *Sitin' in a beat up car*
> *Hittin' every two bit bar from here to Texas…*
>
> *Standin' like a hobo in the morning rain*
> *Starin' down a rusty track for one more train*
> *TELL HIM BOYS*

When the "cannonball" - fast train - reached his Beaumont destination, he anticipated one short whistle meaning, STOP AHEAD. Instead, the iron horse shrieked three short bursts, meaning RUNNING THROUGH STOP AT NEXT STATION. So with guitar in hand, Mick jumped from the door! He hit the ground running but as he could not maintain the momentum, he "rolled and tumbled for at least a hundred yards." He touched down hard, landing flat on his stomach. When Mick hit the ground, he knew he was hurt, but he did not realize he had broken his back. Laying low on his stomach, he looked up sheepishly to see if hoboes had witnessed his embarrassing arrival. None were in sight and somehow his guitar had escaped damage. Adding insult to injury though, the jump and tumble ruined his knitted sweater, the last of his English attire.

Newbury passed into unconsciousness for a few hours. When he came to, he "walked into town and went to work at the King Edward Hotel on Pearl

Street, performing for three hours with a broken back. What really hurt was my elbows and knees... They had no meat left on 'em." At a time when *King of the Road* was the number one song in the nation, the road damn near killed Mickey.

*Sail to the ground in one last burst of sound*
*SONG OF SORROW*

*There I was at 24, faded dreams and nothin' more*
*So, I hit the road again, but, oh, that road hits back my friends.*
*IN '59*

*Have you ever seen a freight train rollin' down the tracks*
*Eighty wheels on threads of steel never lookin' back*
*When I hear that whistle it still chills me to the bone*
*SOME MEMORIES ARE BETTER LEFT ALONE*

*When you're afoot there's nothin' as fast as a train*
*FRISCO DEPOT*

*A hobo cryin' I am too tired to roam*
*IF I COULD BE*

*Once I stumbled through the darkness tumbled to my knees*
*THE 33rd OF AUGUST*

Though Newbury would be plagued with back problems for the rest of his days, good did come from the ordeal. The vivid memory would inspire several songs, plus he made an important contact. "The first time I met Jack Clement," Mick said, "was right after I broke my back. He had an office next to the King Edward Hotel." Memphis native Cowboy Jack was a well-known record producer, who had trained under legendary Sam Phillips at Sun Studios, even producing a few sessions for Jerry Lee Lewis. Clement would one day lend an experienced hand to Mick's best friend, the guy who worshipped Hank Williams.

Shortly thereafter, RCA's smooth country crooner who did his first singing work in Beaumont was about to take his final bow. Gentleman Jim Reeves - the balladeer of Galloway, Texas - died on July 31, 1964, when his single-engine plane ran into difficulties during a storm and crashed into dense woods outside Nashville. Fellow singers and hundreds of local residents participated in the search. His body was found on August 2.

One week following the crash, the signing of the Gulf of Tonkin Resolution initiated America's involvement in a war in a country most Americans had never heard of... Vietnam. Somewhere in the distance a lost train wailed one long and one short whistle burst.

Far from Southeast Asia, Acuff-Rose (A-R) was widely recognized in 1964 as the preeminent song-publishing company in Nashville. The firm had been established as the first music publisher and first company to record country music in Music City, USA. Three of the first four members of the Country Music Hall of Fame were associated with A-R. On October 12 when the legendary company was located on Seventeenth Avenue, Mickey happily signed their songwriting-publishing agreement.

The A-R universe was comprised of several stars and star makers, for instance: Roy Acuff, Hank Williams, Don Gibson, Floyd Cramer, Roy Orbison, Marty Robbins, John D. Loudermilk, Don and Phil Everly, Charlie and Ira Louvin, Felice and Boudleaux Bryant and Pee Wee King (who co-wrote *Tennessee Waltz*, the state song for Tennessee). Twenty-four-year-old Mickey was thrilled. These were his heroes and he had joined their club.

A decade earlier when Mick was forming a high school band, A-R founding partner Fred Rose had died, and his accountant son, Wesley, had assumed management of the firm. Ten years at the helm, Wesley was elated to have Newbury on board and wrote, "When Mickey signed our exclusive songwriters contract, I was as excited about him as any new writer I ever heard... I thought he was artistic magic in action... He is as modern as tomorrow and as traditional as yesterday."

After finalizing the Acuff-Rose deal, Mick performed at a few local spots, until he had mustered sufficient gas money for another trip. This outing would prove to be the beginning of an essential journey, one that would bring him face to face with two people who would have profound effects on his songwriting, although for entirely different reasons.

He took off for Houston, stopping by Dallas to visit lifelong buddy Talmage Bell. Talmage introduced him to his new wife Shirley, and she introduced him to her best friend, Detta Beach. Mickey was drawn to the attractive woman immediately. The 5'6" blond had worked as a hairdresser and most recently had gained employment with Delta Airlines as a stewardess. Detta was based in Dallas and Mickey would see more of her... later.

Mickey next went to Houston to spend Christmas with his family, and it was then that he met Townes Van Zandt at a local coffeehouse. Townes came from a wealthy oil family, and his ancestors had played an important part in Texas history. Among the founding fathers of Texas, they founded Van

Zandt County in East Texas, and the county erected statues of great-great-great grandparents Isaac and Francis, who helped draft the state constitution. Royal lineage notwithstanding, the lanky twenty-year-old told Mick he had just dropped out of college to become an itinerant folk singer. He had started playing guitar at 15 after seeing Elvis on TV, and he dug Dylan; but his hero was none other than the Hillbilly Shakespeare, Hank Williams. The men immediately became friends, and one day, Mickey would persuade Townes to join him in Nashville.

But for the time being, they hung out together, enjoying each other's company and artistry. They took in a few acts at local coffeehouses such as Sand Mountain. Townes accompanied Mickey to a favorite hangout, Jones Sound Recording Studio on Houston's North side. The proprietor Doyle Jones and Mickey were friends, and Mickey would occasionally drop in. (Newbury had no financial interest in the business as has been misreported, however there was another Mickey; Gilley and Jones would form a partnership in the mid seventies.) Jones looked forward to Newbury's visits, explaining, "He was a breath of fresh air compared to all the amateurs comin' in during those days. I liked him so much that I did his demo work gratis. Those recordings are beautiful. Just him and that old twelve-string. What a great guy... one of the greatest talents who ever lived."

Still living in the car, Mickey said, "I would write whatever I felt and mail it to Acuff-Rose. I never took on a retainer because I didn't want to be obligated. I never took an advance or a retainer at all the whole time I was there..." Though free from debt and obligation, the other side of the coin... he was broke.

In March of '65, Mickey performed at The Suburban Club in Houston, where he enjoyed a close friendship with manager, Barbara Lucher. Mick would refer to the club as "Richards North Side Lounge" in the song, *If You Ever Get To Houston*. "Everybody called her 'Sam' and we were just dear friends. We often would sleep in the back of the club, as would other employees. Nothin' was goin' on... we just slept. Well one night... Sam and I ended up together." Sam would give birth to Mickey's child, Joe, in Houston, Texas on December 9, 1965. Mickey however would not know about his son for twenty-four years.

> *Winter came to '65; I fought the cold to stay alive*
> *And when I tried to light a fire, I was burned by my desire*
> *IN '59*

In June, Mickey's future wife Susan Pack graduated from South Eugene High School in Oregon. During that summer, ex New Christy Minstrel Barry McGuire's *Eve Of Destruction* became the number one song in the nation.

A few months later, lovely Susan was - in her words - "surprised" to be crowned Miss Oregon at the 1965 state competition. She then participated in the Miss America Pageant in Atlantic City, New Jersey, placing in the Top Ten as a semifinalist.

One month later, Dylan drew catcalls and boos at the Newport Folk Festival when he played *Maggies Farm* electrically... forever blurring the lines between folk and rock. Soon he would release *Like A Rolling Stone*, ending the reign of the 2-½ minute song. Mick applauded these milestones and would soon establish a few of his own.

With Mick's easy manner and Acuff-Rose's effective promotion, Newbury's songs were covered in 1965. RCA's Jimmy Elledge - a country singer-songwriter born in Meridian, Mississippi and best known for recording Willie Nelson's *Funny How Time Slips Away* - was first to cover Newbury, releasing *Just As Long As That Someone Is You*. Mickey had written the disheartened *Someone* in Houston in 1959 before joining the Air Force.

> *I want someone I can talk to when I'm blue*
> *Someone to love me and be true*
> *Yes, I want someone to love and it makes no difference who*
> *JUST AS LONG AS THAT SOMEONE IS YOU*

"Mr. Green Acres" - Eddie Albert was next to cut a Newbury number, *A Man Can Never Go Back Home*. Composed in 1964 and used for a TV show, "*A Man*" demonstrates remarkable maturity in Newbury's writing. These were also his first lyrics to employ personification.

> *It's been a long, long time since I've been this way*
> *There's the old white house where I was born*
> *Now the gates are rusty, the white has turned to gray*
> *The pillars on the porch are old and worn*
>
> *But the echo of the laughter these old walls have known*
> *Fills my heart with mem'ries of the loved ones that are gone*
> *Here in the parlor I stand all alone*
> *In the old white house I once called home*
>
> *The rooms are empty, the house stands all alone*
> *I think I hear my train, I must be moving on*
> *It seems the old white house whispers,*
> *'Friend, you should have known,*
> *A MAN CAN NEVER GO BACK HOME.'*

Ray Peterson followed with another Newbury song, *(I) Wish I Could Say No To You*. True to style, Peterson sang it as a moving ballad with pretty violins in the background. Then, Pat Boone recorded Mick's *Five Miles From Home*. Boone explained that he cut the folksy tune "way back in my Dot Record days." He praised Newbury's artistry, advising the author, "The song was just good craftsmanship, good popular music, and I had some success with it."

Mick's earliest solo records - featuring him as singer - were released in 1965 on Acuff-Rose's in-house label, Hickory. The label was regarded as a country music outlet, because it was an A-R enterprise based in Nashville, and King of Country Music Roy Acuff recorded there. But Hickory's stable of stars also included pop artists such as Sue Thompson and B.J. Thomas, Scottish folk singer Donovan and a psychedelic garage band from Houston, Neal Ford & The Fanatics. And now... Mickey Newbury was in the house. He would sleep in his Pontiac parked behind the Acuff-Rose building, and arrive at work bright and early, ready to record.

On his first Hickory release, Mick performed his own compositions: *Eastham Prison Farm* and *Who's Gonna Cry When I'm Gone*. He did *Who's Gonna Cry* like a Ray Peterson tearjerker, in the vein of *Tell Laura I Love Her*. The topic of side two, *Eastham Prison Farm*, was delivered as a medium tempo rocker. On his initial Nashville effort, Mickey honored his father by singing about the horror of Texas incarceration.

His second offering, written by Acuff-Rose staffers, delivered two brooding numbers: *Lonely Place* (Melson & Montgomery) and *Well I Did Last Night* (Felice & Boudleaux Bryant). Hickory next issued two songs written and performed by Newbury: *Travelin' Man*, a catchy tune seemingly influenced by early Peter, Paul and Mary; and *There Is A Time to Die*, a folksy romp which may draw from Ecclesiastes, Chapter 3.

> *There is a time for laughing*
> *There is a time to cry*
> *There is a time for loving*
> *THERE IS A TIME TO DIE*

Mick subsequently waxed *Anyway You Want Me*, which he had written in 1965. *It May Not Take Too Much*, penned by Joe Melson, was featured on the B side. "*Anyway*" addresses the theme of 1959's "*Someone*," needing a woman, but "*Anyway*" scores much higher on the emotional scale. Mick's spirit, as expressed in the songs, had improved from grief in '59 to enthusiasm in '65:

*I'll be as tall as a mountain*
*I'll be as small as a bee*
*ANY WAY YOU WANT ME*
*That's the way I'm gonna be*

*I'll be as wild as a river*
*Or as gentle as the wind in the trees*
*ANY WAY YOU WANT ME*
*That's the way I'm gonna be*

Two 45's conclude the Hickory output. Mick's clear-as-a-bell tenor delivers *After The Rains* by F & B Bryant as a melodic R&B number, ideally suited for The Platters. The other side features a Newbury work, *Baby Just Said Goodbye*, which became the first minor hit for Roy Acuff Jr. The trippy *Dreaming In The Rain* complete with finger snaps and fuzz-tone guitar came next (Newbury/Dan Folger), while the backside features a pop tune written solely by Folger, *Leavin' Makes The Rain Come Down*.

So... what to make of Newbury's 12 Hickory releases? Most conspicuously, they are not presented as country fare. The songs have a folksy-pop-ballad feel; one is R&B, one is rock and one wanders the hazy halls of psychedelia. Was he searching for a style? Perhaps... more significantly he was communicating in different dialects. Conveyance of plaintive emotion is the common thread that ties the songs together, so when played one after the other, a sense of natural continuity follows. It is a shame Hickory did not fuse them together on an album. Note that three of Mick's final four Hickory releases deal with *the rain*.

Meanwhile in Dallas, the romance between Detta and Mickey began to heat up. "Mickey was very nice," Detta attested. "We'd go to Denny's restaurant all the time and talk and drink coffee. He carried a brown briefcase everywhere containing his music. He kept all these loose sheets of paper with words to his songs in that briefcase. He'd pull out a song and sing it while playing his twelve-string guitar. He always played his own music. The guitar and briefcase went everywhere we'd go. One day someone stole the briefcase and he was very upset."

"We got engaged, and he gave me an engagement ring that I still have. Since I am Catholic, Mickey said he would convert when we married. He wanted me to meet everybody. We went to Nashville and he introduced me to Wesley Rose. We also went to Houston so I could meet his parents. It was raining when we drove down there. They lived in a little cabin in the Big Thicket and they were nice to me. His dad (Milton) was real quiet..."

74

Mickey pulled into Dallas many times to see Detta. Though he had little money - "I can stretch twenty dollars for months!" - he always found a way to gas up the car for the 700-mile jaunt to The Big D. Friends and family meant more to Mick than moola. Detta had different ideas, though, and was about to shake his foundation. "We knew when we married," she explained, "I would have to quit my job with Delta. Stewardesses then were required to be single. That was fine with me as I'm from the old school. I believe the man should work and bring home the bacon. I wanted to stay at home and care for the kids and the house."

"And that was the problem... He was always broke! We never went to a movie or did anything. He liked to talk and drink coffee at Denny's. And play his songs. Because of this, I broke off the engagement. I was insecure, I guess, because of his lack of finances and I broke off our engagement. He was very upset. I married someone else a few months later."

There is another side to the story, though, and "it" happened not once, but twice... Mickey was twice angry, twice hurt... and consequently... they broke up with each other. Mickey, however, refused to put the story on the street.

> *Detta your needs swallowed me like a wildfire*
> *It was a weed that could not be controlled*
> *Oh the roots were so deep in your unhappy childhood*
> *But I understand now when the WINTER WINDS BLOW*
>
> *Detta I have learned how to deal with my madness*
> *Although at times I swear I do not know*
> *When I am happy or when it is sadness*
> *Do you understand when the WINTER WINDS BLOW*
>
> *I will never know why you ever came into my life*
> *Only to leave me believing you would be my wife*
> *LONG GONE*

Since being discharged from the Air Force, Mickey's clothes and songs had been ripped off. The man was also broke... and not just financially. He had broken his back and broken up with his fiancée. Of these discordant happenings, hell hath no fury like a woman's scorn; and that last blow hit him hard. Mickey did not know what to do. Best friends Talmage and CAG were married with lives of their own. He did not want to return to Houston. "There was no legitimate music business in Houston," Mick would say, plus that would have been too déjà vu.

During this bitter winter of discontent... out there in the cold car... isolated... physically and emotionally wounded... he found comfort in his guitar. Several songs would be inspired by these disheartened affairs, leading Mick to say, "Detta is the inspiration for about half my songs." He would draw from the ocean of melancholy memories time and time again.

*This morning at dawn I pulled into town*
*Had some coffee and talked with some old friends of mine*
*Laughing at all the good times they remembered*
*Then I remembered a time*

*Lord I can see the bright lights back in Dallas*
*Yesterday moves like a dream through my mind*
*I didn't suppose I would ever forget her*
*And you know it took such a long time*

*BUT I DON'T THINK MUCH ABOUT HER NO MORE*
*Seldom if ever does she cross my mind*
*Yesterday's gone and better forgotten*
*Like a poison red berry it clings to my mind*

As winter winds blew and 1966 arrived, Mickey moved to Nashville "at the urging of Wesley Rose." Wesley may have inadvertently saved his life. On the way to Music City, Mickey wrote two songs in the car: *Sweet Memories* and *Funny, Familiar, Forgotten Feelings*. No longer a kid, he had grown increasingly wary of the cold, lonely and treacherous road. Texas was a painful memory and he was more than ready to move on.

*I don't want me no BIG CITY WOMAN*
*If you love the bright lights you can stay*
*'Cause I'm findin' my way back to Nashville*
*We'll be gone before the dawn meets the day*

Though Mick had danced with a few demons, the experiences made him stronger and a better dancer. Plus he was holding one helluva trump card. Pat Boone, Jimmy Elledge, Eddie Albert, Ray Peterson and Roy Acuff Jr. had covered his songs, and though the recordings enjoyed limited success, Mick knew something was going to happen. Something big. In Nashville. He could feel it.

**Mickey circa 1968**

# Chapter VI: *Paris In The Twenties*
## 1966 - June 1968

1966 was the year the music industry noticed Mickey Newbury. Two heavyweights, Don Gibson and Dean Martin, heard a demo of Newbury's *Funny Familiar Forgotten Feelings*, and both singers expressed a desire to release it. According to legal right of first refusal, the songwriter can approve the first artist to cover a song. After the initial release, the song goes up for grabs.

Newbury was faced with the most important decision of his young career... Gibson or Martin? The latter - a Buckeye from Ohio - enjoyed renown as an international celebrity of song, screen and TV. Two years earlier, Martin had scored the runaway hit of his career - his theme song - *Everybody Loves Somebody*. "The Dean Martin Show" had premiered on television in late '65, and the ratings quickly went through the roof. His portfolio included 36 movies, among them "Ocean's Eleven" and "The Silencers," a spy spoof starring Martin as ultra cool secret agent, Matt Helm. Dean Martin - "Dino" - was a charter member to Sinatra's illustrious Rat Pack. The man was absolutely at the top of his game.

But Mickey aspired to become a successful songwriter like his Acuff-Rose associate. "When I first met Don Gibson," he informed Hit Parader, "I couldn't even talk." Signed to RCA Nashville in 1957 by Chet Atkins, North Carolina born Gibson had scored 11 Top Ten singles including *Oh Lonesome Me* and *I Can't Stop Loving You*. The second was a Newbury favorite, as arranged and performed by his hero, Ray Charles. It would also be a feather in Newbury's cap for Gibson to release *FFFF*, as it would mark the first song Gibson had recorded which he had not written. Newbury respected Gibson immensely; they were frat brothers, and they were Southern Boys.

The decision came down to friendship. Gibson recorded *FFFF* that February, and it shot to the Country Top 10. To show appreciation, he would cover a dozen Newbury songs - more than any artist. This scenario stands as a shining example of how Nashville stars shared the spotlight in the era when they took care of their own. At the other end of the spectrum - perhaps from disappointment - Martin never recorded the song. Years later Mick would say, "That was the best deal I ever made in my life."

After it scored as a country hit, Mick told Wesley Rose not to worry, "Some pop guy would pick it up." Time promptly proved him right. Tom Jones - "The Voice" - recorded *FFFF* in April, and it rocketed up the pop charts in several European and Latin countries, becoming a world hit, though it barely broke the Top 40 in the USA. The release followed on the heels of his number one smash successes, *It's Not Unusual* and *Green Green Grass of Home*, thus providing enormous exposure to Newbury as a songwriter. Over the next few years, Jones would cover six Newbury songs including *Weeping Annaleah* and *I Wish I Could Say No To You*.

Besides recognition, *FFFF* brought awards and rewards. The song won three BMI awards for Mickey, and his writing career was off and running. He cashed his first big royalty check of $8,000, and with loose hundred-dollar bills in a brown paper bag; he purchased a gold Cadillac Eldorado hardtop. (The car was not a convertible, as has been misreported.) And then... he wound up sleeping in it! "Since I knew I'd still be living in my car," he said, "I wanted something dependable." Mickey was proud of his Caddy, and he and Ramblin' Jack Elliot spent hours in it cruisin' Broadway.

Most importantly, people got their first taste of Newbury's music. Dave Laing wrote, "With its languorous melody and melancholic lyrics, *Funny Familiar Forgotten Feelings* set the pattern for much of Newbury's oeuvre." In good time, after paying a few more dues, Mickey would master the ability to marry "languorous melody to melancholy lyric." This was merely the first opus.

> *Last night, quietly, she walked through my mind*
> *As I lay searching for sleep*
> *Her soft hand reached out, she whispered my name*
> *As she brushed a tear from my cheek*
> *And then those FUNNY FAMILIAR FORGOTTEN FEELINGS*
> *Started walkin' all over my mind*

The celebration came to a sudden stop, as tragedy struck a few weeks after Mick's 26th birthday. "I never will forget when Roy Orbison's wife died (June 7 in a motorcycle accident). I spent a solid week with him after she died. In fact, Don Gant and his wife and Roy and Claudette were all together. A guy ran a stop sign and hit her. She died almost immediately... in Roy's arms. I stayed with him and all I could say to him was, 'You got to get hold of yourself 'cause of these kids... ' (Two years later) Roy was in England when the house caught on fire. They called me at (my cabin on) Centerville Lake. They wanted to know if I knew where Roy was, and I said, 'He's on tour in England.' They said that his kids (Roy Dwayne, eleven, and Anthony, eight) had burned in the fire... I couldn't even go to the funeral... What would I say to him?"

Several months after Claudette's passing - at the insistence of friends - Roy began dating. Mickey remembered, "He was driving this Ferrari. If I had a girlfriend, Roy'd get 'em. He'd keep 'em 'till he got tired of 'em and throw 'em away, and then I'd go find me another girlfriend... then I'd come back and he'd have 'em. And I know I was prettier than him! It had to be the car... He was the best singer and played such great guitar. A lot of people are not aware of how good he was on guitar." Orbison's operatic singing and superlative guitar playing scored several hits, enduring songs that are part of the collective psyche.

*Pretty Paper* - written by Willie Hugh Nelson - was one of Orbison's more woeful numbers. Nelson was a fairly successful songwriter and recording artist at the time, with a small but devoted cult following. He also did some pig farming in nearby Ridgetop, Tennessee. Nelson's latest LP effort, "Country Music Concert," had just been overseen by RCA's renowned producer, Charles Felton Jarvis.

Jarvis had produced albums for Elvis Presley, Skeeter Davis and Nashville's street singer, Cortelia Clark. Nicknamed "Fel-Tone" by Fats Domino, he shared his office with an exotic pal... a pet anaconda. On a pivotal day in 1966, the first meeting between Georgia native Felton and Mickey transpired. He sang a few compositions for Felton, accompanying himself on the beat up twelve-string. Felton was impressed, saying, "I had already listened to about a hundred different songs that day and at that point I thought I'd had about all I could stand. As soon as he opened his mouth and started singing, I just about jumped over the desk. He was great! Right then I knew I wanted to record Mickey Newbury." The men became friends, and over the next few years Mickey would just drop in. Felton nicknamed him, "The Mick."

Another key meeting followed in Nashville, as The Mick met Texas native Kris Kristofferson when he was on his way back to West Point to teach English. After earning a master's degree in English literature from Oxford in 1960, Kristofferson married in California and then joined the Army. He became a helicopter pilot, rising to the rank of captain before receiving transfer orders to The Point. But Captain Kristofferson heard a different drum... actually an acoustic guitar. He wanted to be a songwriter. Brand new to the Nashville scene in 1966, Kristofferson was given the five-star tour by personal tour guide, Mickey Newbury.

"Kris is a great guy," Mick stated, "a complicated character. He has a gruff exterior and a heart of glass. He wants everyone to love him, at times to his detriment, and is a fiercely loyal friend. As a songwriter he is as good as he wants to be... He's one of those guys that I honest to God knew was a star the first time I saw him... I knew that film was where he needed to be. I took him by the hand and walked him through the town... We were just really close friends..."

"Kris' life," Mick continued, "was kind of mapped out for him by his family, you know. His mother turned her back on him. He and his father got back together the year his father died. And I was really glad to see that 'cause it was tearin' at him... Kris' wife knew exactly what had to be done. I think Kris still loved Fran when they got a divorce. She just couldn't stand it, you know. And you can see... goin' from an officer's wife to livin' in a shack in Nashville, and Kris workin' as a janitor. She just couldn't deal with it. And Kris was gettin' no support from his family."

Kristofferson wound up working as a janitor at a local Columbia studio where Johnny Cash, Lefty Frizzell and Simon and Garfunkel recorded. He wisely used that opportunity to learn the recording business and make contacts. It paid off. Bob Dylan recorded "Blond On Blond" while Kristofferson worked there, and he would point to Dylan as his "single greatest influence." But it was Newbury who taught him the ropes. "We became real good friends," Kristofferson advised the Houston Post. "God, I learned more about songwriting from Mickey than I did any other single human being. He was my hero and still is."

Far from Nashville in style and miles, The Beach Boys released "Pet Sounds" in May of '66. It became a Newbury favorite and is regarded as the first concept rock album. Music was changing rapidly, and the business experienced stellar sales in 1967, a landmark year. For the first time in America, more albums were sold than singles: 192 million compared with 187 million. In dollar value, LPs represented 82 percent of the pie, driven by The Beatles release of the revolutionary "Sgt. Peppers Lonely Heart's Club Band," their answer to "Pet Sounds." Meanwhile, the first half of '67 saw Jimi Hendrix release three Top Ten singles in the U.K., redefining the role of the electric guitar.

Mickey listened attentively to the new music. Sonically and lyrically, the blues with a beat had evolved to a personal and political platform to express (scream) concerns of the sixties generation. Songs dealing with LSD, LBJ, segregation, free love and Viet Nam had replaced light-hearted fare such as *Don't Be Cruel*. Dylan opened the door on liberal lyrics in the sixties with "Your sons and your daughters are beyond you command." The More Melodic Beatles then blew the door clean off its hinges with "Look for the girl with the sun in her eyes, and she's gone." Meanwhile, Mickey wrote a song expressing the horrors of LSD, and Hendrix allegedly commented a year later that the song *Just Dropped In (To See What Condition My Condition Was In)* was his favorite.

During the era, the voice of America's youth cried out, and one youthful voice caught Mick's attention. Though a man of twenty-six, he had fallen head-over-heels for a Nashville high school sophomore... a mature, good-looking fifteen-year-old. The show of affection had to spark at least a low-level conflict with Newbury's colleague and Lana's father, Willie Nelson. Mick said he told Willie, "I'm not going to lay a finger on this girl until she turns 18 and then she's mine!" As a caring father, Willie had a tough time dealing with the situation.

Phil Sutcliffe reported in <u>Blender</u> magazine that Mick "courted Lana until deterred by Dad's cogent arguments - and his Colt .45." Mick said the narrative was hogwash... that Shotgun Willie never drew on him. Lana concurred, "Dad never pulled a gun on Mickey. He took us on a little ride and told us we weren't to see each other again until I was 18. I was 15 at the time." What transpired is locked away in the hearts of the players. "I loved her," Mick confirmed, "but I never touched her." Three years would be a long time; in fact it would be forever.

> *Willie sits and wonders at the words he cannot rhyme*
> *I am not in prison, I am only doin' time.*
> *SO SAD*
>
> *Hear the sound of no sound at all*
> *But the sound of my heart breaking into*
> *You say forever; Well, HERE'S TO FOREVER and you*

Through two key relationships... Detta a love gone bad... Lana a love he could not have... Mickey completed advanced studies in Heartbreak, gaining empathy necessary to become a proverbial heart surgeon. Unlucky in love thus far, he was about to meet The One.

About the time Mick wrote *Just Dropped In*, Susan Pack joined The New Christy Minstrels. The group included Kenny Rogers and members of the future First Edition, Mike Settle, Terry Williams and Thelma Camacho. They were working the college circuit, putting on hootenannies, and Susan would remain with the Minstrels for roughly 18 months. The group went to Nashville in '67 to perform at Vanderbilt University and to lay down a few tracks in a local studio. Kenny - no longer "Kenneth" - Rogers used the opportunity to introduce Mickey to one of the Minstrels, beautiful twenty-year-old Susan.

It would be an understatement to say Mickey was smitten by the intelligent, gorgeous woman with the long red hair and non-assuming inner strength. And as for Susan... she was quite taken by the perceptive blue-eyed handsome gentleman, resplendent with charisma and humility. Still, they would not date for a year or so. How fitting Susan belonged to a group named after the 19th century minstrel troupe that popularized the songs of Stephen Foster, Mickey's favorite songwriter. Shortly after meeting Susan, Mick's career took off. *Oh! Susannah* indeed.

Jimmy Elledge had been first to cover Newbury's *Time Is A Thief* (on Hickory), and though the record did not chart, exposure was provided. 1967 came to a dramatic close as "King of Rock and Soul" Solomon Burke waxed the song, and it went straight to number one on the R&B chart, Mickey's first number one. Burke was not only one of the great showmen of the era, but a minister of the church and father of 21 children.

Mick's ship came in again in early '68 when Don Gibson and Dottie West performed a duet of *Sweet Memories*, and it entered the Country Top 40. Andy Williams was next to cover the ballad, taking it all the way to the top slot in the Easy Listening category. Williams even used it as his TV show theme song. A decade later, Willie Nelson would hit his first Country Number One homerun with... the same *Sweet Memories*. (He originally covered it on the '68 LP, "Good Times.") Where this accomplishment stands among musical pillars is difficult to say, but has another song charted higher three times by as many artists? The achievement may be unprecedented.

Eddy Arnold would be next to earn Mick number one honors in February of '68 with a smooth country cover of *Here Comes The Rain, Baby*. Then in March, Kenny Rogers and The First Edition scored a world hit - their first hit (number five on the U.S. rock chart) - with the psychedelic growler *Just Dropped In*. Rogers had labored assiduously for more than a decade, and his group's interpretation of Newbury's song struck pay dirt. "Kenny is a hard worker," Mick affirmed, "and he has great musical instincts."

Illustrating the strange times and perhaps Rogers' instincts, the song's promo was filmed in a taxidermy shop with The First Edition looking into the heads of dead stuffed animals. They performed the rocker next on the Smothers Brothers Show with Tommy Smothers introducing it as a "weird messed up song." Evidently it connected, as Johnny Cash invited The Edition to perform it on his show.

Mick's standing as a songwriter had skyrocketed in 16 weeks by authoring three number ones and one number five - across four different charts. As people on sidewalks and country roads were singing his music, America was living a hellish nightmare. On April 4, 1968, The Reverend, Dr. Martin Luther King Jr., in nearby Memphis to lead a peaceful demonstration of striking sanitation workers, was murdered by a racist. Two months later, Senator Robert Kennedy was gunned down in Los Angeles while seeking the Democratic nomination for the Presidency. Tragically, the American troop count in Vietnam reached more than half a million, while CBS anchorman Walter Cronkite - raised in Houston - summarized daily, "And that's the way it is." No wonder people were singing *Sweet Memories*.

In the midst of the mayhem, "Hair" opened on Broadway. Opponents tallied three quick strikes against the musical. Strike one, the use of rock music in a musical went against traditional show tunes, with customary song titles such as *Singing In The Rain* and *I Could Have Danced All Night* becoming *Hashish, Sodomy, Going Down, White Boys, Colored Spade, Holy Orgy* and *Walking In Space*. Strike two, open nudity and strike three, desecration of the American flag on-stage angered many, while the whole controversy turned "Hair" into a battle cry for proponents of the First Amendment. The sixties were upon us, and by this time it was personal.

In the Age Of Disagreement, Newbury's music reached out emotionally to opponents and proponents, whether their penchant was for pop, rock, country, easy listening or rhythm & blues. These genres covered tremendous territory, collectively accounting for a significant number - if not a preponderance - of the old, young, conservative and liberal.

> *They tell me right is right, so why is left all wrong*
> *That's why the mockingbird refused to sing his song*
> DON'T WANNA ROCK

And music had a bona fide purpose during the Age Of Disagreement. As early rock 'n' roll had served to break the humdrum of the Eisenhower era, hula-hoops and black and white TV, late sixties music was spiritually medicinal in its purpose. People desperately craved harmonious communication to cope with the terribly discordant times, and radio stations became beacons of sanity, broadcasting soul food to a multitude.

The troubled times set the stage for the singer-songwriter with a story to tell, and it was then that Newbury, Nelson, Kristofferson, Bobby Bare, Tom T. Hall and others roamed Music Row. They represented a new breed of Nashville songwriter. "It was a different kind of writing - the people that I ran with," Newbury explained to The Tennessean Showcase. "There was a lot of creativity, and people use to write from their own experience; they didn't write from a trick phrase." Attracted by the innate, folksy honesty of country music, they were writing country songs influenced by literature and the era's social upheaval. "The purpose of music," Mick said, "is to allow someone into the feelings of another person who's going through the same things... Artists were writin' the music for one another and not tryin' to write it for any kind of record cut..." Newbury was combining a love of writing poetry with a diverse musical background gleaned in Texas and England.

Following the half-dozen successive hits, Newbury was the hottest songwriter in Music City... and the Big Dog took notice. At the end of April, Steve Sholes, the first producer elected to the Country Music Hall of Fame, signed Mickey to a five-year contract with RCA Records. "I was the second person that Sholes signed to RCA after Presley. I had the biggest royalty in Nashville... I got the same advance that Elvis got... (Sholes had signed Presley to RCA Victor on November 21, 1955 in Memphis, acquiring his Sun Records contract for $35,000.) RCA was really anxious to sign me because I had written so many hits that year."

Billboard ran a picture of the signing, showing six smiling signors: Felton Jarvis (RCA Producer), Chet Atkins (RCA Divisional VP), Wally Cochran (RCA C&W Promotion Manager), Bob McClusky (Acuff-Rose General Manager), cousin Jay Boyette (Mick's Business Manager) and the man of the hour - a beaming and goateed Mickey Newbury. Mick had already established himself as an A Team songwriter for the industry's top firm. This ceremony was the capper. He was now an RCA Man.

Hit Parader described the details of Mickey meeting the top dog: "One of Newbury's Nashville friends, RCA A&R (Artist and Repertoire) Producer Felton Jarvis brought the talented young singer / composer to the attention of Chet Atkins and to a contract through an unusual, impromptu audition. During one of Newbury's visits to Felton's office, Steve Sholes happened in on his way to a meeting. Following the round of introductions, Felton suggested that Mickey sing one of his songs - but just one. After the first half dozen Newbury numbers, Steve postponed his meeting and stayed on to listen for the next hour and a half." The man who signed Presley was shocked. The hottest songwriter in town was also a spellbinding singer.

Sholes held a top RCA executive post, having worked there before World War II. "He was like a God," Mick clarified. Sholes was Chairman of the Country Music Association in 1961 and 1962, inheriting the gavel from Wesley Rose. He holds second place as producer of the most number one singles, and all 16 top hits are Elvis recordings. (George Martin, who produced The Beatles, holds first place with 23 number ones.) Sholes also claims the distinction of bringing Mr. Guitar Man, Chet Atkins, on as a protege in the fifties, using him as the house guitarist on recording sessions. He later put Atkins in charge of RCA Nashville when he was promoted in 1957. Time would prove this move to be one of his wisest financial decisions.

In the mid fifties, country boys - Elvis, Carl Perkins and Jerry Lee Lewis - made the jump from rockabilly to rock 'n' roll, and country music almost dried up. By the early seventies, this trend had reversed with country songs such as Kristofferson's *Me and Bobby McGee* being performed by rock singers, such as Janis Joplin. But in 1957, RCA faced a serious decline in country music sales in the face of rock and roll's stunning success.

As a reaction to plummeting country sales, Chet Atkins, helped craft the soft-edged, often lush, Nashville Sound; using string sections, pop backup singers and lots of echo to make records that appealed to older listeners not interested in rock music. It was a compromised style, though, which worked so well that it almost killed off hardcore country. A handful of artists such as Webb Pierce and Ernest Tubb were able to stay the course, but mostly the formulaic Nashville Sound was the dish of the day.

Ultimately, this brought country music a wider audience and was a giant step in mainstreaming the genre. Without the direct involvement of Atkins, country music might never have crossed over into the pop charts. He produced hundreds of hits for most of RCA's Nashville acts, including Elvis Presley and Eddy Arnold, and discovered a wealth of talent, including Don Gibson, Floyd Cramer, Charley Pride, Waylon Jennings and Bobby Bare. He was responsible for such groundbreaking country-crossover records as *The Three Bells* (The Browns), *He'll Have To Go* (Jim Reeves), *Oh Lonesome Me* (Don Gibson) and *Bye Bye Love* (Everly Brothers).

Years later, when asked to describe the Nashville Sound, Atkins reached into his pocket to retrieve a small handful of coins and began jingling them around as he replied, "This is the Nashville Sound." Commercialization indeed: RCA held one hell of a hand. The Nashville Sound reversed country music's decline in sales, which was inversely related to Elvis' unparalleled success. Jingle, jingle, jingle... It appeared as though RCA could do no wrong. And in the golden age of the singer-songwriter, they had Newbury.

In 1968, Nashville showcased an astonishing 265 publishing houses, 15 recording studios accounting for roughly half the nation's records, four record-pressing plants, more than 700 songwriters, 1000 union-affiliated musicians and an estimated 200 professional artists. Mickey compared Nashville then to Paris in the Twenties, to the Moveable Feast described in the novels of Ernest Hemingway and F. Scott Fitzerald. "It was an age of miracles," Fitzerald wrote; "it was an age of art; it was an age of excess, and it was an age of satire (read as 'wit')."

*Paris in the '20's, why it can offer plenty*
*To a young man with a vision so they say*
*With a friend named Fitzerald, I am headed for the old world*
*On a merchant steamer bound for Biscay Bay*
*HEAVEN HELP THE CHILD*

There was a sense of excitement. A creative energy illuminated the town, and make no mistake about it, several artists were lit too. Befitting the significance of Newbury's surname, Nashville in the late sixties was characterized by innovation just bursting out of tradition. His remarkable harvest in the fertile period is illustrated by the number of copyrights filed. During his 10 years in Nashville, 1964-1973, Acuff-Rose copyrighted 81 Newbury songs. More than half of the output, 43 songs, was registered over three years, 1967-1969. A creative energy and spirit did flow through the town. Friendships and synergistic relationships made Nashville a great place to be, where the bohemians were happy to help one another. Consequently, while a generation was turning on, tuning in and dropping out, Newbury was busy writing songs. Which is not to say he did not partake.

Now and then, Mickey would drop in at the Boar's Nest, "a place where you can get together with people and rap." On a typical evening, Kristofferson, Webb Pierce, Willie Nelson, Roger Miller, Faron Young, Harlan Howard, Waylon Jennings and Little Jimmie Dickens might come by for a cool one. (The Boars Nest from the "Dukes of Hazzard" TV program was named in honor of Sue's place, and Waylon sang the show's theme song.) The place was home to Sue Brewer, a single mother, who opened her home, heart and pocketbook to many a struggling singer. Artists congregated at Sue's home to share songs, stories and friendship.

"I was one of Sue's struggling songwriters in the early sixties," Mick remembered. "Sue not only worked nights as Manager of George Jones' Possum Hollow (a Nashville nightclub), but she also worked for Faron Young's Music City News to help support all of us." And Kristofferson added, "Sue's place is one of the special shrines to the soul of country music. If it hadn't been for the Boar's Nest, I know I would never have written the songs that I did."

The artists frequented popular gathering places along lower Broadway, between Fifth and First. Ryman Auditorium on Fifth Avenue was home to the Mother Church of Country Music, the Grand Ole Opry. Crossing the alley to 422 Broadway, to the two-story Tootsie's Orchid Lounge, they would slip a quarter in the jukebox and enjoy another cool one, cheerfully served by Miss Wanda with the big smile. (Too many cool ones though and Tootsie would eject the drunk patron... with the aid of a hatpin.) Willie Nelson got his first songwriting job after singing there, while wife and kids waited out front in the car. Roger Miller reportedly wrote the Smash hit *Dang Me* while sitting in a booth in the dimly lit inn. Scribbling lyrics on a cocktail napkin, Miller may have bellowed out, "What rhymes with purple?" On one imaginative evening... he came up with the answer. "Syrple... maple syrple."

Crossing the street to 417 Broadway, they could pick up the latest LP at Ernest Tubb's Record Store, a great place for conversation and pontification. About then, a down-and-out picker often discovered Tootsie Bess had slipped him a ten-dollar bill. Still headin' east to the Linebaugh Cafe on lower Broadway, they would devour delicious down-home delicacies such as fried chicken made-from-scratch biscuits, mashed potatoes and grits, washed down with a hot cup of strong coffee. And while being served, the waitress would call 'em "honey."

After dinner, if one were in a pensive mood, he might leisurely make his way across First Street. Standing in Riverfront Park, once a wharf, the mighty Cumberland River that brought the first settlers to Nashville, lies straight ahead. One century earlier, Mickey's Great-Great Grandparents - Thomas and Polly - had plowed their Overton farmland near the same ol' river.

> *You remember the old town here yesterday?*
> *The walk from the Ryman to the Linebaugh Cafe?*
> *We would stop in at Tootsie's and Tubb's on the way,*
> *And slowly head East down to First and Broadway...*
>
> *Hey look at that ol' river, Bud, how it keeps rollin on by.*
> *If it was a clock I could stop, I would try...*
> *I would let it roll down on about '65.*
> *Perhaps I would not feel so old...*
> *A LONG ROAD HOME*

With long hair and a beard, Newbury was enjoying coffee at a local cafe. Eyeballing the apparent hippie, the manager growled, "We don't want your business!" Mick asked if that included his friends, to which the manager snarled, "Yes!" Because of that mandate, students from Vanderbilt University - Mick's friends - marched in protest in front of the cafe. Chet Atkins also posted a notice on the RCA bulletin board stating it would be appreciated if RCA employees would refrain from visiting the restaurant, as they had thrown out "one of our own." Mickey remembered how "it almost broke the cafe... the most popular cafe in Nashville at the time."

The cafe manager had been aware of hippies for about two years, as they increasingly appeared in the news and sightings had become commonplace. Beatle George Harrison made headlines in August of '67 - the Summer of Love - when he took a trip to San Francisco to see what the hippies were up to. Mickey and Roger Miller and a few other Nashville cats made the pilgrimage, too. Mick headed up to Haight-Ashbury to check out the "real" flower children. "I got there a little bit late," he said. "They had all moved to Oregon... but at least a song came out of it."

> *Yes Frisco is a mighty rich town now that ain't no lie*
> *Why they got some buildings that reach for a mile into the sky*
> *Yet no one can even afford the time to tell me why*
> *Here's a world filled with people and so many people alone*
> *FRISCO DEPOT*

"I was about as much of a hippie... I probably was... I don't know... I kinda had one foot in one world and one foot in the other world, you know." Spurred on by the era's paraphernalia, affected by profound personal and societal (here comes the greatest of sixties catchwords) "changes", Newbury related to both sides of the fence... and the different points of view influenced his music.

> *What mattered was the thought and not the rhyme*
> *ORGANIZED NOISE*

Ralph Emery nailed the point by referring to Mick as the first "hippie cowboy" in his book, <u>More Memories</u>. William Hedgepeth expanded on the topic in a <u>Look</u> article, writing, "Mickey's physical concession to countrydom is that he wears cowboy boots and has 'Mom&Dad' tattooed on his arm. Otherwise, he is mildly long of hair, uses a classic-style guitar and punctuates his thoughts with 'man.'" This helps to explain why silver-tongued Kristofferson called him, "One of the most confoundingly complex bundles of contradictions walking the streets today."

Writer Dave McElfresh would hit on the same issue: "Singer / songwriter Newbury is, in a number of ways, far from representing the typical Southern music writer. He plays a gut string classical guitar, has tonsils so pure and powerful he could probably sing opera, and writes songs so delicate they radically stretch country's shitkickin' honky-tonk persona in the opposite direction."

It is just not possible to pen Newbury in a single corral, such as folk or pop or country. His output is too diverse. He spun his delicacies not only for Music Row country performers, but for many artists of different styles. "At one time," Newbury recalled, "I had four songs on the charts, one each in a different chart." The songs simultaneously held top positions with styles as disparate as: *Just Dropped In* **Pop/Rock** by The First Edition, *Sweet Memories* **Easy Listening** by Andy Williams, *Time Is A Thief* **R&B** by Solomon Burke and *Here Comes The Rain Baby* **Country** by Eddy Arnold. This is an incredible achievement, unduplicated by anyone.

Mickey partially explained the basis for the accomplishment to Bill Grine. "So here's what happened. Growing up in country music, being subjected to the blues for that short period when I was a teenager, and then the rock era. You go through that, man, and you got an education that kind of... well, there has to be a product that comes out of it that's a combination of the three." Simply put, Mick was not just a country writer. He was however a smart country boy... a sophisticated cowboy to some... an intelligent maverick to others. An assimilator. A freethinker.

His success as a genre crossing songwriter was paying off financially, too. A mid '68 Harper's article stated, "Two years ago, Newbury literally was on the street; today he owns a gold Cadillac convertible, a sharp wardrobe, and an apartment in Nashville. His income for this year may exceed $50,000." According to the U.S. Census, median male annual income in 1968 was $7,660. Allowing 10 percent for inflation and cost-of-living increases, Newbury's $50,000 in '68 becomes $1 million in 2004. Furthermore, entertainers of the era made a fraction of the megabucks garnered by today's celebrities. Point is... Mick was becoming well established. Fame and fortune were smiling, and he was delighted to share the wealth. If a friend needed monetary assistance, he could count on Mick. And many did. Two years after being broke, he had fixed himself. Humpty Dumpy was lookin' good.

He felt however that he knew where to draw the line. As Mick explained to Nashville Scene, "One year back in the sixties, I turned down about a million dollars in commercial contracts. Miller Beer, Coke, a wine company - all that kind of stuff. Publishers don't like missing out on that, but to me it was real unacceptable... I still don't like to see my heroes doing that stuff. I want to be fooled into thinking that they're doing their music because they love it and not just for the money."

Complimenting - or in some circles, complementing - his songwriting skills, Wesley Rose gave Mick a song to complete, which had been partially written by one of Mick's heroes. When Hank Williams was found dead in his car, a shoebox was discovered containing his unfinished *Cowboys Don't Cry*. Mick completed the song a few years later, and Waylon Jennings covered it. But as Mick did not like how he had finished it, 25 years later he would redo the song. Mick sang it to the author once over the phone... Simply beautiful. Perhaps one day it will be released.

*COWBOYS DON'T CRY, so they tell me*
*Ah, but here's one that's lonesome tonight*
*The love that would shine*
*When she was all mine*
*Is now drifting away with the light*

*Sometimes I think of my heartache*
*Rememb'ring the love we once knew*
*It's then they roam*
*So far from my home*
*There's nothing else left now to do*

*Listen to me all you cowboys*
*When I die will one of you sing*
*I'm going away*
*Where the whippoorwills stay*
*And bury my guitar with me*

Speaking of cowboys, hippies and poets, Mick pleaded with Texan Townes Van Zandt to come to Nashville. Townes told writer Peter Blackstock, Mickey "heard me at a joint in Texas when I was a young hippie, and he said, 'You've got to come to Nashville.'"

"I had no idea what he meant," Townes informed Paul Zollo. "I didn't know about going to Nashville, making a record, getting a publishing deal or anything like that. He could have said, 'Come to Seattle' and it wouldn't have made any difference to me." The reply? "Sure man, I'll go anywhere." The outcome of the visit - with Newbury as tour guide - was Van Zandt's debut album and masterpiece, "For The Sake Of The Song." "I got here and just kind of fell in," he explained to Zollo. "I didn't have to knock on any doors or anything."

Stylistically a cross between Bob Dylan and Marty Robbins, the record was produced by Mick's Beaumont buddy, Cowboy Jack Clement, and released in 1968 on Kevin Egger's Poppy Records. The LP's extensive liner notes were written by Mickey and state, "Perhaps the 21st century musicians will sit and chat about the troubled times of Bob Dylan; the heartaches of Hank Williams and Don Gibson; the imagination of Paul McCartney and John Lennon. These were the men that opened doors. John Townes Van Zandt was one that walked through... Townes Van Zandt. The man. My friend."

Mickey would express his feelings about Townes from then on to anyone who opened the door. "I'll tell ya, man, the person who's influenced me more'n just about anybody else is somebody I'm sure you've never heard of.

Guy name of Townes Van Zandt. Incredible poet. Townes is somebody who looks like Hank Williams, even writes like Hank Williams probably would have written. But I tell ya, I think Townes is better. I consider him in the same category as Dylan and McCartney."

The respect was mutual. Townes mentioned the way Mickey's voice touched him... "It was really funny trying to explain. I can't call it 'explain' but I'd tried to tell Jeanene (Townes' wife) about the sound of Mickey's voice and the guitar on a good night at the same time. It's hard; you can't do it. It's like from outer space. I've heard about people trying to explain a color to a blind person. Like Helen Keller. There's no way to do it."

Newbury was silently managing Townes at the time to ensure Gnashville did not chew him up. When Van Zandt's stock rose, the label wanted to pull him out of Nashville and relocate him to New York, closer to the intellectual folk movement of Guthrie and Dylan. Mickey thought this would be a great disservice to Townes and told him so. "They didn't know what to do with him," Mick stated, "and I told Townes that, you know. In fact the guy offered me $100,000 for Townes' contract. I turned it down then tore up the contract and gave it to Townes... to prove to him what I was tellin' him was true. Didn't do any good... he still went."

Mick could have used the money, but he refused to accept compensation for harm he felt the move would cause his buddy. He gave Townes his freedom but would not abandon his friend at any price. They would co-write two songs together, *Mister, Can't You See* and *The Queen*.

Another Newbury friend, Sammi Smith had dropped out of school at age 11 and began singing professionally at age 12. Discovered in '67 by Marshall Grant - Johnny Cash's bass player - Sammi was persuaded by Cash and Grant to move to Nashville. She met Mickey in early '68 "when he was still living in his car," and Sammi remembered, "Mick stayed with me for a while. I had this little place down in the lower Broadway area, and he would just drop in. He and Kris and Townes and Johnny Darrell and many others would come by and visit. They'd pass the guitar and try out new songs on each other."

"Those good sessions," Mick reminisced, "were always the thing that really expanded your knowledge about songwriting... A situation where artists were hangin' out together and learnin' from each other and being fired by someone else."

"We supported one another," explained Sammi. "We were a big, extended family, and we would do anything to help one another. Mickey helped everybody all the time. He helped me just by being born. That was the best part of my life." Sammi would gain international fame a few years later with her recording of Kristofferson's *Help Me Make It Through The Night.* Her passionate interpretation made the song a number one country hit and a Top 10 pop hit, earning Sammi a gold record, a Grammy and CMA's selection as Top Female Vocalist of 1970. She would release three songs penned by Newbury.

In the city described at the time as a "country Greenwich Village," good Karma ran rampant. "When I met Guy Clark," Mick stated, "he wasn't even a songwriter... He was an art director for a TV station." Mick would lend the burly Texan a big hand. In a candid interview with Al Moir, Clark confirmed, "Mickey was the reason I moved to Nashville. I met him through Townes Van Zandt, and it was he (Newbury) who persuaded me to move here... and it was through him that I got my first cut by the Everly Brothers." Considering the number of artists Mick was bringing to town, he could have opened a travel agency. "Nash-Visits By Newbury" would have done well... except for one detail... The clients were broke.

Similarly, Lee Fry said he will never forget how Mickey helped him. "Guy Clark and Townes Van Zandt convinced me to play my songs for Mickey... which I nervously did. Mickey then asked me if I would 'mind' if he demoed my songs, explaining, 'If they hear me, they will listen all the way through, and they will appreciate what a writer you are.' Just the idea that Mickey's voice would carry my songs was something I would personally treasure... even if no one else liked them... So I agreed immediately! He demoed them on my portable Sony reel to reel... (I learned later he hated to do that outside a studio.) Waylon Jennings heard the first song - *The Hunger* - and wanted to record it the same night... and did! That got me established in Nashville as a songwriter. Later Mick told me, 'If you want to thank me, just pass on the same help to someone else along the way... as best you can.'"

That's how it was during Newbury's Nashville in the Sixties, like Paris in the Twenties, a cultural utopia of artistic camaraderie... friends helping friends. An entire artistic community playing "Pay It Forward." Years later the movie so named became a Newbury favorite, and he would watch it over and over. That's understandable. And sad. It made him homesick.

# Chapter VII: *His Master's Voice*
## 1968, July - December

Mickey went to Los Angeles in mid '68 to do the Joey Bishop Show. Susan Pack was in L.A. then, as she had grown tired of the road, had left the New Christy Minstrels and was staying at Kenny and Margot Rogers' house to watch their kids. Kenny informed Susan he would like her to go out with Mickey. A four-hour discussion ensued, and at last she gave in. They went to see the movie "2001" and listened to Mick's music afterwards. Though Mick and "Susie" enjoyed a memorable evening, they would not see each other again for 18 months.

> *Called a friend in Frisco*
> *He said she was in L.A.*
> *Here I am in Alabam' two thousand miles away*
> *Oh I got them Mobile blues today*
> MOBILE BLUE

When he returned to Nashville, current <u>Billboard</u> and <u>Cash Box</u> weeklies caught his eye. The July 15 editions featured the first Newbury advertisements and were titled, "MICKEY NEWBURY IS NOW!" Showcasing a smiling Mick decked out in ivy league sports coat and high turtleneck, full-page spreads trumpeted his debut single, *Are My Thoughts With You / Weeping Annaleah*. In vogue copy next to the picture read, "This great new star, reflecting on the mirrors of the mind, captures the vibrations and total awareness of today on his first Victor single."

Mick co-wrote *Weeping Annaleah* with Acuff-Rose pal, Dan Folger. Besides sharing a few songs, the Texans shared an apartment for six months in Nashville's Executive House Apartments. "Mickey started *Annaleah*," Folger explained, "and then I came in and together we worked up the music and the words for the choruses, and named it." The flipside - *Are My Thoughts With You* - was penned exclusively by Newbury.

The subsequent issue of <u>Billboard</u> favorably reviewed the release: "The successful pop-country composer out of Nashville comes on strong in this performing debut on RCA that should meet with immediate pop play and sales impact. Powerful rhythm ballad material and performance." A few collectors have discovered the record was released in a four-color picture sleeve in the USA and Germany. The songs would be covered by about 15 artists, including: Tom Jones, Etta James, Earl Scruggs, Linda Ronstadt, The Box Tops and The First Edition.

During this time, <u>Hit Parader</u> reported that Newbury was working on a major classical piece with Tupper Saussy, conductor of the Nashville Symphony, who provided accompaniment on the RCA single. Tupper's concept in music served up a smorgasbord-concoction of pop, jazz and classical. A classical release from Newbury would have been interesting, but it never happened.

Tupper first met Mickey at RCA in Nashville and wrote: "He really liked a piece I'd just recorded under Felton Jarvis and Chet Atkins. His encouragement developed into a friendship. Mickey was commuting between Houston and Nashville in those days. He spent many nights in our guest bedroom, which he regarded as blessed relief from living in the legendary El Dorado Cadillac. My whole family loved Mickey. We loved when he came, hated when he left. I wrote about this in *Little Sparrow,* which Don Gant sang with the Neon Philharmonic." Tupper and wife Lola had two children, a house on Nashville's posh Belle Meade Boulevard and a pet monkey named Thelonious Monk.

The first nation-wide article featuring Newbury appeared in <u>Harper's Magazine</u> in July of '68. It was reprinted in <u>Life Magazine</u> and condensed in the October issue of <u>Reader's Digest</u>. Titled "Inside The Grand Ole Opry," by Larry L. King, the piece presented a brief history of country music, the popularity of the Opry, Nashville's importance and Newbury's arrival in Celebritydom. Newbury the star was receiving national and a bit of international exposure.

Then as the world watched, the Chicago riots stole the Democratic Convention spotlight in August. A few months later, Mickey's friends, Roy Rogers and Texan Dale Evans hosted the first televised Country Music Association Awards Show in Ryman Auditorium. Perhaps Roy was wearing Mickey's boots that evening; as they shared the same boot maker and shoe size; the sole mates exchanged boots regularly. The CMA had hired Rogers to host the CMA Show to broaden the appeal and audience of country music, a goal already affected by Newbury's songwriting.

Meanwhile, RCA recorded Newbury. During his tenure there, the company would release one Newbury album and three singles: (1) *The Queen / Organized Noise,* (2) the afore-mentioned *Are My Thoughts With You / Weeping Annaleah* and (3) *Sweet Memories / Got Down On Saturday (Sunday In The Rain).* The last two 45's were drawn from Mickey's much-anticipated album, "Harlequin Melodies."

**ALBUM # 1** Harlequin Melodies (RCA LSP-4043) was Newbury's first album and features eleven songs, nine written and two co-written by him (underscored): (Side 1) Sweet Memories, Here Comes The Rain Baby, <u>Mister Can't You See</u>, How Many Times Must The Piper Be Paid For His Song, Are My Thoughts With You (Side 2) Harlequin Melodies, Funny Familiar Forgotten Feelings, Time Is A Thief, Good Morning Dear, <u>Weeping Annaleah</u> and Just Dropped In (To See What Condition My Condition Was In). The LP was released in the UK as "Funny Familiar Forgotten Feelings" to benefit from the Tom Jones hit single.

Halleluiah! Newbury's first album! A time for celebration... a joyous occasion... Five songs had already been huge hits for other artists... A sure thing... Could not miss! Wait... hold the horses... return the party favors and cancel the caterers. The album flopped. It not only missed the charts by a mile, but the songs sound mediocre at best. Mick would apologize on BBC Television a few years later, "For those of you who went out and bought it... I'm sorry!" Huh? What in the world went wrong?

Everything. For starters, "Harlequin Melodies" was recorded at RCA's recently completed Nashville Sound Big Studio, now called Studio A. "It looked like a basketball court," Mick explained. "Was like tryin' to make love on a sidewalk... You could get lost in there. It was not comfortable."

Mickey had second thoughts about even making the album, stating, "If I can't get involved with people that are close to me, then I sing badly. I was even reluctant to make a record... The 'Harlequin Melodies' album was the first time I ever tried to work with a group... work with somebody backin' me up. 'Cause I break time and everything you know, just from being use to workin' by myself... In this album, it was like I was in a cage tryin' to listen to what everybody else was doing."

Nevertheless, <u>Billboard</u> magazine (8/17/68) gave the LP a glowing review: "Mickey Newbury makes an auspicious debut here. He's extremely effective as a vocalist and the songs, which are of his own composition, blend words and music with striking impact. Among the highlights are *Are My Thoughts With You, Just Dropped In* and *Funny, Familiar, Forgotten* (sic) *Things.*"

<u>Billboard</u> was way too kind. Most songs feature middle-of-the-not-sure-which-road arrangement and sound muddy, as if they were hit with a double dose of Dolby. Surprisingly, RCA's patented, oft-pretty Nashville Sound is a no-show. The productions are boring, confused, overbearing, monotonous and distracting, causing writer Peter Blackstock to pooh-pooh the album as just a collection of "songwriting demos." A Newbury signature song at the time, *Funny Familiar Forgotten Feelings*, for instance, is cloaked insipidly in bland attire. Mickey explained, "The only song that I had any input on was

97

*Sweet Memories*, and I just did it with a guitar and a bass." Still, RCA's production of *Sweet Memories* is immensely inferior to the version Mick would release in 1973. The album's namesake, *Harlequin Melodies*, is the sole cut delivered in an aesthetically pleasing package.

RCA dressed *Just Dropped In* in lame, embarrassing psychelelia to emulate the First Edition's successful hit, which had reached number five on the charts. Regrettably, these psychedelic readings lose lyrical significance. The First Editions' version - so catchy, so hip, so cool - Mick's message is missed as one gets caught up in the infectious ear candy: "Yeah, yeah, oh yeah, what condition my condition was in!" The punch line is not Newbury's; it was added by the First Editions. Then there's the RCA production - so bad - nobody cares to listen.

The lyrics detail the horrors of LSD, **not** its pleasures: "Someone painted April fools in big black letters on a dead end sign / I had my foot on the gas as I left the road and blew out my mind..." "It was not a drug song advocating the use of drugs," Mickey said. "It was a drug song telling people of the horrors that drugs will do to you... Some people jumped out of buildings... That song was about a country boy's attitude to a bad acid trip. There were so many pro-acid songs then, that I thought someone ought to show the other side." After all, according to Mickey, it was written after he spent "a night in hell."

Psychedelic rock is the wrong vehicle to deliver the message. Reflecting the writer's intent, Acuff-Rose cut a demo acetate in 1967, promoting the song as a measured bluesy number. The promo reflects Mickey's vision. "I like to have my music down as close as like I hear it in my head," he explained to <u>Country Music People</u>. He next performed it on a 1983 Bobby Bare TV Special as slow R&B and then rereleased it on a 1994 album in the same genre. RCA failed to see Mickey's vision... They went for the gold.

RCA did advertise the album. Besides running full-page spreads in <u>Billboard</u> and <u>Cash Box</u> for the single *Are My Thoughts With You / Weeping Annaleah*, RCA promoted "Harlequin Melodies" in several publications. A full-page ad on the cover of <u>GO</u> - a Hollywood weekly - and in <u>Country Magazine</u> featured Mickey's album picture underscored with Madison Avenue glitz: "Mickey Newbury paints lovingly on the canvas of your mind. With tender and bittersweet strokes of his voice, Mickey applies eleven colors of love in this new Victor album..." So RCA did promote "Harlequin Melodies," though much like a Hallmark card.

Newbury looks mad as hell on the album cover, and the picture is worth a million words. Mickey explained, "I get on the plane with Felton and we fly to New York City and meet with the President of the company... just a hell of a nice guy... Harry Jenkins was his name. I had been askin' Felton, 'How they gonna market me? 'Cause I don't want to look like a country artist.' And Felton says, 'We'll take care of it.'"

"So we're goin' down to where they're gonna shoot the photograph and I tell Felton, 'If they put me next to a hay bale or a horse, I'm gonna catch a plane back to Tennessee'... 'cause every act in Nashville was next to a hay bale. And I'll be damned if we didn't walk in there and there was this wood... this barn wood wall they we're gonna put me against... and that's what's back there (on the album cover). And the Art Director asks me, 'Where's your uniform?' And I said, 'What uniform? I don't wear a uniform.' He was lookin' for the cowboy hat and cowboy clothes and boots and sequins and all that you know. And so Felton says... 'cause he can see that I'm upset... 'Have you guys heard this album?' And they're all sayin', 'Well... uh... er... uh... we haven't had a chance to really sit down and listen to it yet.' So Felton says, 'Well let's go in and listen to it first.'"

"So we parade down to this office and listen to it, and this guy says... it could have been Harry or whoever it was makin' 'em pop to... He says, 'Go down the street down here to on the corner of so and so and there's a guy who's got a bunch of Nehru shirts'... He says, 'Bring me eight or ten of 'em.' He says, 'What size do you wear Mickey?' I didn't even know what a Nehru shirt was you know. I said, 'Well size small.'"

"Well they come back with all these Nehru shirts. So now I've got this funny lookin' shirt on with this big ol' amulet you know that's hangin' around my neck... I finally picked this one Nehru shirt out... and I looked at myself and I thought, 'That looks so ridiculous.' And everybody says, 'That looks great! That looks great!' And I said, 'Really?'"

"I had this real short hair," Mickey explained to Oregon Public Broadcasting years later. "If I'd had long hair... and had that on... It's like... OK can you imagine a businessman with a businessman's haircut... dressed in some of those wide pants that my seventeen-year-old son wears? That's what it was like. You know... there's somethin' wrong with this picture. They then took me in and leaned me against that barn wood wall... And when they did... I looked over at Felton and that's the picture. So I'll never forget how I felt when I turned and looked at Felton."

The cartoonish measures are made understandable by a Wesley Rose comment: "Mickey is as modern as tomorrow and as traditional as yesterday." Trying to capture that concept on canvas, they threw a Maharishi shirt on a Texan and stood him next to a barn wall.

<u>Look</u> magazine explained the situation subjectively: "Mickey is part of the poetic fringe of country composers today, filling simple old melodic forms with original imagery and highly subjective, often soulful feelings."

Dave Mc Elfresh hit the mark too, reporting three decades later: "Years ago, some on-the-money journalist referred to Newbury as 'the Robert Frost of country music' - which still stands as the most succinct line of music criticism this writer ever read. The Nashville-by-way-of-Texas legend starts off one song - *The Piper* - with, 'Morning came and found her at the window with her nose pressed to the glass / The dew was like a broken diamond necklace left scattered on the grass... ' If such lines came from the obtuse mouth of Garth Brooks or his ilk, they'd sound like Sylvester Stalone reading Dostoevsky." In 1968 though... RCA had no idea how to portray *that* on an album cover. Frankly, it isn't any easier today.

<u>Harper's</u> contributing editor, Larry L. King wrote the album liner notes. Sent to Nashville in February of '68, his once-in-a-lifetime assignment was to report on what was happening there musically. King talked with the great names and wrote, "I heard their famed sounds: Chet Atkins, Marty Robbins, Flatt and Scruggs, Eddy Arnold, and countless others. These were old and special heroes of mine, and so I was well-prepared to be impressed by their art. Nothing, however, prepared me for Mickey Newbury..."

"Mickey picked up his guitar to sing two songs he had written and which were at the time climbing the charts, *Funny Familiar Forgotten Feelings* and *Just Dropped In...* The rare combination of Newbury's perceptive lyrics, his pure and seeking voice unaided by vocal trickery or echo chambers, and his own easy and personal way with the guitar... Mickey Newbury - I said then and reaffirm now - was the most talented man I had encountered in a city famed for its unusual musical talent... To hear Mickey Newbury sing his own compositions - giving them the emphasis, interpretations and soul their creator intended - must be something like hearing Mark Twain read aloud from <u>Life on the Mississippi</u> or <u>Letters from the Earth</u>. Twain, however, couldn't handle the guitar. Newbury can."

**"Unaided by vocal trickery or echo chambers,"** Newbury and guitar blew King away, causing the Harper's writer to praise him as "the most talented man" he had encountered. Just Newbury and guitar, he said. "Harlequin Melodies" probably would have been a blockbuster... if RCA had recorded just Mickey and guitar. Perhaps a violin could have been added, maybe even a little bass. Twenty years later, in 1988, Newbury would do just that... and a masterpiece would be created. But such a simple, folksy approach would not have been fashionable in 1968... not after Dylan went electric... and not in RCA's Big Studio.

Mickey referred to a song's many possible arrangements as "the different ways of dressing your children." RCA dressed his songs like the Festrunk Brothers - two wild and crazy guys - in polyester print shirts and tight striped pants. RCA's dreadful production of "Harlequin Melodies" constitutes perhaps the biggest boondoggle in the history of commercially recorded music. Newbury's career as a recording artist should have taken off with the release of the album. Too bad Ralph Peer didn't produce it... Less would have been so much more.

Though the LP was filled with songs that became hits for others, it produced no hits for Mickey. Addressing the issue, Peter O'Brien wrote, "Despite his admiration for Jarvis' production skills, I do not think Mickey Newbury was best served on 'Harlequin Melodies' by the consistently intrusive and irrelevant arrangements inflicted on the songs by Tupper Saussy and Cam Mullins. The quality of the songs was self-evident reinforced by the fact that every one of them has been covered by other artists."

The songs have been recorded by 150 artists, including: Lulu, Pat Boone, Box Tops, Tom Jones, Ray Price, Don Gibson, Ray Charles, Floyd Cramer, Wayne Newton, Joe Simon, Sue Thompson, Joan Baez, Brook Benton, Glenn Yarbrough, Vicki Carr, Brenda Lee, Jerry Reed, Dottie West, Eddy Arnold, Larry Butler, Jimmy Elledge, Etta James, Willie Nelson, Linda Ronstadt, Andy Williams, Roy Orbison, Solomon Burke, Anita Carter, Everly Brothers, Englebert Humperdinck, B B King, Jim Ed Brown, The First Edition, Buffy St. Marie, Tennessee Ernie Ford, Jack Blanchard & Misty Morgan and Jerry Lee Lewis (first to cover *Just Dropped In*).

Although many of these artists are renowned as exceptional singers, Allen Harbinson announced in a <u>Goldmine</u> article: "Not one of those singers sang Newbury's songs as well as he did." Whether Harbinson's statement indicates superior voice quality, remarkable range or perfect phrasing, the author concurs, as did "Fel-Tone" Jarvis, who proclaimed, "Mickey Newbury sings his own songs better than anybody."

Newbury's vocal control and stylistic versatility enabled him to sound like George Jones, Ray Charles, Roy Orbison, Stephen Foster and on occasion when the subject required a folksy delivery, Bob Dylan. How might Newbury's singing be described? Though surefire words do not exist... imagine Luciano Pavarotti... had he grown up in Houston listening to AM radio during the forties and fifties. Critics have long praised Newbury's voice:

> Peter Blackstock wrote, "Musically his melodies frequently echo with a melancholy longing ever so eloquently expressed by his soaring, achingly sweet singing. Rarely has such a heavenly voice been

possessed by an artist whose reputation is so firmly grounded in his songwriting credential... Despite his reputation as a 'songwriter's songwriter,' Newbury was also blessed with an angelic tenor voice."

In a <u>Popular Music and Society</u> essay, George H. Lewis noted, "Newbury is not only a great songwriter, but also possesses one of the most emotively distinctive voices in all of pop music."

Bill Donoghue - 'fesser Mojo - shared his opinion, "Mickey Newbury is a unique singer/songwriter. Nobody sings his songs as well as he does; yet he is the one person who has been unable to get a hit with them."

Rod McKuen waxed poetic in describing Mick's singing: "His voice always reminded me of those lonesome whistles I used to hear as freight trains climbed the hill where I lived and worked as a ranch hand one summer. A long melodic sigh as the machine came up the mountain. He has one of the best sets of pipes of any male vocalist I've ever heard, his voice can give a low almost inaudible purr one moment and in the next soar as if he was aiming for the back row of a football stadium."

Writer Kurt Wolff declared Newbury was blessed with "a strong, versatile tenor voice that has to be one of the most beautiful to ever pass through Nashville - full of dusty melancholy, sad longing and a piercing haunting glow."

Larry Kelp described Newbury in the <u>Oakland Tribune</u> newspaper as, "One of America's best composers, and possessor of one of the few perfect voices in any kind of music."

Buzz Cason briefly summarized his feelings: "I had the pleasure of singing on several of his records. One of the Greatest if not the Greatest singer of our times." And Alan Rhody added, "He could've also sung in the days of no electricity with no problem. His voice was a rarity in itself."

Tim Veazey decreed, "If Frank Sinatra would've hopped a few freight-trains, written his own songs and had more passion, maybe he could've been Mickey Newbury. Mickey could wrench more emotion from one line of a song than many can an entire repertoire. He was equally at home at either end of the musical emotional spectrum. He played the guitar like a piano and sang as if his parents were Tony Bennett and Billie Holiday..."

Robert Adels wrote in <u>Country Music</u>: "Newbury's voice is almost too sweet to be human... And while many other performers have had and will continue to have hits with his songs, you truly haven't heard them until he's done them for you."

When requested to describe Newbury's singing, Sammi Smith stated, "I love fine things. They draw me like a magnet. There's a glaring difference between Tiffany and Wal-Mart, Balenciaga and Aunt Suzie's Sewing Class, Waterford and Jelly Glass and Mickey Newbury and anybody else who ever drew a breath."

Finally, Waylon Jennings summed up simply while hosting the TV show, "Nashville Now." Introducing Mickey, he quipped, "If you don't like to hear Mickey Newbury sing, then you're not American."

Though peers and critics agree he was a great singer, Newbury was the sole artist who did not get a hit with a Newbury song. He was a respected and thriving songwriter, well known in the industry. Three of his peers... an inner circle of sorts... enormously successful as songwriters... in time would wax the most Newbury covers. Don Gibson recorded 12 Newbury songs, and Waylon Jennings and Roy Orbison each covered nine. (It is intriguing that "The Big O" recorded nine Newbury songs, yet released only four... )

When Mickey played his latest creation for the inner circle, they would often exclaim, "Man, that's great! I wanna cut it!" Their many visits to the Newbury songbook represent the highest accolade these legends could bestow upon their friend. Nevertheless, Newbury was nearly invisible outside the tight circle of Music Row publishing houses. RCA had the opportunity to change that... and failed. But everybody and every company make mistakes. Perhaps RCA was on the upswing of a steep learning curve. Perhaps. Circumstances though were about to throw Newbury a few curves he would not be able to handle.

During the album's production, Felton was hospitalized with kidney failure. "That was rough," Mick explained, "he couldn't get in the studio." And then... Steve Sholes, Mick's only other friend at RCA - who signed him in '67 - died of a heart attack in a taxicab on the way to a recording session. Chet Atkins immediately succeeded Sholes in the executive hierarchy, but Mick did not know Atkins well at the time.

Mick hated the album, and since he was given no creative control, it was easy to blame the company. (Had the album succeeded, this would be a different book.) "I had my own vision about what I wanted to do with my music... and I didn't want to do what the other guy had done... If they wanted cookie cutter music... I was just the wrong guy to talk to..." RCA would not be talkin' to him much longer; the final straw was about to fall.

Felton had produced several sessions for Elvis, and "E" was taken with Felton's high-octane energy and charisma. He had been an Elvis fan for years, even releasing a song titled, *Don't Knock Elvis* (Viva 1001, Tecumseh Records). In Peter Guralnick's outstanding Elvis biography, <u>Careless Love</u>, Guralnick describes the first meeting between the two men: "From the moment that Elvis first arrived at the studio at around 8 PM there was no question that he was taken with the hopped-up, almost hyperactive enthusiasm of this skinny young producer (Felton) - it was a hell of a relief after Chet's damned indifference..." Guralnick goes on to describe them as "not only friends but musical allies," adding that Felton thought meeting Elvis "must have been fated."

After Elvis' triumphant '68 Comeback Special and after the success of *In The Ghetto*, he again became Nipper's pet project and priorities were rearranged at once. Therefore, Felton, who was then producing Newbury, Cortelia Clark and a few others, was asked by His Master's Voice to produce Elvis exclusively. Elvis, Guralnick wrote, "wanted Felton with him not just when he recorded but when he appeared in Vegas, and if he were to go out on the road, he expected him to be there, too - he wanted Felton, in other words, at his beck and call." This was a dream come true for Felton, but as he and Mickey shared a great relationship, Felton asked him what he should do. Always one to put friends first, Mickey told him not to pass up the opportunity. He didn't.

When Newbury signed RCA's five-year contract in 1967, he made an oral agreement with Sholes. The accord allowed him to get clear of the label if Felton could not produce him. Since Sholes had died, Chet Atkins - who was running RCA then - attested to the verbal agreement, which the lawyers accepted as binding. Though senior management pleaded with Newbury to stay, he chose to leave. "At the time," The Little White Wolf declared, "I was very independent. I always have been independent but I was independent for that time." (At about the same time, Don Gibson also left RCA and headed to Hickory Records.)

Mick left RCA for three reasons: lack of creative control, dissatisfaction with the cacophonous "Harlequin Melodies" album and strike three, loss of his beloved producer. In essence, he felt nobody in the corporation understood him, and in 20/20 hindsight, the relationship was just not to be.

Mick would express second thoughts in later life. "I was probably foolish for leavin' because we might have gotten something worked out there... because to have that kind of committment from a big company was a lot more of a big deal than I thought it was at the time... I just did not know anything."

*I was almost 30 going on 14*
*Hocked my gold watch and bought some blue jeans*
*Jumped a slow freight train to Alabam*
*Told my junkie friends in Milwaukee*
*For the last time friends you will see me*
*I am headed south to find out where I am...*
*1 X 1 AIN'T 2.*

"I didn't know anybody else there... If I had known Chet better, I'd have probably stayed at RCA... But, I didn't have any sense... I didn't realize anything... You know I turned down many million-dollar deals... I don't know where my head was... If I had taken any one of those deals today I would have the money to do anything I want to do... But I may not have any song to sing today if I'd took that million dollars... From that time on, I never gave up creative control again, except for one time, and I was sorry for that."

Kristofferson summed up simply, "Mickey always went his own way." And Mickey confided to <u>Country Song Roundup</u>, "I guess I'm hardheaded, that's one thing. I've been careful with decisions I've made and if I made them, I went ahead and went through with them."

**Working on a song on the houseboat Pappydad**

# Chapter VIII: *Looks Like Rain*
# 1969

It was not as if the sky had fallen when Mickey walked out on RCA. Au contraire. He had friends, clout, respect and money - ingredients that when mixed together can serve up a hearty helping of arrogance. The move in fact asserted his independence and embolded him to stand alone as a singer-songwriter. Embarrassed by the "Harlequin Melodies" product, Newbury vowed to do better. Much better.

*For things that are strong soon find a way to stand alone*
*IF I COULD BE*

The year saw the first human walk on the moon and Richard Milhous Nixon inaugurated as the 37th President of the United States. At the opposite end of the spectrum, the crowning conclusion to the Age of Aquarius came on the weekend of August 15 in farmer Max Yasgur's pasture in Bethel, Sullivan County, New York. The Woodstock Music and Art Festival attracted nearly 500,000 free spirits who laughed, played and got rained on at the greatest rock 'n' roll party of all time.

Mick signed with Mercury Records at this time, because good friends Jerry Kennedy and Bob Beckham were there. Kennedy had signed Newbury's friend Roger Miller to Smash-Mercury six years earlier. The move must have felt like a coming home of sorts, as Mercury had been Mickey's recording label during his years with The Embers. But those days were light years away.

He was living in a secluded cabin on Center Hill Lake, 100 miles east of Nashville. Mick also made home of a private 36 foot RiverQueen houseboat called "PappyDad," moored in the Cumberland River 25 miles northeast of Nashville. He would take the boat out on the Cumberland, to nearby Hickory Lake and points farther on. Good buddy Frank Ifield - an Acuff-Rose writer who recorded five Newbury songs - fondly remembered, "just drifting and dreaming while fishing from his boat on old Hickory Lake." But mostly, the boat stayed at the dock, and Mickey spent much time on board, writing songs. The houseboat nourished his wandering ways, providing ideal accommodations to Newbury's free spirit. Plus he loved being on the water.

Mickey would wake many mornings to find Kristofferson sleeping on PappyDad's deck. During one get-together on the boat, Nashville artist Rudy McNeely remembered an inebriated Kristofferson, who leaned back a

107

bit too far and fell in the water. Pulling himself onboard - his drinking glass full of the lake - he growled, "Damnit Newbury! Now I've got proof you've been watering down the booze!" Kristofferson spent time in hot water, too, washing dishes at a local joint.

Mickey and Kris went to LA in September to write a John Hartford TV special. They had met Harford (the added "t" was the brainchild of Chet Atkins) in Nashville when he was working as a deejay at WSIX and as a session man. Kristofferson remembered the trip: "Mickey and I were different. Hell, I was a drunk, you know, and I went and hung out in the bars where the action was. Mickey was more of a stay-at-home. We were kind of an odd couple. He would stay at home and do that music over and over in his head. And I'd come in all wasted from The Palomino... and I'd have about two hours to sleep before we went to work on the Hartford special... and I'd be woken by this God-awful noise of the full volume version of some intro to some song. And he's askin' me, 'Serious what do you think about this intro to this next song on 'Looks Like Rain?' And I'd say, Mickey, I've heard that a million times..."

"Mickey meant so much to me as a songwriter. I learned so much from him. When I came to Mickey, I'd been struggling along there for a couple years already and already lost a family and any reputation I carried. And I learned a lot from Mickey... I learned more about songwriting from Mickey Newbury than anybody I can think of... If he listened to the songs after I knew him, I'm sure that he would recognize certain Newbury influences... Mickey is just as much of a natural phenomenon as a songbird, you know... To me, he was a songbird... He comes out with amazing words and music... I'm sure that I never would have written *Bobby McGee*, *Sunday Morning Coming Down*... if I had never known Mickey."

Having time off from the Hartford production, Mick and Kris decided to pay Kenny Rogers a visit. To Mickey's delight, Susan Pack dropped in, and they talked for four hours that evening. He realized then that she was more than special. Their paths would cross again in three weeks.

During the trip, Mick persuaded Roger Miller to record *Me and Bobby McGee*. Kristofferson started writing the song while driving between Morgan City and New Orleans. "It was raining," he said, "and the windshield wipers were going. I took an old experience with another girl in another country. I had it finished by the time I got to Nashville." Mick knew the song was a hit the first time Kristofferson sang it, but persuading Miller was another matter entirely. "I literally had to grab Roger by the ears to make him listen to it." Following Mick's recital of the now famous lines, "Busted flat in Baton Rouge, headin' for the train / Feelin' nearly faded as my jeans," the King Of

The Road exclaimed, "Hey, that's pretty good!" Mick answered, "I've been tryin' to tell you that for three months, Roger!"

Miller promptly went into the studio and cut it. Newbury, Kristofferson and Billy Swan sang backup as The Swanettes, and they had a ball doing it. Janis Joplin later recorded the song, and it reached number one on the rock chart, her only number one. Tragically, the recording first appeared on her posthumous LP, "Pearl." Though many a flower-powered hippie misunderstood the lyric, "Freedom's just another word for nothin' left to lose," *Bobby McGee* became an anthem during the latter years of the hippie movement. Kristofferson's career was launched.

There is a bit more to the story, one missing piece. "I was the first one to cut *Me and Bobby McGee*," Mick informed Jack Bernhardt during an interview. "I carried it around with me for... I really basically wanted to get a major artist to cut it 'cause he (Kristofferson) needed that as a credential, you know." The question then is... where is that recording? Newbury-Miller-Kristofferson-Joplin fans would love to hear it.


**ALBUM # 2** Looks Like Rain (Mercury SR-61236) was Newbury's second album and includes nine songs written by him: (Side 1) Write A Song Song, Angeline, She Even Woke Me Up To Say Goodbye, I Don't Think About Her No More, T. Total Tommy, (Side 2) 33rd Of August, When The Baby In My Lady Gets The Blues, San Francisco Mabel Joy, Looks Like Baby's Gone.

Released in the fall of '69, "LLR" was the first of Mickey's three Cinderella Studio albums. A decade earlier, session guitarist Wayne Moss had transformed his ordinary garage in Madison into a production studio, hence "Cinderella." Since then, Grand Funk, Joe South, Mike Nesmith, Billy Swan, Leo Kotke, Charlie Daniels, Ricky Skaggs, Nancy Sinatra, Steve Miller Band, Tony Joe White, Jerry Jeff Walker, John Hartford - playing banjo and dancing on plywood, and many others have recorded there. During a 2002 interview, Moss confirmed the use-to-be-garage as the oldest continuously operating studio in the Nashville area. "It's not in the phone book, he explained. "Never has been. Word of mouth is what has kept us alive." Cinderella story indeed... In 1969, though, when Newbury recorded "Looks Like Rain" there, Cinderella was just a basic four-track recording studio.

Recording engineer Mike Considine came to know Cinderella then. He contracted the studio because he "loved the sound Newbury was getting out of the place." Recalling a late '69 visit, Considine described the setup: "Once we hit the area, it became apparent to me we were in a residential zone. I had thought the studio would be in some commercial building. I was shocked at first when we pulled up in front of Wayne's home. Then we walked to the back to a building that looked to me to be a garage of some sort. Sure enough that was the studio. I think it may have been a chicken coop at one time. The control room was right inside the door. Off to the left was the playing room. I don't recall any isolation booths at all. This was really down home and I loved it. The place had a feel to it. A music feel to be exact! There was magic in that place..."

Guitar picker and audio magician Wayne Moss was well known in Nashville circles as a brilliant engineer... "Great ears!" Considine attested. But as his production house was outside the Nashville system (and with it, the profit), the setup was regarded contentiously by more than one hardliner. Didn't matter to Mick. With Moss' technical support, he would find his singing style, guitar technique and trademark recording methods; and the patented sound would carry forward to albums over the next three decades. In Cinderella, Mick would begin to make his own music.

Since the reel-to-reel recorders accommodated just four tracks of audio, a supplemental method was desired to augment the number, so the production could be layered over more than four sessions. The recording of LLR was therefore ping-ponged - recorded from one multi-track machine to another - to increase the virtual number of tracks. Though effective, the laborious process increases noise and tape hiss; thus Mickey used rain sounds to mask the imperfections. "Rain and static sound exactly the same," he affirmed.

"On the trademark thing, the rainfall and train effects and so on started with the Mercury album... I like it. It provides a flow. You can have two very disparate numbers, but it eases you through, from one song to the next... Every bit of verse is helped by different stock images. The rain, for instance, is one of those - rain to connote sadness when used in conjunction with tears - rain to remind yourself of gloominess. Funny thing is, that subject seems to be almost universally applied; it is one of the favorite devices of Japanese poets."

"The sound effects on LLR came from another Mercury act, The Mystic Moods (their 'One Stormy Night' LP). The first time I heard them used was on Rod McKuen's albums of poetry and prose. After many nights on my boat listening to the 'roughs,' I decided to use sound effects... one, to cover all the hiss... two, I liked the way they framed the songs, allowing me to ride along seamlessly from story to story. After that, I continued to use sound effects or musical interludes... dogs... trucks... the Gulf... and the wind chimes hanging from my boat... We got sound effects from everywhere. I even went out and bought 100 crickets in a quart jar... They got loose in his

- Moss' - echo chamber. So for a month after that, in the middle of his session, there would be a 'bing.' Ha ha ha."

And as far as the train goes, it evokes a feeling of farewell, with swift movement to another place and time. Rain and trains work well together to stage an intimate mood that is sustained throughout the LP. Mickey added a dose of reverb - then called "echo chamber" - and the result is haunting. Liner notes state the album was produced by Jerry Kennedy (of Shreveport, Louisiana) and Bob Beckham and engineered by Wayne Moss and Charlie Tallent. Make no doubt about it, though unstated, twenty-nine-year-old Mickey Newbury served as Executive Producer.

Nashville's contemporary elite contributed on LLR: Wayne Moss, Chet Atkins and Jerry Kennedy on guitar (Kennedy played the toe-tapping guitar work on Orbison's *Pretty Woman*); David Briggs, Norbert Putnam and Farrell Morris on keyboards; Kenny Buttrey on drums, Buddy Spicher on fiddle and Charlie McCoy on harmonica. Chet and Mick had become friends since Mick's departure from RCA. Though Chet was aiding and abetting the competition - a few hardliners would have said enemy - his vision was much broader than such parochial concerns.

String sounds on LLR - and the two following Cinderella releases - were steel and electric guitars overdubbed. To make a steel guitar sound like a violin or cello, players used a device 12" long by 4" wide, operated by footswitch. This was necessary as a string section had not been budgeted, plus there was insufficient room in Wayne's cramped studio to accommodate a cello. Mickey also employed a sitar - played by Jerry Kennedy - an extremely radical move for a Nashville songwriter of the era.

"I didn't use any drummers because the drummers couldn't play with me... because my tempo changes... I started with my guitar and built from there... The musicians had a hell of a time playin with me... There's no bass on that record except on one song... It's Charlie McCoy on his knees playin' the pedals with his hands on an organ... I think about some of the stuff we did to put that album together... It is amazing... It is insane what I went through to put that album together..."

"There was some such strange things that happened when I started mixing that thing and flying in the sound effects... The train whistle would be on the exact note that I wanted it to be on... Some of the weirdest things... It was like God reached down and touched me, you know..." LLR used the sounds of rain, thunder, trains and wind chimes to set its dark, pensive, intimate mood. These effects seamlessly link the perfect songs on LLR into one conceptual whole. Mickey said the album was really just one long song. George H Lewis makes the point perfectly clear in a 1998 article, "He has been an innovator and pioneer in molding thematic and sonic linkages that have made his own albums emotional and conceptual wholes - not mere collection of songs - ever since his release, in 1969, of 'Looks Like Rain.'"

In a Hit Parader interview, Mick acknowledged the heavy influence of two pioneers. "I can remember my father singing all those old Jimmie Rodgers songs. Lately that old country blues has been influencing everybody. I've been using it in my own songs for the last two years." He also credited Woody Guthrie's disciple: "A writer has a lot more freedom now because of Dylan. He opened the way in country music as well, because country writers always wrote about the everyday hangups between two people. Now you can write about things you feel inside, from your imagination. A lot of my songs are from dreams." (The second song on the album, *Angeline*, is a "dream" song.) Incidentally, Dylan visited Mick on the houseboat, while Dylan was recording his country album, "Nashville Skyline." Talk about a guitar pull...

Dylan's influence can be heard on LLR, especially on T. *Total Tommy* and *San Francisco Mabel Joy*, which may be the greatest folk song ever written. Many peers would agree. Years later while rehearsing in Canada for a TV gig, Larry Gatlin would tell Mick, "It's my favorite song... Of course you know I think it's the best song I ever heard in my life. I try to write it every time I sit down to write a song."

Before he began writing *Mabel Joy*, Newbury stated that he knew everything about it. The song just ran out of his mind as fast as he could write. This is extraordinary considering the song's novel-like saga and its wonderful usage of alliteration: "Stunned and shaken someone said, 'Son she don't live here no more.'"

As he explained during a 1970 interview, "90 percent of my songs I've written in five minutes and maybe I've changed some words here and there... I never start with a title... I never know what a song is gonna be about until it's written." Mick echoed the point to Rolling Stone a few years later, "Songs have always had a way of writin' themselves in the back of my head."

But where do the stories come from? "As to the body of the subject matter," Mick told Country Song Roundup, "I think I draw about 100 percent from my own experiences." "There's a similar story - to *Mabel Joy* - in my background," Mickey confirmed to Omaha Rainbow, "but I don't know whether it has a connection or not. I tell you what it's almost like. We have lived lives over and over again, and very similar things happen to us over and over again in all these lives, and we cope with them in different ways in each life... I know a story very similar to that in my immediate being, in my family, yet it's not the same story. The lessons are the same."

*YOU ONLY LIVE ONCE IN A WHILE*
*So live for today you're alive*
*Between the first step and the last smile*
*We only live once in a while*

*Ain't it funny how we always say in times of leaving*
*Say in times of leavin' we will be comin' back one day*
*GONE TO ALABAMA*

Other early influences stand out as well. *Write A Song Song* contains poetry suggestive of The Beats: "Sitting in the dark-in the darkness of my room / I wonder why I look the sky look the sky / Begins to softly cry." Classic country is well represented by a "she left me" song - a tearjerker, *She Even Woke Me Up To Say Goodbye*. Finally, *When The Baby In My Lady Gets The Blues* harkens back to Mick's doo-wop days with The Embers.

The man had a memory like an elephant and drew lyrics from experiences. Mickey discussed the story behind *Poison Red Berries*, aka *I Don't Think Much About Her No More* with <u>Country Song Roundup</u>. "I went to Sammi Smith's house once to pitch a song, and she had one of those berry bushes in her yard. She told me not to touch the berries; the red ones are poisonous. I forgot about that until years later, when I was searching for a line equating poison with a lost love." Under an angelic chorus and over a bed of organ-funeral music, Mickey sings the song's crux: "Yesterday's gone and better forgotten / Like a poison red berry it clings to my mind."

"I probably heard that album more than any human being on the planet," Kristofferson said. "Newbury is such a resolute artist; he is never going to compromise his vision of what the whole picture should be. And so you got this Newbury picture with sound effects and beautiful melodies and singing, and he keeps working on it and working on it, and he was driving me crazy at one point." Maybe that explains why the album liner notes, written by Kristofferson, state, "Perhaps... he is a visitor from outer space."

Extraterrestrial or not, critics praised the seminal contribution. George Lewis wrote, "Coupled with Newbury's darkly romantic writing, emotionally vulnerable vocals and brilliant music textures, the album easily outclasses anything coming out of Nashville at that time with the exception of Bob Dylan's 'Nashville Skyline,' recorded at about the same time, and with many of the same musicians. But whereas Dylan was attempting to create a country album from his evolved folk perspective, Newbury's agenda was larger. Drawing on an eclectic musical background, he fashioned a complex whole from many sonic parts."

Country Music People noted, "The results on the 'Looks Like Rain' album were superbly simple, yet effective... The sound is acoustic and deliberately underplayed - letting the mood and Newbury's lyrics gently draw in the listener."

Kristofferson stated in the liner notes, "They (the arrangements) sub-consciously intensify the moods of the songs - sounding at times like the ancient echoes of a forgotten past, and at others, like the dark mystery of space."

A discerning commentary came from Newbury's friend - Jimmie Mac - former Nashville songwriter, and one of America's top DJs at KDAV, Lubbock. Jimmie said, "Looks Like Rain is not something folks 'get.' It's something a broken heart experiences. Don't try to understand sunlight. You'll go crazy. Just bask in its warmth."

Thom Jurek might have summed it up best: "It (LLR) is a sound that seemingly comes from inside the mind of the listener as much as from the speakers on the stereo... His lyrics are, like all great truths, deceptively simple... 'Looks Like Rain' is a perfect record. It is so fine, so mysterious in its pace, dimensions, quirky strangeness, and charm, that it defies any attempt at strict categorization or criticism; a rare work of genius."

As a technical accomplishment in 1969, LLR is a marvel. Mickey's friend and renowned Bay Area radio personality Ron Lyons comments. "Looks Like Rain should have won at least a Grammy for 'Best Engineered Recording.' With multi-tracking and overlays and only three or four tracks to work with, matching the levels (volume) on all tracks, and constantly dubbing them back and forth to get the final mix, and also equalizing the voices is fraught with hazards. Mickey told me that 'God must have been guiding his hands the way it all came together.' I have listened to 'Looks Like Rain' musically, emotionally, and technically over and over again and except for some cheap vinyl Mercury used in those days, it is almost flawless in execution."

Working with little budget and against the Nashville wind, Newbury experimented with technical gimmickry in ways only The Beatles would surpass. But The Beatles received boundless support from their label. Newbury didn't. Certain conservative Nashville nabobs would have enjoyed seeing the heretic tarred, feathered and run out of town. Perhaps these good ol' boys got to Mercury. Even before LLR was released, according to

114

Newbury, Mercury's president and co-founder Irwin Steinberg told Wesley Rose in an airplane on the way to England that he was "disappointed" in the album. Said he thought Mickey was going to be like a Jerry Lee Lewis. Furthermore, he barked, "That's the biggest piece of shit I've ever heard in my life!" Rose asked, "Did you ever listen to him before you signed him?" "No," Steinberg replied, "I just took the word of other people."

When word of the conversation got back to Newbury, he confronted Steinberg. The men were shortly in an argument, which ended with Newbury telling him to "kiss my ass... It was really just a total miss so I got out. I raised so much hell with the label, and I bought my album away from them. I got it released from the label." Eight years later, Mickey explained himself to Country Music People. "There was a lot of conflict between what I wanted to do and what they wanted me to do which caused me to ask for a release, because that was the early times of the change in Country Music, and it just wasn't accepted by a lot of the established people in Nashville." And so a disgruntled Mickey Newbury left Mercury in search of greener and friendlier pastures.

> *I burned that highway down in '69*
> *Yes I burned that four-lane highway down in 1969*
> *I never do look back*
> *I do not see that railroad track*
> *Burned that highway down in '69*
> *IN '59*

LLR experienced disappointing sales due in part to Mercury's disinterest and lack of promotion. And as Mickey explained to Country Song Roundup, "I had some complaints on my album that the songs were too long and everything. I know that and I'm sorry that disc jockeys couldn't play them. I understand their problems. They got commercial spots and everything. I've got a lot of friends in radio and I've talked to them and I know what their problems are. They gotta understand also that I've gotta do what I feel. If it's not gonna be salable then I'm sorry... You can't worry about keeping up with the trends. If you do, you'll always lag behind."

LLR did sell well in the San Francisco area, due in large part to KSFO DJ extraordinaire, Bobby Dale, who would play the complete album on the air. Twenty-five percent of Mickey's sales were in the Bay Area, where he loved working at the Fairmont and the Boarding House. "In the early seventies," Mick explained, "I was big in San Francisco, where I often performed. Tower Records was nothing then, just one store with about a dozen employees. The owner, Russ Solomon, asked me to come by and say hello to his employees. I did, and performed for just them for a couple of hours. I guess they loved me as their token redneck - Texas drawl and cowboy boots." For that act of kindness, Solomon would one day stock Tower stores worldwide with Newbury's CDs.

How amusing Steinberg remarked he thought Newbury would be "like a Jerry Lee Lewis," as The Killer was first to cover *She Even Woke Me Up To Say Goodbye* from LLR, and it quickly hit the number two spot on the country chart. Jerry Lee also so named an album. Thirty-one artists have since covered the tune: from Brook Benton to Jerry Garcia of the Grateful Dead to Keith Richards of the Rolling Stones to Don Williams. The song's wonderful melody and aching-heart lyrics - "Baby's packed her soft things and she's left me" - make it one of country's best.

Several people told Newbury that *San Francisco Mabel Joy* would flop. "Everybody said, 'What're you gonna do with a five-minute song?' I said, 'I don't know, sing it I guess'... It's sold 55 million records so far. It's been on the biggest albums in history. It was on Joan Baez' double platinum album ('Blessed Are' - which also contains Mick's *Angeline* and *The 33$^{rd}$ Of August*). It was on a John Denver platinum album ('Some Days Are Diamonds'). It was on a Kenny Rogers multi-platinum album ('The Gambler' - which has sold 35 million copies)... So I'm glad that I wrote the song that would never get recorded."

By recording on his own terms outside the mainstream system - well outside the box - Newbury was called a "quiet outlaw," years before the "outlaw" term existed. He resented the label since he was simply making a record the best way possible. In the process, though, he declared his independence; LLR stood on its own ground... nonconforming to the formulaic Nashville Sound. Though LLR was released only one year after "Harlequin Melodies," their sound, feeling, maturity and quality are light years apart. It's hard to believe they are products of the same person over any time span. Still upset over the RCA fiasco, Newbury told BBC Television, "Looks Like Rain is really my first album as far as I'm concerned."

After the release of LLR, Kenny Rogers telephoned Mickey in October to ask him to meet Susan's airplane. She was coming to Nashville, he explained, to put together The Good Time Singers, urgently needed to sing backup for Tennessee Ernie Ford. And so, as Susan deplaned, a grinning Mick was waiting and his greeting stunned her. "You know if you stay, this is gonna be wrong, so we're gonna do it right. We're gonna go get married right now!" Susan told him, "You are crazy!" He replied, "Yeah, but that's what we're gonna do." They were married by 3 PM that day in Gallatin, Tennessee.

Though they had spent only eight total hours together in the two years since they had met, Mickey said, "She walked in and it was like BANG! And she felt it too, you know..." Susan said she gave up her professional career as soon as she was married, "and I never looked back... It wasn't like I was missing anything... I had traveled the world, and I had sung in some fantastic places... It wasn't even a consideration... I wanted a marriage and children."

"I never thought about marrying Susan, I just did it," Mickey told <u>Rolling Stone</u>. "You'd think a man of 30 would have had more sense. But I've lived my whole life by movin' strictly on emotions and makin' snap decisions." That decision, Newbury reflected, proved to be a turning point. "I had what I wanted - Susan and freedom. It was probably the happiest period in my life. I laid out in the sunshine, fished, read, wrote and didn't worry about anything."

*Then Susie you found me when I was hopelessly lost*
*And I did not know where to go*
*You had the answer and we came together*
*But Susan I needed you too long ago*
*WINTER WINDS BLOW*

*The tight circle draws close but somehow I know it's all right*
*There is never the feeling of chains but a refuge from night*
*I find myself seeking her hand as I drift off to sleep*
*Had I never known her God only knows where I'd be*
*SONG FOR SUSAN*

Mickey would convert to Susan's religion, as she was a faithful practitioner of the Mormon faith, and they wanted their children raised in one church. Within Christianity, Mickey was not spiritually pedantic. In his heart he accepted Jesus Christ as his Savior, and he felt the details that divide many people are window dressing. The man was more interested in the light beyond the window.

*Every time it rains Lord I run to my window*
*WHY YOU BEEN GONE SO LONG*

**Relaxing on Old Hickory Lake**

**Milton, Mamie, Mickey and Susan**

# Chapter IX: *An American Trilogy*
## 1970 - 1972

By the 1970's, the term "rock & roll" had become nearly meaningless. The decade saw the breakup of The Beatles and the death of Elvis Presley, robbing pop music of two major influences. Jimi Hendrix, Janis Joplin and Jim Morrison of The Doors - three main figures in sixties rock - would die from reported and controversial drug overdoses. Pop music splintered into a multitude of styles: soft rock, hard rock, folk rock, punk rock, shock rock, country rock and the flamboyant dance craze of the decade, disco. But whatever genre one preferred, rock music was big business. Country music also was undergoing a splintering, spurred on by individuality and rebelliousness.

In the seventies, Nashville's patron Gaylord Enterprises invented the Oprylandia empire and shaped the city's country music tourist business by contributing to the economic revival of the downtown riverfront, sending boats up and down the river, modernizing the Ryman Auditorium and moving the Grand Ole Opry. Music had become monstrously huge business and was responsible for Nashville's multi-million dollar tourist industry.

But even to his detriment, Newbury refused to play the game. Though invited many times to appear on the Opry, he declined. Why would he turn down an offer to play the world's greatest stage? Because the penny-pinching Opry paid performers a pittance of profits. It was a matter of principle. The ugly subject generated heated exchanges between Mick and publishing bosses, clever Wesley Rose and hard-hitting Roy Acuff, who was by no means a wimpy musician. Before being anointed King of Country, Acuff had been drafted to play baseball for the New York Yankees in the early twenties when Babe Ruth was there. He even ran for Governor of Tennessee and nearly won. Serving as a permanent Opry member, he was primarily responsible for the Opry's success and prominence. Regardless of Acuff-Rose's persuasive tactics, Newbury would not concede. "I won't do the Grand Ol' Opry," he explained to <u>Omaha Rainbow</u>. "They know how I feel about them; I've told them before. I won't play there because I don't feel like they have sufficiently paid their artists since the conception of the Opry. They've made money without any of their artists realizing any of the profit."

He played other venues. In the early seventies, he put on a few concerts at the informal Exit/In, which <u>Country Music</u> called, "far and away the best club in Nashville for live music... fast becoming one of the top clubs in the country." Located about five minutes west of the Ryman, the Exit/In featured such acts as John Prine, John Hartford, Bill Monroe, Waylon Jennings and Willie Nelson. Mick also played the Hermitage Landing and Barn Dinner Theater, the last with Roger Miller as a private show for Vanderbilt Medical School.

On April 22, 1970, Mick appeared at The Bitter End East, the first "country" act to work there, and in a write-up of the show, <u>Billboard</u>'s Nancy Erlich referred to him as a "country-folk singer." <u>Country Song Roundup</u> caught the show too and wrote, "Mickey is an exceptional entertainer as is evidenced by his performance at the Bitter End in New York where he held the audience in the palm of his hand." Mick would introduce Kristofferson to club manager and soon to be owner, Paul Colby, and then "Kris wound up working there."

About this time, Ray Charles recorded two Newbury songs, *Sweet Memories* and *Good Morning Dear*, on the LP, "Love Country Style." (He also released an album titled "Sweet Memories," containing its namesake on the London label). In short order, the men would become friends, leading Mick to say, "Ray has more charisma than anyone I've ever met." Liner notes in a future Charles box set would state, "Newbury had made a name for himself in Nashville in the late 1960's as a composer of strong, nontraditional country fare... His best-known song at the time was probably The First Edition's pop/psychedelic novelty 'Just Dropped In,' but Newbury's work was far more noteworthy for the melancholy he could evoke through songs like *Sweet Memories.* Surely that capability attracted Charles, whose inclusion of two Newbury originals spoke volumes about Ray's ever-contemporary ears..."

Contemporary artistry, in a stylistically modern sense, translated to blatant sacrilege in many Music City circles. For that reason, Mick needed to connect to a modern-day recording company, not chained to Nashville tradition. About six months after leaving Mercury, he signed with Elektra Records. Jac Holzman was running it then, and they were more receptive to experimentation and change than other companies. "Lonnie Mack introduced my recording of "Looks Like Rain" to the VP of Elektra, Russ Miller," Mick said; and Miller would explain that when he first heard the music, "I was so moved I cried."

"The next thing I knew I was swept up in a whirlwind," Mick continued. "I was the first act signed from Nashville by Elektra." Elektra purchased the LLR album from Mickey for $20,000 more than he had paid Mercury to buy it back. Moreover, the contract gave Mick the right to produce his records or hire producers, plus no roadwork - no touring. An amazing deal for an artist of that era.

Mick made clear his feelings about his new label to <u>Country Song Roundup</u>: "I felt an immediate rapport with the people I met from Elektra, which is something I find very important. I've been in this business long enough to realize that you don't sign with a company, you sign with people. Musically they understand what I'm doing, plus I am able to consider these people as friends... On a serious note, the early days on Elektra were indeed ground breaking, and a wonderful time to be in the record industry. Jac was truly a visionary. By way of historical note, he started Elektra records in The Village in New York, selling his records from a bicycle. By 1969, he had such diverse acts as Theodore Bikel, Judy Collins and The Doors."

"Jac knew where the music was heading... He saw a trend towards country/folk and signed a little group of studio musicians called The Eagles. The roster included all of these people along with Bread and Carly Simon. Great times. At one point, in that small L.A. office, the label was doing more business than any two of the majors combined, due to the genius of Jac and the dedicated artisans he surrounded himself with... not to be confused with the artists. Elektra was like a family."

Jac felt the same for Mick and journeyed to Nashville to see him. "Mickey," he advised the author, "was a craftsman songwriter, never far from a song in some aspect of formation. Facile and fastidious, Mickey tuned and burnished each song until it shown. There was no excess, no unsightly ornament in his work and that is why his songs speak so intimately to us today. I wasn't much of a Nashville cat, but I loved the music. And there was nothing more seductive than spending an evening on Mickey's houseboat. One of my fonder memories is sitting with him and Susan on their houseboat and softly sailing on one of the rivers near Nashville on a summer evening. There was a rich feeling of the South, very strange to a Northerner, but totally captivating. The lake, the quiet, the magnolia... Mickey singing... it doesn't get any better. And... Susan bakes one helluva pecan pie, the best I ever tasted."

Peaceful moments on the river were interrupted by backlash from an insane political proclamation. President Nixon announced on April 30, 1970 that he had ordered American troops into Cambodia to take part in a major military action. The statement, for lack of a better word, bombed, setting off nationwide protests against the Vietnam War. Then on May 4, a demonstration by students at Kent State against the War ended in tragedy when the Ohio National Guard opened fire on protesters killing four students and wounding nine others. Protests occurred nationwide in response to the tragedy. As the counterculture movement shifted into high gear, nearly five million American students joined the national student strike. Former Supreme Court Justice Earl Warren said Kent State sparked the worst

American crisis since the Civil War, and <u>Business Week</u> magazine warned: "This is a dangerous situation. It threatens the whole economic and social structure of the nation."

Against this setting of social and political pandemonium, Elektra booked Mick at a new club in West Hollywood, just down the road from The Troubadour on Santa Monica Boulevard. "We were staying in Jac Holzman's apartment in L.A. while Mick performed at the Bitter End West," Susan stated. "Mick didn't know what he wanted to sing. We spent one entire rainy day sitting in the apartment while he played through every arrangement of every song that he was thinking about doing. He never went on stage with a planned set. He always let the 'spirit move him.' He played three songs (*Dixie, Battle Hymn of the Republic* and *All My Trials*) that afternoon, but not together. He was pretty quiet, except for the music."

Later that Saturday evening while backstage at the Bitter End, Mick was conversing with comedian David Steinberg about current headlines. Whites in integrated Southern schools, Mick explained, were insisting on using *Dixie* as the school-fight song, while blacks were protesting, as they saw it as an anthem of white supremacy. At the same time, the singing of *Dixie* had been banned in some Southern states, as a mistaken statement of the civil rights movement. Nothing in the song made it the exclusive property of bigots or extremists, Newbury protested. He then advised Paul Colby he was going to sing *Dixie*, as a protest against censorship. Fearing a riot, Colby turned white and pleaded with him not to do it. Mick told him to call the riot squad.

"It was one of those, kind of, happening nights, you know, where everybody in the business comes in. Joan Baez was there, and Odetta and Cass Elliott - bless her heart - and the Mamas and the Papas" and Mick's wife Susan. "Streisand came by," Susan remembered, "and tried to talk Kristofferson into leaving with her, before Mick sang. Kris declined and my admiration for Kris jumped a notch."

"Originally, Mick continued, "I intended to do (just) *Dixie*. It had the connotation of being a strictly Southern song that was associated with racism... I thought it was unfair so... In the middle of the show I started to do *Dixie*." "Everybody was holding their breath," Susan recalled. "I was sitting next to Odetta, and I have to admit I turned a little green. What happened in the next seven or eight minutes was magic."

The *Dixie* Mick presented that evening was not the rousing, rebel yell, battle march version, but the slow, heartfelt, melodious tune that we know today. Only by slowing it to a quarter-time ballad, could Newbury illustrate its true beauty and meaning. "I got through with the *Dixie* part of the song and I looked down and Odetta was sitting down in the front row and she had tears in her eyes." As writer Dorothy Hamm would summarize, "He changed a song that some consider divisive into a song of unification."

Only when he began singing *Dixie,* did it dawn upon him to add *Battle Hymn of the Republic* and conclude with the antebellum *All My Trials.* Mickey explained, "*Dixie* just continued on, you know... the other two songs just happened to find their way in the song... and it wound up being a trilogy." The impromptu arrangement just came together on that magical night and in one moment of brilliant inspiration.

"When I got through with that song, the place was like completely silent ... Seemed like it went on for 30 seconds... And then I mean to tell you they stood and screamed and hollered like you would not believe... It was the most electrifying experience I ever had in music..."

Grateful a riot had been avoided, Paul Colby would voice his recollection. "When he finished, he didn't know if he was going to be applauded or if the stage was going to be rushed. The applause was thunderous." And Susan would add the finishing touches: "By the end of the song, there was absolute silence in the club... not one clinking glass. Odetta was crying; Cass was crying, and then people were on their feet. A standing ovation that lasted at least two minutes. And that Newbury grin... he knew he could do it."

"A lot of people," Mick explained, "were not aware that President Lincoln requested *Dixie* to be performed on the steps of the White House the day the Civil War was over. Historically it goes a long way back... and it was written by a man (D.D. Emmett) from the North of the United States... *Battle Hymn of the Republic* was written by a man from the South. I know the song was written for a Broadway play. (Music for *Battle Hymn* is credited to a Southerner from South Carolina, William Steffe in 1856. The lyrics were written in 1861 by Julia Ward Howe, a northern Transcendentalist from Boston, as a poem to compliment Steffe's infectious melody.) And *All My Trials* was initially a Jamaican slave song... It was called *All My Sorrows.*"

"African-American slaves of the era adopted *All My Trials* as a song of sorrow. The Confederacy took *Dixie* as a marching song, while the Union identified with *Battle Hymn of the Republic*... So there were the three components of the Civil War." In four minutes and fifty seconds, Mickey wove them into *An American Trilogy*, eternally bonding minority, Southern and Northern issues into a common lament; and in so doing, he helped diminish the Mason-Dixon Line. The song has become "the ultimate example of Americana," Brian Hinton wrote. "It somehow evokes the birth of modern America."

"I just put together songs from three separate factions in the Civil War, to show that they were all really fighting for the same thing," Mick told <u>Disc</u>. "It's not my triumph though," he humbly added. "It's the beauty of the songs."

### AN AMERICAN TRILOGY

*Oh I wish I was in the land of cotton*
*Old times there are not forgotten*
*Look away look away look away Dixieland*
*Oh, I wish I was in Dixie away away*
*In Dixieland I take my stand to live and die in Dixie*
*Dixieland that's where I was born*
*Early on one frosty morning*
*Look away look away look away Dixieland*

*Glory glory hallelujah*
*Glory glory hallelujah*
*Glory glory hallelujah*
*His truth is marching on*

*So hush little baby*
*Don't you cry*
*You know your daddy's bound to die*
*All my trials Lord soon be over*

A bit later when *Trilogy* was released as a single and as part of the LP, "Frisco Mabel Joy," the song was promptly banned in the Southern states that had banned the singing of *Dixie*. "Most of the reaction I got was from the black community. I got sued by a branch of the NAACP in Missouri. They didn't understand what I was doin' with it at all. I decided to rearrange *Dixie* and make a ballad out of it. It was my way of taking a certain group's marching song away from them." For the record, the year was 104 AK.

"There were racial connotations and there were anti-war statements they thought - there was a lot of controversy about it," Mickey told <u>Country Music People</u>. "It took almost a year before people realized I had no intentions of making any deep political statements - philosophical maybe, but not political. I don't get involved in political statements unless they're cloaked in some kind of emotional statement because I don't believe you can preach to people's intellect and change them. You can only change them by your actions or letting them feel what another person feels through your music. We're not logical creatures; we are emotional creatures."

Newbury approached political statements in songwriting in a different way. "Instead of making an intellectual statement, you made an emotional statement. If we were gonna talk about racism, we wouldn't try to tell you how bad it was... We would introduce you to a black man. Make you be friends with him." For good reason, <u>Tennessean</u> Staff Writer Peter Cooper referred to Mick as "a communicator of soul and emotion."

> *I was just a boy the year the Bluebird Special came through here*
> *On its first run south to New Orleans*
> *A blind old man and I we came to Guthrie just to see the train*
> *He was black and I was green*
> CORTELIA CLARK

A few days prior to the Bitter End engagement, Mick appeared on the Skip Weshner Show at KRHM in L.A. Skip was married to Lynne Taylor of the Rooftop Singers and hosted the popular program, which featured artists such as Dylan, Hoyt Axton, John Denver, Gordon Lightfoot and Joni Mitchell. Susan and Russ Miller accompanied Mick to the radio station, where he gave an interesting interview and performed five songs. Skip taped the session, and it may be the earliest surviving recording of a live Newbury performance.

At one point Skip asked, "How tall are you?"
"Five-eight," Mick replied.
"Oh come on!" said Skip.
"That's all," Mick confirmed.
"Well," the host declared, "If somebody asked me how tall is Mickey Newbury, I'd say I don't know, six feet or six-one... I guess it's the way a man projects."


**ALBUM # 3** Frisco Mabel Joy (Elektra EKS-74107) contains the following songs: (Side 1) An American Trilogy, How Many Times (Must The Piper Be Paid For His Song), Interlude, The Future's Not What It Used To Be, Mobile Blue, (Side 2) Frisco Depot, You're Not My Same Sweet Baby, Interlude, Remember The Good, Swiss Cottage Place, How I Love Them Old Songs. (Released also as Newbury's sole Quadraphonic LP under Elektra EQ-4107.)

Whereas "Looks Like Rain" presents a sophisticated air of folksy rebelliousness, "Frisco Mabel Joy" uses folk, country, bluegrass and balladry to showcase Newbury's poetry. The album was his second offering from Cinderella Studio - by then a sixteen-track facility - and his first release on Elektra. The label did a good job promoting the release - sending to select radio stations, for example - a stereo reel-to-reel tape (WS 5156) containing six 60-second FMJ advertisements.

Mixed at Jack Clement Recording Studios, the album became Mick's only LP to crack the National Top 100 (#29 on the Country Chart and #58 on the Pop Chart), selling 120,000 copies and becoming his best-selling record. Ironically, FMJ's initial sales spurt resulted from the song medley he had arranged but did not write, *An American Trilogy*. Sales could have been better," Mickey explained. "It would have been a perfect bicentennial record, but I just never thought about it - I just do things when they come; it was just four years too early."

First-time listeners are drawn to the album's lush string arrangements, a Cinderella Sound that represented Newbury's take on The Nashville Sound. He let the cat out of the bag in 1977, advising Omaha Rainbow, "All the string sounds on the 'Frisco Mabel Joy' and 'Heaven Help The Child' albums are all pedal steel. That big instrumental sound after the *Trilogy*... it's all steel guitars, there's not a string or horn there. Actually, it's not just steel, there's electric guitar as well. Charlie McCoy, Weldon Myrick, Wayne Moss. I record by doing the vocal with just acoustic guitar first, then everything else is overdubbed. That way at least you know what you're getting when you're laying it down. Every instrument has a reason for being there."

Mickey would be credited for the far-reaching influences of his employment of pedal steel. The Pedal Steel Guitarist reported, "Mickey is generally considered to be the first artist to 'crossover' (go from the Country to the Pop charts) using a Pedal Steel. Before this, if a song contained a Pedal Steel, it had to be Country, and, had very little chance of being played on Pop stations. 'Course, after Mickey did it, many other artists such as Bob Dylan, Joan Baez, Judy Collins, the Carpenters and many more have successfully used Pedal Steel to create the sound that identifies them with Country / Rock / Folk." Naturally, it took a Hipbilly to lead the way.

One extraordinary song on FMJ grabbed writer Don Negri's attention. "*Frisco Depot*," he wrote, "should be required listening / reading for anyone aspiring to be a real songwriter (as opposed to tunesmith). Supposedly a reference to a visit to San Francisco by Mickey in the late sixties, the City by the Bay becomes a metaphor for the distances that separate us from our dreams, from each other, and from ourselves. This is a richly layered song, as each stanza, feeding lyrically off the preceding, develops a new, yet complementary theme. The choice of words, their positioning - the way they play off each other - are simply masterful."

It is public and private when Mick sings *Frisco Depot*; he is nursing his broken heart and the listener's, too. Haunted by the past, he could authentically tap into all the pain he ever felt. He conveys the plunder melodically through heart-stabbing poetry and a glorious voice with penetrating honesty. Raw emotion is communicated; barricades are dissolved and his personal pain becomes the people's currency.

The emotional maturity of these songs is amazing, considering Newbury wrote several during his mid-to-late twenties. He had the emotional ability to reach the depths of any song, and a cry in his voice that just breaks the heart. Still, how can a young man write, *The Future's Not What It Used To Be*? The subject should be exclusive property of the elderly:

> *I never thought I would live to grow old*
> *Oh the past cut a hole deep in me*
> *Shackled and chained to a ghost that remains*
> *I am haunted by her memory*
> *THE FUTURE'S NOT WHAT IT USED TO BE*

*Remember The Good* - Mamie's favorite ballad - was covered by Mick's favorite balladeer, Roy Orbison. Like Orbison's *Running Scared*, it is structured as a crescendo rising to a climactic last verse. Writer Mark Brend would critique the song in a fashion uncharacteristically emotional for a British journalist: "If you're not trembling and goose-pimpled when Newbury hits the high notes in *Remember The Good*, you've got a cold, cold heart." (Brend would go on to form a British band named... "Mabel Joy.")

Mick explained the basis for one song on the album. "I got married and I tried to write some love songs... It's not a time to write sad songs you know. So, I set out to write some love songs and I couldn't do it. But I did write a happy song." *How I Love Them Old Songs* sends one on a happy, honky-tonkin' romp in the country, as he sings: "Ah when I hear that double-eagle guitar / It makes me think how trouble free girl we are." The verse may refer to John Phillip Sousa's song, *Under the Double Eagle*. Bluegrass and country guitar players adapted the march king's catchy tune, and a generation of pickers believed that when one could play it, he had arrived as an accomplished guitarist. Many artists, including Norman Blake and Willie Nelson, have covered the Sousa benchmark.

Changing voice and style, Mick presents *Mobile Blue* as a Dylan-esque foot-stomper. Finally, *The Piper* raises the ante on the proposition that poets are born and not made.

> *Mornin' came and found her at the window*
> *With her nose pressed to the glass*
> *The dew was like a broken diamond necklace*
> *Left scattered on the grass*

*She slipped from my side*
*She stands at the window and watches the rain*
*Lord I wish I was blind*
*And could not read her mind and see all her pain*

*But from here where I lie I can see*
*The tears in her eyes as she quietly cries*
*Out for him not for me*
*HOW MANY TIMES MUST THE PIPER BE PAID FOR HIS SONG*

The album would produce more than 210 cover versions, primarily due to the widespread appeal of *An American Trilogy*, and that topic will be discussed later. *How I Love Them Old Songs* would be picked up by 23 artists including Bill Monroe, Gene Vincent, Carol Channing, Tompall Glaser, Daliah Lavi and Jim Ed Brown. *Remember The Good* and *Mobile Blue* would be waxed by more than 25 performers, for example Brook Benton, Wayne Newton, Eddy Arnold, Waylon Jennings, Claudine Longet, Glen Yarbrough and Crow (David Wagner). Robert Forster and Roger Miller would also record songs from the album.

Reviews of FMJ were positive. Karen Berg wrote in <u>Rolling Stone</u>, "If you get into Mickey Newbury you can really get hooked... He's never mawkish. He's cathartic and his melodies clear the head of clutter. And can he ever sing. First he's sweet like an angel, but then he dips sexily into the lower register or a faster tempo... He's a master of the ballad, but that's not to say he can't rock... To me, he is a major talent... He should get the national recognition he's due." <u>Rolling Stone</u> also included FMJ in its poll of the best albums of the year.

Albert Hall wrote in a December '71 <u>Country Song Roundup</u> article, "Yet his drive, his ambition, his need for expression enabled him to endure this experience (past hardships) and become what he is today... one of the finest songwriters on the face of the earth."

And in early '72, <u>Crawdaddy's</u> Jill Franeberry hit the bull's eye; "Mickey Newbury is the Robert Frost of song, finding the core of emotions with lyrics that are simple, yet so complex. Every fiber of song is woven with the sweet sorrow of memories, exquisitely carried by that voice, so boyishly sweet, yet heavy with wisdom."

Finally, in April '72, the Staff Editors of <u>Hit Parader</u> printed a review so flattering... it comes across as advertisement. "A while back Mickey released an album on Mercury called 'Looks Like Rain.' The music industry just went walking around shaking its collective head saying, 'Newbury has done it all this time.' All of us at <u>Hit Parader</u> thought it was the finest album we ever heard and thought it couldn't be topped. But it was. By Mickey Newbury. His new album on Elektra, 'Frisco Mabel Joy,' from which was culled the smash single, *An American Trilogy*, is not just an album - it's an experience. Mickey Newbury has been known for his genius within the industry for a long time - now he's getting the widespread recognition he's deserved so greatly."

During the album's production, Mickey suffered a scare when good friend and producer, Dennis Linde, became ill and almost died. The déjà vu scenario carried his thoughts back to two years earlier, when Felton Jarvis nearly died and Steve Sholes did die around the production of "Harlequin Melodies." Mick must have felt jinxed, but this time he did not have to face the music alone. He had Susan, his bride of six months.

In the November '70 issue of <u>Country Song Roundup,</u> Mick beamed, "I'm one of the few guys in the business that's really happy. I'm really happy. I've got a beautiful wife. I live on a nice boat. I got what I want. I can go where I wanna go and I haven't always been this way and I appreciate it... I don't drink. I feel better in the last year and a half, or two years, than I ever felt before in my life... I was rundown."

> *There was a time I spent my nights in a bar*
> *Playin' that old jukebox until the honky-tonky locked up*
> *HOW I LOVE THEM OLD SONGS*
>
> *And then I met a lady in time she made me forget*
> *Her love set me free*
> *THE FUTURE'S NOT WHAT IT USED TO BE*

The Newburys had moved to a Nashville suburb in Hendersonville, making their home on a dammed-up river called Old Hickory Lake. They acquired a vintage Mercedes and exchanged the 36-foot PappyDad for a 50 footer. The new houseboat had two 350 horsepower engines, and Mick pointed out, "We could go 40 mph. The boat was a deep 'V,' like a cruiser except wider... You could take it in the ocean." They took several trips in the craft, once over 500 miles en route to the Birthplace Of Jazz, New Orleans. The course to The Big Easy would have carried them over the Cumberland, Ohio and Mississippi Rivers, though they stopped just short of the "Mighty Mississip."

> *Now he's steamin' down the river just inside of Memphis*

*Breathin' in the sweet southern scene*
*And he's leavin' all his troubles in the present*
*Bound down to old New Orleans...*

*Lazy Mississippi moving mightly slow*
*Like that old blackbird walking down the road*
*Able when the times get rough*
*To just pick up and go further on down the line*
*APPLES DIPPED IN CANDY*

Working and living outside Nashville caused people to talk, Mickey explained to Skip Weshner. "People thought I was a hermit because we stay on... I got married... We stay on the houseboat and don't get into town much... I don't know how it got started 'cause I don't think I've ever given anyone the impression that I didn't enjoy their company or didn't want anybody around... But word got around that I was a recluse, and Johnny Cash made the statement that I had a sub-machine gun mounted on the front of the boat!"

"And Russ Miller (of Elektra) sent Lonnie Mack down to see me a few months ago - a great guy you know. When Lonnie came back, Russ asked if he got out to see me, and he said 'no.' Everyone in town told Lonnie I was hard to get and they couldn't find me... And so I told Russ, 'Nobody ever bothers to look in the phone directory... 'cause my number's listed!"

"I wish," Mick told the author, "I had kept a diary of who visited us on the houseboat: Bobby Dylan, Joan Baez, Ray Charles, Art Garfunkel... everybody..." Mick was delighted to invite people on board. "The first time I met David Allan Coe was at the Marina. He sat in that old hearse for two days before I decided to find out who or what he was looking for. I made a cup of coffee... walked up the hill to his car and said, 'Hey man, can I help you find someone?' He said, 'Yeah, I'm lookin' for Mickey Newbury!' 'Well,' Mick replied, 'You're here.' He looked a little bit confused... I was not this sad, suffering, sorrowful songwriter he had in mind. I invited him to the boat for a cup of coffee and we have been friends since."

At 30, Mick had made many friends and he was satisfied with his career. "I'm now in the process of making some new goals. I've met all my goals that I wanted to make. I've done everything I've wanted to do musically. Just like I wanted to be a writer and I wanted to get some certain people (Willie Nelson, Waylon Jennings, Don Gibson, Ray Charles, Roy Orbison) to cut my songs and I've done it. I think now what I'd like to do is to get into position to be able to write my own songs and record them and have them sell. Of course that's what everybody'd like to do. I'd like to do it without going through the other stuff. Maybe I can and maybe I can't..."

Industry heavyweights continued to notice Newbury. Elvis recorded *An American Trilogy* on June 4 in RCA's Studio B. The Nashville session was filled with many musicians who had worked with Mickey at Cinderella: Chip Young on guitar, Norbert Putnam on bass, Davis Briggs on piano and Charlie McCoy on organ and harmonica. Incidentally, *Trilogy's* first movement, *Dixie*, is also the name of Elvis' first girlfriend, but it was Elvis' wife Priscilla who took the song to him. Presley's *Trilogy* would be released in February of 1972.

Tennessee studs and stars were familiar with Newbury's music, including "The Man In Black." During his ABC show on October 7, 1970, Johnny Cash and the Tennessee Three performed Mick's *I Don't Think About Her No More*. Referring to Newbury as a "poet," Cash would one day remark to Nashville friend, Judy Wirths, "Nobody could ever put words together like Newbury." Meanwhile, Mickey and Susan celebrated their first anniversary.

Tragedy struck two days before Christmas, when Willie's house in Ridgetop, Tennessee, burned down. "Everyone was safe," Blender magazine reported, "but Nelson plunged back into the ruins. 'I went in through the back door and headed for my guitar case.' Inside the rescued case was 'Trigger,' his now-trademark Martin classical guitar and two pounds of Colombian tea." Ironically, he had just written a song called *What Can They Do To Me Now*. After the fire, Willie, family and band returned to "God's Country," aka Texas.

To take a break from Nashville and spend Christmas with Susan's family, the Newburys headed 2,500 miles northwest to Eugene, Oregon. While there, Susan was drafted to star as Treacle The Fairy in a Christmas play for children at the University of Oregon. Her younger sister played a princess part; their mom Mary served as director, and local DJ / Newbury fan, David Apple, was anointed king of the fable. Mick enjoyed the production from the safe confines of theater seating. He enjoyed Oregon too, an invigorating breath of fresh air and wide open spaces.

Though fresh air was not part of the deal, New York's Bitter End East brought Mick back to perform over six evenings - October 10th through the 15th, 1971. Between shows, he would hang out at the Lone Star Café on Bleeker Street in Greenwich Village, enjoying strong coffee and conversing with anybody at hand: mayor, hippie or postman. He once treated a bowery couple to breakfast at the Lone Star, and the experience is referenced in his song, *Genevieve*. Mick wrote about another incident in the Big Apple, and vertically challenged individuals may appreciate it. "I even thought once about filing a federal lawsuit while sitting with my feet six inches off the

ground and my legs dead to the knee in a public john in New York City...
Ha... Ha!"

Following the Bitter End gig, Mick appeared at Lenny's On The Turnpike, a
famous jazz showplace near Boston.  He and Kristofferson had been the
only non-jazz entertainers to play there.  The assistant manager told The
Pedal Steel Guitarist, Lenny's "had never seen such enthusiastic response
as Newbury received."  Mick worked the club with "a really nice kid" who one
day would become a famous celebrity.  "Jay Leno's first show," Newbury
explained, "was opening for me at a little club called, Lenny's.  A hell of a
nor'easter dumped about 12 feet of snow on the ground... I had trouble
getting there from the motel, which was located just behind the club... So
we had three or four people at each of our two shows.  Jay was really a nice
kid.  He was real thin and wore these black blue jeans."

After Boston, Mick performed at The Great Southeast Music Hall in Atlanta,
where the opening act was Tom Waites.  Mick also played the Quiet Night in
Chicago, where he met Steve Goodman, who was only locally known at the
time.  Steve informed Mick that he was his second favorite songwriter; John
Prine was his favorite.  The two men became friends immediately.  Three
decades later, though, Prine would disagree.  While performing at a bar in
Galway, Ireland, he would say, "Mickey Newbury is probably the best
songwriter ever."

On December 4th, Newbury's *American Trilogy* entered the Top 40 at
number 37, eventually reaching number 26.  Remaining in the Top 40 for
seven weeks, the song would prove to be his only hit single.  It hit number
one in Dallas selling 50,000 copies in two days.  "I've never really had a
major record," Newbury told the Omaha Rainbow.  "It bugs me some, but I
expect it, I understand the problem.  I accept it and deal with it, because it's
my own choice I do it this way.  But it bothers me, yeah... So all I can do is
hope that word of mouth and time will take care of it."

A freezing winter brought in 1972, as Guy Clark and Susanna were wed
January 14th on the Newbury love boat on Old Hickory Lake.  Townes
served as best man.  "Susanna and I stayed on Mickey's houseboat until we
found a place of our own," Guy commented to Al Moir during an interview.
Mickey had been spending more time on the boat too, as he wasn't enjoying
Nashville so much by then.  Plus the old back injury was acting up.

Elvis waxed a Wagnerian, bombastic version of *An American Trilogy* (RCA
74-0672) on the 16th of February at the Hilton Hotel in Las Vegas, and it
became his first flop, barely penetrating the American charts at number 66.
Still, Mick advised Disc, "When Elvis recorded it, I was knocked out."  The
song did climb to the Top Ten in the UK, reaching the eight spot.  Elvis

would eventually make *Trilogy* a signature song, taking it to international heights of popularity. After its absurd banning in a few Southern states, "Elvis," Mick exclaimed, "made the song respectable."

The song has come to be associated with Elvis, eagle cape and all, sadly as a caricature. Biographer Peter Guralnick described Elvis' unforgettable presentation against the unfurling of the American flag: "At the conclusion of *An American Trilogy*, as the chorus swells, the percussion rolls, we are about to go into the 'Glory, glory, hallelujah' peroration, and Elvis stands there meditatively, eyebrow cocked, his mind for a moment seemingly on destiny, as the music once again takes him far, far away."

Royalty rights to *Trilogy* almost went far, far away, as well. Elvis' manager, Colonel Parker, would try to buy the rights, but Elvis - "Bless his heart!" - would not let him. It is remarkable Elvis stopped him. Ex carnival barker Parker, Chet Atkins once pointed out, "Got a helluva kick out of just beating you in a deal, any kind of a deal." *Trilogy* has since become Elvis' seventh all-time moneymaker, appearing on countless worldwide albums, compilations and videos. American writers, however, are not paid royalties on most offshore issues.

**ALBUM # 4** Sings His Own (RCA LSP4675) contains the following songs: (Side 1) Sweet Memories, Good Morning Dear, Just Dropped In, Weeping Annaleah, Time Is A Thief, (Side 2) Funny Familiar Forgotten Feelings, <u>Sunshine</u>, <u>Got Down On Saturday</u>, Are My Thoughts With You, <u>The Queen</u>.

Attempting to prosper from Mick's somewhat successful FMJ album, RCA released "Sings His Own." A 1972 <u>Billboard</u> article hailed the album as "A <u>Billboard</u> Pick" and stated, "Not merely a reissue, this LP is more of a genuine service that RCA is providing…"

Nonsense! The album was yet another embarrassment from The Big Dog. It was mostly a reissue, containing just three unreleased songs - underscored above - from Newbury's '68 RCA sessions. One song, *The Queen* is a pretty piece that was co-written with best friend Townes. Mick wears a black Stetson on the cover, and he looks like an annoyed tough guy. The hat had been a gift from Elvis to Felton to Mick.

In October, Mickey returned to a country he knew and loved, England, to make a few performances following the Top Ten unveiling of *American Trilogy*. On the 17th, he appeared on the BBC London TV program, "Old Grey Whistle Test," singing *Trilogy* and *The Piper*. Interviewed by renowned host Bob Harris, Mick looked young, happy and handsome. The program also featured performances by The Band and Santana. Next, he appeared in concert on the 20th with fellow Elektra artists, Harry Chapin and Plainsong, at Queen Elizabeth Hall in London. A promo EP was issued containing Mick's *Remember The Good* and songs by Plainsong and Chapin. Mick made his final appearance on British TV on November 4, performing *Trilogy* on the BBC London program, "Parkinson." The program featured famous actor Douglas Fairbanks.

Returning to America, Mick performed at the Big Sur Festival in California with the undisputed diva of folk music, Joan Baez. Good buddy Kristofferson, Taj Mahal and Blood, Sweat & Tears also participated. Because Mickey did not take the stage until late in the day, he grew very cold waiting his turn, and body shivers made it hard to play the guitar and sing. He would refer to it as "the worse musical experience of my life." The concert was released as a double LP, "Big Sur Festival (One Hand Clapping)," and included a large poster featuring Mickey with the other celebrities. He performed two songs, *Mabel Joy* (a duet with Baez) and *33rd of August.*

**VIDEO** "Mellow Memories" is Mick's earliest video, later released as "Rock And Roll Call." The compilation of hit songs is a terrific slice of music from the late sixties and early seventies, with performances by Neil Diamond, John Denver, Brian Hyland, Helen Reddy, The Association, Sonny and Cher, Nitty Gritty Dirt Band, Tommy James and the Shondells and Diana Ross and the Supremes. Newbury closes the program with a concept video, one of the earliest by a "country" artist. Ghosted against a video backdrop, he plays guitar and lip-synchs the three components to *American Trilogy*. For 1972... a decade before the arrival of MTV... two decades before digital delivery... Newbury's music video is a slick production.

*An American Trilogy* has become Newbury's most covered song, released by at least 155 artists (4/1/04). Genre crossover is extraordinary. Variations range from Presley to The London Symphony Orchestra, to Dread Zeppelin, to Enrique Chia, to Manowar (heavy metal), to Johnny Cash and on to Tanzorchester Klaus Hallen (a Rumba!)

*Trilogy* also impacted outside America. "The last time I was in Ireland," Mick recalled, "I went to a club and they closed all of the clubs over there with it, with the *Trilogy*. They all stand up - it's like an anthem, you know. It was really strange. It's been a very mystical kind of experience putting together those three pieces."

Though the song helped Mick's pocketbook, "Funnily enough," he explained, "it was probably very detrimental more than a help, because it was a reworking of other songs and it was not indicative of what I really do."

At 33, Mick knew what he wanted to do.  Fortunately, he was still young enough to try.

# Chapter X: *Poeta Nascitur Non Fit*
## 1973

In early January, Mickey attended the 2nd Annual Elektra Records WEA Distributors Convention in Phoenix, with fellow Elektra artists Bread, Judy Collins and The New Seekers. During this era, Mickey performed in San Francisco frequently, where he was one of the hottest acts. Jeff Yeager, Elektra's Promotions Manager, explained how Mickey would sing "anywhere and for anybody." He once booked him into a Bay Area synagogue with an audience of 1,000 people. Yeager remembered it was raining and that Mickey performed beautifully for over an hour, making it "one of the most spiritual events I ever witnessed."

The nation experienced a spiritual rejuvenation of sorts on March 29 when the Vietnam War officially ended. About the time the last U.S. troops left Vietnam, Mickey, Susan and Wesley Rose flew so far west, they ended up in the East. Far East, that is... to The Land Of The Rising Sun. Using the Big Island of Hawaii as an intermediary stop, Mickey paid a visit to friend, Jerry Bird. "Most folks," Mick said, "will never know he was the creator of one of the sounds of the islands, the steel guitar... a sound created by my friend Jerry Bird right in Nashville, Tennessee." After a week of fun in the sun and romantic evening luaus, Susan and Mickey continued on to Japan, where Mickey competed in the Second Annual Tokyo Music Festival, organized by the Tokyo Popular Music Promotion Association. On arrival at the airport, he was met by many fans, and Susan was "showered by roses."

Many artists - officially 609 - entered the world song contest, 373 from countries outside Japan. A few of the participants included Mac Davis, Paul Williams, George Clinton, Vikki Carr and Olivia Newton-John. After days of competition, the field was narrowed to 31 finalists. When Mickey's turn came, he performed his three-generational ballad, *Heaven Help The Child*. Playing guitar and singing beautifully over dramatic orchestration and background singers, Mickey Newbury, entry number 397, won first place plus a cash prize of 1 million yen ($10,000). A more important announcement came from Susan. She was carrying their first child.

*The seventies were kind to me; I was young... I was free.*
*Had it all, and then some more. I could walk through any door.*
*IN '59*

**ALBUM # 5** Heaven Help The Child (Elektra EKS-75055) contains the following songs: (Side 1) Heaven Help The Child, Good Morning Dear, Sunshine, Sweet Memories, (Side 2) Why You Been Gone So Long, Cortelia Clark, Song For Susan, San Francisco Mabel Joy.

"Heaven Help The Child" became the third and final release from tiny but mighty Cinderella Studio. The album bears the Newbury stamp of saying complex things simply while never oversimplifying complexity. The LP is full of memorable music and lyrics, songs whose passages can be recalled after one listen.

The title song, *Heaven Help The Child* is Newbury at his most poetic, a multi-level odyssey woven from threads of life as seen through his eyes. In an interview with Martin Neil, Newbury described the song as "a sequel" to *An American Trilogy*. In a style reminiscent of Hemingway, the ballad speaks of "1912 in New York" and "Paris in the twenties," then rolls into "War is hell to live with," dramatically concluding with Scottish poet Robert Burns' *Auld Lang Syne*. Between "Paris" and "War," Newbury injects an amazing passage: "We're all building walls / They should be bridges." The lyric ranks with the top writing of Thoreau or Lennon/McCartney or Shakespeare. Frankly, it seems biblical, akin to New Testament parable.

*Heaven's* melody - complete with the ringing of church bells - is gorgeous, and Mick's singing is stunning. Chris Fraser of Australia is the only artist who has covered it, and he does an inspired interpretation, speeding up tempo to suit his style. Chris said, "Every time I do it on stage, I get something happening inside me which is almost as good as sex." It's difficult to imagine any artist performing the song like Newbury. It is antiwar folksy - Dylan's province - but Dylan couldn't hit the tonal quality of Newbury's high notes with the aid of an Eventide Harmonizer. It's a soaring ballad but not subject matter Orbison advanced. In one word, inimitable... in another, Newbury.

After hearing Newbury perform the song, British writer Martin Neil gushed, "While all those in the room were speechless... it answered any questions I might have had about his future direction. He's going up, and his sensitive insight will take a lot of people with him." ("Gushed" is a term not normally linked with British journalists... )

The musicians enjoyed making the album, particularly one song, a toe-tappin' steel rocker. Pickin' and grinnin' on the bluegrass standard and bar-band classic *Why You Been Gone So Long*, this may have been Area Code 615's finest hour. Wayne Moss, David Briggs, Charlie McCoy, Welden Myric, Norbert Putnam and Bobby Thompson were members of the outlaw clan 615. As pure backup artists, their goal was to bring rockabilly back, using the down-home sound of bluegrass, mixed in with steel guitar. On this run through The Smokies, they succeeded wildly.

"Nashphilharmonic" - mentioned in the liner notes - was not a reference to a band. It was, Mick explained, "a catch phrase I created to include all the musicians I was working with, both past and present." Four years had passed since they had worked together on the painstakingly produced "Looks Like Rain." The musicians had become friends, professionals on the same wavelength, and their cohesiveness is evident at first listen.

*Why You Been Gone So Long* would become Newbury's second most recorded song with 59 covers. Mick's friend, Johnny Darrell was first to cut it, performing the tune as semi rock. He so named a 1973 album, and referred to Mickey as "an under-appreciated genius." Phish, Big Smith, Brenda Lee, Carl Perkins, Insane Pony, Bill Anderson, Anita Carter, Smithsonian Institute, Jerry Lee Lewis, Larry Jon Wilson and Clarence White and Ry Cooder - of Byrds fame - would also cover the song.

Along with *An American Trilogy*, *Sweet Memories* is recognized as a Newbury signature song. Mick released it originally in '68, but as he detested the RCA production, he recut it on "Heaven." A wise decision, as the newer version cancels out the earlier one. Nearly 50 artists have since recorded the song, and six have so titled an album: Ray Charles, Curt Ramsey, Sue Thompson, Willie Nelson, the Everly Brothers and Tumbleweeds - a country music group from The Netherlands who performed on the Opry. Acuff-Rose also had the song translated to Spanish by Mario Molina Montes, though covers of *Dulces Memorias* have not been registered.

*Sunshine* and *Good Morning, Dear* would be released by more than 10 artists, among them Juice Newton, Ray Stevens, Gene Vincent, Ray Charles, Roy Orbison and the Box tops. Pat Boone recorded *'Dear'* - his second Newbury cover - "in one of my most enjoyable Nashville sessions when I was with Mike Curb at MGM." He advised the author, "Indicative of Mickey's later writing, *Good Morning, Dear*, was more than a song - it was, and is, a slice of life. Just like his *American Trilogy... Dear* touches you in a surprising way, and surely springs from personal life as Mickey has lived it, and that makes it really precious. Mickey Newbury is a poet," he added. "There are good songwriters, and there are poets, and Mickey is both..."

About a year before "Heaven's" release, the Newburys had been in San Francisco while Mickey appeared at the Boarding House for one week. Returning to Nashville, they were saddened by an obituary in the <u>Nashville Banner</u>. Mickey's friend, Cortelia Clark, a sixty-seven-year-old blind man who lived on Jefferson Street and sang for years on the Fifth Avenue sidewalk, had perished in a trailer fire. He was attempting to fill the tank of a kerosene heater when the stove exploded. "In a steady rain," the paper reported, "the casket of Cortelia Clark was carried to the grave by strangers, funeral home attendants and gravediggers." Cortelia had won a Grammy in 1966 for a live original folk street recording produced by Felton Jarvis. To honor his departed friend, Mickey wrote one of his most beautiful ballads, *Cortelia Clark*. Newbury said he did not know it was about Cortelia until the final verse was written. The song contains one of Newbury's most illuminating verses: "He was black and I was green."

> *I read it in a week-old paper*
> *No one made it for his wake*
> *Or laid a single flower at his feet*
> *He was just a blind old beggar*
> *People said but Lord I'll wager*
> *He will not be beggin' on your streets*
> *You will find him Lord this mornin' steppin' from the dark*
> *Save a street in Glory Lord for CORTELIA CLARK*

*San Francisco Mabel Joy* on "Heaven" is taken without alteration from the '69 Mercury album "Looks Like Rain." The song was not overdubbed, as has been misreported too many times. It is amusing the way apocryphal information gets passed along. Including *SFMJ* on "Heaven" connected the dots. Why? For one, Mick's LP, "Frisco Mabel Joy," did not contain its namesake. And two, Newbury was saying hello to Mercury in his special way. The man was having fun with an inside joke.

Elektra promoted "Heaven" as they would promote a release from The Doors or The Eagles. Large color posters measuring 20" X 26" were folded and shipped to record stores and used as give-aways. Postcards with the album cover shot were mailed. Tabloid-size 11"x14" full-page advertisements were run in <u>Billboard</u> and <u>Rolling Stone</u>. The <u>RS</u> ad appeared in the March 15 issue under a Latin header, "Poeta Nascitur Non Fit," meaning, "Poets are born, not made."

Commensurate with target marketing and audience receptivity, initial exposure for the Cinderella trilogy of albums came from underground FM stations, rather than country media. Former <u>Rolling Stone</u> Editor, Ben Fong-Torres remembered, "Mickey Newbury was a favorite, not only of mine... but at free-form stations around the country." Writer George Lewis offered an insightful précis, "Given the stunningly original songs that this trilogy of albums contains, it is perhaps understandable that they were far too innovative for the record (and traditional broadcast) industry to successfully handle at that time." And Mickey as usual gave credit where due: "Prior to me or anyone else, Dylan had written long songs that received no airplay, but could not be ignored.  Underground radio was born, opening a door for the writer refusing to be constrained by the three-minute format.  Music was never the same."

Though the trilogy of albums is brilliant, no hits were produced for Newbury.  The music was too sophisticated, the themes too complex.  His writing went beyond universal appeal, and that left few people who could appreciate it.  In 1975 he explained to Rich Wiseman of <u>Rolling Stone</u>, "Now I could get a hit single, man... I know so much about this business and I've done it for other people.   But unfortunately I can't without compromising myself.  'Cause I'll tell you the honest-to-God truth - I'd have my name on less than one percent of the records that go gold.  I would love to have a bigger audience.  But I can't bend what I do to reach two million sixteen year-olds."

Shortly after "Heaven's" release, Mick performed in Pittsburgh to a boisterous crowd of 15,000.  When he appeared on stage, the audience began to laugh, as he was sporting a GI haircut white-walled on the sides.  "My scalp was showing through on top."  He began with a rowdy reading of *How I Love Them Old Songs*, to which the audience began stomping and clapping madly.  They were so loud that they did not hear him change gears and begin singing from *Heaven Help The Child*, repeatedly: "We're all building walls; they should be bridges."  When the audience finally did notice what he had done... what he was singing... they gave him a standing ovation.  A few days later, Mick performed at a cancer benefit at Vanderbilt University with Joe South, Ray Stevens and Roger Miller.  The following day's headlines in the <u>Nashville Banner</u> read, "Newbury - Short On Hair - Long On Talent."

Mickey next performed at Arlington Stadium then home to the Texas Rangers baseball team.  Show promoter and Newbury friend Roy Stamps remembered, "In the spring of '73, I called him and told him to name his price... I was doing a package show and he was going to be on it.  I'll never forget that he asked for $4,000 and a plane ticket.  It was more than I was paying anyone on that show, but I said okay and I think it freaked him out a little.   The show included Rick Nelson, Sammi Smith, Bobby Bare, Willie Nelson, Johnny Darrell, Ferlin Huskey, Billy Joe Shaver and a new kid named Larry Gatlin.  Although the attendance was disappointing, the show was very well received and Newbury just knocked everyone out.  The roar that night at the Holiday Inn was something that dreams are made of...  Mickey sang for five hours in the hotel room... not another person even picked up a guitar."

"The funny thing was the phone call I got from Gatlin the next morning.  He asked me not to book him on the same show with Mickey... as 'our music is just too much alike.' Larry could only pray that his music would be compared to Mickey's."

Gatlin agreed. "In 1971, Dottie West told me I looked enough like Mickey that I had to be able to write songs. (Dottie introduced him to Mick's music, starting with "Looks Like Rain.") I might have looked like him, but I sure couldn't write like him. He was one of a kind..." In another decade and in another country, the two men would do a show together... at Gatlin's request.

Stamps remembered another outing with Newbury in 1974. "Mickey, Bill Joe Shaver, Rodney Crowell and Guy Clark did a songwriters gig at the Granada Theater in Dallas. The other guys on stage kept moving their stools around so they wouldn't have to follow The Mick."

**ALBUM # 6** Live At Montezuma Hall / Looks Like Rain (Elektra 7E-2007) was issued as a double-gatefold LP. The first record in the set, "Montezuma," contains the following songs: (Side 1) How I Love Them Old Songs, Heaven Help The Child, Earthquake, Cortelia Clark, I Came To Hear The Music, San Francisco Mabel Joy, (Side 2) Bugger Red Rap, Bugger Red Blues (The Truck Song), How Many Times (Must The Piper Be Paid For His Song), An American Trilogy, Encore, Please Send Me Someone To Love, She Even Woke Me Up To Say Goodbye. Songs included on the second record, LLR, are discussed in Chapter VIII.

"Montezuma" was recorded live in Montezuma Hall at the Aztec Center, San Diego State University in March 1973. Rumor had it that the KPRI radio station employee, who taped the concert for future FM broadcast, would release it as a bootleg. Therefore, Elektra immediately negotiated rights to the recording and packaged it with a rerelease of the '69 Mercury issue, "Looks Like Rain." Because many Newbury fans then discovered LLR for the first time, the original Mercury LP became a hot commodity, fetching a street price of $300 and up.

Mickey did not appreciate bootlegged product. Dressed in coat and tie and sporting the GI buzz-cut, he made practice of just dropping in on record stores. If illegal LPs were offered for sale, he'd flash phony identification and deadpan in his best Texas drawl: "My name is Special Agent Sims - from the Department of Interior, Division of Recordings, Tobacco and Gaming Control (or some such nonsense). You're in violation of Code 541A, intent to sale illicit audio product. This carries a minimum fine of $10,000." Reduced to a whimpering mass, the owner would begin to plead and offer excuses. Agent Sims would counter, "Tell you what we'll do. If you burn the unlawful merchandise, we'll let it slide this time. But we'll be checking on you in the future!" As Mick sped away, a stream of rising black smoke split the jagged sky.

For legitimate radio station promotion, Elektra issued "Montezuma" as a single LP (EK-PROMO 20), titled, "Mickey Newbury Recorded Live At Montezuma Hall, San Diego State University, March 6, 1973." Duplicating the contents of the commercial "Montezuma," it features a black front cover and Mickey's FMJ picture on the back. Because few were distributed, it has become a valuable find for collectors.

As "Montezuma" features Newbury performing his ballads on a box guitar, many fans for the first time heard the classics stripped to the basics... without accompaniment from Nashville's best. And fans love the album, not only for the exquisite live takes, but also for Mick's warm sense of humor. *Earthquake* and *Bugger Red Rap* are notable examples. The concert-opening remark is always good for a laugh, as well, "The guy sittin' right about out there... you left the seeds in that stuff man!"

Reviewing "Live At Montezuma Hall," George Lewis wrote, "Hearing several of the earlier trilogy songs (from LLR, FMJ & Heaven) here stripped of their elaborate production values underscores both how good the songs themselves are, and the strength and emotive ability inherent in Newbury's voice... These minimalist acoustic versions are wonderful, and a side of Newbury that few are aware of... This disc then is a revelation."

The album and others showcase Mick's ability to make cricket noises, crow like a rooster, honk like a car horn, bark like a hound dog, hoot like a great horned owl, yodel-whistle like a rapping bluebird, laugh like a freight train and howl like a freight train. He could not however outrun a speeding freight train... He tried that once! The human effects machine could even imitate the resonance of a Salvation Army trombone. Newbury's sonic mimicry sounds like the real deal, not an animated adult at play. Perhaps the skills are a carryover from the doo-wop days, when The Embers relied on vocal prowess for ornamental effect.

This one-man band did not tune a guitar in the traditional way, but developed a distinctive sound. "It's because of the tuning I use," he explained to Peter O'Brien. "Till recently nobody else used it, but now Larry Gatlin, Red Lane and a few people are using it. I made up the chords for that tuning that never have been used before. I hope it's a trademark. What I was hoping was that the minute I hit my guitar, people would know it was me before I ever started singing."

Mick played in a "dropped D" tuning that gives the guitar a darker, more vibrant sound. The tuning may have originated in Kentucky and Mississippi in the early 1920's. In today's modern rock era, dropped D has become a common tuning for the guitar, utilized by Steve Vai, Joe Satriani, Eddie Van Halen and many others.

Since Mick could not read or write music ("Can't read a lick... I don't even know the names of the guitar strings!"), his friend - music teacher and guitar maestro Jeff Stave - provides the dropped D tutorial. "Start with a regular tuned guitar. That will be: 6/E, 5/A, 4/D, 3/G, 2/B, 1/E. Lower the 6th string two half steps or frets to D. It will be an octave lower than the 4th string. Now finger:

String / Fret / Finger
2 / 3 / 2
3 / 2 / 1
4 / 4 / 3

Finger pick on the 4th, 3rd, 2nd, 3rd strings in that pattern order while doubling the 4th string with your thumb on the 6th string. This is the basic D chord. Change chords by moving your left index finger to other bass strings on the second fret, always leaving your other fingers in place. Don't play the first string (E) much. Keep it simple, no more that two notes at a time. For the G chord, simply cover the 6th string on the 5th fret and leave the 2nd, 3rd and 4th strings open. Mickey plays equally well in the keys of G and D with this tuning. Capo up if need be. If you strum, use your wrist as a mute on occasion." Mick added, "The way I play guitar is difficult, because you got to be able to blunt certain strings."

Mick simplified the explanation: "Pick your guitar up... Play a D chord... Now... drop the big string until you have a full D chord. With it tuned this way... you now only have to practice until you pass out! Heh... heh... jus' kiddin'. (He was not kidding. 'Sometimes,' he said, 'I play the guitar so much that the calluses on my fingers have to be filed off!') Start there, exploring by simply moving one finger at a time to different positions until you start to hear something familiar." Newbury's Basic Songwriting 1A - Chapter One - requires playing as long as necessary, often for hours, until hearing "something familiar." As he informed <u>Hit Parader</u> in '69, "The root of my melodies comes from harmonizing with the guitar."

His lack of formal music education might have been a blessing. "Mickey was not limited by the constraints of the musical language," Stave explained. "Where those with a formal musical background feel the need to move in obvious, acceptable progressions, Mickey could go where his heart led him." Mick would grab the guitar, close his eyes and harmonize for

144

hours on end. "I'll sit around with a guitar and do a melody for days," he told Country Song Roundup (June, 1977). I'll gradually fill in the words to match the rhythm of the song. MMMMM... sometimes, a few words... sometimes a little melody... then at other times everything... all at once. Just no rules! Occasionally, I'll go through an exercise to find a word. I'll write skeletons. Say I'm writing a melody. The song is already there; my problem is getting it. What I'll do is get at it a piece at a time. I'll sit down and take the first line, and maybe one word will *leap* out. Then I'll find the words to put around it. Once I get those, I can pull a thread out of it..."

Kristofferson learned the importance of the melody with the words; "It was the first thing I picked up from him. It just blew me away, when he got it just right, how simple lyrics and simple melodies worked in a way to break your heart." Mick's example of such a song? Modestly, he illustrated the point with a non-Newbury composition. *Danny Boy*, he said, "is one of the most perfect marriages of a melody and a lyric... which is very unusual."

He once explained the task this way: "When I write a song, I write the melody first. It's like the words are being said in the melody, so my job is finding out what the words are." This laborious process - the gestation of Newbury's art - would ultimately deliver a perfect melding of melody and words. Sometimes five minutes... sometimes forty years... in due course a Newbury song was born.

The delivery was almost as painful to watch as it was for Mickey to experience. Good friend Marty Hall explained, "To my observation, his songwriting typically would begin with a sweet bit of melody and a line or two. He would then build on the lines until he had the basic structure of a song completed. Once he reached that point, the editing began, and it could go on literally forever. If there were ever a song he completed perfectly and forever, I did not know it. Mickey accepted the fact that he would only rarely come to a point of complete satisfaction with his own work, but that only meant that a truce with the musical universe was in place until a better word or verse struck him."

"On a new song, Mickey would write verse after verse, carefully crafting each, and then he would assault each verse with his terrible swift pen, frequently abandoning entire verses and reordering the remaining verses. The words would transform, the verses would transform, and the song would transform. All of this was exhausting, and when it was over, it was typical for Mickey to need sleep. When he would awaken, he would start the process all over again, frequently going back to the discarded and previously edited verses and bringing them to mind yet again... He was as cruel a master as one could possibly have on his own work. He would hold himself to a standard that would frighten away the most gifted songwriters in the world. He would not compromise what he did, and if that meant throwing a verse away, or working at it 12 times to just get one portion of one line in just the right fashion that he wanted it, he would do it. He was absolutely committed to the quality of his craft."

Critics, peers and friends appreciate the results. Staff Writer Peter Cooper observed in <u>The Tennessean</u>, "Among writers, Newbury was a giant, a master of craft..." Songwriter and friend Gove Scrivenor summarized the results simply, "No one will ever possess his way with words and melody."

Whether verse and melody floated around Newbury's universe until captured is not the point. When he sensed a song was out there or in there, delivery became the mission. This is not the same as pulling an obstinate rabbit from a hat, but is more akin to a sculptor envisioning a carving in untouched, virgin stone. Except Newbury did not work in just three dimensions. His domain was the fifth, and he humbly described himself as "just a conduit." "Good writers can't take any credit for their work," he explained. "All they can do is take credit for workin' hard for the people who receive it."

> *Starin' out the window all I wish is*
> *I could hear the words I'm hearin' in my head*
> THE SAILOR

Connotations and associations came to mind as he wrote, but some layers were not evident. Newbury frequently discovered new levels of significance in his work. "Not only do I continue to find new meanings... My songs are like a priest and psychiatrist rolled into one... waiting only for me to ask a question." Townes Van Zandt said, "His voice is like from outer space," and Kristofferson wrote, "Perhaps... he is a visitor from outer space." From outer space or inner space or a conduit to the fifth dimension... Newbury's music is art... uniquely beautiful art... expressed as a fusion of sincerity and simplicity.

Capturing the art on paper is at best problematic. In 1970, Acuff-Rose printed the first Newbury songbook - a valuable find for collectors - promoting 64 songs with a limited distribution to singers and songwriters. Transcribed in the basement of the old Acuff-Rose building by an elderly woman, the accuracy of chords and words is only close. Jeff Stave explains, "As I have been interpreting Mick's music from an early songbook, I noticed some of the odd and difficult key signatures for the songs that he sent up to Acuff-Rose. Typically, he would write a song, capo it up to where it best fit his voice, put it on tape and send it in. The piano transcribers would not be attuned to this and would put it down in whatever key they heard E flat, E, F, whatever. Then they would use generic chord symbols on the score that could never be associated with Mick's sound." Incidentally, one of Mick's dreams was to release a "Mickey Newbury Music Book" bound beautifully in dark leather, containing songs he had recorded. Perhaps one day it will be available.

In November, Mickey performed at a Country Party Benefit for Pacifica Radio Station KPFA-FM in Berkeley. Rolling Stone described it as a "warm set from Mickey who then introduced a series of surprise guests: Rambling Jack Elliot, just in from Hawaii and mildly high on acid, who told about falling in love with a waitress last year at the Boarding House while listening to Mick sing; he was joined by Tom Jans who did a quick set of his own."

When Mickey returned home, he and Susan received an early and glorious Christmas present, as son Chris was born in Nashville on December 12. Mickey instantly altered priorities, as nothing mattered more to him than Baby Chris and Susan. He became a dedicated Papa at once.

Susan stated, "Anything that Mickey takes on, he's obsessive about it. When we had a child, he was obsessive for a year. I mean the first year Chris was born, he never left that child's side, ever... Was the same way about playing chess - morning, noon and night, playing golf - 54 holes a day or writing music... That's just a part of his personality. It's not just the music. I think also as I saw how the music was *cleansing and healing* to him, then that's not a problem to see him spend that kind of time."

As a sensible explanation, a bipolar personality is characterized by shifts between extreme episodes of mania and depression, usually with periods of normal mood in between. Mickey battled deep depression by writing songs, or as he referred to the self-prescribed antidote - Robbing The Dragon. "I spend maybe two months in the year, when I'm extremely depressed, in writing," Mick explained to Al Moir. "It has become my crutch. The guitar is what I run to when I am sad." Mick was able to make the demons stop dancing by stealing their music.

Manic tendencies represent the other half of the bipolar equation, and addictive-obsessive behavior is the rule rather than the exception. Mick acknowledged this by saying, "I have an addictive personality." He realized he should take medication, but refused, as it would stifle his creativity.

The author raises the issue only to lower it. The man's music can be most appreciated by understanding the good and the bad, the lows and the highs, encountered along his way. Mick would write, "Without the good, without the bad / There would be no need my friend / To remember when."

147

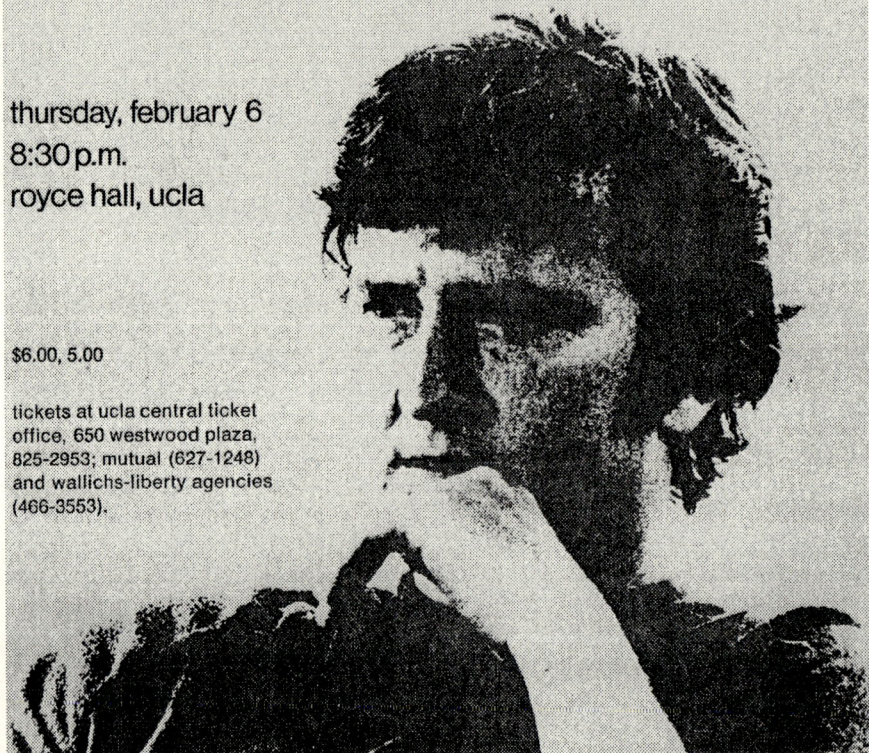

ucla committee on fine arts productions presents

## —— LOS ANGELES DEBUT ——

singer/songwriter
# MICKEY NEWBURY

with
# LARRY JOHN WILSON

thursday, february 6
8:30 p.m.
royce hall, ucla

$6.00, 5.00

tickets at ucla central ticket
office, 650 westwood plaza,
825-2953; mutual (627-1248)
and wallichs-liberty agencies
(466-3553).

## Chapter XI: *I Came To Face The Music*
## 1974 - 1975

Following Chris' birth, the Newburys moved from the Tennessee houseboat to a two-story house 40 miles outside Eugene in the forest foothills of Vida, Oregon. It is amusing at least, ironic at most, that Vida signifies life in Spanish. It was an easy drive from the new home base to the Pacific Ocean or the Cascade Mountains. They were close to the beautiful McKenzie River, and important to Mickey, he was near a gorgeous golf course. One thing he wasn't ready for... four feet of annual rainfall.

They moved to the Land of Gold and Opportunity on intangible grounds, not for all that glittered, but for all that mattered. Mickey would say they relocated, "So that our children would be near their grandparents," Susan's parents. But it was much deeper than that. First, Mickey and Susan did not want their children subjected to Guitar Town's glitzy environment. As son Chris would say 30 years later, "Growing up and where we've been and the style of life we've lived was very anti-celebrity I guess you could say... Grandma and Grandpa (Pack) come over... Cousins come over... and we stuff ourselves with apple pie, pumpkin pie, turkey... Very typical normal family life."

> *I don't need me no Cadillac automobile*
> *I don't need me no pocket full of cash*
> *BIG CITY WOMAN*
>
> *Love is all that matters*
> *A FATHER' PRAYER*
>
> *Susie's in the kitchen doin' dishes*
> *Chris and all his toys have gone to bed*
> *THE SAILOR*
>
> *I will build us a cabin here in the tall wood*
> *Bottom land cedar and Snake River stone*
> *We will sit by the fire won't the juniper smell good*
> *OVER THE MOUNTAIN*

(Cedar is abundant in Oregon and used in cabin construction. The Snake River forms the northeast border of Oregon with Idaho.)

Second, Mickey was not happy in Nashville. Not at all. For starters, he never overcame the disappointment with RCA and Mercury. Moreover,

Music City had ceased to be like Paris in the Twenties, becoming more like Berlin in the Thirties. Music dictated by executive order, composed by committee, left little to nothing for artists to share. Corporate cowboy clones were just redoing the last hit. Newbury wouldn't play the game.

> *They all want a puppet on a string*
> *They don't want a boy that only sings*
> *They want so much more*
> *They will show you to the door*
> *TELL HIM BOYS*

Mickey sorrowfully remarked to Albert Hall in a '71 interview, "I remember how we all use to get together to talk and play our latest songs for each other... now there doesn't seem to be as much time for that sort of thing. I find myself spending more time with people from out of town than the people that live here since they're usually too busy." The Pipers of Music Row Inc. had become more concerned with turning a profit than creating art. One year earlier, Mickey told Hit Parader, "This recent recognition of Nashville has caused some of the people in the music industry to forget what made their music good in the first place. It's becoming more businesslike and less easy going." Confiding in the author, he said simply, "I'm divorced from Nashville now."

> *The road down to Nashville's like crystal and stone*
> *I'm LEAVIN' KENTUCKY, I'm goin' back home*

(Crystal is clear, and stone is hard... in other words... clearly hard.

> *PEOPLE ARE TALKING, people will talk*
> *When they got nothing new to say*
> *Tell them I'm dyin', tell them I'm dead*
> *Tell them I'm simply gone away*

> *So, Que Paso? to the Hotel California.*
> *Adios to the Mason-Dixon Line.*
> *IN '59*

Twenty years later, Nashville Scene would report, "Although he rarely performs and seldom records, Newbury never quit music. He just quit the music business... 'I'd hate to have to write for money,' Newbury said, explaining that he deliberately left Music Row to avoid falling into the habit of cranking out formulaic songs for country singers. 'That would kill me, I think.'" Anyway, Newbury never was so much of Nashville as in it.

Though he left Nashville, the industry benefited enormously from his contribution. Kurt Wolff summarized in a 1997 article, "Newbury was a major player in a musical revolution of sorts that swept through Nashville... revitalizing country music with fresh ideas; acknowledging a broader range of influences - psychedelic rock, folk, blues, R&B - and ultimately winning the industry a much larger fan base in the process."

Alan Rhody agreed, "I thought about him and his friends and all the good they brought to this place - Nashville - when they came here in the sixties. That just made it seem even more like the wasteland it's become today. No heart. No soul. The complete opposite of Mickey Newbury."

And writer George Lewis added to the discussion, "It is obvious that Newbury's work, most especially in the late sixties and early seventies was essential material, pushing these country and pop artists who listened to broaden their musical horizons... and showing those who would take up the challenge that, even in Nashville, one did not necessarily have to sell one's soul for a song. Newbury didn't. He took what he needed from Music City, moved to Oregon and raised a fine family." In the end, Newbury followed his principles, summarized by one of his favorite expressions: "Success is when a man gets what he wants. Happiness is when a man wants what he's got."

> *There's a blue moon in Kentucky*
> *I'm on this two-lane out of town*
> *Just one stop to pick up my lady*
> *Population three more down*
> *THE SILVER MOON CAFE*

> *Well congratulations, say you're moving out of town*
> *You say you have a 14 month old son*
> *Well you know I always said one day I'd like to settle down*
> *Seems like I was always on the run*
> *HOW'S THE WEATHER*

On the way to Oregon, the Newburys stopped by Houston to visit family and friends. While in town, Mick dropped in on an old friend, Doyle Jones, proprietor of Jones Sound Recording Studio. Musician and writer Claude Wooley worked there at the time, and years later he would write: "When Mickey arrived, he had with him his lovely wife Susan, and their son Chris, who was a babe in arms and their first born. Doyle made our introductions and proceeded to put on the master tape that Mickey had just finished in Nashville. The album that would soon be released was entitled, 'I Came To Hear The Music.' My musical life has never been the same since I heard that tape. For the next hour, the songs that poured into my ears and straight to my heart left me so humbled and spellbound, that I realized at that moment, I only *thought* I was a songwriter. I knew I was in the presence of greatness. That night when I returned home I still heard those songs in my head..."

**ALBUM # 7** I Came To Hear The Music (Elektra EKS 7E-1007) contains the following songs: (Side 1) I Came To Hear The Music, Breeze Lullaby, You Only Live Once (In A While), Yesterday's Gone, If You See Her, (Side 2) Dizzy Lizzy, If I Could Be, Organized Noise, Love Look (At Us Now), Baby's Not Home, 1 x 1 Ain't 2. Elektra also planned to release the LP as a quadraphonic recording under EQ-1007, though it never happened.

"I Came To Hear The Music" was produced by Newbury's friend, Chip Young, who plays guitar on several Newbury releases. The back cover captures Mickey, Susan and baby Chris in a picture of familial contentment. Appropriately, the Jordanaires sing backup - as this is a spiritual release. Religious and Christian motifs permeate Newbury's music, and this album is one of his most ethereal proclamations. Several songs praise God, establishing a contemplative mood via verse perfectly matched to melody:

*Did God make time to keep it all from happening at once?*
*I CAME TO HEAR THE MUSIC*

*I believe in His wisdom*
*God set aside this time*
*To let us all go home to yesterday*
*BREEZE LULLABY*

*God it takes a long time*
*YESTERDAY'S GONE*

(*Yesterday's Gone* also includes the verse: "Tomorrow the son will be born...")

*Without love good God where will he go*
*DIZZY LIZZY*

Throughout the production, Newbury changes genres as best suited to deliver the subject. *Breeze Lullaby* is presented as a Viennese concerto. One of the first songs he wrote, *Baby's Not Home*, rolls into the rudest, wildest sax break ever. *Yesterday's Gone* harkens to the early meditative style of Cat Stevens - not surprising as Cat's "Tea For The Tillerman" was a Newbury favorite - plus the song's closing orchestration would be right at

152

home on a Moody Blues album. *1 x 1 Ain't 2* evokes pictures of Li'l Abner and Daisy Mae kickin' up their heels. "*1 x 1 Ain't 2*" explained Mickey, "is a real old song, '64 or '65. The oldest song I've recorded. Billy Swan was the one who talked me into doing that. One of the sweetest guys that ever lived, most real. One of the few guys I've known for all these years that hasn't changed... He's a fantastic guy."

*If You See Her* addresses complexity through verses so simple, so mercurial... so Newbury:

> *Everything I told her then was true*
> *Everything was true at the time*
> *But time has a way of changing everything*
> *Truth has a way of changing all the time*

*Dizzy Lizzy* features an intro of swirling guitars and horns evocative of George Harrison's *What Is Life* and a Beatles-like handclap around the rocking beat, which slows suddenly to a country trot. And the chorus? "Rock 'n' roll ain't nothin' but the blues with a beat." Then the tempo speeds up again. Newbury was having fun here, as the songs exude professionalism of the highest order. How high is that? Measuring most artists to Newbury is like comparing a pre-schooler's finger-painting to a da Vinci.

The album is a seminar in musical diversity. We are taken from rock to country to mountain music to folk to chamber music to pop ballads. Somehow it all works together because it's all honestly Newbury. As Elvis biographer Allen Harbinson wrote, "In fact, only Elvis had managed to equal such diversity, but Elvis didn't also *write* his songs." Though diversity derives from aptitude and ability, diversity was Newbury's problem with radio stations. One dominant characteristic of his music is eclecticism, and that's what made his albums unattractive to strict radio formats. "As a songwriter Newbury had the popular touch," English critic Mark Brend wrote. "As a recording artist he was out on his own."

Though programmers were unsuccessful in pigeonholing Newbury's oeuvre, songs from the LP struck a harmonious cord with a diverse group. *Love Look At Us Now* was covered by OBE Edward Woodward, celebrated British actor of stage and screen, famous for performing Broadway-type musicals. Johnny Rodriguez, the Mex-Tex balladeer, was first to make the pretty song popular, and it would be covered by country soulman, Joe Simon. Glenn Barber scored a minor country hit with *You Only Live Once In A While*. Johnny Van Zant, of Southern rock persuasion and former lead singer of Lynyrd Skynyrd, would release *Yesterday's Gone*; while *If You See Her* would be picked up by Waylon Jennings, Johnny Rodriguez and Petr

Spaleny, a well-known Czechoslovakian crooner. *Baby's Not Home* was performed by Roy Head, Don Gibson and Sue Thompson; and finally, *1 x 1 Ain't 2* would be interpreted by Neal Ford & The Fanatics - a first-rate psychedelic garage group - who did the recording work at Doyle Jones' place.

Consider the superlatives required to discuss the album: simple, complex, mercurial, meditative, psychedelic, spiritual and ethereal... folk, pop, rock, soul, country, mountain and chamber music... wild sax, Mex-Tex, Southern rock, Broadway musical and Viennese concerto... Beatles, Slovakian, Li'l Abner, Moody Blues and da Vinci. Perhaps a pigeonhole the size of a Wal-Mart might accommodate Newbury's categorization. No wonder DJ's in a 10x10 studio had a tough time.

Reviewing "I Came To Hear," Robert Adels wrote in Country Music: "If *As Time Goes By* had never been written, if inebriation brought about sensitivity as easily as it does sentimentality, then every drunk in the world would be begging for one more song from Mickey Newbury's new album. The LP is elegantly soppy and properly brilliant 'let's-hear-that-one-again kind of music... If you've heard Mickey Newbury, you've got to have one of his albums. And if you've got one, chances are you've got the whole lot of 'em."

Following release of the album, the curtain rang down on the last Ryman Opry show on March 15. The closing song, *Will the Circle Be Unbroken*, featured Hank Snow and Johnny Cash, but the entire Opry cast raised their voices in tribute to The Mother Church of Country Music. The Opry would move from Captain Ryman's Auditorium to the modern, safe confines of the Opryland complex, just up the Cumberland River on the outskirts of Nashville. Lower Broadway would soon become a bizarre parade of bums, drunks, hookers and tourists, prowling up and down the filthy sidewalks, visiting the go-go-joints, massage parlors, blue movie houses and porno shops.

> *The man in the grey flannel suit dares not walk on this street*
> *Does anyone know what became of the old Opry?*
> *THE NIGHT YOU WROTE THAT SONG*

Scores of Secret Service agents were in town on the Opry's opening evening at its new location. At the urging of Republican Roy Acuff, President Richard Nixon unfurled a yo-yo onstage before sitting down to play the piano. In the VIP audience, reported Country Music, were "country music moguls, local business people and other bigwigs, Opry sponsors, journalists and politicians (four Governors, two Senators, and thirteen Congressmen); not quite your average Opry crowd." Nixon's performance - the first Presidential Opry - failed to muster sufficient support. A few months later he resigned the Presidency due to the Watergate scandal. Adding insult to injury, it is doubtful the Opry paid him.

The Newburys moved about the same time as the Opry. They relocated just up the McKenzie River on Leashore Drive in the town of Springfield - Lane County - a peaceful Oregon community with 30,000 residents. Mick's new home was situated one mile from Eugene, the state's second largest city. He could still hear the whistle blow, as Amtrak, Southern Pacific and Burlington Northern maintained Springfield schedules.

Forty-eight inches of rain fell annually... mostly it seemed when Mick was in town. For good reason, the University of Oregon's sports teams are referred to as Ducks. "Eugene," Mick explained during a concert, "is a lot like San Francisco was... except that it rains all the time. And I really don't like the rain. It follows me wherever I go... It's really the strangest thing. I can be gone for weeks and it'll be sunshiney... And the plane lands and it starts rainin'."

> *It will drive you insane*
> *To search the sky in vain*
> *For a sunny day*
> *THAT'S THE WAY IT GOES*

The hot sun was shining in late August when Willie Nelson hosted his annual picnic in Liberty Hill, Texas, and guest artist David Allan Coe performed. Coe momentarily turned his back to the audience while on stage, and a photographer snapped the picture. Coe was wearing a black leather jacket that proudly displayed the colors of his biker pack. The name of the motorcycle gang? The Outlaws. The press picked up the photo, and lo and behold, Willie and Waylon promptly became the Outlaws of Country Music.

The term "outlaw" had been introduced in 1972 following Waylon Jennings' hit, *Ladies Love Outlaws*. Journalist Hazel Smith is credited with coining the phrase "Outlaw Country" in '73. By 1975, Nashville had grown giddy over the term. Outlaw was the perfect promotion tool needed by marketeers to exploit this new dangerous brand of music, which spiked country with rock and roll, R&B and badass attitude. Nashville's "new progressive breed" of singer-songwriter was hyped as an establishment rebel, and the buying public swallowed it whole.

Sammi Smith began performing with Waylon and Willie when she moved to Dallas in '73, leaving Nashville around the same time as Mickey. Waylon enjoyed her performances so much he nicknamed her "Girl Hero," and Sammi would name a son after Waylon. The outlaw movement would climax in '76 with RCA's release of a double LP, "Wanted! The Outlaws," featuring Willie, Waylon, Tompall Glaser and Jessi Colter - Waylon's fourth wife. The cash-in compilation of previously released cuts arrived just in time to grab the first platinum record ever awarded a country album. The set includes Mick's *Why You Been Gone So Long* performed by Jessi.

It is no surprise they drew from their buddy's catalog. Newbury had recorded "Looks Like Rain" in '69 on his terms outside the Nashville system. For that declaration of independence, he was called a "quiet outlaw" seven years before "Wanted." But as Mick had merely made a record the best way possible, he resented the outlaw label. Still flying under the Nashville system's radar years later, he earned further distinction as an "outlaw's outlaw." As Sammi Smith pointed out, "Mickey was THE original outlaw. He made you think about outlaw... in the first place."

Mick explained his strong feelings on the matter to Peter O'Brien, "All this stuff about 'the new breed of singer / songwriter is just publicity. That aggravates the hell out of me, people who jump on the bandwagon like that... It's just categorizing again, making a new pigeonhole to stick somebody into. You got to be dressed a certain way, you got to be a drinker and a hell raiser, cuss and make an ass of yourself, act like a kid. I've told 'em I quit playing cowboys when I grew up. Its show business turns me off."

A few months later, Outlaw Coe released an LP "Dedicated to Mickey Newbury," titled, "The Mysterious Rhinestone Cowboy." The back cover features a letter from Coe:

> "Dear Mickey,
> Once upon a time I thought freedom could be measured by the scars upon my hand and the promise of a good woman's love. But I was in prison then. Freedom is knowing how to remember the weight of your chains after they have been removed, for each man feels his own pain in prison and each man must pull his own time. People talk to me about freedom... Hell, I've been in prison all my life. My music is free now but I haven't forgotten those chains, those bars and the demons that danced inside my brain. Thanks for helping me through the hard times. Your friend,
>
> David Allen Coe"

Mick would in turn share his feelings for Coe: "If you can get around all the crust, a very feeling soul lies beneath that mask. He is also one of the most gifted singers I have met on my journey. Maybe too gifted..."

The next few months would put Mickey to the test. After all these years, he and Milton had come to terms. Though Mickey experienced his share of hell during the younger years, he had grown up and grown strong, maturing beyond most bad memories. Milton was proud of his successful boy, and the good son reciprocated by helping his folks. He and Susan presented them with the most precious gift, a beautiful grandson, nine months old by this time. Mickey helped his parents financially too, surprising them with a new boat, for example. Then out of the blue, Mamie called with shocking news, "Your Daddy has had a stroke."

"I still remember," she explained, "how devastated I was and how hopeless Milton seemed... It is so hard to see someone you love slowly go away from you, even though they are still breathing. They are there, and yet, they are not there."

> He worked and sweated all the years to finally find it out
> He was once a man but twice a child
> APPLES DIPPED IN CANDY

Mickey was having a hard time physically, too. Since the '63 jump-from-train spinal injury, he had suffered excruciating back pain, which he faced with under and over-the-counter medication. Lately the pain had intensified, so in November of '74, he went to Nashville for back surgery and to work on the next album, "Lovers." Following a successful surgery, Mick curbed his dependence on drugs.

Shortly thereafter, he participated in an anti-drug campaign by contributing to an LP compilation, "Get Off II." Distributed to radio programmers only, the album's four-dozen public service announcements - PSAs - are delivered by rock, pop, and folk artists including: Yes, Poco, Genesis, America, Al Green, Beach Boys, Gregg Allman, Chuck Berry, Deep Purple, Dave Mason, Steve Miller, James Taylor, Bill Withers, Jackson Browne, Fleetwood Mac, Gladys Knight, Herbie Hancock, Curtis Mayfield, Pointer Sisters, Linda Ronstadt, Carly Simon, Jackie Wilson, Johnny Winter, Peter Yarrow, Jose Feliciano, E.L.O., Seals & Crofts, Three Dog Night and Jesse Colin Young.

On the hard-to-find LP, Mickey presents a 30 second anti-drug statement over a bed of his *1 x 1 Ain't 2*: "This is Mickey Newbury. The first thing that comes to mind is... I wanna help my friends kick the habit. Once you ever start chippin' on heroin, you got it. I mean you may kick it physically, but mentally you're 50 years old... And the minute that you're down, the first thing that comes to mind is heroin."

Early '75 found Mick in the hospital with pneumonia, from being out late at night with friend and producer Chip Young, "running around in a thunderstorm, trying to record rain sounds for 'Lovers.'" Susan Newbury explained, "They were almost struck by lightning which would have assured their place in musical history... People love a sad story." Then, while recording "Lovers" in a dark studio, Chip stepped on and ruined Mick's favorite guitar, which Mick had used for "Montezuma." It was the expensive Ramirez guitar, a model used by Segovia. Chip knew how Mick felt; a few years earlier, Elvis had accidentally destroyed Chip's guitar during a karate exhibition in the studio.

Mickey loved guitars and said, "Every guitar has its own voice. Some are so beautiful they could bring a smile to a dead man's eye... and yet... when they open their mouth to speak... others... look like they have been used to cut Johnson grass for years but sound... oh they cannot be replaced. The first guitar I fell in love with was a small Martin. It was broken by a good friend of mine in a drunken rage... as was my heart. I found another one years later and it was stepped on in a studio in Nashville. I swore I would never fall in love with another guitar. But... I did."

**ALBUM # 8** Lovers (Elektra 7E-1030) contains the following songs: (Side 1) Apples Dipped In Candy, Lovers, Sail Away, When Do We Stop Starting Over, Lead On, (Side 2) How's The Weather, If You Ever Get To Houston, You've Always Got The Blues, Let Me Sleep, Good Night.

"Lovers," produced by Chip Young and released in February, was the last of Mickey's Elektra recordings. They again used Youngun Studio and most of the musicians from the preceding LP, "I Came To Hear The Music." Mick explained that as he was drinking excessively, his "voice was off." On top of the booze, he had been hospitalized with pneumonia, had endured painful back surgery and his father had suffered a serious stroke. It is no revelation the album contains his weakest singing. A glance at the front and back album cover presents the mood. The man was facing the music.

*Hand me another I'll swallow that mother*
*Soon I'll be higher than the sun ever rose*
*We've had a showdown and I'm feeling mighty lowdown*
*HAND ME ANOTHER OF THOSE*

*Night and day is all the same*
*Pourin' whisky on the flame*
*Burn another memory from my mind*

*Through the years she moved uptown*
*While I came a long way down*
*MAKES ME WONDER IF I EVER SAID GOODBYE*

Being a Newbury product, however, the album reaches several high points. *Apples Dipped In Candy* became his third trilogy. Its center selection would be right at home on the "King Creole" soundtrack; it's easy to imagine a gyrating Elvis growling the riverboat chorus: "Apples dipped in candy, sweet potato wine / One is for your belly (baby!), the other's for your mind." And the jazzy interlude is played sensationally by Mister Guitar, Chet Atkins.

*Lead On* is delivered as an old time gospel hymn with traditional passages ("Jesus do you still know me / Here I stand ragged and worn"), and flavored with Newbury seasoning ("Like an orphan left to wander / Like a sailor lost in a storm"). *Let Me Sleep* contains a one-of-a-kind rarity for Newbury... a drum solo. (Most Newbury songs are so laid back, they have no need for a drummer.) Against Newbury's swirling tenor, drums pound out a hypnotic rhythm that could be titled, "Drums of Insanity."

The album's title song, *Lovers*, is a pretty ballad with lyrics immediately recognizable as Newbury's: "To think they once tore down a wall for a door / But now they don't speak anymore." The verse was inspired through actions taken by Mickey's pal, songwriter Hank Cochran. According to the story, Hank and pretty singer Jeannie Seely - the first lady to wear a miniskirt on the Opry - lived in adjoining apartments in Nashville's Executive House Apartments. Hank eventually grew tired of having to go out into the hall and knock on her door... So one day he borrowed a chain saw and cut a hole in the wall between the two rooms. Though Hank's amorous actions were impressive, the story required a bit of a rewrite. "To think he once chain sawed a wall for a door" does not have the same sweet ring.

After Hank solved his problem and Mick romanticized the line, the song would spawn covers by Charlie Rich, The Kingston Trio, Cliff Richard and Olivia Newton-John. Mickey had met Olivia - "a sweet and lovely teenager" - at the Song Contest in Tokyo, and she included *Lovers* on her 1975 album, "Clearly Love," which went gold and to the number 12 spot in the United States. Other songs from the LP would be picked up by Charlie Pride, Don Gibson, Bobbie "Blue" Bland, B B King and Kate Ceberano / Wendy Matthews. The last two recorded *You've Always Got The Blues* as the soundtrack for the Australian Broadcasting Commission's eight-part TV series, "Stringer."

The album concluded an era, as it marked Mick's final release on Elektra. It had been a good run during a pivotal period in American music. Newbury's five Elektra albums influenced scores of country artists to reach beyond honky-tonk twang, while hundreds of artists in other spheres would interpret his country material. As stated by Mark Brend in Record Corner, "Newbury produced some of the most intriguing country music ever made. Or at least, it was described as country music as a matter of convenience. In fact, Newbury's great run of albums on the Elektra label in the mid seventies trampled all over the defining boundaries of that particular musical idiom... with plaintively soulful vocals, vast orchestral arrangements, sound-effects and instrumental passages linking songs..." Peter Blackstock efficiently summed up in "Farther Along": the period 1970-1975 "was a fertile time for budding songwriters, and Newbury was the best." Country music was the indisputable benefactor. Its audience increased exponentially, while the music industry as a whole benefited enormously.

Ironically, the Country Music Association - who never honored Mickey Newbury - can be used to illustrate the point. The CMA Awards show erupted in controversy in 1975 when John Denver was named Entertainer of the Year. As presenter Charlie Rich read that Denver was the winner, Rich set the envelope on fire with his lighter. The event climaxed a year of tension between the CMA and major country artists, who criticized the organization for nominating performers identified with pop music. Mickey however was one who bridged the genre gap. When not feuding, Rich and Denver recorded his songs.

Newbury built bridges with music, not walls. *Sweet Memories*, for instance, has been translated to many genres. The song became Number One Hits for Andy Williams - easy listening and Willie Nelson - country. Several artists identified with specific fields have covered it: Lulu - pop, Joan Baez - folk, Brook Benton - soul, Etta James - funk, B B King - blues, Brian Collins - reggae, Don Gibson - country, Hank Holler - polka, Roy Orbison - pop/rock, Bill Woody - disco, Ray Charles - R&B, Buffy St. Marie - folk, Lawrence Welk - easy listening, Ricky VanShelton - modern country and Anita Carter - traditional country. Longfellow proclaimed music to be the universal language, and Mickey Newbury demonstrated total fluency.

Coinciding with the release of "Lovers," Mick toured for three months at Elektra's insistence to promote the album. On February 6, UCLA presented him in concert at Royce Music Hall, a show opened by Larry Jon Wilson. Fan Charlene Gordon was there and wrote, "It was wonderful!" The ticket price? $5 and $6... Lois Spencer attended the "amazing concert" too. "My hubby and I did go backstage into a room," she reminisced, "where Mickey and Kris Kristofferson were greeting people. I stood in line to shake hands with Mickey like a bobbysoxer meeting Frank Sinatra. I couldn't believe that someone so talented and famous would be so accessible. Little did I know..."

Next appearing on Dinah Shore's television program, Mick and Dinah made a duet of *Sweet Memories*. Fan Dale Hamilton caught the show and said, "It changed me forever. I went out that afternoon and bought every Newbury album I could find... no easy accomplishment in Cleveland, Ohio!" Still, Mick would add, "I didn't like TV then... It had such bad sound." Dale would one day meet the love of his life through a dating agency. Seems he was looking for a lady who appreciated Mick's *Mabel Joy*. Deborah answered the call and they were promptly married.

Dinah introduced Mick to Johnny Carson, a man Mick described as "a nice guy." Then on March 13, he was a guest on Carson's Tonight Show in L.A. with Ronald Reagan, who was between jobs as Governor of California and President of the United States. Carson yielded the floor to the minstrel from Texas, who brought down the house with a reading of *An American Trilogy*.

Next, Mick performed at The Cellar Door in trendy Georgetown, the Exit/In in Nashville, the Great American Music Hall in Atlanta and finally at venues in Phoenix and Berkeley. At the end of the engagements, America withdrew from Saigon on April 29, leaving the old noncommunist capital to fall to North Vietnamese tanks. Saigon would hurriedly be renamed Ho Chi Minh City.

> But now I'm without a cause to be all caught up in
> For the blacks have their freedom and the reds are our friends
> And we've ended a war we could not seem to win
> And the folk singer's out on his ass once again
> My how the times they have changed
> THAT WAS THE WAY IT WAS THEN

As America was withdrawing from Southeast Asia, an exhausted Mick performed for one week in San Francisco. Rich Wiseman reported in Rolling Stone, "Toward the end of a successful week's run at the Boarding House, he was announcing his conditional retirement from the live stage. Pulling another Camel from the breast pocket of his burgundy bathrobe, balladeer Newbury, 35, a native of Houston and an established songwriter for 10 years, explained himself, 'Unless something happens between now and 1976 when my record contract is up,' he said, 'I'll probably quit performing and just record on an album-to-album basis. I'm hating what I'm doin' now.'"

"Now that he mentioned it, the wear could be seen on his long, taut face. He hadn't slept much during the week, and had eaten even less, shedding 10 pounds he didn't have to lose. 'It's not that I don't enjoy playin' 'cause I do,' he continued. 'But in a club situation when I'm tired and can't put out, man, then it's painful... The only way I can get into my songs is to totally rewrite them in my head as I sing them. That's drainin.' That's why a writer / artist eventually burns out.'"

"Hardly a devastating schedule, but for Newbury, enormously respected in songwriter and critic circles though still virtually unknown to the public, this half-dozen date mini-tour represented his most sustained foray into in person performing since the era when he sang with a teenage rock group called The Embers."

Though he had performed on scores of stages over the course of his career, it had always taken a rear seat to songwriting. Mick made these appearances at Elektra's dogged insistence to promote "Lovers." He hated touring though and said, "Man, it's goin' against the grain... Anybody who wants to be a songwriter or singer... you can't do both. It takes the same creative energy out of you to perform your songs as it takes to write a new song." Incidentally, in 1975 he estimated that he had toured "about eight months total" over his career.

> *People tell me the way that you're livin's the way to live*
> *Oh what I'd give to live that way*
> *Bogalusa, Tulane to Monroe, then to Memphis*
> *Your night life's changin' day to day*
>
> *Willy nilly to where I wander*
> *Stay on the go*
> *I know what gets that FM play*
> *We got a show in San Francisco*
> *You know that we need to one day plan to do L.A.*
>
> *I see so many faces in the crowd*
> *They start to look the same*
> *They like their music loud*
> *But oh I'm so slow to change*
>
> *People say the way that you please them*
> *Is to become a rock musician, so they say*
> *Sit in your room and count your money*
> *It's so much fun and all you got to do is play*
> *ON THE ROAD*

Immediately following the Boarding House gig, Mick reappeared on the Johnny Carson Tonight Show on May Day with Lola Falana. Performing *Lovers* and *How I Love Them Old Songs*, Mick would say, "Johnny didn't know I was country till I'd been on his show two or three times." He appeared in concert the following evening with John Stewart at the Santa

Monica Civic Auditorium, and then he was featured on the Smothers Brothers Television show on May 5. A few days later, Mick was Bob Hope's guest on a Special with Kay Starr and Nancy Wilson.

The depressing events of the past months plus a demanding road schedule sent Mick searching his past for consolation. He returned to Mobile Bay, Alabama, to visit the old homestead and perhaps to unearth a piece or two of his childhood. He had fond memories of Aunt Marie and Aunt Laura, their delicious candy red apples and beautiful unspoiled beaches. "This was just really a wonderful place to be as a child... It had all these huge ol' oak trees and magnolia trees... You could just leave the house and go down and there were the white beaches... and I love it! Well I made the mistake of goin' back... I went down there... And where the farm was... All the industry had polluted Mobile Bay... And there was oil comin' up on what was the beach... And it was all eroded... And there was this ugly grass growin' up with oil on it... so I wrote this song about that."

> *Ain't it funny how we always say in times of leaving*
> *Say in times of leavin' we will be comin' back one day*
> *And ain't it funny how I now find in my time of grievin'*
> *What was really leavin' was not me but Mobile Bay...*
> *GONE TO ALABAMA*

**At a benefit concert on San Carlos Reservation, Arizona, 1978**

# Chapter XII: *A Fiddle Of Gold For A Soul*
## 1976 - 1979

A new way of communicating - a contagious CB Fever - gripped the country in the seventies. The Citizens Band radio, a short-range, two-way voice communications system around 27 megahertz, initially became a favorite tool for truckers. The general public soon followed, and sales peaked in the mid seventies with about seven million units sold per year. As part of the attraction, CB users adopted special monikers, identifying themselves with "handles," thus providing a shield of anonymity and, sometimes, a spark of harmless fun.

Mick's handle was "PappyDad... my Grandfather's name." From his Springfield home, he reportedly operated an illegal five-kilowatt linear CB transmitter with a 40-foot antenna. Legal power levels ran at four watts, and illegal systems typically utilized as much as 100 watts. Mick's rumored 5,000-watt rig - way outside the norm - was referred to as freebanding. Thought it is said he "could talk to truck drivers in Canada," 155.3 miles is the maximum CB distance permitted according to FCC rules. The Commission also makes it clear that music, whistling and sound effects should not be transmitted. Wonder if Newbury complied? As he was spending more time at home, he missed his music friends, and DXing with other operators eased his mind.

*Spends all his miles on the dials of a poppin' C.B.*
*THE NIGHT YOU WROTE THAT SONG*

Mick was frustrated and reaching out helped. His record label had changed considerably over the past six years. Shortly after Mick signed with Elektra, Jac Holzman sold the company for $10 million, though Jac would remain at the helm for three years. With the increased sales brought on by Bread, Harry Chapin and Carly Simon and the label's affiliation with Atlantic and Warner Brothers, Elektra became more than a support group of artists and artisans. It became big business. Jac needed a break by 1973 and went to Hawaii for an extended vacation. David Geffen took over Elektra then, merging - some would say submerging - it with his Asylum label. Geffen remained in control until '75, when he left to become vice-chairman of Warner Brothers pictures. Joe Smith assumed power, and during his reign, Elektra became more like a conventional record company and less like an inspired idea.

During the year, Mickey worked on a few new songs at Elektra, as his singing voice had returned to top form. Texan singer-songwriter Rock

Killough was introduced to that voice one evening. "It was June 26, 1976. Mickey was sitting in the grand salon on Hank Cochran's yacht and he was singing when I stepped on board. He sang for four hours. I'd never even heard of the smallish man in black with the thoughtful sad songs and the glorious tenor voice. But, we became friends that night and I became an eternal fan." Mick and the yacht's owner were also good friends; Hank Cochran was the writer of such standards as *I Fall to Pieces* and *Make the World Go Away.* Perhaps that evening they spoke of the current Kristofferson-Streisand movie, "A Star Is Born."

When Mickey returned home, Susan gave him wonderful news. She was carrying their second child.

In October, Newbury signed with ABC Hickory Records, who paid Elektra $500,000 for his back catalog. As Hickory served as Acuff-Rose's in-house recording label, the journey though far from complete, had gone full circle. For the first time in a decade, Mick had all eggs in one basket - except for the two inconsequential RCA albums. He liked getting back to basics, explaining, "I fired my manager. Fired my accountants, the whole thing. Started out all over again. I really don't need a manager."

Mick and Susan's first daughter Leah was born during the winter of 1977 in Springfield on February 11. Big brother Chris, then three, was delighted to welcome his new playmate, nicknamed "Annaleah" in reference to Mickey's song, *Weeping Annaleah.*

> *Well, yesterday's gone forever and ever and never to be again*
> *Oh, you look for the sunshine*
> *That brought warmth to your mind*
> *But find only rain*
> *Sleeping Annaleah*
> *WEEPING ANNALEAH*
>
> *Oh di lo de lea I am GONE TO ALABAMA*
> *I am gone to Alabama I am gone to Mobile Leah*

About the time Leah arrived, Mick was name-checked in Waylon's number one song, *Luckenbach, Texas*: "Hank Williams' pain songs and Newbury's train songs..." Meanwhile, the success of "Saturday Night Fever" marked the high point of the disco craze; and yes, Newbury's work was even covered in the polyester environment. Bill Woody released an LP titled, "Organized Noise" with six Newbury songs interpreted as disco dance tunes.

**ALBUM # 9** Rusty Tracks (ABC Hickory AH-44002) contains the following songs: (Side 1) Leavin' Kentucky, Makes Me Wonder If I Ever Said Goodbye, Bless Us All, Hand Me Another Of Those, People Are Talking, (Side 2) Tell Him Boys, Shenandoah, The Lucky Old Sun (Just Rolls Around Heaven All Day), Danny Boy, In The Pines.

Side one of "Rusty Tracks" was recorded mostly at Elektra under the production of Mick's buddy, Bobby Bare. Because Elektra had no intention of promoting the LP, Mick arranged for ABC Hickory to acquire the masters as part of the back catalog. Mick went straight to work at Hickory on the rest of the album with staff producer Ronnie Gant. Released in January 1977, it consists of original material and original treatment of old standards.

Mick and the "Rusty Tracks" producers assembled a legion of Nashville's best musicians, including Norbert Putnam, Buddy Emmons and Buddy Spicher. Strings were beautifully arranged by Alan Moore; backing vocals were aided by Larry Gatlin and Janie Fricke. And Newbury's singing is just mesmerizing.

The songs carried on with perceptive lyrics, masterly delivered in memorable melodies. *Makes Me Wonder If I Ever Said Goodbye* and *Leavin' Kentucky* are notable examples.

> *God I'm just one man*
> *I wish I was three*
> *Take a forty-four pistol to me*
> *Put one in my brain for her memory*
> *One more for my heart*
> *And then I'd be free*
> *LEAVIN' KENTUCKY*

Traditional ballads - produced by Gant - such as *Shenandoah*, *Danny Boy* and *That Lucky Old Sun* were performed with such emotive phrasing and powerful singing that Mick accomplished what an artist strives for in the cover of a standard: he made the songs his own.

Reviews of the new songs were favorable such as The Pedal Steel Guitarist, who wrote, "Trying to pick a favorite song from this album, would be like trying to choose a favorite child. I love them all but, each for a different reason. To comment on Mickey's singing on each song is not necessary. He sings as usual - GREAT! Mickey is not only a great songwriter, but, he is also a powerful singer." TPSG also wrote, "*Bless Us All* gives another insight into the compassion Mickey has for people." And reviewing the album, writer Russell Shaw's commented, "When any songwriter is asked who their favorite composer is, the name Mickey Newbury comes to mind."

Johnny Rodriguez, of Mexican-Irish decent, scored a number two country hit with the album's *Makes Me Wonder If I Ever Said Goodbye*, titling it, *I Wonder If I Ever Said Goodbye*. Born in Sabinal, Texas, Rodriguez became country music's first Hispanic singing star, popularizing the Mex-Tex style two years before Freddy Fender's initial success. Texas Ranger Joaquin Jackson discovered Rodriguez in 1970, while Rodriguez was singing in jail for pilfering and barbecuing a goat! Rodriguez does a fine job with Mick's music and covered five more Newbury songs: *Hand Me Another*, *Poison Red Berries*, *If You See Her*, *Love Look At Us Now* and *Leave Me Tomorrow But Love Me Tonight*.

Newbury friend Keith Bowman mentioned how he played his first Newbury album 'till "you could drive a freight train around the grooves." The cover of "Rusty Tracks" illustrates the notion colorfully, with a red locomotive doing double duty as a record player tonearm. The slick art deco image could be captioned with a classic Newburyism: "Sometimes I wonder if I'm writin' the song or if the song is writin' me."

Wonder if Mick watched TV on March 2? Jay Leno made an auspicious debut on Johnny Carson's "Tonight Show" that evening... tall, longhaired, scarecrow-skinny and funny. Five years earlier, the comedian had opened for Mickey at a jazz club in Boston.

On April 11, Mickey performed at the UK Ninth International Festival of Country Music at the Wembly Arena with Don Williams, Don Gibson, Crystal Gayle, Jean Shepard, Conway Twitty, Carl Perkins, Jody Miller, Don Everly, Loretta Lynn, Billie Jo Spears, Emmylou Harris and George Hamiltion IV... An Acuff-Rose songbook titled, "This Is Mickey Newbury" containing 11 songs was offered for sale there, and it may be his only commercial songbook.

For the festival, Mickey, Susan, Don Everly and Dorothy Ritter - Tex' wife - flew to London together on the Concord. "This was the first year the Concord flew," Mick said, "and was one of the highlights of my life in the clouds." While in England, the Newburys stayed with good friend, Frank Ifield who had been in Nashville with Mickey at Acuff-Rose. Nearly a decade had passed since the two men had "just drifted and dreamed while fishing from Newbury's boat," and Ifield commented, "I was privileged to have him stay with me at my home when we last worked together at Wembly." Ifield covered five Newbury songs, and Newbury (with Dan

Folger) wrote one of the songs, *Maurie*, specially for him.  After returning home, Susan returned to the University of Oregon to obtain a teaching certificate.

Mickey made many friends outside the music industry, away from Celebrityland.  Dave Franklin of The Woodlands, Texas wrote, "Before I'd ever heard Mickey perform, I'd met him, played golf with him, he'd been to my house and I'd been with him to Miss Mamie's.  Then in 1977, I went to a show featuring songwriters.  The show included Willie, Larry Gatlin, Merle and many others.  The audience included lots of muckety mucks from the business world who thought what they had to say was more important than what the singer had to sing, so it was pretty noisy.  Anyone who saw Mickey perform years ago knows what comes next."

"It's Mickey's turn, he steps on stage wearing a white shirt and carrying his guitar.  Nothing on the stage but a stool.  Then he sits down and starts tuning and suddenly what the loud mouths had to say wasn't so important.  No one talked 'til Mickey left the stage.  Maybe even more telling was later that night at a guitar pull in one of the hotel rooms.  As the guitar was passed from Gatlin to Willie, etc, the people in that room were quiet.  When Mickey took the guitar, it changed from quiet to reverence.  Funny thing was, when Mickey was through, nobody wanted to take the guitar.  Shortly thereafter, I was playing in their songwriter's golf tournament, paired with Larry Gatlin.  Larry was in awe of Mickey and his talent.  This was at a time when the Gatlin Brothers had number one songs and albums all over the place.  Mick was still his hero."

Super-hero to a multitude, Elvis, appeared in his last concert on June 26, at Market Square Arena in Indianapolis.  The final song he performed was *Can't Help Falling In Love* and not *An American Trilogy*, as has been misreported by this author and others.  Elvis died 51 days later, on August 16 in Memphis, at the young age of 42.

Mickey learned of Elvis' death after completing a round or two of golf at Louie Prima's golf course in Mandeville, Louisiana.  Dismayed, but not surprised, he was affected enough to bow out of evening dinner plans with friends.  A decade earlier and shortly after scoring four top hits, Mickey left RCA because Elvis would receive their beloved producer's exclusive attention.  Ironically, Mick's masterpiece arrangement, *An American Trilogy*, became a show-stopping signature song for Presley plus one of the final encore songs he did perform.  When Col. Parker attempted to finagle the song's copyright and royalties, Elvis would not permit it.  The King protected Mick, and the relationship ran far deeper.  Before Elvis was controlled by the Colonel, Elvis was mentored by Sam Phillips of Sun Records, who spoke fondly of Mickey, as "one of the greatest songwriters and performers... a rare talent."

Mickey respected Elvis and spoke fondly of him. While touring England in 1993, Mick dedicated a performance of *American Trilogy* to the memory of Elvis, "The greatest Rock 'n' Roll artist..." In 2000, Mickey would write, "There's not enough time or space here to put into words what I know about Elvis Presley. His producer (Felton Jarvis) was one of my best friends, as were many of the musicians (Chet Atkins, Chip Young... ) he carried with him, all the way back to the fifties."

"I feel it would not be appropriate to discuss inside information about his private life... I can tell you what has been said before with certainty. He was a prisoner in his own home, due in great part to the self-interest of many around him. What he needed in his life more than any one thing was a good 'No Man.' Unfortunately, 'Yes' was all anyone was allowed to say. His talent was great, his life sad, not to be desired by anyone wanting one peaceful moment in this world. God bless him... I pray he has now found that peace." Though invited to Graceland several times, Mickey never accepted. Too bad. He would have made a great No Man.

> *Elvis died in Memphis; boys, they nailed him in one hand*
> *SO SAD*

Two months after Elvis' passing, Mick played the Bread and Roses Festival of Acoustic Music at the Greek Theater in Berkeley. During the three-day event, several performers shared the stage including: Dan Hicks, Pete Seeger, Joan Baez, Hoyt Axton, Tom Paxton, Jackson Brown, Arlo Guthrie, Richie Havens, Josh White Jr., Buffy Sainte-Marie, Jesse Colin Young, Ramblin' Jack Elliott, Country Joe McDonald and Robin Williams (and His Merry Band). The event was chronicled on a compilation LP, featuring Newbury's *San Francisco Mabel Joy*. Philip Elwood of the San Francisco Examiner caught Mick's performance and wrote, "The warm, mellow, sentimental, soft-voiced Southerner brings an intimacy to a concert even when it is outdoors and has thousands attending."

**ALBUM # 10** His Eye Is On The Sparrow (ABC Hickory HA-44011) contains the following songs: (Side 1) Juble Lee's Revival, Westphalia Texas Waltz, Wish I Was, His Eye Is On The Sparrow, (Side 2) The Dragon And The Mouse, Gone To Alabama, It Don't Matter Anymore, I Don't Know What They Wanted Me to Say, Saint CeCelia, Juble Lee's Revival Shout.

Ronnie Gant put together a stellar ensemble for 1978's "His Eye Is On The Sparrow," just as he had accomplished for "Rusty Tracks." Alan Moore returned as well to arrange and conduct the strings. The two albums could have been released jointly as a double LP, as their sound, mood and feeling are similar. Mick wrote all songs on "Sparrow" except for the traditional title track, which feels like a Newbury piece of music. These autobiographical compositions are seminars in literate poetry, fused to beautiful melody.

> *Jesus sat quietly his head in his hands*
> *A man in the very back row*
> *Turns to him pleading can you understand*
> *I put more on her back than her clothes*
> *JUBLE LEE'S REVIVAL*

*Juble Lee's Revival* is a fine example of superb song craftsmanship. Of course Jesus The Carpenter would sit "in the very back row," but is there another man in the back row with Him? Who turns to whom? "I put more on her back than her clothes" can be read many ways. It means providing more than can be seen, be it burden or assistance. The line also means dispensing lashes or harsh treatment. Finally, someone may be begging Jesus for forgiveness or mercy ("Turns to him pleading...") But if Jesus is making the statement, the context becomes spiritual or soulful... as clothes cannot compare to what He gives.

The next song can also be interpreted on many levels. Three decades earlier - as Mickey was taking violin lessons in Houston - Cotton Collins, a fiddler for the Lone Star Playboys, composed a no-name waltz. After a dance, local Westphalia citizens suggested the tune be titled *Westphalia Waltz*. Many artists including Roy Clark, Tommy Hill, Bob Bellamy, Merle Travis and Pee Wee King recorded and popularized the pretty song. Mickey however had other reasons for referencing Westphalia. The tiny Texas town is located 75 miles north of Paige, where Great Grandparents Stephen and Sarah worked the land and raised a slew of children. Sadly, Sarah died in a San Antonio mental hospital a few tears before the waltz was named - on what would have been her 100th birthday. Mick also completed boot camp in San Antonio, so mentioning the city carried personal significance. Connecting the dots between the three points - Westphalia, San Antonio and Houston - forms an equilateral triangle around an area that is the heart of Newbury country.

### WESTPHALIA TEXAS WALTZ
*He said to her my little darling*
*Why you're as lovely as I did recall*
*Her eyes brightly sparkled like diamonds*
*As the tears started slowly to fall*

171

*Oh yes I can clearly remember*
*She said in a slow Texas drawl*
*She cried as she surrendered*
*To the strains of the Westphalia Waltz*

*He stood as the sun in the morning*
*Rose up on Wichita Falls*
*And there in the dim light she watched as*
*He sauntered on off down the hall*

*He said to her my little darling*
*You are as lovely as I did recall*
*She cried as she remembered*
*The strains of the Westphalia Waltz*

*Yes I can clearly remember*
*That night in San Antonio*
*She cried as she surrendered*
*To the strain of the Westphalia Waltz*

The spirit of the song though is more profound. The third verse reads, "He stood as the sun (Son) in the morning / Rose up on Wichita Falls." The wordplay appears to be a biblical reference, as in John 8:12, Jesus said, "I am the light of the world. He who follows Me shall not walk in darkness, but have the light of life." Also, Wichita Falls is in north central Texas about 20 miles from the Oklahoma border, and acts as Gateway to Texas from the North. "Sun" (Son), "Rose up" and the northerly gateway appear to point to the resurrection. Also, the album's front cover scene shows a distant sign atop a high-rise building, proclaiming, "Jesus Saves."

The third verse continues, "And there in the dim light she watched as / He sauntered on off down the hall." Saunter means to walk at an easy, unhurried pace. A lesser-known Middle English definition is "walking about musingly." The word is derived from saint, as holy men were thought to spend much of their time in this manner. At first reflection, "down the hall" appears equally superficial, but Newbury's poetry is often deeper than initial thought. A hall is a connecting passage with an entryway to another place...

The chorus concludes, it seems simply, with, "She cried as she surrendered / To the strains of the Westphalia Waltz." On the ground level, strains signifies great physical or mental stress. (Perhaps she cried and surrendered because the ordeal was too much to endure; it was just too painful.) Up one level, the word means a sustained musical note or

172

movement, as in melodic strains of the violin. (Perhaps she surrendered because the waltz was so lovely; thus, she submitted to its beauty.) Strains, however, also denotes removal of something from the unwanted rest of it; a cleansing or purification process: like separating grease from gravy, sand from water, spirit from body.

Though perhaps coincidental, West in *Westphalia* may allude to death. In everyday hobo lingo, Westbound is a train a hobo dies on - from the sun setting in the west. Conceivably, the beautiful waltz addresses suffering, bodily death - listen to the eerie sounds beneath the pretty instruments at 3:30-3:59 - and spiritual rebirth, appropriately concluding with a soulful Ray Charles-like shout. This is not just Newbury country. It's his realm.

Mick used simple words to address matters of great complexity. "The easier a song is to sing," he informed <u>Country Song Roundup</u>, "the easier it will stick with me, because my mind has a tendency to gravitate towards simplicity... Sometimes though, I can't stay simple; the subject I'm writing about calls for a more complex interpretation. Maybe that's why some people have said that my writing is not commercial."

The next song, *Wish I Was*, is pure Newbury, an intoxicating swirl of instrumentation and powerful voice, while the message is unadulterated humility: "A grain of sand is all I ever wanted to be." Though at first listen, it comes across as a fun children's song, *The Dragon And The Mouse* is so much more ("He was so terrified...") *Gone To Alabama* is delivered as foot stompin' mountain music, with a unique message: The world changes and we don't. ("What was really leavin' was not me but Mobile Bay.") *It Don't Matter Anymore* - which friend Johnny Darrell would cover - and *I Don't Know What They Wanted Me to Say* are sad songs about friends not sticking around through the thick and thin; but that's okay, as "Hope remains only God knows how."

The song *Saint Cecilia* draws from passages of Christian sanctity. In the third century and on her wedding night, Cecilia told her pagan husband Valerianus an angel guarded her body; therefore he must not violate her virginity. She sent him to see Pope Urbanus who baptized him, and Valerianus returned home a Christian. An angel then appeared and crowned the two with roses and lilies. Cecilia's followers soon grew, and the Roman prefect condemned her to death. As Cecilia sang in her heart to God only, she is sanctified as patroness of church music and is often glorified in fine arts and poetry. The day of St. Cecilia - virgin and Christian martyr - is celebrated on November 22. *Saint Cecilia* is another example of Newbury's multi-level poetry delivered as a charming sonata:

*St. Cecilia's in her garden pickin' paper violets*
*For all the wide-eyed children sadly clingin' to her dress*
*Singin' blessed be the heavenly to Hell with all the rest*
*Her salvation is her virtue her sin her emptiness*

*Cryin' I'm unfeelin' she turns into her shell*
*Well how can I be like Jesus I have just begun myself*
*To find my own way back at times I think*
*I know me well*
*But at other times a stranger stands*
*Where my body fell*

*Save the children save the children*
*Said the captain to the crew*
*For there can be salvation only for a precious few*
*Who would leave this sinking ship and build a balsa wood canoe*
*And sail with me across this mighty water*

On February 18, 1978, Hattie Louise Tatum - better known as proprietor of Tootsie's Orchid Lounge - succumbed to a long-fought battle with cancer at Vanderbilt Hospital. The news saddened Mick, as Tootsie was "one of the good ones." She helped many struggling songwriters and loved those who did the same. Ernest Tubb - who owned a record store across the street from Tootsie's - sent to her wake a huge floral heart, pierced in the center by a gigantic hatpin. It seemed to Mick as if the support community of camaraderie was disappearing. In addition, his last two albums had experienced disappointing sales. A depressed Mickey Newbury would give up touring for several years.

*Surely I will never see tomorrow I will be dead*
*What a way to go I know that I was so foolish he said*
*Then he broke down and cried*
*THE DRAGON AND THE MOUSE*

*I think it's time for me to lay it down*
*Close the door and never turn around*
*Maybe all the good in life is free*
*What I've paid for was not good to me*
*Friends all tell me how much I have changed*
*I tell them no one stays the same*
*They turn and walk away*
*I DON'T KNOW WHAT THEY WANTED ME TO SAY*

*All the friends I thought I knew*
*They dwindle down now to a precious few*
*Feel like an aging LA whore*
*IT DON'T MATTER ANYMORE*

("Aging LA whore" may be a disillusioned reference to Mick's masterwork, *San Francisco Mabel Joy*.)

Contributing to Newbury's disillusionment, the business side of music was showing more Mr. Hyde than usual. Mick hated the predatory nature of his industry, advising Jodi Krangle during an interview, "I would sooner be robbed by a fan than a company. The fan may be broke and have but one choice. There is no excuse for the way the songwriter is robbed by everyone from the record company to the broadcaster by the pure bottom line... greed."

"Like all of us," he told the author, "I have been so disappointed in so very many people over the years, who became corrupted by money and betrayed a trust. I might do that too if I were fast enough, but I'm not. My mind thinks in 3/4 time. But I was never disappointed in Roger Miller, Roy Orbison, Dan Blocker, Don Williams, James Garner, Dinah Shore, Ray Charles... They stayed true to their art, true to their friends and true to themselves."

One torrid affair broke Newbury's heart and pocketbook. As copyrights on his songs rested with Acuff-Rose, the firm as publisher and Newbury as songwriter agreed to split royalty payments on a 50/50 basis. The agreement, Mick explained, wasn't worth the paper it was written on. "Everybody," he said, "sued Acuff-Rose over unpaid royalties: Don Gibson, John Loudermilk, Roy Orbison..." Orbison would sue for $50 million, half of which was claimed for punitive damages, a new precedent in music business litigation. "I was the only one who didn't sue him," Newbury confirmed. "We're talkin' about millions of dollars. Wesley Rose screwed just about everybody."

*They tell me ol' Bud Rose hocked his guitar*
*Bought a ticket to Nashville to become a big star*
*Now he works on a bottle, and he lives in a car*
*Do you still have your dreams?*
*A LONG ROAD HOME*

("Bud Rose" is a triple play on words: First reverse their order for insight into Newbury's humor. Next "Bud" is slang for buddy or friend, and then there is also his buddy, Wesley Rose.)

*Here's to the piper, Bud, the bastard's been paid*
*A LONG ROAD HOME (*as recorded live in 1998)

*I never met a stranger 'till I knowed him for a time*
*THE SAILOR*

*The red necks are drawin' their lines up in East Tennessee*
*Their cannons are primed; they are fit to be tied I believe*
*The man in the gray flannel suit does not walk on this street*
*Does anyone know what became of the old Opry*
*Tomorrow is out of sight; yesterday's dead and gone*
*You never knew how right you were*
*THE NIGHT YOU WROTE THAT SONG*

("Gray flannel suit" is used with deeper purpose than as a description of clothing. "The Man In the Gray Flannel Suit" - after the fifties bestseller of the same name - became a catchphrase for corporate anonymity. In other words, Mick did not identify the flimflam man. Plus by this time, A-R had lost its distinctiveness... The firm was nothing special.)

Newbury would not acquiesce to peer pressure or economic incentive to join the A-R lynching party. He took the high road. At the peak of the lawsuit hysteria, he was asked by The Pedal Steel Guitarist, "Was there anyone, in particular, who helped you in your career?" Yes, Newbury replied, "I received a lot of encouragement from friends. But, all of the actual help came from right here (in Nashville), from Wesley Rose and his organization." Mick refused to kick the man when he was down.

He refused to compromise core convictions. Granted, Southern pride and lack of business savoir-faire played a big part, but Newbury refused to follow his greedy industry's rules, expectations and formulas. A maverick song-scribe, he was not shy about expressing deep distrust of the music industry. Yet he managed to exist in it - not of it - writing and recording songs that express his vision. For love and respect of craft, he walked away from millions of dollars. He would not give in to the moneymen.

Newbury explained himself to Country Song Roundup in 1977, "In my own view, once you write your first song for money, then you are copping out - you're in the business of mass appeal." Newbury clarified the point to Nashville Scene, "I love to write, and I never had to do it for a living. I was just fortunate enough that sometimes one would be bad enough to be commercial, so I was able to build enough of a catalog to make a good living whether I do anything or not."

He restated the belief in '98. "After I took payment for my first performance, I believe I sold out. I would love to write and record and give it away to all my friends." As man must eat in order to create, his philosophy is indeed a high pillar. To Aristotle, music was the most moral of the arts. Mickey agreed and his actions spoke louder than words. He drew a deep line in the Tennessee mud, separating the essential - I must make money to eat - from the celebrity mania - If I do it their way, I will become a money-makin' star.

AAMCO made him an incredible offer. They would give him big bucks to alter a classic song for TV commercials. *Just Dropped In To See What Condition My Transmission Was In* was a brief conversation... Newbury just said no.

Though detrimental to his career, Mick refused to appear on the grandest country music stage - the Grand Ole Opry. Based on his judgment that the Opry paid performers poorly - while the Opry pocketed a pretty profit - he refused to play their game or their venue. He just said no.

When John Loudermilk, Don Gibson, Roy Orbison and others went after Acuff-Rose, Newbury did not join the posse. "We're talkin' about millions of dollars," he explained. Didn't matter. He just said no.

Mick valued people more than money. In her autobiography, <u>Nickel Dreams</u>, Texan Tanya Tucker offers a vivid example: "When I came in for sessions or song meetings, I stayed at the Spence Manor, a Music Row hotel. They tell about the time Mickey Newbury was walking along 17<sup>th</sup> Avenue toward the Spence and saw George Jones stagger out of a car and into the lobby of the hotel. George hadn't closed the door of the car and he'd left a paper bag filled with money lying open on the seat. Mickey shot up to George's room and handed him the bag. 'What the hell is this and why're you throwing it around your car seat?' Mickey asked. 'Oh, yeah,' the Possum says. 'I forgot about that. Waylon loaned me $50,000 last night.'"

Newbury would not sell out. In the late sixties, Nashvillains offered $100,000 for Townes Van Zandt's contract. He just said no, and then he tore up the contract. He gave Townes his freedom but would not abandon his friend at any price. "He likes to stand up for the underdog," Mamie affirmed, "and would never do anything to hurt anyone intentionally."

Neither saint nor fool, Mickey Newbury, refused to two-step. The Taurean was the epitome of gutsy - and stubbornness - personified. Family, friends, the sake of the song and Matthew 16.26 mattered to him. The devil had to find a different dance partner on several occasions.

*Well I once had a good woman*
*But I treated my good woman wrong*
*Sad to say she left me today*
*Yes my good woman is gone*
*Same song and dance*
*And THE TWO STEP GOES ON*

At the request of a friend, Mick did one gig in 1978. Sammi Smith organized the benefit concert for the Apache Nation at San Carlos Reservation in Arizona. Johnny Rodriguez and Johnny Cash - who helped bring Sammi to Nashville a decade earlier - performed at the full day spring festival. Sammi's friend and Newbury fan Mary Frank Andrews was there and said, "Though Mickey performed at an outside venue, he sang intimately for over an hour... just as if he were in a small cabaret. God, he was so good."

**ALBUM # 11** The Sailor (ABC Hickory HB-44017) contains the following songs: (Side 1) Blue Sky Shinin', Let's Have A Party, There's A Part Of Her Still Holding On Somehow, A Weed Is A Weed, Let It Go, (Side 2) Looking For The Sunshine, Darlin' Take Care Of Yourself, Long Gone, The Night You Wrote That Song.

"The Sailor" became Mick's third and final ABC Hickory album in as many years. Some of the songs were recorded at Jack Clement Studios in Nashville. After the LP's release, the label was acquired by MCA, owner of Universal Studios and Seagrams - the whiskey company. MCA immediately rereleased Mick's ABC Hickory LPs: "Rusty Tracks," "His Eye Is On The Sparrow" and The "Sailor," hot-stamped as MCA-802, MCA-803 and MCA-804.

"Lovers" and "The Sailor" are Newbury's low ebb of the decade. He acknowledged, saying, "I know I put out some bad albums." With 1979's "The Sailor," Mick delivered such mainstream country compositions as *A Weed Is A Weed*, *Blue Sky Shinin'* and *Looking For The Sunshine*. Produced by Ronnie Gant with strings - 14 players - again arranged by Alan Moore, this is a brief album, clocking in at just over 27 minutes. Though Dennis Wilson is one of the backing vocals, Mick's signature between-track transitions are missing.

The album yielded covers by Frank Ifield, Janie Fricke, Marie Osmond, David Frizzell, Tammy Wynette, Kingston Trio, Billy "Crash" Craddock and Glen Campbell with The Nelson Riddle Orchestra. *Blue Sky Shinin'* appeared on Marie Osmond's '86 album, "There's No Stopping Your Heart" that enjoyed considerable chart action.  The Kingston Trio covered *Looking For The Sunshine* and so titled an album.

Two songs from "Sailor" are wry examples of Newbury's witty writing:

> *Well you know the crop by the seeds that are sown*
> *Do all your planting with care*
> *Water and ground will make anything grow*
> *But A WEED IS A WEED anywhere*

> *The red necks are drawin' their lines up in East Tennessee*
> *Their cannons are primed; they are fit to be tied I believe*
> *THE NIGHT YOU WROTE THAT SONG*

("Their cannons are primed" is terrific wordplay: Geared up or prepared to fight is one meaning.  But canons with one "n" signifes standards or laws; perhaps Mick was alluding to the Acuff-Rose legal hassles.)

On Mick's 39th birthday, *In The Navy* by Village People and *Shake Your Body (Down To The Ground)* by The Jacksons peaked at number three and seven on the pop singles chart.  Mickey may have joked about the silly songs to Mancil Davis, his partner at a golf outing at the Trophy Club in Dallas.  Perhaps contributing to the era's musical silliness, Mickey appeared in his first movie.  Mickey - as Deputy Webb - and Susan appeared in "Swim Team," a really bad B fiasco, directed by James Polakof.  According to the film's liner notes, "The Whalers school swim team holds a record of zero wins in seven years.  Their team captain is hung over, the star swimmer is practicing her stroke on the coach and the team mascot is belly-up on the beach.  It's a funny case of sink or swim for the new coach who wants to transform this group into a real swim team."  Mickey and Susan enjoyed taking part in the movie, even if a farce.  They enjoyed doing things as a couple, plus the experience broke up the routine.

Mickey would weather a tempest of ups and downs over the next few years, starting sadly when his Dad Milton passed away on May 29, after suffering a second stroke.  Mamie confided in the author, saying, "I was so proud of him, especially his loyalty to all his family... He went to prison to save a cousin.  He was the love of my life."  Milton was buried on Memorial Day.

> *He worked his fingers to the bone to make that shotgun shack a home.*
> *He kept his sadness deep inside; had that dream the day he died.*
> *IN '59*

Mick and Susie celebrated their tenth wedding anniversary in October. Though traditional and modern gifts include tin, aluminum and leather, he gave her a pretty song. "It became a family joke," explained Susan. "If there was an anniversary or birthday coming up, the kids would go shopping and Mickey would go writing... He knew I was happier with a new song than anything from a store." Mickey explained the strategy during a Bay Area concert. "Being the cheapskate that I am... see it's cheaper... I mean I can just slide back in a little dark corner... and come out... and I'm a hero for a year!" His gift to Susie this year was titled, *I Still Love You After All These Years*.

*Patiently you waited for so long*
*Stood beside me knowing I was wrong*
*Through all my confusion*
*You could hear the perfect song*
*I STILL LOVE YOU AFTER ALL THESE YEARS*

As 1979 came to a close, the CMA awarded Willie Nelson the coveted Entertainer of the Year Award.

**Too Tall Mick with Guy Clark at the Birchmere**

# Chapter XIII: *After All These Years*
## 1980 - 1987


In 1980, the film "Urban Cowboy" fueled an explosion of interest in country music. Starring New Jersey native John Travolta, who spent evenings at Gilley's nightclub in Pasadena, Texas (a suburb of Houston), the movie caused record and tape sales to surge by more than 50 percent. Cowboy boots, Wrangler jeans and flashy hats became the uniform of the night. The horse of choice for these slick new outlaws? A hot pickup.

One year later, MTV made its auspicious debut, and then all hell broke loose in 1982. The Gloved One, Michael Jackson released "Thriller," then the best selling album of all time, spurred on by a young generation's MTV worship. Good for business but bad for music, MTV is today in 79 million homes in America and has 271 million viewers worldwide. It is seen in 70 percent of countries.

The Nashville Network played follow the leader on March 7, 1983, beaming country music programming into millions of homes. Due to network exposure, video turned into an essential marketing tool, elevating the importance of a performer's appearance. Conversely, the importance of the song declined as slick productions featuring cowboy clones, hot chicks, fast cars and cool effects mesmerized a worldwide audience. Moonwalkers and phony cowboys were not Newbury's cup of tea. Musically, the era and he were poles apart.

In the autumn of 1980, Wesley Rose brought a ray of sunshine into Mick's world when he invited him to attend the 11th annual celebration of the Nashville Songwriter's Association International (NSAI). Susan would not be able to make it, as seven-year-old Chris was in school; and three-year-old Leah was everywhere. Mickey asked best friend from The Embers days, CAG, to accompany him to the ceremony.

The banquet, show and ceremonies were held at Nashville's Hyatt-Regency Hotel. Wesley and CAG were seated at a table with Mickey when Susan waltzed in to the ballroom. Mickey was surprised and happy to see Susie, though he had no idea what might unfold. His old friend Ralph Emery served as emcee. (Renowned as a TV host and WSM DJ, Emery had won Country Disc Jockey of the Year six times.) Songwriter Hal David, President of the American Society of Composers, Authors and Publishers, presented the keynote address.

Suddenly, against a stirring medley of Newbury songs, Elvis' *An American Trilogy*, Tom Jones' *Funny Familiar Forgotten Feelings* and Andy Williams' *Sweet Memories*... the announcement came: "The next inductee into the Songwriter's Hall of Fame... Mr. Mickey Newbury!" As more than 500 songwriters, publishers, artists and industry members stood and cheered wildly for the youngest inductee ever, Mickey was presented with the Manny - for manuscript - Award. That was Mick's second surprise of the wonderful evening.

In nominating Newbury for the Hall of Fame, composer Joe Allison called Newbury a "writer's writer" who influenced other songwriters "with his genius level of standards of excellence." Wesley Rose concurred: "October 12, 1980 will always be remembered as a very special day in our industry. That's when Mickey Newbury was inducted into the Songwriter's Hall of Fame. No honor in our business was ever more deserved as evidenced by the standing ovation he received from his peers who had bestowed upon him this most prestigious honor. I could not have been more elated had he been of my own flesh and blood. As was mentioned on this occasion, 'His family of musical brainchildren will live among us for all time to come.'"

Sixteen years after Mick signed with Acuff-Rose, he received official validation from his industry and from his peers. A few days later, he phoned Townes Van Zandt to thank him for the inspiration.

Mickey would lose a few close friends in 1981. His buddy Felton Jarvis had endured debilitating kidney problems for a decade, requiring dialysis therapy; and during a peak of the illness, Elvis located a replacement kidney for him and even paid for the transplant. At long last, at the end of his pain, Felton died in January after suffering a stroke in December. Then, Sue Brewer, owner of the Nashville Boar's nest and patron to struggling singers, died of cancer. Ten years later, she would be inducted into the Nashville Songwriter's Hall of Fame, though not as a songwriter. The Father of Rock, supernova William John Clifton Haley, also died that year. His career had tragically spiraled downward in a flurry of financial woes, divorce, tax problems, alcohol, and a lonely death in Texas at age 55.

*Haley died in Corpus Christi*
*Died without a dime*
*SO SAD*

**ALBUM # 12** After All These Years (Polygram / Mercury SRM1-4024) contains the following songs: (Side 1) The Sailor, Song Of Sorrow, Let's Say Goodbye One More Time, That Was The Way It Was Then, Country Boy

184

Saturday Night, (Side 2) Truly Blue, Just As Long As That Someone Is You, Over The Mountain, Catchers In The Rye, I Still Love You (After All These Years).

"After All These Years" returned to the solid foundation of lingering lyrics and orchestrated melodies. Produced by friend, Norbert Putnam, "Years" features Dave Loggins on harmonies and guitar. The glorious album radiates a longing for days gone by and includes two of the prettiest songs ever written: *Song of Sorrow* and *I Still Love You (After All These Years)*.

>*Just the thought of you still takes my breath away*
>*After all these years what more can I say*
>*You are the light that guides me*
>*Through my darkest day*
>*I STILL LOVE YOU AFTER ALL THESE YEARS*

*The Sailor* is a deep song, painted with broad strokes with metaphorical allusions to heaven, hell and earth. Using the intro from *Wish I Was*, the overture begins with a prayer for humility, "A grain of sand is all I ever wanted to be." The subject is then embodied in the first verse: "Oh my daddy was a sailor." Mick verbally confirmed that "daddy" refers to Jesus, while His home is depicted in the lyrics, "Tell me then where could I go / But up into the sky."

Hell on earth is proclaimed through brilliant wordplay: "Here I am in Nashville town / Bow-deep in the mud." (Though written lyrics state "Nashville Town," Mick sings "Jackson Town." They are one and the same; Andrew Jackson, seventh President, practiced law at 333 Union Street in Nashville.) Earthly ties are lovingly portrayed by "Susie in the kitchen doin' dishes / Chris and all his toys have gone to bed." Mick's longing to know Jesus or desire to capture perfect prose may be indicated in the concluding lines, "Starin' out the window all I wish is / I could hear the words I'm hearin' in my head."

*The Sailor* contains brilliant lyrics, simply delivered:

>*Turnin' at the gangplank he looked me in the eye*
>*He said learn to read the truth son it lies between these lines*

The usage of "lies" is clever wordplay. The word signifies that truth can be found between or amid the lyrics. A second meaning of lies is as an untrue statement. The double entente is not accidental. A Word Man in the Shakespearean sense, Newbury's brutal editing process painstakingly considered language angles and perspectives. Writer Don Negri referred to Newbury as "a linguistic alchemist," and good friend, Marty Hall emphasized the point: "Mickey considered himself a student of language and could speak at considerable length about the derivation of words and sounds. He was quite amazing in this respect. And he cared deeply about the use of words. He said to me once that as songwriters we are 'stewards of words.'"

"The truth son it lies" is this poet's way of expressing the basic precept of Christianity, as stated in Proverbs 3:5-6: "Trust in the Lord with all your heart, and <u>lean not on your own understanding</u>; in all your ways acknowledge Him, and He will make your paths straight."

> *Say you double-headed eagle*
> *Say you can teach me how to fly*

"Double-headed eagle" could be a reference to "double eagle," a 20 dollar gold piece first issued to the public in 1850 following the California Gold Rush; metaphorically then, it may mean money or riches. The term might also allude to the song "Under The Double Eagle" - the benchmark Sousa piece, used by pickers to acknowledge a master guitar player... metaphorically then, mastery of music.

Double-headed eagle is also the oldest crest in the world, a symbol of power more than 2,000 years before the building of King Solomon's Temple. It is an accepted emblem of Masons, the oldest and largest worldwide fraternity dedicated to the brotherhood of man under the fatherhood of a Supreme Being. Below the Masonic double-headed eagle is the phrase, "Spes mea in deo est," which means, "My hope is in God." When Mick sings, "Say you double-headed eagle / Say you can teach me how to fly," perhaps he is communicating a fundamental cabala. Faith in God can teach us how to fly.

In the end, he leaves it open, allowing the listener freedom to interpret what will "teach me how to fly." Riches, music or God... King Solomon pursued the subject as well. The song is a fine example of how Newbury's music can get to the bottom of things but also lift us up to the highest heavens.

Newbury remarked to friend - Georgia farm boy Steve Enfinger - "My music won't be understood 'till after I'm dead." It frustrated Mick that most people do not understand the message, though many feel it. As spiritual conviction is emotionally conveyed, writer Moshe Benarroch hit the bull's-eye when he stated, "Personally, listening to him just fills me with joy and hope. There is something deeply religious in his songwriting and singing, remindful of a prayer."

> *Does she know now what the words I sing mean*
> *IF YOU SEE HER ask her for me*

Two songs on the album, *Let's Say Goodbye One More Time* and *That Was The Way It Was Then*, are sincere offerings from the heart of a card-carrying romantic.   *Over The Mountain* is an idyllic promise of pastoral happiness, capped with a passionate display of Mick's signature yodel whistling.    Co-written with friend Joe Henry, lyricist-poet-novelist of Colorado, the song would also be at home on Dave Loggins' archetypal LP, "Apprentice In A Musical Workshop."

> *I will plant us a garden here next to the forest*
> *Dig us a well there with water so pure*
> *Water so pure and as sweet as the sunrise*
> *OVER THE MOUNTAIN*

On the tenth album since leaving RCA, Mickey connected a few dots.  In 1965, RCA's Jimmy Elledge became the first artist to cover a Newbury composition with, *Just As Long As That Someone Is You.* Mickey had written *"Someone"* in Houston in '59 before joining the Air Force, and he performed it here for the first time.  Also, just as *San Francisco Mabel Joy* did not appear on the album "Frisco Mabel Joy," *The Sailor* was excluded from its LP namesake, appearing here instead.

Norbert Putnam produced the album at the Bennett House, in Franklin, Tennessee - 20 miles south of Nashville.  While in the area, Mickey and fellow Hall-Of-Famer Dallas Frazier conducted a songwriting seminar at Acuff-Rose for the firm's staff writers.   Singer-songwriter Tony Baker remembered, "We went into the bowels of Acuff-Rose for a demo session and I was almost in a swoon from exposure to such skilled and perfect artistry, such obsession with authenticity and quality.  Mickey would, again conspicuously ask my opinion between takes, as if it mattered, which I'm sure it did to his mind.  Doing what he could to give me stock and currency among this elite group, but I was so out of my league.  We arrived at the cabin in the wee hours of the morning and, because his friend was trying to sleep on the couch in the den, we retired into the bathroom to talk.  Mickey sat on the commode and I sat on the floor and we talked until almost daylight.  It remains a favorite memory of mine."

It is a twist of irony that an album titled, "After All These Years" would carry the Mercury name, Mickey's label during The Embers era and his first label after RCA. (In 1960, the Netherlands based company Philips acquired Mercury records, later reorganizing as Polygram / Mercury.) "Years" would become Mick's last album of new studio recordings for 15 years; not until 1996 would fans hear fresh compositions from Newbury. Marking the end of an era, "Years" expresses a spiritual longing and sentimental reminiscence.

The chroniclers would review Newbury's works, giving credit where it was due. "Simply put," Don Negri summarized, "Mickey Newbury is one of America's finest singer-songwriters. In the years between 1969 and 1981 Mickey recorded 10 excellent albums, several of them bordering on brilliant... A poet and a visionary (i.e. the ability to see and describe what escapes you and I), Mickey's songs are a kaleidoscope of American images." And George H. Lewis would add, Newbury's 10 albums "comprise one of the most brilliantly original and important bodies of work of any contemporary popular artist."

As summer came, Mickey attended Willie's golf gig, held this year near Mickey's old stomping grounds, 25 miles north of Houston. Golf pro Dave Franklin was there and wrote: "In the early eighties, Mickey was in The Woodlands for a Darrell Royal-Willie Nelson Golf Tournament / party / drink 'til dawn / pick and play get-together. I was sitting in the lobby of the hotel having a beer with him when Dave Loggins joined us. This was shortly after he released 'The Apprentice.' Dave and Mickey were talking about new songs, and it was decided to take a guitar into the men's room and have a listen. The next hour was absolutely magic as these two giants passed the guitar back and forth inside four walls of tile. It was the most incredible hour a music lover can imagine."

Golf played a major role in Mickey's world, as reported by Eugene's local newspaper, The Register-Guard: "While songwriting was Newbury's passion, playing golf was his avocation. He often could be found on the links at the McKenzie River Golf Course and frequently played in celebrity golf tournaments around the world." He played when he was in good spirits. "When I'm happy," Mick said, "I don't feel like writing songs. I wanna be out playin' golf, you know. It's when I'm sad and don't feel like doing anything else that I write... So... I'll sing somebody else's happy song 'cause obviously they didn't want to play golf. They wanted to sit down in a dark, dingy studio and write, *Oh What A Beautiful Morning!*"

Franklin remembered how Mick "Played golf the way he did everything... intense... totally involved... constantly questioning himself, 'Now why did I hit the ball like that?' For instance, Mick explained to Roy Stamps, "How much trouble he was having just hitting the ball... hook one time, slice the next. He went to the golf pro for advice and was told to try another set of clubs... ladies clubs! Mick said he didn't care for the idea, but he followed through with the suggestion and his golf game improved." That's not quite the whole story though. "At one time," Susan explained, "there were 400 golf clubs in our bedroom... on top of the dresser, under the bed, in the closet. He was always looking for the 'perfect' club. He even tried to get Barney Adams to make a Mickey model."

"Mick was a very good golfer," Stamps added, "and playing at Willie's is always a race against the sun... Willie calls it speed golf... If you can't find your ball in 60 seconds, you just drop one where you think your ball went and hit again. Willie always marked his ball with a 'W.' Now Mick was an accomplished forger and carried an extra ball like Willie played, with a forged 'W.' Well, on a par three, Willie hit his first shot over the green and into the woods. Willie never saw where it went. Mick hit his shot on the green, about 10 feet from the pin. While Willie was looking around the green and in the traps, Mick put the forged ball in the cup and started yelling. 'Everyone,' Mick said, 'danced around and traded high fives.' A few holes later, while Willie was lining up a putt, Mick told him the truth. Willie cussed and missed the putt, while Mick and the others were laying on the ground laughing. I don't think Willie ever played with Mick again."

Another golf story comes from Ron Lyons: "Mick and James Garner finished a round of golf and went into the coffee shop still wearing their gloves. Several ladies nearby were oohing and aahing over James (Jim) Garner."

Mick:   'I really have to thank you, Jim.'
Jim:    'What for, Mickey?'
Mick:   'Well, for helping me to get this new hand.'
Jim:    (picking up on it right way) 'It was my pleasure.'
Mick:   'Not every friend would help a guy like that.'
Jim:    'Don't think anything about it.'
(There is a pause as people continue to watch.)
Jim:    'Something wrong?'
Mick:   'Well, it's nothing really.'
Jim:    'Come on, if something's bothering you... '
Mick:   'No, no... Never mind.'
Jim:    (sounding a bit exasperated) 'Come on. Out with it.'
Mick:   'Well Jim (holding the gloved hand up), it's a girl's hand'!"

Golf helped Mickey unwind, and he played continually in the eighties. On November 15, 1982, however, he happily left the clubs at home to accompany Susan to a Springfield hospital. A few hours later they celebrated the arrival of beloved son, Steve.

Six months later, Mickey's mother would marry Harry Crawford in New Braunfels, Texas. "Harry was a handsome man," she said, "and he was very good to me. He was tall and slim. His hair was originally black, but at

52, it had turned to silver. It was very thick, and looked almost like angel hair, that they used to put on Christmas trees. But his mustache and sideburns were still black... Milton was my great love, but I loved Harry in a much different way." Mamie would maintain use of the Newbury surname.

As the compact disk player was being unveiled across America, Mickey flew to Nashville in March. While there, he put down a few experimental tracks, first takes, for what would lead to a future album, "In A New Age." The early effort, produced by Larry Butler, features new age synthesized sounds. "I was so drunk then," Mickey explained. "I hate those cuts and never want to hear 'em again."

> Then a storm in '83 caught me too far out to sea
> I hit a reef, and I ran aground on the streets of Guitar Town
> IN '59

While in Guitar Town, Mick appeared on the "Bobby Bare and Friends" TV show with Harlan Howard. Mick was in excellent form, performing *An American Trilogy* and smidgens of seven songs, including his only televised performance of *Just Dropped In*. Bare was in awe of Newbury's talent, pleading with him to continue playing.

Mick's business manager to be, Bob Rosemurgy went to Nashville then to meet him. Because Acuff-Rose left him in the lobby for six hours, he went home. Mick would jokingly say, "Rosemurgy came to see me all the way from Michigan, and the guy left him sittin' in the lobby at Acuff-Rose... And he just got back on the plane and went home... He gave up real easy... So we didn't get to see each other for 20 years... Thanks a lot Rosemurgy! That's just when I needed a friend... Why do you think he left you sittin' out there in the lobby? Nobody liked me then! Didn't want me to have no friends... Ha ha..." Bob would not give up though. Their paths would cross a decade later and a few blocks away.

From Nashville, Mick flew north to Canada at the invitation of a friend. Texan Larry Gatlin was booked to appear on the CHCH-TV program, "In Session," in Hamilton, Ontario. The station at the time was running an excellent series where popular performers named their major influence, and they would arrange for them to play together in a pre-taped 30-minute television special. Gatlin - who had recorded a string of number one hits including *All The Gold In California* - chose Mick. On December 15, 1983, they rehearsed, jammed and bantered back and forth for two hours in the TV studio, performing their own songs and harmonizing together on a few others.

Mick sang *Lovers, Mabel Joy, Wish I Was* and *An American Trilogy*. Setting the Ovation guitar aside, he did an early version of *Workin' Man*, accompanying himself on his new toy, a Suzuki Omnichord OM-27 Electronic Autoharp. Mick referred to the pear-shaped, lap-held synthesizer as a "lazy man's instrument," and during this period he was rarely without it... He carted it to golf courses and even played it on airplanes.

Returning to the guitar, Mick and Larry called and answered on *Ain't No Blues Today* and then together did *Sweet Memories* as a gorgeous duet. The mood between the two men was friendly and playful. Larry seemed to be seeking Mick's approval, while Mick appeared paternally supportive and appreciative. During rehearsal, Larry called Mick his "hero," and after singing one of his own compositions, said, "Just help me do it half as good as Newbury and I'll be satisfied." After they traded licks on *Ain't No Blues Today*, Larry informed Mick, "I'd like to take a tape recorder or a piece of paper and just walk around in your brain for a couple of hours."

Returning to the West Coast, Mick ran into an old friend from the RCA days, composer/arranger Tupper Saussy. Though they had much to discuss, the encounter was laden with mixed emotions. "Tupper was really a good guy," Mick explained, "a little bit left of center though. He got involved in a tax evasion mess, as he refused to pay taxes. Last time I saw him was in the early eighties in San Francisco. Was on his way to Paris. Still runnin.'" Perhaps Tupper was searching for his old company. General Electric had acquired RCA and sold the home entertainment division to Thomson Consumer Electronics in France. Still... it's hard to imagine Nipper as a coiffured poodle.

Mick flew to the Pacific Rim in 1984 to fulfill a dream down under, a concert trek through Australia. "Roger Miller and Kenny Rogers were there," Mick stated, "and I spent a lot of time with them. Roger, (his wife) Mary and I were guests of (Australian outlaw DJ) John Laws so far back in the bush, John had to send a helicopter after us. It was a pleasant but very full time." John Laws was impressed as well and wrote, "Mickey would have to be one of the most decent, regular fellas that I ever met in my life... with a big heart and a big ability to write and sing music... Roger Miller considered Mickey one of the great songwriters... P.S. Me and Mickey and Roger had more than one drink together." Down under, indeed.

While in the region, Mick zipped over to New Zealand to perform on the TV show "That's Country." Returning to Australia, he co-wrote half a song with local artist, Doug Ashdowne. Mick would draw inspiration and "bits" from the effort to fashion a song in the second millennium, to be titled, *I Don't Love You*. His final appearance on the Continent of Contrasts was staged at a popular folk club in Melbourne, The Troubadour, founded in 1978 by

Newbury fan, Andrew Pattison, because "it would be nice to have somewhere to go and listen to some gentle acoustic music." Newbury fan and "Aussie" minstrel, Chris Frasier, fondly recounted how, "Mick's last concert at The Troubadour went on to all hours of the morning. By then he had lost his voice, so when he wanted to hit a high note, he would just put his hand in the air, and the audience would clap."

Returning to America, Mick laid down at least seven songs in a Nashville studio session. Produced by Larry Butler, the songs were not released. Mick's friend Jonmark Stone played guitar on *Why You Been Gone So Long* and *Mobile Blue*, and during the sessions, Johnny Cash, Waylon Jennings and many others dropped in to say hello. "It was an awesome experience," Jonmark remembered, "to spend an evening with Waylon and listen to him talk about Mickey's songs, cut by cut, album by album. I mean what a huge fan he was." Waylon covered nine Newbury songs: *Mobile Blue, Sweet Memories, Frisco Depot, Cowboys Don't Cry, 33rd of August, If You See Her, Let Me Stay Awhile, San Francisco Mabel Joy* and *You're Not My Same Sweet Baby*. *Cowboys Don't Cry* is the song that was left "half unfinished" by Hank Williams and completed by Mickey. Waylon's waxing of *Let Me Stay Awhile* ranks as one of the best covers of Newbury's material. Waylon does a superb job with Mick's music; his trademark guitar style coupled with the rich, deep voice adds to the ballads.

While in Nashville on November 5, 1984, Mick appeared on "The Door Is Always Open," a televised guitar pull hosted by Waylon and featuring Webb Pierce, George Jones, Faron Young, Willie Nelson, Roger Miller, Harlan Howard, Kris Kristofferson and Hank Williams Jr. The men came together to pay tribute to their friend, Sue Brewer, who had passed away three years earlier. Waylon referred to the gathering as an "organized riot." Following the tribute, Mickey appeared on "Yesteryear in Nashville," a TV show hosted by Archie Campbell.

In early '85 Mickey received news that stole the wind from his sail. Wesley Rose was entertaining an offer from Opryland USA, owner of the Grand Ole Opry, to acquire the Acuff-Rose catalog of 20,000 copyrights including 300 Newbury compositions. Rose eventually accepted the deal at a price of $22 million, even though he had assured Mick that "one day" he would be given managerial reigns to the company. "Mickey signed with Acuff-Rose because of Wesley Rose," future business manager, Bob Rosemurgy explained. "And stayed there because of him. Mickey gave up lucrative recording contracts because of Wesley's promises, which were never fulfilled."

> *I am dead in Tennessee, they buried me alive*
> *And I am SO SAD... SO SAD...*
> *The best I had... is all I have...*

While Rose's bank account bloomed, Newbury's wilted. Stemming from a budding commitment that never matured, Newbury felt betrayed. And then, to add insult to injury, the IRS showed up and picked the garden clean. "All of that came together at one time... So I wasted what should have been the best years of my life just fightin' off the wolves... Plus I was too old... Nobody wanted me anymore."

> *Wolf is scratchin' at my door Lord Lord*
> *I can hear that lonesome wind moan*
> *WHY YOU BEEN GONE SO LONG*
>
> *Castles of sand stand but not for too long*
> *What's here today tomorrow is gone*
> *LET'S SAY GOODBYE ONE MORE TIME*
>
> *I have had mountains and mountains and mountains*
> *in the palm of my hand*
> *TIME WAS*

As an even thornier issue, Newbury - an inveterate nonconformist - had little desire to see new work released in a pop culture climate controlled by an increasingly cynical and money grubbing music industry. He was becoming increasingly disenchanted.

> *Stack of bills get higher but I don't works no more*
> *CATCHERS IN THE RYE*
>
> *Do you ever have a longin' for a pure and simple time*
> *When all we had between us was a dream and one thin dime*
> *We were flat out on the highway with no place to be but gone*
> *SOME MEMORIES ARE BETTER LEFT ALONE*
>
> *Oh if I could fly I would close my eyes*
> *Spread my wings and fly away from all this pain*
> *Search the stars and find a place in space and time*
> *I am seeking shelter from this chillin' rain*
> *Honey there's a storm comin' sure and certain*
> *Gonna turn this dusty highway into forty miles of mud*
> *A STORM IS COMIN'*

Mickey explained how, "I got mad at the IRS one time... I was just really cranked 'cause they had come in and robbed my bank account, you know... And checks were bouncin'... And I was sittin' at the piano and I was just red in the face and I said" (I wrote):

193

*The taxman came and he took away everything I made today*
*Said he could not take my IOU*
*I said 'Son in 1963 I was where you were too young to be'*
*For apple pie in my red, white and blue*
*And furthermore I volunteer with eight young men we commandeered*
*A worn-out truck eight men have tried the truth*
*Now you're tellin' me today it did not matter anyway*
*Well the hell with you and the hell with Uncle Sam*

"And then I went all the way through the whole thing about why we left Europe in the first place and came here in 1628... And when I got through, Susan said, 'What are you going to do with that?' I said... rip, rip, rip... and I threw it in the trashcan, you know. Because it was born out of anger. Those kind of songs need to be written to get them out of your refrigerator, because they spoil all the other food in there. If you take something out of the refrigerator and it's a little bit moldy, throw it away. Out of about 1,000 songs I've only thrown about 25 or 30 away."

"One of them was a suicide song. And it was so powerful that I was afraid of it. And I knew it was a hit. It hurt to throw it away, you know. That goes against all of your nature... your capitalistic nature! I needed that money real bad at that time, you know. But I threw it away because it made my mother cry. And I promised never to sing it again... But I threw it away 'cause I was afraid that it would cause someone to commit suicide..."

"Songs can be healing or they can be damaging, and the responsibility of a songwriter is to always leave hope in his songs. That sounds corny, but it's for real. That's your obligation. Your obligation with art... it should be uplifting and not something that drives you in the ground." Shakespeare wrote that music is the "food of love." Mick agreed.

Resulting from struggles with life, business and the IRS, Mickey would compose some of his finest songs in the eighties, such as *Ramblin' Blues*, which could not have been written under more positive circumstances. "Adversity for a songwriter," he explained, "is much like a good fire in the winter. You must stay just far enough away to feel its warmth... If you can take something bad and make something good out of it... it cheats him (it robs the dragon)." Consequently, this period of personal difficulty created a productive environment for songwriting, though fans would not hear the new songs for a decade.

In the same vein, Mick advised Pembroke Picker, "From a creative standpoint, I wish Roger Miller had not made it big for another six years. I'm not saying he didn't pay his dues. He did! Playing fiddle for Minnie Pearl, drumming for Ray Price... But, he made it so big, that his writing suffered, because the pressures were so great. I believe he could have written so many more great songs. You see, writers are set free from molds, by people who are not afraid to do something different... It's the writer who has the guts to expand and open more creative doors, who really contributes." Miller did that well before the arrival of stellar success.

As 1985 came to a close, the annual CMA Awards Show was co-hosted by another individual who was "not afraid to do something different," Newbury's former apprentice, Kris Kristofferson. As Mick watched the CBS presentation, perhaps his thoughts were drawn to cold mornings when he found Kristofferson asleep on his boat deck.

**ALBUM # 13** Sweet Memories (MCA-945) contains the following songs: (Side 1) An American Trilogy, Good Morning Dear, If You Ever Get To Houston, She Even Woke Me Up To Say Goodbye, Dizzy Lizzy, (Side 2) Sweet Memories, Remember The Good, Sunshine, The Future's Not What It Use To Be, How I Love Them Old Songs.

"Sweet Memories" was the first Newbury album in four years, though it offered nothing new. The LP contains ten songs, eight from the Cinderella Studio trilogy of Elektra albums, making it a poor man's "Volume One Best Of" collection. The album fueled fears among diehard Newburians that Mickey was finished with the business. Mickey did not release the album. Why did MCA? In 1977, Mickey signed with ABC Hickory who purchased his back catalog from Elektra. Two years later, ABC Hickory was acquired by MCA. So MCA controlled Newbury's back catalog except for the 1968 / 1972 RCA and 1981 Polygram material.

On April 6, Mick appeared at the Picker Poet Reunion Concert, broadcast by Berkeley's FM Pacifica. He brought the house down with six songs: *Genevieve, The Piper, Wish I Was, Ain't No Blues Today, San Francisco Mabel Joy, That Was The Way It Was Then* and *I Don't Think About Her No More.*

Next, he performed *Wish I Was* at the Austin Opera House on April Fools Day, 1986. Other performers included Roy Head, Ray Wylie Hubbard and Asleep At The Wheel. Backed by the de facto house band, First Take, the live show would be released in a compilation album: "Texas, A Musical Celebration, 150 Years." As Austin has been mentioned, to set the record straight, Mickey Newbury never was invited to appear on "Austin City Limits."

195

On September 17, Mick reunited with a good buddy from the Nashville days. The owner of the Birchmere club in Alexandria, Virginia, had been after Guy Clark to persuade Newbury to perform there. Guy's persuasive tactics worked. They played the Birchmere together over two evenings, alternating separate sets.

Mickey met a fellow in November who would become a trusted companion. "Learning that I was a songwriter," Marty Hall recalled, "our mutual friend, Jim Bradley, invited me to call Mickey. So I called him and we spoke for an hour or so, agreeing that it would be best for me to come up and bring with me a song or two for him to hear. In a few days I drove from Eugene to Vida and met Mickey, Susan and the children. Susan was in major Mom Mode."

"After initial pleasantries, Mickey and I adjourned to the Secret Compartment, Mickey's dimly lighted rough-cedar-and-skylight studio, which was jam-packed with a daunting assortment of instruments, tapes, records, boxes, lyric sheets, audio gear and antiques. From the disarray appeared two chairs facing one another and nearly touching. Mickey sat in one as he grabbed a customized Ovation guitar and patted the other chair in indication of where he wanted me. Just as I sat down he closed his eyes, pitched back his head and started singing, *Wish I Was.* I have never recovered from the impact of that moment. It was large, very, very large. At once I realized many things, not the least of which was that my life would be forever changed. And indeed, it was."

Over the years, Marty continued, "Our conversations ranged from music to poetry to mathematics to visual art to medicine to weather to love to creation. Mickey was well read, decidedly of an opinion about most things, yet always interested in what else might be possible. He was constantly in scan mode for new possibilities and how to apply what he knew to the craft of songwriting and music production."

Mick's life was changing too. First, meeting Marty was very large and he made that clear, "Marty is a dear friend of mine. He is just the neatest guy you'll ever meet in you life..." When not writing songs, Marty does charitable work for hospices, and he supplies musical instruments to orphaned children in Central America.

Mick's life would be altered on December 10th when Susan gave birth to their final child, daughter Laura Shayne. Astrologists take note: three of five Newbury children were born under the Sagittarius sign. Besides Laura Shayne, Joe and Chris were born on December 9 and 12. "Three of our children," Susan said, "were due on Christmas Day!" But there are more kids, she explained. "We have five children of our own, and lots more that call us Mom and Dad." Like good friends Roy Rogers and Dale Evans, the Newburys raised several foster children.

> *I'm an orphan child lookin' for a home*
> *IF I COULD BE*

Over the next few years, Mick appeared on several TV shows including the ever-popular "Nashville Now," hosted by Ralph Emery, who was married to Mick's friend Skeeter Davis. Dressed in sharp suit and silk tie, Newbury brought a touch of class to the country programs, while his performances of *An American Trilogy* drew standing ovations. Though he wished to perform other songs, the hosts would not let him. They insisted on *Trilogy*. Emery always added a personal request: "One of my favorite songs... Mickey please play *Sweet Memories!*"

> *Say, does anyone know what became of Ole Ralph Emery*
> *THE NIGHT YOU WROTE THAT SONG*

Following the 1987 Willie Nelson golf invitational, a concert was held at the Paramont Theater in Austin, Texas, where Willie's guests performed. Roy Stamps remembered, "I had the pleasure of sitting backstage with several people who had never heard Mickey in person. He sang three or four songs and just blew everyone away."

Then in August, a Muscle Shoals, Alabama - 125 miles south of Nashville - session produced an LP that remains unreleased. To be titled, "Old Friends and Golden Bridges," eight songs were recorded: *Old Friends*, *Long Gone*, The *Piper*, *Westphalia Waltz*, *Rainy Day Blues*, *America The Beautiful*, *When My Lady Gets Her Blues* and *Pledging My Love* (written by Johnny Ace). Mickey performed *America* beautifully and respectfully; and as a tender touch, a children's choir accompanied him. The song should be released.

Winter of '87 found Kenny Rogers hosting the CMA Awards Show. Airborne Records was launched shortly after that, becoming the first label to be funded through an initial public stock offering. On November 13, Airborne started with half a dozen performers, among them two Mickeys... Newbury and Gilley. Meanwhile, MCA controlled the bulk of Newbury's albums, and so for the first time, he was totally separated from his catalog. Nevertheless, it would not stop him from releasing a new album of old songs.

197

# Chapter XIV: *In A New Age*
## 1988

ALBUM # 14 In A New Age (Airborne AB-101) contains the following: (Side 1) All My Trials, Cortelia Clark, Willow Tree, The Sailor, Frisco Depot (Side 2) Poison Red Berries, Lovers, San Francisco Mabel Joy, An American Trilogy.

"In A New Age" was Mick's last album issued on vinyl. Released also as his first compact disc (Airborne ACD-101), it went to market in the medium's early longbox packaging. The Nashville-born Airborne label began operation seriously undercapitalized, experiencing financial problems and folding shortly after "Age" was released.

"They wanted to name this album 'A Legend In A New Age,'" Newbury remarked to The Tennessean Showcase. "I said, 'You can name it that if you want, but I can't introduce it like that from the stage or tell anybody what it's called.' It kind of puts you in a weird place." Mick stated repeatedly an artist could not be a legend "until he's dead." The album had been a Newbury concept and work-in-progress since 1983 Nashville sessions with Larry Butler. "They're all old songs," Mick said. "Originally, I just sat down at Larry Butler's studio and sang whatever came to mind - that was the order and everything."

It all came together in 1988 in Nashville when Chet Atkins introduced Mickey to violin virtuoso Marie Rhines. Marie holds a Master of Music Degree from Yale and the New England Conservatory of Music in Boston, and she is a composer with 22 awards from ASCAP. Marie has performed at Lincoln Center, and she also originated the successful "Folk Heritage" program on National Public Radio. Surprising to Marie, Mick was already familiar with her music when Atkins introduced them. "We have one of your albums at home," Newbury told her, "And we love it!" Shortly thereafter, they were in the studio. Accompanied by Rhines on violin and playing the Photon guitar given to him by Atkins, Mickey and Marie completed "In A New Age" in one day, on March 2.

The gut-string Photon guitar, equipped with an early and buggy MIDI device, enabled the triggering of cosmic-like sound effects. Once Mick obtained the hi-tech instrument, the Suzuki Omnichord was relegated to the closet. During a "Nashville Now" TV episode, Mickey gave Ralph Emery the short story of how the guitar came to be a prized possession. "When Chet showed it to me, I told him, 'If you don't give it to me, I'll kill you." Chet obliged... though there is more to the story.

When Chet demonstrated the guitar to Mickey, he immediately fell in love with it. Marie Rhines was there and remembered, "I was present during most of the negotiations over the new Photon guitar with Chet. I do distinctly remember Mickey offering to give Chet timeshare in the country in Kentucky or some such place, and they went back and forth with Mickey offering Chet all kinds of deals and prizes in return for this guitar. Chet was positively determined that he was only going to loan it to Mickey overnight. Chet kept saying, 'But Mickey, I just got it and I haven't even had a chance to play it myself. I need it. Please.' I began to really feel sorry for Chet, as I could see the handwriting on the wall, with Mickey so much in love with this guitar. I knew it was only a matter of a few more hours and Mickey would win. I think they may have even resorted to tossing coins, or some such tomfoolery. But Chet went out of the room mumbling something like, 'but it's mine.'"

"You see, it was Chet who brought me over to meet Mickey that very day, so I heard all this delightful banter back and forth between the two of them, upstairs in Greg Humphrey's studio. We even recorded our very first three or four songs we ever played together on that same night. Chet agreed finally to let Mickey have it, I think in the end because Mickey just charmed him... I remember Mickey asking me to forgo any payment for the Bluebird (their first concert) so as to make enough money to pay Chet for the guitar, which I happily did, knowing how happy it was making Mick to play with it, and that we were going to have plenty of time to concertize in the future."

This was a dream come true for Marie, as before they met, Mickey was her musical hero. Marie had completed advance studies in Cambridge, England a decade earlier, and Newbury's music helped her get through the experience. "I think I played it every day as I was so homesick for America. Hearing Mickey sing filled my heart with images of my home country and I would feel better. I don't know what I'd have done without Mickey that year."

So all necessary pieces were in place: Marie Rhines - thanks to Chet, the Photon guitar - thanks to Chet and Mickey - thanks to Susan. Finally, the way in which "Age" was produced is how RCA should have produced Mickey 20 years earlier. The album presents nine of his classic songs in simple settings that emphasize his heart-stopping vocal abilities. If ex RCA senior executive Chet Atkins were attempting to even the score, he succeeded... "In A New Age" is a masterpiece.

Mick's first new studio album in seven years was coordinated by Owsley Manier and produced by Greg Humphrey at Master's Touch Studio in Nashville. Though Larry Butler served as Executive Producer, he was not in the studio during the sessions. "I never met him," explained Rhines. "He did not even know about the recording session at that moment. Mickey had already recorded an album with Larry. It was ready for pressing, and they had spent a huge amount of money preparing to release it. Including studio cost, musicians, etc., some figure like $50,000 was thrown out. But Mickey was not at all happy about the accompaniment on this album. He was actually quite miserable about it and wanted to erase the whole thing."

"When we met," continued Rhines, "he was ecstatic to say the least, as he said it had always been his dream to do an album with solo violin. So the very day we met, he invited me to the studio to play through the exact same songs that Larry Butler had produced on the ignominious master hoping to replace what Larry had produced with the new one with my solo violin. It was sort of like an underground session, as nobody was supposed to know we were doing it. I just did what Mickey asked."

"When I arrived at the studio at 11 AM, I remember it was quiet, no one around, except Mickey - who had set up two chairs in this big empty studio, facing each other with two microphones. I sat down, and then we began to play and never stopped until side one was done. Owsley was in the studio at that time along with the recording engineer and also Mabel, the owner of the studio. We returned after a brief lunch, sat down and went through the exact order of side two never stopping the tape until we finished the final song. Done. Mickey loved the results."

Transitions and effects were added afterwards, but in just another day at the office, Mickey and Marie laid down nine songs in two short sessions without splices. Mickey liked to say, "It took me one hour to do it." In 1997 he explained himself to No Depression, "If I go in the studio, and we don't get it in the first or second take, I pass it up. It's a method that I've pretty much always followed. I can't go back and sing something over and over again. I don't know how in the hell anybody does it."

Owsley Manier, the Project Coordinator, was there as well and remembered how it came together. "I went to see Mickey, and discovered there was this bogus album that was going to be released on an independent label of old demos with alleged in a new age sounds, that was just horrendous. And I suggested to Mickey once I had found out that the record company had printed the paper but not made any CDs or LPs or cassettes. (A few LPs were inadvertently released in Canada - *Author*)... I said, 'Let's just go in with you and Marie and we'll rerecord this...'"

"We got a studio, and we had to do this immediately (as studio time was expensive; the cover and label were already printed, and the 'bogus' record was ready for pressing). We went in and recorded the album nonstop in the same order (as the original album - to match the cover's song list which was already printed). While Mickey and Marie were playing, the train sounds and all those sound effects were playing to them live in the studio through the monitors, which sort of inspired this kind of feel and flow and tempo... And then we finished the whole thing (adding production effects) in 24 hours and that was it."

Once the new master was completed, one high hurdle remained. Larry Butler and Airborne executives would have to be convinced to use the new master in place of the one ready to be released. "It would take some diplomacy," Rhines explained. "I, being the new kid on the block, was deemed satisfactorily uninvolved enough with everyone, never having met Larry Butler, to represent Mickey in the meeting with Owsley. Basically, three Airborne execs sat on one side of the desk, and we (Owsley and I) on the other, and I proceeded to explain as gently as possible how much it would mean to Mickey if they would agree to the new master."

"They turned on the tape machines and played each and every singe cut back to back comparing both masters for several hours. It was the first time I heard the original Butler produced sessions. They sounded quite fine to me because Mickey's voice was, as always, spectacular. But he wanted his new sound with the Photon guitar and solo violin to represent the direction he wanted to go. I hoped they would understand how much it mattered to Mickey to finally get the sound he desired, and that it would certainly be an inspiration for Mickey to want to tour with his new sound; sell more CDs and bottom line - make more money for the company..."

"When I left that meeting I had no idea if our 'New Age' sound would get past those doors. Back in the studio Mickey, Owsley, and I began our vigil, which lasted for two or three days, if I remember correctly. The news finally came. Larry Butler approved Mickey's new sound and would be willing to issue this new master. Mickey was thrilled. To this day, I have never met Larry Butler. I hope one day to have the pleasure. I heard only good things about him from everyone at that time. Mickey just wanted to branch out in a new direction."

Of great relief to fans, the album was not new age in style, but a presentation of familiar songs in a new era, as the LP was a reworking of nine songs from previous albums. Mickey did not need to run multiple takes, as he knew these songs, his "children." A majority were recorded during the Cinderella Studio days, yet Newbury, an extraordinary interpreter, made them fresh again... He made you hear the lyric.

The album opens with new life - "Hush little baby, don't you cry" and closes with death - "You know your daddy's bound to die." Between the beginning and the end, Newbury focuses on the center of his attention: God, trains,

Gnashville, perpetual rain and unconditional love.  He presents the subjects with the authority of stars who made him a legend on Music Row.

These songs are not for the mass market, explained Tom Geddie of <u>Buddy</u> magazine, as they are "too beautiful, too dark, and too reverent for today's cynical society that seems to want candy-coated songs."  The songs can make one vulnerable and strong at once.  Most folks can't decipher the dichotomy... the bipolarity... the transception.  From listening to Newbury, one gets the feeling he's listening to an old friend... maybe, even a reflection of oneself.  His lyrics are personal - from the soul - and easily transferred to familiar feelings and thoughts - for the soul.  The imagery has a natural feeling and is really transposed emotions, feelings put into words.  The complexity works simply because it's honest.  "The tools of a writer are truths," Mick said, but as an even more basic explanation, he wrote, "The reason I am able to 'master the complexities of the common man' is... I am."

Allen Harbinson wrote in a 1990 <u>Goldmine</u> article, "It must have taken a tremendous amount of confidence, or a peculiar kind of artistic naiveté, for Newbury to imagine that he could not only reclaim the song (*Trilogy*) from Presley but match his own original performance.  But when he begins ('In A New Age') with *All My Trials*, his singing of the lyrics, 'If life was something that money could buy / The rich would live and the poor would surely die,' has a naked, anguished beauty of the kind that could make grown men weep."

**ALBUM # 15**  "In A New Age" (Airborne ABL-61000) was released on LP and cassette (ABT-61000) formats about the same time as the afore-mentioned "Age" (AB-101).  Referred to as the "bogus" album by Manier, Plan B (Butler's?) was to offer it experimentally using Canada as a test market.  Mickey, however, changed his mind.  "I never want to hear it again," he explained.  "I threw the damn cassette down on the ground and stomped on it."  Recalled immediately after release, a few copies escaped collection, and these rarities - especially sealed - are desired by collectors.  The two albums - different as they are - share the same cover artwork, Paul Harmon's painting of a view of the moon from his "Prehistoric Landscape" series.

The "Canadian" album results from expensive post-production overdubs of 1983 sessions, produced by Larry Butler.  Newbury sings the nine songs in the same sequence as on the American issue, but the Canadian version features new age sound effects - Yamaha DX Series synthesizer - in place of Marie on violin.  Mick found the over-embellishment objectionable.  But as voice tracks were laid down in 1983 - except for the inferior final two that were recorded in 1988 - Mick sings as a higher tenor; and consequently, his voice is more youthful.  Mick's voice changed, becoming deeper about 1986.

On several tracks, he seems just about to lose control of his anguished phrasing, but true to Newbury form, he does so on key.  Two songs, *Poison Red Berries* and *Frisco Depot*, distinctly display the torment.  He sings these songs as if he wanted to put all the pain he had ever felt into them.  When he scream-sings, "And Lord I can see the bright lights back in Dallas," he's not just telling us about his broken heart; he's singing of Everyman's heartbreak.  This gut-wrenching honesty simultaneously conveys a feeling of strength - the nerve to tell the story - and weakness - immeasurable pleading.  The nakedly spiritual drama plays out against heavy rain, Old Testament thunder, new age sound effects and a melodic backdrop of Mick's rhythmic guitar, not the slick Photon but his trademark classical acoustic.  The musique concrète and refined rawness make these two Newbury tracks - his most haunting.  They take one all the way into the ether.

> *Lord, when you're chained there's nothin' you cherish like freedom*
> *When you're free it seems that you're hell-bent for chains*
> *You dance with your demons till you get strength, Lord, to beat 'em*
> *Then you deal with the devil for the salvation you sold*
> *FRISCO DEPOT*

Travis Corder nailed the point in a <u>Music Row</u> article, referring to Newbury's music as a place of terrifying beauty.  He wrote, "Newbury's songs don't make excursions to the dark side, they live there.  He is willing to bring his insights to us.  Newbury makes terrifying, warts-and-all reality beautiful, and that's sweet medicine some folks still eagerly want to swallow."  These perceptions are the basis for his powerful, hypnotic lyrics, which fully captivate and charm the soul.  Granted, Butler's post-production embellishments are over the top, but Newbury's singing... his phrasing... are right on target.  The truthful emotion... perfectly delivered... overpowers the distractions.  Yes, the prettier and safer American masterpiece "In A New Age" can make grown men weep.  But the alternative Canadian issue can make 'em scream.

> *There on the dark side of the world*
> *Trying to pull up to the day*
> *Turn around, come back, please don't leave me*
> *CLINGING TO THE EDGE OF THE WORLD*

To promote the "American" album, Mickey and Marie conducted a six-city tour in June, which included Nashville (Polk Theater, Exit/In and Bluebird

204

Cafe), Alexandria, Virginia (Birchmere), San Francisco (Great American Music Hall and the Venetian Room), Los Angeles (Roxy), Houston (local club) and Austin (University of Texas). The tour was sponsored by the National Academy of Songwriters.

Before the trip, Mick told <u>The Tennessean Showcase</u>, "I'm not really an entertainer; I'm a songwriter. I haven't done much of it and I'm not really inclined to do it, but I don't have anything against it." In fact, Newbury was a riveting performer whose lack of show-business razzle-dazzle made his music stand out all the more. His performances did not include mirrors, light shows or swirling smoke. He did not moonwalk, strike a pose, wear tight pants or thrust his hips. But for any soul fortunate to catch a performance, the experience was mesmerizing and unforgettable. "He's as effective in a room as he is on record," Kristofferson swore. "He's a powerful performer." Mickey preferred the warm atmosphere of respectful listening rooms to arenas and honky-tonks, once saying, "I tell my audience stories, and have no desire to be background music for conversation, dance music in a lounge or the latest fad."

Luckily, the Bluebird was packed that night in June, as Mickey and Marie needed to raise money. "It was at the Bluebird that Mickey inaugurated the Photon guitar in public," Rhines recalled. "I always remember our first concert as a fundraiser to buy that guitar from Chet. As a matter of fact, Mickey Rooney, John Prine and other well-known writers and producers were in the audience. I have a picture of Mickey showing John how to play the guitar on stage, after he invited John to come up front and play. It was a wonderful night. Our one and only Bluebird flight."

"He particularly loved *Danny Boy*," continued Rhines, "which I first played with him at the Bluebird. I just began it, never having actually played it in my own concerts ever before, but with Mickey sitting right there next to me leaning back with a big smile on his face, I just had to improvise on the melody for him. Notes came out of my violin sort of on their own, and I remember how I felt I had never really heard *Danny Boy* until that moment."

Newbury's friend - singer/songwriter Jonmark Stone was there and remembered. "I'll tell you about my favorite Bluebird night... Mickey called to say he was doing a show and that he'd put Bree and I on the 'get in' list at the door. Turned out we had a small table up front... From the first chord, as always, he was awesome... He played for an hour and a half or so and called up John Prine... Then he called up John Loudermilk who played so many self-penned hits it was hard to keep track. Next, he invited Delbert McClinton up to the stage. Fantastic. Much to my surprise, Mick asked me up next. After I had dazzled everyone with a medley of my hits (not), Mick got back up and gave us another half set. What a night! I believe he really enjoyed the show, also. I can still see that famous ear-to-ear grin."

They played the Birchmere on the 17th. Rather than allowing Marie to drink water from a glass set on the floor, Mick surprised her by suddenly disappearing off stage and re-emerging carrying a tray with Perrier water and a red rose. "I was stunned and so surprised having never been treated so royally on stage before. But that was Mickey. Always taking good care of me wherever we toured. The gesture was sincere yet mischievous, in true form." After her thirst was quenched, they performed several songs including *Lie To Me Darlin'*, *You're My Lady Now* and *Amazing Grace / House Of The Rising Sun*.

After the Birchmere show, Mick and Marie flew to San Francisco where they appeared at the Great American Music Hall and the Venetian Room. "Mickey played at one of the most beautiful venues in the world," Marty Hall remembered, "the Venetian Room at the Fairmont Hotel. Mick was opening for Karla Bonoff, and his performances with Marie Rhines were seamless and entrancing. I remember Mickey's children being there. Susan sat next to me and we both leaned next to each other in the middle of one of Mickey's songs asking each other if we knew why and how he was changing one of his songs on the spot and unrehearsed. How he was able to do that, especially while keeping Marie in some sort of telepathic musical alignment, is still a mystery. In any event, it all worked fine and sounded wonderful. When we asked Mickey about it, he simply said, 'Oh, did I do that?' Yeah Mick, you did that." Marie remembered, "Every concert with Mickey was like soaring with an eagle and so easy. I remember how we basically never had to talk about any part of the music. We just went out there and began to play."

"Mick's performance," Marty continued, "blew away the audience. He was at his best. He was in fine voice, he was feeling pretty good, and his vocal texture matched the content of much of his lyrical content. In short, his performance was perfectly believable and that was evident to the audience. And Marie's contribution to Mickey's performance was nice, too, particularly in that setting, where the subtleties of her strings and her harmonies were not lost. The newspaper's review accurately reported Mickey's performance as overshadowing Karla Bonoff."

Concluding the San Francisco leg, they headed south to The City of Angels. Robert Hilburn of the <u>Los Angeles Times</u> caught their concert and wrote, "Wearing a dark suit and tie as he walked on stage at the Roxy, the gray-haired Newbury, now 48, looked more like a successful executive than a one-time member of a revolutionary Nashville songwriting contingent that helped enrich both country and pop music... In his early seventies appearances here, there was a delicate, timid edge to his manner that made him seem like a man who didn't quite know his place or standing in the pop world. Time, however, has given Newbury a security about his work."

After the show, an old friend in a black leather jacket wandered backstage. Jay Leno, who opened for Mick at Lenny's On The Turnpike two decades earlier, had enjoyed the concert. Rhines wrote, "He and Mickey seemed to have quite a lot to say and it was like a high school reunion between them." Also in the audience that evening, Terry Moore (the Hollywood starlet who knew Elvis and Marilyn, dated James Dean, married Houstonian Howard Hughes and made a slew of flicks in the fifties) stopped by to say hello. Mick and Marie were hungry, but Leno could not offer transport as he had arrived on trademark Harley. Terry offered to treat them to dinner anywhere in the city. Though they could chose from the classiest bistros in L.A., Mick and Marie were craving more meager fare. So Terry instructed her Rolls Royce driver to take them to... Denny's.

Mick and Marie flew to Houston the next day to make one performance at a local club, perhaps Rockefellers. Terry Moore decided to accompany them. Afterwards, they traveled to Austin to put on a concert at the University of Texas, and later that afternoon, they were interviewed live on NPR radio at the University of Austin. On August 9, Mick and Marie performed six songs on "New Country," a Nashville TV show as promotion for "In A New Age."

Because his music was popular in the Eastern Block - Poland, Hungary and Czechoslovakia - a Polish promoter arranged for Mickey to perform at a fall festival. The event was sponsored by Polish National Radio - Polskie Nagrania, Marlboro cigarettes and the U.S. Information Service. "I wanted to go. It was just before the wall came down, just before the Revolution (of 1989 in Eastern Europe). There were guards and machine guns everywhere, but I wanted to do this in support of Lech Walesa, the leader of the Solidarity movement. (Walesa had received the Nobel Peace Prize in '83, and in 1990 he would be elected President of Poland.) Marie and I played one concert to 30,000 people in a huge stadium. It was quite an experience."

A few festival performances would be released in a 1990 Polish compilation, titled, "Country Piknik." The rare LP presents 11 artists, including Mick and Marie performing *Shenandoah* and *She Even Woke Me Up To Say Goodbye*. Marie also fiddles up a hot reading of *Big Rock Candy Mountain*.

"It was a complicated five-hour drive," Marie explained, "through tiny villages to get to the festival site, less than 40 miles from the Russian Border. People had saved up three months salaries in some cases to afford the ticket price for the outdoor three-day festival, and most slept in campers and tents in surrounding fields by the lake. It was a pretty, pastoral site. But there was tension everywhere, beginning even as I had walked through the Warsaw airport, where the shelves had been bare and I'd searched hard to find a drinking fountain. There were moments of sadness seeing people who had nothing, and who only wanted to hear a few strains of American music to keep their spirits up. There was a sense of unrest in the air. I was told there had been no meat available to eat for three months. There was virtually nothing for sale in any store in Warsaw, just empty shelves everywhere. All the churches were boarded up, with communism still in full force. (Mick did stumble on one open church there, and he would tell the story of how an organ playing *Ave Maria* moved him to tears.) There was literally nothing to buy in any store, anywhere, except I remember someone selling some bootlegged cassettes of Roy Orbison, which we bought on the street to do our bit to help the economy. Music seemed to obliterate the despair, and people were happy for three full days, walking around in their cowboy hats and Texas boots. Where they ever got them, I can't imagine, with no money. From the response, I know they loved Mickey."

Mickey persuaded Marie to wear a cowgirl outfit onstage. "I felt like Dolly Parton," she exclaimed, "but I was there to entertain and uplift at a very dark hour. You see, I had already traveled behind the iron curtain years before the Poland trip and had stayed for weeks in communist countries. So this was not a new experience for me. Owsley (Manier) asked me to go out on stage and perform a solo set of fiddle tunes, which I did before the rather boisterous Poles in the throes of war."

"I remember after the Sunday evening concert joining everyone downstairs in the lounge at the hotel, where it was an extremely celebratory mood with everyone drinking quite seriously... if you can imagine the final night of a three-day festival in the provinces near the Russian border, with vodka flowing. I excused myself at a respectable hour in the midst of all this revelry, saying, 'see you all at breakfast.'"

While Marie was touring with Mickey, Susan began teaching fulltime at Thurston Middle School in Springfield. Mick and Marie became good friends and enjoyed a professional relationship... Period. But how did Susan feel about her good-looking husband gallivantin' around the world with the lovely violinist? "Susan doesn't have a jealous bone in her body," Mick exclaimed.

Though it may sound trite, the Newburys' marriage was based on love, respect and trust. And, as daughter Laura Shayne explained, Mick even made it difficult to argue: "Anytime my parents would get into an argument (which wasn't often) my dad would break in - mid argument - with 'I love you darlin.' He'd make sure it was dripping with Southern twang... how can you fight with a man like that?"

Mick said he stayed true to Susie, and he offered several examples of his faithfulness. "Once while performing at the Bitter End," he advised, "this beautiful chick came on to me. I mean to tell you she was drop-dead gorgeous. Was tempted, but I didn't go after her! Just had to wait seven minutes... and then I was okay."

> *Well now I thought I had heard it all*
> *And then this woman in a Texas drawl*
> *Said 'now honey can't you shake that thing?'*
> *I said 'I was only hired to sing.'*
> *SHUCK AND JIVE*

And during a 1996 concert, Mick stated, "My wife does not take my writing personal, thank God. One of the first things I told her... I said, 'Susie, I don't have any control over what I write, you know.' That's really the honest to God truth. I really don't. So I can't really be concerned about a lot of things. I mean I just have to let it go."

The year 1988 came to a close with shocking news when Roy Orbison died unexpectedly of a heart attack at age 52. U2's Bono summed up many feelings when he said, "His great gift was to turn the pain and bad luck that he experienced into ground breaking songs." Mickey wrote, "HANDS DOWN... NO QUESTION... Roy Orbison was the best singer ever captured on record... I suppose Roy was my favorite singer... I know he was one of my best friends and I miss him every day."

**Jesse Winchester and Mickey - June 16, 1989**

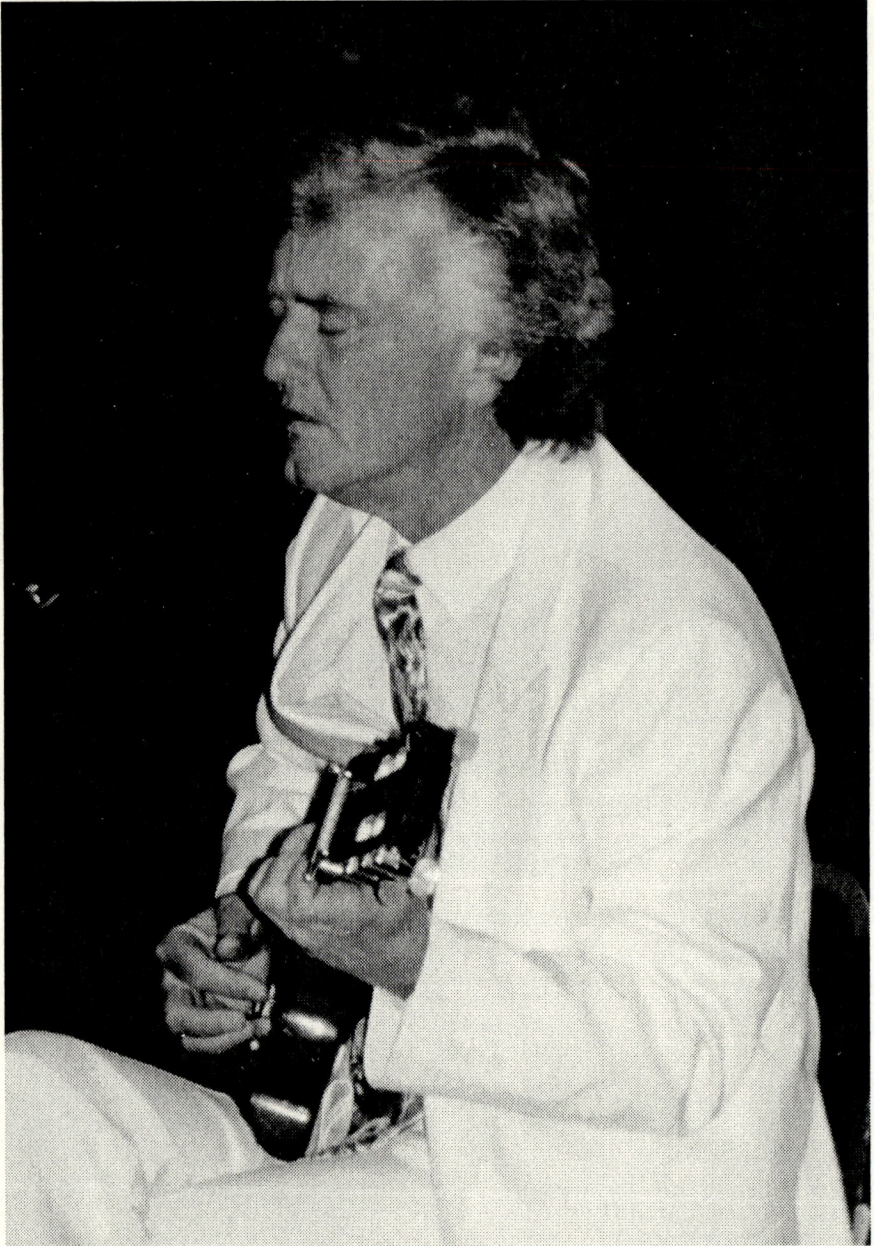

**Mickey at the Birchmere**

# Chapter XV: *It Plays For Him*
## 1989 - 1994


"Yo! MTV Raps" was launched in 1989, marking rap music's arrival in the mainstream. Mick did not care for the melody-less genre. (Try to hum a rap song... seriously... try it.) He also opposed spoken, sung or printed word that condones violence or disrespectful behavior. Meanwhile, he continued to play his brand of music, performing six songs on Mountain Stage Public Radio, including *Ramblin' Blues* and *Please Send Me Someone To Love*.

One evening while relaxing at home, Mick answered the telephone. Introducing himself in a Texas accent as Barbara Lucher's son, Joe announced with affecting resolve, "You're my Dad." He was speaking the truth. In 1965, Mick and Barbara had ended up together following Mick's performance at her club in Houston. She would, however, not let on that Mick was the father until 16 years had passed in the boy's life. Now a young man of 24, he wished to meet dad and dad wished to meet son. And so, Mick and Susan brought Joe from Texas to Oregon.

They immediately enrolled him in a local technical school and helped him to repay a $10,000 debt. "Susan was more than understanding," Mick proudly stated. "She became a second mother to Joe and did everything possible to help and support him." Responsibility was accepted - not only because it was the right thing to do - but also because they wanted to assist Joe. Mick was proud of all his children.

Mick returned to the Birchmere in Alexandria, Virginia on June 16, his third and final engagement there. Having played the venue with Guy Clark (1986) and Marie Rhines (1988), he shared the stage this time with Jesse Winchester. Born in Shreveport and raised in Memphis - like many young Americans - Jesse had held personal distaste for U.S. Government policies on the Vietnam War. And so to avoid the draft, he moved to Montreal, Quebec in 1967. He was able to return to the United States a decade later when draft dodgers were granted amnesty. Jesse and Mick performed over two evenings at the Birchmere, putting on separate sets.

In October, Mick played The Sweetwater Saloon in Mill Valley, located eleven miles and one bridge from downtown San Francisco. David Grossman opened for Mick and remembered, "Don Burnham, my roommate at the time said it was going to change my life, and it did. I have never seen a solo performer since or before who moved me more."

Following the Sweetwater gig, Mick played the Bread & Roses Festival at the Greek Theater in Berkeley. Founded in 1974 by Mimi Farina, Joan Baez' sister, Bread & Roses is a Marin County based organization that brings light and music into prisons, hospitals and nursing homes. "Mickey was a lifetime supporter of Bread & Roses," Marty Hall explained. "I can remember seeing here and there in his studio congratulatory letters and awards given him by the organization. He opened the '89 show, playing his then-rare MIDI Photon guitar with orchestral sound effects. As it turns out, the same section of highway we took to get from the airport to the venue collapsed shortly afterwards in the earthquake (of October 17) affecting the Bay Area."

"At the festival it was obvious that Mickey was respected by virtually everyone in the business... Boz Skaggs, Bonnie Raitt, Graham Nash, David Crosby, Jennifer Warnes and others were there and all of them paid homage in one way or another to Mickey. Kris Kristofferson performed too, and Mickey made special effort to introduce us. The affection between them was obvious and warm." Years later, Mick would tell the author, "I just wish Kris and I had been able to spend more time together. We were just really close."

Mick returned home following the shows, and Marty recalled "one freaky night" in November. "Mickey asked me to bring some equipment up to his studio in Vida to help him assemble a tape for Howard Thompson, whom Mickey had known from his days at Elektra. It was one of those nights the Eugene Chamber of Commerce hates to admit constitutes the majority of our Novembers, with horizontal rain and 35 degrees."

"Virtually everything went wrong in our studio efforts, starting with spilling coffee into the mixing console. We played back the master tape from one deck and recorded the output of that deck into the input of Mickey's Nakamichi cassette recorder, which had a feature allowing us to monitor the output amplitude as we recorded. Essentially we were listening to and seeing the finished tape as we were recording, just as Howard would be listening to it in New York in a couple of days."

"At long last, we finished the recording at about 11 PM. Through an abundance of caution, we decided to listen to the finished tape all the way through just to make sure everything was okay for Howard, and then things really got freaky. We turned on the machine, and there was dead silence. Yes, the tape was completely blank, even though we had seen and heard the same tape playback just minutes before. Blank, that is, until the very last phrase of the very last of the four songs on the tape."

"The last tune was *Old Friends*, which ends with the words, 'That's all I have to say.' So what we had was a tape, which was utterly silent for 20 minutes and then has Mickey singing, 'That's all I have to say.' Well, that was about all Mickey and I had to say for the evening, too. On the way out, we noticed that my digital watch and the clock in Mickey's studio had gone backwards one hour. Mickey said stuff like this happened to him all the time. Not to me. It was a freaky night, and I was very glad to get it over and done."

Working with Mick's equipment was always an adventure. "When I met Mickey," continued Marty, "his studio was populated with a Synthaxe - a netherwordly prehistoric version of a MIDI guitar. Soon followed a hot-rod Kurzweil K250, and then another hot-rod Kurzweil 250. The term 'hot-rod' used to describe any Mickey Newbury instrument is redundant, for each and every instrument ever used by Mickey Newbury was immediately altered, modified or in some way Mickey-fied such that it would not work easily in any other setting whatsoever. We went through stand-alone sequencers, drum machines, sound modules, effect synthesizers, and then we embarked upon computer-based sequencers. Mickey was quite eclectic, never more so than with respect to curious items of recording gear."

On April 26, 1990, Wesley Rose, the major force in Nashville music publishing for four decades, died at age 72. Shortly thereafter, Mamie's second husband, Harry Crawford, died with lung cancer in Houston. "He passed away so young," she said, "and only seven and one half years after our marriage... It was such a sad situation." As Mamie's heart was breaking, her silver-haired firstborn hit the big five-o.

Meanwhile, Mick flew to Orlando, Florida, to put on a TNN TV special at the Cheyenne Saloon and Opry House. Dressed in sharp black suit and silk tie and escorted by two beautiful bodyguards, he arrived at Nashville Network's "Church Street Station" by elegant horse-drawn carriage. He opened the program with a rousing *Wish I Was*, and then introducing *Sweet Memories*, stated, "Please buy it. I've got five children and they need the money." Wrapping it up with a warm reading of *America The Beautiful*, Mick suggested the song would fare well as America's second national anthem. It is an unambiguous testament to his modest nature to begin the presentation with "A grain of sand is all I ever wanted to be" and end it with, "God shed his grace on thee." While the man was performing with panache and humility, *Vogue* by Madonna - flamboyance without humility - peaked at Number One.

After the touring was done, Mick was happy to return home. Daughter Laura Shayne remembers going to the airport to meet his plane: "I can still

215

see him walking towards me. He always carried himself in a way that even a stranger would stop to watch him pass by. Such confidence intertwined with such humility. His pace always quickened when he saw me."

**ALBUM # 16** Best Of Mickey Newbury (Curb D2-77455) contains the following songs: 1. An American Trilogy 2. Danny Boy 3. Blue Sky Shinin' 4. Makes Me Wonder If I Ever Said Goodbye 5. Shenandoah 6. She Even Woke Me Up To Say Goodbye 7. Ain't No Blues Today 8. Sunshine 9. Hand Me Another Of Those 10. It Just Doesn't Matter Anymore 11. Gone To Alabama 12. Any Way You Want Me.

Mickey was never paid royalties on this 1991 album, reportedly unauthorized from Curb Productions. Chairman and Founder, Mike Curb had formerly served as President of MGM Records and producer of the Osmond Brothers. Though it did bring fans a few new songs, as a "Best Of" collection, the release is a terrible misrepresentation.

The music industry by this time had become a textbook model of macroeconomics, statistical probability and bell curves. Epitomizing created demand, Garth Brooks released "No Fences," the first country album to go multi-platinum. Based on produced, as opposed to achieved, success of artists such as Garth and Madonna, stockholders and venture capitalists in the music industry seemed to be marching to R.O.I. Their Piper had become the only corporate goal, Return On Investment. The five-year focus was on maximizing profit, not in developing talent. If a commercially successful work happened to be artistic, it was coincidental; as art is by nature, subjective, and never part of a business plan, by nature, objective. Newbury and oeuvre didn't fit the bill. He would not join a march of dimes and he would not acquiesce to "friends" in low places.

Evidently, he was no longer a priority in Acuff-Rose's business plan. As Mick had grown tired of the firm's passive to listless marketing of his catalog, he was self-publishing his songs. Why split the pot with a partner who stacks the deck and fails to ante up? Newbury eventually tired of turning the proverbial cheek.

Still, as clichéd as it may sound, Mickey was a dyed-in-the-wool practitioner of the Golden Rule. He had become friends with Eugene's Nic Knievel, brother of America's legendary daredevil, Evel. A concert organizer and owner of a recording label, Nic introduced him to local resident Karen Schaal, a singer / songwriter who went by Tess Turner as a stage name. Shortly after that, at Nic's request, they went into the studio to work on her album.

216

Released on the NJK Knievel label, "Merry Merry Christmas" contains 14 traditional holiday tunes. The CD was recorded at Pacific Media Production, mixed at Bill Barnett's Gung Ho Studios in Eugene (October 27-29) and engineered by Michael Edwards. Vocals are credited to Turner and to her "special guest star, Mickey Newbury," who sings on four numbers. Mick added his vocal overdubs in his home studio.

The album begins with the title track, *Merry Merry Christmas*, an R&B doo-wop piece written by Turner, which she and Mick perform as a rockin' duet. (Years later, the song would enjoy a classical remix with acoustic guitars, violins and crashing drums.) They continue trading lines on the bluesy *Have Yourself A Merry Little Christmas* and the shocker of the set, *Stille Nacht / Silent Night*. With roots from the Old Country, Tess delivers the opening and closing verses to *Stille Nacht* in German, while Mick reverently lifts up the middle part: "Silent night, holy night / Shepherds quake at the sight / Glorious stream from heaven afar / Heavenly hosts sing alleluia / Christ the savior is born / Christ the savior is born." It is astonishing how magnificently Newbury performs the passage, changing enunciation to fit the mood, from plain-speaking Texan to highbrow Englishman. He sings the song operatically and passionately, soaring in the multi-octave style of a world-class tenor.

His only solo outing here is a heartfelt reading of *O Christmas Tree*, an ancient carol that first appeared in Germany during the Middle Ages as *O Tannenbaum*. Though countless lyrical versions exist, the selected lines feel like a Newbury piece of music: "Your boughs are green in summer's glow / Do not fade in winter snow..."

The album's cover shot shows a fair-haired Tess, a pretty woman who looks a bit like Judy Collins. Her voice is suited to warm ballads, as made crystal clear on *Silver Bells* and *Stille Nacht*. Since she included a few songs in German and a few up-tempo polka interpretations, the album was aggressively marketed in the "German Athens" of the USA - Milwaukee, Wisconsin. Few Newbury fans are familiar with the exceptionally rare collection, a Yuletide treat for sure.

"The CD was done quickly," Tess explained, "because we were on a limited budget and Christmas was just around the corner. Unfortunately Mickey got sick; otherwise he would have performed on more songs. He taught me many things in the brief time we worked together... He taught me never to use the word 'yes' in lyrics... He had the incredible ability to take *Mary Had A Little Lamb* and turn it into a masterpiece. (In the CD liner notes, Tess thanked Mickey and added, 'With you, 1 + 1 = 3!') But most importantly, he was always very, very sweet. Even after our project was done, he would call me out of the blue just to say hello."

217

In November, Mick appeared in Nashville at Owsley Manier's Exit/In and at 12ᵗʰ and Porter - a gig opened by Rudy McNeely. Playing the Photon-midi rig, Mick performed *Poison Red Berries, Just Dropped In, 'Frisco Depot, Lie To Me Darlin', Good Morning Dear* and *She Even Woke Me Up To Say Goodbye.*

Even though his new songs were not being released, Mick was still composing. When daughter Leah was 14, she wrote, "His head bowed over that bent piece of wood, and he reminded me of a child with his favorite toy. He plucked out notes here and there and, after about a minute and a half, had shaped it into an elegant, haunted tune. He always had the talent to do that. As I sat and watched my father hover over that guitar, he seemed suddenly so old, and yet, at the same time, younger than myself. I listened, and something was different; his voice seemed a stranger and yet, at the same time, the golden tone was so familiar."

"The moment froze and we were both caught in time... daddy and me. His eager blue eyes peered out at me over a pair of cheap reading glasses that were perched on the end of his nose, and he winked. When he sang, deep lines etched the outer corners of his tightly shut eyes and his mouth, which was partially covered by the shadow of gray whiskers grown a few weeks earlier. The melody filled the room, enveloping me in sound and intertwining with the musky scent of 'Old Spice' and cigarette smoke. I sat and inhaled the pure genius of my surroundings. Every couple of measures, he would glance up at me to make sure that I was still listening, and to search my face for a reaction. It seemed that with one harsh gesture I could crush his enthusiasm like an autumn leaf. He was so sensitive to criticism. His forehead creased deeply as he stumbled over a few lines, which he quickly rewrote, and then regained rhythm, that quickly, that easily."

"Everyone needs a hero. He is mine. He lacks in some things, but one thing my father does not lack is love and wisdom. He has done what few have managed; he has mastered music, and it plays for him. He is far from famous, but who needs the world's recognition when the appreciation lies within your own four walls?"

**VIDEO** Don Dortch interviewed Mickey in 1992, and the session became part of "A Songwriter's Seminar," a VHS commercial video featuring songwriting comments from Newbury and Hank Cochran, Steve Cropper, Harlan Howard and Max D. Barnes. The 55-minute video presents a relaxed and gray-bearded Newbury offering sage advice to aspiring writers.

In the fall, Mickey performed at a special benefit concert in Eugene. The goal was to raise money to purchase a custom fitted vehicle for local resident Linda Robeson, who had been injured in a skiing accident at Williamette Pass. Organized by Nic Knievel, the event was staged at the Hult Center for Performing Arts. As show time approached, Nic fell under the weather, so Marty Hall took the bull by the horns, assuming responsibility for the event. Tess Turner and local artists opened the show, and then Mickey performed a stirring set. Former Miss. Oregon and ex New Christy Minstrel Susan Newbury sang a song, too.

Sad news arrived on October 25 when Roger Miller died of throat cancer at age 56. A week later, his wife Mary (a former member of Kenny Rogers and the First Edition) held a memorial service for him at a place Roger knew well, the Ryman Auditorium in Nashville. A few days later - on October 30 - Acuff-Rose celebrated its golden anniversary, and then three weeks later, the firm's co-founder and Opry star... King of Country Music... Roy Acuff passed away. Acuff would be featured on a postage stamp in 2003 - the centennial anniversary of his birth in Maynardsville, Tennessee.

To commemorate Acuff-Rose's half century in business and loss of its founders, Opryland Music Group released a double CD with 51 songs. The 1992 "Anniversary Collection" included three Newbury songs: *Sweet Memories* performed by Mick, *An American Trilogy* performed by Elvis and *Just Dropped In* performed by Kenny Rogers and T.F.E. Only Orbison had more songs included, with four. Oddly, Opryland chose Mick's '68 rendition of *Sweet Memories* from the RCA period, rather than the superior '73 recording from "Heaven Help The Child." This is, however, the sole domestic CD release of Newbury's '68 material. The set also includes performances by Don Gibson, Patsy Cline, Patti Page, Willie Nelson, Marty Robbins, Ricky Nelson, Fats Domino, the Everly Brothers and many others. Songs in the "Anniversary Collection" are outstanding and substantiate lyrics from a 1993 Uncle Tupelo tune: "Name me a song that everybody knows / And I'll bet you it belongs to Acuff-Rose."

Mickey next performed four songs - most notably *Genevieve* - at the Frank Brown Songwriters Festival in Gulf Shores, and the performances would be released in a cassette compilation. The Songwriters Festival draws thousands of people and is a ten-day happening, beginning on the first Thursday in November. It is "dedicated to the real architect of the music industry, the songwriter." Owned by Mick's good friend, Joe Gilchrist, the Flora-Bama serves as de facto headquarters for the event. Half the lounge is situated in Perdido Key, Florida and the other half is in Alabama. "Just inside the front door, a vending machine dispenses cigarettes, candy - and guitar strings."

219

Guitarist Jack Williams met Mickey at the festival, respectfully describing him as "the complete performer." Ross Jaburg interviewed Williams and wrote, "These people (at the festival) lean on each other and feed from each other. They write together and there is cohesion among people here. There are probably close to a hundred songwriters within a few miles of this place tonight, and the comment, 'This is the way Nashville used to be,' is heard occasionally. The atmosphere here just seems to inspire collaboration and inspiration. About halfway through the festival, Newbury told me, 'I've written two songs since I got here, one with Hank (Cochran) and another with Bertie Higgins on the phone.'"

Mickey was back in the saddle again. For three decades, he had yearned for the artistic camaraderie of Nashville in the Sixties. He loved mentoring artists, especially younger ones. His altruistic actions helped make Gulf Shores in the Nineties a representation of Paris in the Twenties. "If it weren't for Mickey and his music," Gilchrist said, "none of this would be the same, neither the Flora-Bama nor the Frank Brown Songwriters Festival." Plus Mick loved the area's beaches, climate and delicious seafood... especially oysters-on-the-half shell.

During Mick's Flora-Bama show, a Green Beret Vietnam Veteran began heckling him, advising the audience he was "going to kick Newbury's ass." (To quiet the non-confrontational rowdy or run-of-the-mill drunk, Mick would ask the soundman to turn Mick and guitar down; until eventually... the audience would ask the obnoxious one to hush.) Man-to-man, Mick coldly informed the Beret at intermission, "I've known many tough men, but I've never known one tough enough to swat down a .44 slug." The Beret behaved from then on, and Newbury bought him a drink.

A contradiction exists between Newbury's comment to the heckler and an earlier statement that he opposed spoken, sung or printed word that condoned violence. Granted... he was aware of the conflict, concomitantly holding abhorrence for and fascination with violence. He experienced his lion's share of brutality during the teenage years, explaining, "I grew up in a knot 'cause I hated to fight... I hated violence, yet it came automatic. If I hadn't dropped out I might of killed somebody. I was so paranoid that I had gotten a pistol... I became my own psychiatrist." Mickey traveled with a pistol during later years and was able to mask the paranoia, but it was there.

> *I put my dangerous feelings under lock and chain*
> *Killed my violent nature with a smile*
> *Though the demons danced and sing their songs*
> *Within my fevered brain*
> *All my God-like thoughts are not defiled*
> *THE THIRTY-THIRD OF AUGUST*

A few months after the Flora-Bama gig, the Great Flood of '93 would leave thousands of Midwest families homeless. River levels set 100-year to 500-year records. The result was catastrophic flooding along a nine-state area of the upper Mississippi. In all, 17 million acres were inundated, causing $12 billion in damages and 48 deaths.

*That river is no stranger*
*It's anger knows no bounds*
*Honey there's a big storm comin'*
*Gather up the children*
*Head for higher ground*
*A STORM IS COMIN'*

The Farm Aid organization was there to help farm owners, and Mickey did his part, traveling to Ames, Iowa, to perform at Farm Aid VI. The eleven-hour show was a reunion among several longtime Newbury friends including cofounder Willie Nelson and fellow Highwaymen, Johnny Cash, Waylon Jennings and Kris Kristofferson. Townes Van Zandt was there, too. Other performers included six-time veteran Neil Young, Bryan Adams, Bruce Hornsby, Dwight Yoakam, Ringo Starr, Sawyer Brown, Merle Haggard, Arlo Guthrie, John Mellencamp, Martina McBride, Alice In Chains, Charlie Daniels Band, Asleep At The Wheel, Roger Clinton (the President's brother) and Tom and Roseanne Arnold - who performed the theme song from "Green Acres." Roughly 36,000 people attended the nationally televised event, at Iowa State University's Cyclone Stadium on April 24. Covering the benefit, the July '93 issue of US magazine featured a hilarious picture of Mickey giving Lyle Lovett a kiss.

At the last minute, Mickey agreed to tour England with Texan Don Williams. The two men had met in Nashville in 1969, when Newbury was one of the hottest songwriters in town and Williams worked as a staff writer for Jack Clement and was just getting started as a solo act. During the seventies, Williams became the most popular country singer in the world with 17 number one hits including *Amanda, Tulsa Time* and *Some Broken Hearts Never Mend.* In 1980, he was voted Artist of the Decade by England's Country Music People.

Throughout the 21-day tour - sponsored by the UK Division of Acuff-Rose - Newbury opened, coughing between songs and continually using an inhaler. Though Williams was worried about Mick's health, Mick sang beautifully. Long time fan Tracey Godley was there and wrote, Mickey "stole the show for us and so many people..." Country Music And More wrote, "I once saw Mickey in concert as opening act to Don Williams and he made Don look *as if he was on speed!* As a performer he was one of those artists who you had to sit and listen to. No big production, no flamboyant show - just these rather special songs... From the seventies up until today... he is probably the only songwriter who could guarantee to have a song played at any C&W festival / event in Britain."

During the troupe's stop in the city of York, Mick asked writer Al Moir to accompany him on a "five-minute sound check" in an empty 2000-seat auditorium. Moir was in for a surprise. "Mickey sang and played for a full 90 minutes to an audience of one. Eventually, he had to leave the stage because the audience was clamoring at the doors. When I asked him why he had honored me with such a performance, he replied, seriously, 'I would rather sing for one person who is listening than be played for a million who are not.'" Perhaps Mick was playing for ghosts of decades past. While stationed in England 30 years earlier, he frequently visited the historic garden city of York. In 1998, songs from the UK tour would be culled to make a Newbury album. About the time he returned home, Susan received a Master's Degree from the University of Oregon.

1994 kicked off as Ryman Auditorium reopened as an entertainment venue, and in July, Mick happily reunited with good friend Kris Kristofferson. They played songs and golf at a Squaw Valley, California resort, and Mick said, "He assumed I'd quit writing, so I played him about 40 new songs... I believe Kris will write a great book before he dies. He has prepared his entire life to do so. (Reportedly, Kristofferson is working on his memoirs, tentatively to be published by Hyperion in 2005.) If he was not married to Lisa... and I not to Susan... I would fight him for her... and whip his old ass. I love his mother-in-law almost as much." But Mick and Susan were married and happily celebrated their silver wedding anniversary.

**MOVIE** Though never payed for his bit part, Mickey appeared in "Skins" - aka "Gang Boys" - starring producer Wings Hauser and Linda Blair. The movie deals with a dysfunctional family that through a hate crime finds love again. Mickey played a crazy street preacher and had his hair dyed white. Hobbling across a Hollywood street at night - cane in one hand, bible raised in the other - Reverend Newbury scream-preaches the word of the New Testament, Matthew 5:39 and 5:44:

"Love your enemies! Do good unto those who would curse you! Pray for those who would wish you ill will! He is coming! If a man slaps you on the cheek (here he slaps his face hard), turn your other cheek! Listen to me brothers! For how could I know beauty without having first known ugliness? How could I know the light without having walked in the darkness? Yes brothers, listen to me if you have ears. He is coming!"

Now across the street, Newbury turns his attention to a man leaning on a streetlamp, eating a sandwich.

*Newbury:* "What do you think brother? I don't believe he's ever left here."
*Man:* "Brother all I've got is a cold cheeseburger and a sore ass from riding the Greyhound all night. OK? I ain't got no money!"
*Newbury:* "I don't want your money. Just a few kind words."
*Man:* "You want a kind word? Hollywood. God bless you."

Better lines could not have been scripted for his role. Friends know he was a religious man... not fire and brimstone, verse and chapter, but in a way that can be described as spiritually perceptive. He made many mistakes but did his best to live by his priorities - God, family and friends. In a world intoxicated by celebrity, Hollywood starlet Terry Moore said she, "didn't know anyone who worked harder at not being a star than Mickey." Marty Hall concurred, "I never saw Mickey not be completely humble."

Indeed, some of his best performances were offstage. "If I wanted to make money," he proclaimed, "I could have been a preacher. I'd a made more money than any television preacher alive... because I'm not only a student of the bible, but I can write songs and sing songs... You know I could have been the richest preacher that ever walked this earth... But we all got to die one of these days... And you better be a good preacher you know." Newbury's idea of a good preacher? "There's not a hair's difference between Billy Graham and somebody laying in an alley, and Billy Graham knows that. When I met him, I was prepared to not like him because most famous people are in it for the money. But he was an impressive man."

"I occasionally speak to God... occasionally every other hour. I never ask for anything but his blessing and the wisdom to be the vessel he intended. I have no fear of death because I am certain you cannot kill a Christian. If every soul in the world wants to live his or her life in doubt and fear... have at it! We all have the freedom of our will. I will not... will not... be afraid... Many people who go to church are afraid to die. I'm not."

> *Sunday morning found him lyin'...*
> *SAN FRANCISCO MABEL JOY*

To illustrate the point, Newbury wrote a reply to the author's expressed fear of flying: "It has been my observation... most folks go through life fearing the very things... in probability, that will never touch them. 'Death' or our departure from this... at times... most difficult life is God's plan for a better life and yet... is looked on as something to fear. Faith is the only answer... Faith in something we cannot see. It is difficult... I cannot see the radio wave but I know without a doubt it exists... The proof... I have heard the radio. So... when someone tells you they will worship only what they can see... pity them, their ignorance, for what is unseen is just as real and... at times... ALL that is Real. Have faith, for nothing on this earth but your fear can harm you."

*LEAD ON I will follow*
*Although my wayward ship be tossed and rolled*
*I will find no shelter from this troubled sea*
*No other place on earth to save my soul*

During the author's visit to Mickey's home in Springfield, he demonstrated "how energy flows between people." At a distance of one foot, he asked me to look him straight in the eyes. He gazed at me with one eye for a few seconds and both eyes suddenly. When he turned full vision directly on me, the energy flow was immediate and intense. Mick explained his view that people are "on different frequencies" and one's frequency is transmitted by this energy. We can however be on the same wavelength as another person, man or woman, and this serves as a basic explanation of soul mate. The Radioman explained this is how prayer works - how Jesus hears everyone - sort of like a spiritual, wideband radio transceiver. The proposition that thought travels is not a novel concept. The narrative, though, illustrates how Newbury dug deeper into established hypotheses.

*Starin' out the window all I wish is*
*I could hear the words I'm hearin' in my head*
*THE SAILOR*

*I know your sorrow I know your pain I know your need*
*THE FUTURE'S NOT WHAT IT USED TO BE*

*I wish that I*
*Could not read her mind*
*And see all her pain*
*HOW MANY TIMES MUST THE PIPER BE PAID FOR HIS SONG*

**ALBUM # 17** Nights When I Am Sane (Winter Harvest WH 3301-2) contains the following songs: 1. Just Dropped In... 2. The 33$^{rd}$ Of August 3. East Kentucky 4. Nights When I Am Sane 5. Heaven Help The Child 6. Genevieve 7. Easy Street 8. Apples Dipped In Candy 9. You're My Lady Now 10. San Francisco Mabel Joy 11. Earthquake 12. Saint Cecilia 13. Four Ladies 14. What Will I Do.

"Nights" was Mickey's first live album since "Montezuma," 21 years earlier. The 1994 album was one of his least favorites ranking up there - or down there - with the RCA atrocities. Mick was joined by lead guitarist Jack Williams, a man Peter Yarrow - of Peter, Paul and Mary - describes as "the best guitarist I've ever heard." Coincidentally, Jack once backed up The Coasters; and in 1957, The Embers opened for them. Newbury said, "Jack was a bass player in a rock band in his earlier days. I believe Jack could play anything he chose to. He is an arranger... and piano player to boot. Also a fair road warrior... and all around good guy." Mickey and Bob Rosemurgy met at this Nashville concert, which was recorded live in Nashville's Hermitage Ballroom on March 12, 1994.

"Catie and I were standing in the lobby," Rosemurgy remembered, "when the elevator opened and Mickey walked out carrying his guitar. I said 'hi' and he said 'hi.' He said, 'I'm Mickey Newbury.' I said, 'I'm Bob Rosemurgy.' He said, "Are you the lawyer?' I said 'Yes.' That was the start of what became a dear friendship and a most interesting period in my life."

"Rosemurgy called in November of '93," explained Owsley Manier. "I said I've given up on getting Mickey a 'real' record deal... Gonna start a little label. So he (Rosemurgy) was our first stockholder, and his investment paid for the recording of 'Nights' and the video taping." Rosemurgy is a successful Escanaba, Michigan attorney whose practice areas include civil litigation, product liability, medical malpractice, commercial litigation, wrongful death and trial law. "He's one tough lawyer," Mick said. "They call him Ayatollah Of The Midwest." He is also a lover of Newbury's music, having been a huge fan since the early seventies.

The name "Winter Harvest" was Mick's idea. Marty Hall remembered, "What kicked off the label was Steve Earle's agreement to record 'Train a Comin' for Winter Harvest, this reportedly as a personal favor to Mickey for 'being there' for Steve in darker days in Steve's life... (Son of an air traffic controller, Steve met Mick at Guy Clark's house in Nashville, as Steve was making his first tape.) What ultimately emerged was an impossible-to-foresee set of very fruitful relationships with Bob Rosemurgy, Paula Wolak, Jack Williams and Michael Charles McDonald."

"Steve Earle," Rosemurgy continued, "was very young when Mickey was in Nashville... Mickey knew him and liked him. They didn't have any contact in later years, just due to distance and careers not for any personal reasons... In one of life's ironies, Mickey and a few others started Winter Harvest. Mickey's 'Nights' was the first label release. The second was Steve's 'Train a Comin,' which revived Steve's career. I know Steve wasn't all that thrilled with his time on the label and left to start his own (E2), but the label got him back on his feet and recording / touring and performing again. So Mickey had a big part in that."

**VIDEO** Nights When I Am Sane (Winter Harvest WH 3301-3) is a film of the "Nights" concert. Mick hated the way his hair looked. After the movie "Skins," he could not get the white dye out, so he had his hair cut short and dyed brown. This was his look when the video was made, and Jack Williams would tease him about the "orange hair." After the harsh treatment of his tresses, according to Mamie, "His hair never came back like it originally was."

On September 18, Mickey performed at the Ace of Clubs in Nashville, where he "alternated cigarettes with an inhaler all night long." Like Chap Stick, the inhaler had become a regular fixture, necessary as the coughing fits had intensified. Obviously he was ill, though the severity of the illness was not known.

During the trip, Mickey appeared on "Nashville Now" with special guest host, Waylon Jennings. Introducing him, Waylon quipped, "If you don't like to hear Mickey Newbury sing, you're not American." Mick stole the show with wonderful readings of *An American Trilogy* and *Genevieve...* leading Waylon to exclaim... "You see why I wanted him on the show!"

Some Time in the early 70.s

*Mickey Newbury*

East Kentucky threads of willow
down a red, railroad track
dusty highway take me to Denver
I will not be comin back

to the mountains of Colorado
like a bandit I did run
but the beauty of the mountain
could not undo what I had done

East Kentucky I knew your daughter
in the early mornin rain
in the shelter of the tall pine
I did love her with no shame

**Mick's handwritten lyrics to *East Kentucky***
**(His name did not appear originally; he autographed it as a gift.)**

228

At the Flora-Bama, 1997

**Immediately following Mick's final performance at the Flora-Bama, he hugs Mary Anne Potter, while his proud Mama looks on.**

# Chapter XVI: *Lulled By The Web*
## 1995 - 1999

In early 1995, Mickey was diagnosed with pulmonary fibrosis, a nasty disease similar to emphysema. Most pf patients first suffer from alveolitis, an inflammation that scars the lung. Once scarring sets in, medications can do little to help. Symptoms include continual cough and breathlessness, a vicious cycle leading to depression. Breathlessness reduces the ability to exercise, causing patients to become deconditioned. Being depressed and deconditioned lower the ability to fight back. This is a devastating disease that grows worse daily.

"Mickey always had respiratory problems," Mamie stated, "and should never have taken up the cigarette habit. But in those days, we didn't know they were so dangerous. In fact they allowed them smoke breaks when he was in the service." This was a nightmare of the most horrible kind for Mick's mom, who had already endured the loss of two husbands. "Newbury men," Mickey explained, "are like comets. We burn brightly but not for long."

At 55, he was distressed by the news. Mickey wanted to see his children grow up, and he longed to grow old with Susie. He was concerned over the ongoing ability to pursue his craft and the long-term effect on the family's finances. Symptoms would make it difficult to focus on songwriting and difficult - as well as painful - to sing. Consequently, his livelihood was seriously jeopardized when retirement was just around the corner and Leah was deciding on a college. How Mickey would face the music speaks volumes of his character. Most anyone can sparkle in the sunshine, but true character is illustrated by how one copes with stormy weather. And Newbury's train had just entered the ultimate storm.

> *Yesterday's newspaper forecast no rain for today*
> *But yesterday's news is old news the skies are all gray*
> *ANGELINE*

One stormy actor loved Newbury's train songs, especially "In A New Age," and so Sean Penn arranged for Mickey to perform at the opening of his new nightclub in Santa Monica. There had been, Marty Hall explained, "Previous contact between Sean and Mickey and discussion about Mickey providing music for one or more of Sean's movies." Evidently, he wanted to use *Just Dropped In* for "The Crossing Guard" with Jack Nicholsen, but a Springsteen cut was selected instead. "However, Mickey did agree to open Sean's club for him, and Mickey asked me to join him in Los Angeles. By this time Mickey needed some assistance."

"Owsley (Manier) was there to deal with the house sound, so that left Mickey and me to hang out, which we did. I ran a few errands for Mickey and then dropped him off at his hotel. He was booked into the hotel at the beach called The Shutters (Mick said the hotel - booked by Sean - 'must have cost $5,000 a night') and he was having trouble breathing. It was a very smoggy L.A. week, and Mickey was having to use his oxygen and albuteral treatment equipment more and more frequently, and he needed time to rest. Before I left him, Mickey casually handed me a cassette tape of some rhythm tracks he had been working on in Nashville, asking me to take a listen and let him know what I thought of the tracks. I hugged him and took off, mired in traffic possible nowhere else in the world except at the intersection of Highways 101 and 405."

"The tape Mickey had given me was very interesting and good. And then, buried in the tape, track 13 cued up and an oddly familiar chord progression fired up... Mickey's voice lamenting, 'I saw myself in the mirror just the other day...' Well I just about wrecked the car! He was singing my song, *Twenty Years And Sweet Dreams Ago*, and which I had no idea he had recorded. What a shock!"

"In 1989 I had written *Twenty Years* and taken it to Mickey for criticism and discussion. (The song was inspired by their friend, Carl Gay, of the singing group, The Kimberlies.) By the time Mickey heard the third verse, he stopped the cassette and asked me if I had been reading his mail. He congratulated me on 'getting it,' and he liked it enough to send a copy of the finished demo to Kenny Rogers with a personal letter recommending that Kenny record the song. Mickey commented to me he felt a bit miffed that Kenny did not even acknowledge receiving the package, although we are certain that he did receive the package."

"In any event, there I was, stuck in L.A. traffic in sweet shock that Mickey had recorded *Twenty Years* with the apparent intention to include it on a future CD. I cannot describe with any accuracy the feeling of that moment, which is exactly how Mickey intended me to feel... The fact that something I did mattered personally and artistically to my hero Mickey means more than I can say."

"That evening my best friend, Timothy Drury and I went to Sean's club, arriving about an hour before the official opening. I went to the back room, knowing that is where I would find Sean and Mickey. I walked right past Sean and immediately hugged Mickey, who had a smile the likes of which I have not seen before or since. I have never seen him happier. He only said three things to me, 'Got 'cha, Babe.' You know, I wouldn't have recorded your song unless I thought it stood up as art. I nodded with teary eyes. Then he said, 'I love you.'"

"And that was it. Sean, whom we had ignored during this very personal exchange, took Mickey by the shoulder and conducted him out of the little room and into the crowded club, which was like something out of a novel. There were many people from eastern big cities all decked out in furs and jewels, and there were stars everywhere you looked. I can remember seeing Jon Voight, John Travolta, Rebecca DeMornay, Kevin Spacey, Robin Wright Penn, Quentin Tarrantino and Harry Dean Stanton, and many familiar faces I cannot connect with names."

"The sound system was not good, and Mickey could not hear himself sing. Nor could the crowd hear him sing, and that made Sean mad enough that at one point he stood up before the crowd and asked everyone to quiet down to listen more closely to Mickey. The club's opening was a success, even if it were something less than Mickey's best and favorite live performance. It was, however, a night to remember."

About then, Townes Van Zandt played his last gig on the opposite coast. While he performed at the Bottom Line in New York, Tejano star Selena was murdered in Corpus Christi - the same city in which Bill Haley had died. Selena had been born in Lake Jackson, 50 miles south of Houston, and her posthumous "Dreaming of You" became the first Tejano album to reach number one in the United States. Meanwhile, <u>No Depression</u> hit newsstands. The magazine of the "alternative-country" music movement would feature many excellent articles on Newbury.

**ALBUM # 18** Lulled By The Moonlight (Mountain Retreat) contains the following songs: 1. Three Bells for Stephen 2. East Kentucky 3. Captured In Blue 4. Just Another Lovely Day 5. Blue Sky Shining 6. Freight Train Howlin' 7. Shades of '63 8. Amen for Old Friends 9. Genevieve 10. Sailor Sailor 11. What Will I Do (In The Dead of the Night) 12. Ramblin' Blues 13. Workin' Man 14. The Future Is Not What It Used To Be 15. Time Was 16. Silver Moon 17. Safe Harbor.

Mountain Retreat was formed by Mickey to serve as his music production and distribution company. The label's first release, "Lulled by The Moonlight," was limited to 2000 CDs and autographed. Recorded at the Record Club in Nashville, the 1996 album is dedicated to Mick's hero, Stephen Foster, "Father of American Songwriters," and to the memory of Don Gant, "Foster Father of Nashville Songwriters." Foster's influence on

Newbury may be heard in several songs, such as *Three Bells for Stephen* and *I Still Love You After All These Years*.

Newbury's first new studio album in eight years was mixed in one night, and the cover was done in one day. Mick sold it out of his house, and his phone number was listed in the liner notes. Flora-Bama owner and good friend Joe Gilchrist served as Executive Producer, and he helped by selling the album at the Flora-Bama. Paula Wolak served as main producer, receiving assistance from Jack Williams on tracks 12-14. Mickey wrote all songs except *Captured In Blue* (co-written with Williams), *Freight Train Howlin'* (co-written with martial arts expert Rudy McNeely) and *Silver Moon* (Toni Jolene Clay/J. Weatherly).

Highlights include tracks 2-3, 9 and 11-15. Mickey wrote *East Kentucky* in the early seventies just before leaving Nashville; and influenced by those circumstances, the gripping stunner concludes with the lines, "Dusty highway take me to Denver / I will not be coming back." The ballad *Genevieve* is painted with broad, beautiful strokes and is one of Mick's most poignant offerings. In September of 1994, he performed it live on "Nashville Now," as co-guest Connie Smith - sitting alongside - listened adorningly. Her facial expression said it all: Respect. Connie was visibly moved by the song and looked to be on the verge of tears.

Tracks 11-15 flow seamlessly with common mood, texture, measure and transition. As laments over inevitable losses, the songs address obligations met at too high a price and passionate longings for the past. "Matter of fact," Mickey explained, "the album is kind of retrospective of the different periods I went through musically... I mean all the way from my lounge lizard period when I was a kid... The album followed a sequence of events in my life."

Mick had originally recorded *The Future Is Not What It Used To Be* on his 1970 album, but he was 30 at the time, ostensibly young for such a topic. Here at 56 with pulmonary fibrosis, he scream-sings the song, perhaps for the first time completely understanding the self-fulfilled prophecy:

> *Oh the years they went by I went steadily downhill*
> *'Till I had no place left to go*
> *Made the missions by mornin' made the dives every night*
> *Made a wreck of my body and soul*
> *And then I met a lady in time she made me forget*
> *Her love set me free*
> *Oh we don't have a lot but the future is not what it used to be.*

Tragedy struck during the album's production. "I was visiting with Mickey in Perdido Key in '96," Newbury friend Jonmark Stone explained. "Mickey had invited me to be a part of the recording sessions that eventually became 'Lulled By The Moonlight,' and we had a few great days there before we packed up and drove to Tennessee, expecting to be recording for a couple of weeks. I was very concerned about Mickey. His health was obviously failing, and he spoke openly about the fact that his time was limited. He faced his own mortality with so much left to do. We checked into Opryland hotel late, got a night's sleep and headed off to the studio the next morning. Knowing how important these sessions were, my wife had said before I left Florida that she would never call the studio unless there was an emergency."

"We were recording *East Kentucky* when I was told she was on the phone. My father had suffered a massive heart attack in Virginia. Mickey called the session to a complete halt, took me into a back room and didn't leave my side until we knew fully what was happening. Studio time costs money. He also had musicians and two engineers on hold, and yet there was nothing more important to him than my heart. Mickey taught me a lot that day about living and dying. Friendships like that can't be replaced."

Another musician - bass player Roy Vogt - collaborated on the album and declared, "I was fortunate enough to work with Mickey in the studio and contribute to 'Lulled By The Moonlight.' The man was the truest genius and poet I've ever been blessed to work with in Nashville in over 22 years. I hold the opportunity to play with him and to contribute in some small way to his art as high as anything I've done in this town."

At this point, attorney Bob Rosemurgy - Mickey's friend - began running the record company. Bob explained. "I booked a tour for Jack and Mickey in the Midwest (mainly in Michigan or as Mick called it, 'The Frozen Tundra'). I traveled with them and had a ball. The CD 'Lulled By The Moonlight' came out then... and Mickey had no way to sell it. I got his letters from fans and started a mailing list, connected with songs.com for a website, and started running Mountain Retreat. While Mickey was writing and recording, I was selling CDs... I learned the business from talking to Mickey and others and 'on the job' training... I still know very little about that business, other than 95 percent of the people in it do not do what they say they will do. We've done well getting our music out, and we were able to increase our distribution over time. Mick was the Chairman of the Board and I was CEO, while Susan, Kathrine and Peter (all of Mountain Retreat) helped me greatly... He and I talked about three hours a week or so, and about everything. He loved to argue too, especially with a lawyer."

Following the release of "Lulled," Mickey performed with Jack Williams at the Jubilee Arts Theater in Knoxville and then at the Flora-Bama. During one of the shows, Mickey experienced respiratory failure - he stopped breathing - but true to altruistic form, he later expressed concern for a friend, exclaiming: "I gave poor Jack a heart attack!" Mick appreciated Jack's friendship and assistance, acknowledging, "If not for Jack's help... I would never have been able to go back out on the road these past few years."

Jack loved touring with him, too, and wrote, "Touring alone with Mickey is like being Huck Finn on a raft rolling down Big Muddy in the company of a pistol-totin' riverboat gambler who seems to be on the lam, and who has a thousand, non-stop, unbelievable tales to tell - which so often turn out to be true! Playing with Mickey Newbury is like having a small role in the creation of REAL American folklore; every word and note he sings is as true to the American soul as any that have been written or sung: the American Voice singing the American Poetry. I'm a lucky guy to have been chosen to spend time in such inspirational company!" Jack nicknamed him "Jose Mendelez" - a private joke.

When depression from pulmonary fibrosis hit Mick, he reached out electronically, via the virtual dimension known as cyberspace. Initially envisioning the Internet as a sales outlet for his music, Newbury's first website was located at www.songs.com, and the Front Porch chatroom was born. Songs.com was owned by Gaylord Entertainment, proprietors of the Grand Ole Opry, the Opryland Hotel and radio station WSM.

In short order, Newbury's Front Porch became a popular hangout, and aficionados throughout the world became pals. Not just pen pals, but best friends. Newbury's buddy, Ernie Bunch wrote, "We begin to learn the power of the Internet for bringing like minded individuals together. I still marvel at the sheer number of people who think the same way about our friend as we do... voices in the wilderness brought together to this very special place by technology, and our love for a friend." A few more Front Porch pioneers include Rick Brashear, Dave Franklin, Jim Gatti and Bobby Freemam. Mickey would regularly say, "The purpose of the Porch is to bring friends together," and that his music was the vehicle... not the journey. Old friends would just drop in to post messages to Mick, such as Paul Colby who wrote: "I saw Kristofferson last month at Town Hall in New York. I asked about you and just realized you would be on the Internet. P.S. Bitter End is still kicking ass!"

On New Year's Day 1997, Mickey's heart was broken when another friend - "my brother" - Townes Van Zandt died suddenly. Following hip surgery,

Townes died unexpectedly of heart failure at the young age of 52 at the family's home in Smyrna, Tennessee. His hero and mentor, Hank Williams, had exited the world 44 years earlier to the day. Hank Williams pain songs to be sure.

Months would pass before Mick felt like touring. In the interim, he played a bit of golf and protected Susie's chickens. Mick - and the ultimate surprise - greeted vultures and foxes visiting the Springfield farmhouse. It must have felt wonderful... disconnecting himself from the oxygen machine ... loading the 12-guage shotgun... drawing a bead on the scavenger... Wonder what thought went through his mind right before he pulled the trigger?

Towards the end of 1997, Mickey hit the road with Jack Williams. They performed at the Flora-Bama Songwriter's Festival on November 6. The "Bama" gig was followed by appearances at the Great Southeast Music Hall in Atlanta, the UUC in Augusta, The Handlebar in Greensville, Coastal Carolina College in Myrtle Beach, the Bluebird Cafe in Nashville and a private club in Memphis. "Basically," Newbury explained to No Depression reporter Kurt Wolff, "I'm a writer who sings as opposed to a singer-songwriter. I can sing four or five times a year and be contented. And that's what I've been doing." Though the appearances were hard on Mickey in his weakened state, seeing friends and fans lifted his spirit enormously.

"Mickey was amazed," according to Williams, "to discover thousands of followers who had remained fans of his even after his public 'disappearance.' Some of these people waited in long queues after our concerts toting 18 or so, well-worn Mickey Newbury LPs to be signed, often with tears in their eyes at 'rediscovering' and getting to meet and talk to their long-lost favorite artist."

Almost a decade had passed since he had performed with Marie Rhines at the Bluebird Cafe. Bill Friskics-Warren caught Mick's concert at the Bluebird on December 1 and critiqued the show in No Depression. "After yet another false start, this time on *She Even Woke Me Up To Say Goodbye*, Newbury, who had hoped to tape the show and release it as a live disc, looked as though he was ready to call it quits. That is until some guy, expressing the feelings of most everyone who'd crammed into the Bluebird, blurted out, 'We'll sit here while you write one.' Whether it yielded enough complete takes for a live album or not, the legendary singer-songwriter's rare Nashville appearance offered an intimate, humorous and often moving glimpse of his peculiar genius and spirit. The fits and starts made it all the more personal... Newbury played nearly 20 songs in two hours. Half of his set was newer material, including several bittersweet reflections on mortality and the passage of time."

While in Nashville, he visited old friends, among them, musician-songwriter-promoter Drew Reid, who recalled a curious telephone conversation. "Mickey was in town and had tried contacting someone at Acuff-Rose about some old masters or demos, I'm not sure. He said he told the lady, 'May I speak to so-and-so; this is Mickey Newbury.' She went away for a minute. Mickey was on hold. When she came back, she said, 'Now who are you with, Mr. Newbury?' Mick just hung up the phone."

> *Nobody wants you when you're down and out*
> *Nobody wants to know your name*
> *You're just another face lost in the crowded street*
> *WISH I WAS*

Opryland theme park - a twenty-six year mecca of tourism - closed its rides and shows in early '98 after dwindling from 2.4 million visits annually to 1.6 million. Meanwhile, offbeat moviemakers the Coen Brothers used Newbury's song - the First Editions' version of - *Just Dropped In* for "The Big Lebowski."

About then, Mickey played his final Lone Star concert, ironically where Jimmie Rodgers had built "Blues Yodeler's Paradise" - a house for his family - when he was dying from tuberculosis. Jack Williams was with the ailing Newbury and wrote, "His finest hour in these last years may have been his only Kerrville Folk Festival appearance, where thousands of tearful Texans stood up throughout his other-worldly performance beneath a clear Texas sky. Mickey had come home." Singer-songwriter Cowboy Kent Johnson was there too and said, "He was so good, I cried."

**ALBUM # 19** Live In England (Mountain Retreat MR05192) contains the following: 1. Angeline 2. Amazing Grace / Cortelia Clark 3. Song Of Sorrow 4. His Eye Is On The Sparrow 5. Sailor Sailor 6. Ramblin' Blues 7. Danny Boy 8. Easy Street 9. 'Frisco Depot 10. Shenandoah 11. San Francisco Mabel Joy 12. An American Trilogy.

"Live In England" was culled from Mick's twenty-one-day tour of England in 1993. Good friend Phil Weedon, English photographer extraordinaire, shot the picture used for the cover. Phil explained, "Returning to England after visiting with Mick at the Flora-Bama, I sent pictures taken of Mick's performance to Bob to send to Mick. Well Mick liked them enough to want to use them on the forthcoming CD cover. Up to this time I had been a fan of Mick's for over 20 years and had only recently become acquainted with him. So this was an honor indeed."

"Mick had asked for a picture of the bridge in London to go on the cover with his face over the Thames. I struck lucky first time on a clear, cold morning with the winter sun in the right position over Tower Bridge. We had just got a new computer and, I agreed to design the artwork for the sleeve. It was to be called 'Live In England.' I was new to computer graphics but had some background in design. I didn't however count on the foibles of Mickey Newbury. Many a long evening was spent looking through the computer manual and trial and error played a big part."

"I sent the first draft to Bob via express mail and he sent it to Mick. I can't remember how many times we revised it, seemed like twenty times, but was probably five or six... each expedited by airmail. I recall Mick being very particular with typeface and color of text. The process began to drive me crazy, and there were a few nights when Mick stopped being my 'hero.' Finally, he put all my worries to rest, telling me: 'It's gonna be out there a long time Phil, we should spend the time to get it right.' Today I try to remember this maxim when impatient clients want things 'yesterday.' At last, the final proof was sent. I woke up in the middle of the night in a cold sweat when I realized that I had written 'Live In London' on the proof... I rang Bob; it was corrected to 'England' and at length I slept well. The original proof with Mick's signature and a 'thank you Phil' proudly hangs above my desk."

The "Live In England" album features four songs covered by Newbury not written by him. First, he gorgeously intersperses *Cortelia Clark* with lines from *Amazing Grace*. (*Grace* had been written 200 years earlier by English slave trader turned minister, John Newton.) Mick was familiar with Judy Collins' standard setting version, as they were friends at Elektra when she cut it in the early seventies. But unlike Collins' crescendo of rising choruses... Mick solos it spectacularly.

Newbury's performance of *His Eye Is On The Sparrow* is magnificent, as good as anything Pavarotti. It may have been construed as audacious behavior for an American to perform the Irish anthem *Danny Boy* in the U.K. Mickey knew this and said, "It's a little bit frightening tryin' to sing this song here. I can sing it in The States and get away with it." Perhaps as the Irish had made an anthem of his *American Trilogy*, he was returning the compliment.

**BOX SET** The Mickey Newbury Collection (Mountain Retreat) includes 10 albums released from 1969 to1981: <u>Mercury label</u> - (1) Looks Like Rain; <u>Elektra</u> - (2-6) Frisco Mabel Joy, Heaven Help The Child, Live At Montezuma Hall, I Came To Hear The Music, Lovers; <u>ABC Hickory</u> - (7-9)

Rusty Tracks, His Eye Is On The Sparrow, The Sailor; <u>Polygram / Mercury</u> - (10) After All These Years.

Packaged as an eight-CD collection (the last four albums are doubled up) the Box Set contains 87 different songs. When Newbury was asked which of the songs were personal favorites, he replied, "My songs are like my children. Perhaps some may be prettier than others, but I love each of them just the same." Maybe somebody kidnapped the children, as ABC Hickory/MCA claimed the original masters to <u>all</u> 10 albums (!!!) had been lost or destroyed. "Record business foul play," mused devastated writer-critic Don Negri.

CD mastering then was accomplished with TLC from virgin vinyl thanks to Earl Wynn, Ernie Bunch and Bob Rosemurgy who donated sealed LPs to the cause. Owsley Manier, Rosemurgy and studio specialists undertook the massive project. Transferred on "exquisite equipment" in a Nashville studio, the audio was processed through a special computer. A skilled engineer removed surface noise and expanded the sound dynamics, without altering original music. The Box Set recreates these "lost or destroyed" albums, down to original cover art and song lyrics. While seeking permission or a release from Elektra, Rosemurgy was advised in writing, "Elektra Records does not have an artist named Mickey Newbury." Perhaps the Acuff-Rose receptionist - who had asked, "Now who are you with, Mr. Newbury?" - had changed employers.

The Box Set received glowing reviews. Newbury's 10 albums recorded from '69 to '81, according to George H. Lewis, "comprise one of the most brilliantly original and important bodies of work of any contemporary popular artist... In his music, as in his life, Mickey Newbury has always set his standards high, and it shows from start to finish in this essential collection that sparkles like crystal, but is - at the same time - solid as stone."

And <u>No Depression</u> wrote, "The 10 albums Newbury released from 1969-1981 constitute one of the most remarkable catalogs of music any artist has assembled in this century, a body of work for which he deserves to be remembered and revered... The Mickey Newbury collection is one of those anchors that ground great record collections, a treasure that offers rewarding musical experiences for years to come."

Fans had anxiously awaited the Box Set. Several had played the twenty to thirty-year-old LPs so often that surface noise became a familiar part of the song. "Well his daddy was an honest SSSCCRRRRRAATCH man / Just a red-dirt Georgia SSSCCRRRRRAATCH farmer..." Many fans maintained record players solely to play his LPs. Fifteen years following the advent of the CD, Mick's music was offered in the digital medium. Mountain Retreat did an amazing job remastering the albums, and Newbury fans will be eternally grateful.

After release of the Box Set, on December 19, the House of Representatives impeached President Clinton. Prior charges should have been levied against the Razorback from Hope, Arkansas for discussing the type of underwear he wears - "Briefs!" - and blowing a sax on TV. For the Joy of Sax recital, the rockin' leader of the free world donned a pair of Tom Cruise trademark shades. Risky business... perhaps... but that depends on your definition of "risky." As his fans and staff swelled, Clinton performed an encore at the University of Oregon in Eugene. Mick did not venture out for the gala.

The year 1999 saw a college student in Boston launch Napster, a free online music sharing service that would attract 38 million users. A few months later, the first list of "Newbury's Songs Covered by Others" was posted on the songs.com website by the author. Initially 126 recordings were documented, and Mick would comment, "It brings back a flood of memories. Many of those on the list were my heroes when I was a very young man." The total quintupled five years later - to 670 - meaning a Newbury song has been covered every three weeks for 38 years.

Many artists - 489 unique performers - have saluted 94 Newbury songs. A great songwriter, Don Gibson, is tied for first place with the most covers at 12. Cowboy Johnson, an ex rodeo rider from Texas, released a superb tribute album in early 2004, also containing a dozen covers. Gibson and Johnson are followed by:

* **9** - Waylon Jennings, Roy Orbison
* **7** - Sue Thompson
* **6** - Joan Baez, Thom Fricker, Tom Jones, Johnny Rodriguez, Kenny Rogers, Bill Woody
* **5** - Frank Ifield, Jerry Lee Lewis, Sammi Smith
* **4** - Roy Acuff Jr, Mickey Gilley, Toni Jolene, Brenda Lee, Pat Newbury, Buffy St. Marie, Willie Nelson, Dottie West
* **3** - Eddy Arnold, Glenn Barber, Brook Benton, Box Tops, Jim Ed Brown, Anita Carter, Ray Charles, Don Cherry, David Allan Coe, Clay Hart, B B King, Kingston Trio, Al Murphy, Neal Ford, Wayne Newton, Johnny Tillitson.

Newbury's compositions have crossed many boundaries. The works have been delivered as blues, folk, funk, pop, jazz, punk, rock, soul, bluegrass, Celtic, country, disco, gospel, metal, polka, reggae, rumba, psychedelia, easy listening and R&B. And not just in America but Australia, Canada, Czechoslovakia, Denmark, England, Finland, France, Germany, Ireland,

241

Jamaica, Japan, New Zealand, Netherlands, Norway, Philippines, Poland, South Africa and Sweden. Peer approval indeed... universally so.

*An American Trilogy* is Mick's most covered piece with 155 versions, making it one of the most recorded songs in history. Afterwards, the Top Ten includes: *Why You Been Gone So Long* 59, *Sweet Memories* 47, *Funny Familiar Forgotten Feelings* 45, *She Even Woke Me Up To Say Goodbye* 31, *How I Love Them Old Songs* 23, *Just Dropped In* 19, *Remember The Good* 16, *I Don't Think About Her No More* 13, *San Francisco Mabel Joy* 13, *Mobile Blue* 11 and *Sunshine* 10.

Commenting on the number of covers, Mickey wrote the author, "With all these songs... why don't we have an island somewhere... 'bout 70 degrees all day... cool breeze... blue... I mean BLUE WATER... water so blue it would put Liz Taylor's eyes to shame. Why... why? Oh... and a lot of money to fly all our friends in. Oh OH... enough money to build a house for all of 'em!"

**ALBUM # 20** Lulled By The Moonlight (Mountain Retreat MR02384) is an unlimited, reissue of the 1996 album. This second release was not autographed and not numbered.

**ALBUM # 21** It Might As Well Be The Moon (Mountain Retreat MR7488-2) is a double CD. *Disc 1* is a rerelease of the 1988 American "In A New Age" *with added instrumentation.* (The original '88 Airborne release was available only for a short time as the label folded quickly.) *Disc 2* is a live '88 Newbury concert accompanied by Marie Rhines on violin, and includes the following tracks: 1. Introduction 2. Willow Tree 3. After All These Years 4. Gone To Alabama 5. Apples Dipped In Candy 6. The Piper 7. Lie To Me Darlin' 8. The Night You Wrote That Song 9. Juble Lee's Revival 10. She Even Woke Me Up To Say Goodbye 11. That's The Way It Goes 12. Sweet Memories 13. Ain't No Blues Today 14. That Was The Way It Was Then / Let's Say Goodbye One More Time 15. How I Love Them Old Songs 16. Danny Boy 17. An American Trilogy.

Marie Rhines recalled the concert on Disc 2, "Live from the Great American Music Hall, San Francisco's oldest and most opulent nightclub. I remember every moment of that golden night. It was a memory of pure perfection on stage with Mickey. My sister Beverly had flown in from Boston, and Susan had come down from Oregon." During the *Introduction*, Mickey performed *I Am Just A Country Boy*, replacing traditional lyrics with his own: "I've been to the city / I've seen the city lights / Nothing in this world could be as pretty / As my Susie on a summer night..." Then he dedicated *I Still Love You After All These Years* to Susie, announcing, "And this is for you honey..."

Mick's better half (He often said, "I married way over my head!") began teaching at Agnes Stewart Middle School in June of 1999, specializing in science, math and computers. In October, the couple celebrated their 30th anniversary.

The first gathering of Mickey and Front Porch Friends was held in Perdido Key, Florida on November 5. Someone referred to the group as "Mickey's Family of Friends," and the expression strikes a sympathetic chord. Before traveling from Oregon, Mick stated, "I'm havin' a hard time getting up for the Songwriter's Festival as I'm coming off Pretezone. But I have to be there! Right now I am two years past my scheduled time to depart this planet, so my health is not an issue. My mind thinks in 3/4 time."

"Mickey's trip to Florida," Marty Hall elaborated, "to play at Joe Gilchrist's Flora-Bama was a scary time, for his health was at a low ebb and his spirits were, too. But his website had been so wonderful for him and his fans, and he wanted some way to connect faces with names. I strongly sensed that Mickey had in mind going to Florida and doing the show, then relaxing on the Gulf and slipping away. This possibility was rendered moot by the unexpected arrival of Chris to help his father in Florida. Chris had been in Spain teaching Spanish/English but returned to the United States to be with Mick." Folks were stunned by Chris' appearance. He looked like Mickey at 25, just taller.

Marty also surprised Mick by showing up at a reception the first night in a building across the road from the Flora-Bama - the Silver Moon Cafe. Marty explained, "When Mick arrived, there was a great crush of people greeting him. When he got to me, he grabbed me and said, 'You stinker... I'm really glad you came!' The reception was a tribute of sorts, with emotional performances by Jack Williams, Rock Killough, Jonmark Stone and Larry Jon Wilson. Mickey got up and played too, although his performance was a struggle. He made a brief but beautiful speech, acknowledging how much he is loved." In front of Mamie, Chris and a large gathering of Front Porch Friends, Mick raised his hands, dropped his head and cried, "Look at me Momma. I'm the richest man in the world!" "Just when things got a bit too heavy," continued Marty," he went into 'Little Blue Robin' and instantly changed the mood."

The following evening Mickey performed fourteen songs over a two-hour stretch on the Flora-Bama main stage. Frequently gasping for breath, this would be his last public concert. On stage he joked, whistled and sang beautifully... while taking oxygen. He played guitar and keyboard for some of the newer tunes. The performance also went out live over the Internet. "More than once," Marty said, "I signaled Chris that I thought we should try to gracefully end the performance, but Mickey would have none of that. When the performance ended, Mickey was surrounded with an unending throng of fans who all wanted to visit, hug and get Mickey's autograph. He dug deep and came up with enough energy and love for everyone." And Jonmark Stone remarked, "I don't think I'll ever see a more moving performance than Mick's at the Flora-Bama in 99."

The next day Mick invited a dozen or so friends up for mid-morning celebration. Receiving the guests while dressed in trademark black silk robe and black silk pajamas, he was exhausted, though charming and attentive. High tea was prepared and served by Karen Bull of Australia, Kathy Enfinger of Georgia, Mary Anne Potter of Oklahoma, Susan Williamson of Texas and Valerie Weedon of England. Mick enjoyed the service with a healthy brunch: cottage cheese, plain yogurt and whole white seedless grapes. "Each bite," he observed, "gives one a very distinctive taste." At this point, a hungry Jack Williams announced he would "be going out for steak and eggs." After a memcrable two-hour visit, guests attempted to beg off so Mick might rest. He would not hear of it though, insisting, "Stay... just a bit longer." During the festival, the Newburys resided in Joe Gilchrist's Gulf-facing high-rise condo.

> *No, I'm gonna lay in the sun today*
> *I have a place where I can stay*
> *A house right on Perdido Bay where the folks are good to me*
> *SHADES OF '63*

Mickey wrote a new final verse to *Sweet Memories* before leaving Perdido Key. A consummate perfectionist, the man worked on the song for 35 years:

> *Once again I will close my eyes and fall into my dreams*
> *For in the light of day this life is never what it seems*
> *I find I need a place tonight to run away and hide*
> *From all the sadness and the madness in this world outside*

As technological communities scrambled to overcome impending Y2K issues, 600,000 people in the United Kingdom selected *An American Trilogy* - as performed by Elvis Aron Presley - as the number one American song of the *millennium*. No American song finished higher than the Newbury-Presley classic. The survey, a joint effort undertaken by HMV, Channel 4 and Classic FM, required 12 months to complete. Also "Looks Like Rain" was named third best album of the century by Scandinavia's biggest daily newspaper, "Aftonbladet."

**Mamie, Mick and the author taking in a performance in Cottage Grove, Oregon, August 19, 2000.**

# Chapter XVII: *Silver Moon Café*
## 2000 - June 2001

**A**LBUM # 22 Stories From The Silver Moon Cafe (LongHall/Mountain Retreat 8160 2) contains the following tracks: 1. The Silver Moon Cafe 2. Lie To Me Darlin' 3. It Makes Me So Sad 4. Some Memories Are Better Left Alone 5. Down n' Dirty 6. Why You Been Gone So Long 7. Ain't No Blues Today 8. Ain't No Sunshine 9. Oh Mama 10. Dancing Shadows 11. Twenty Years And Sweet Dreams Ago 12. A Storm Is Comin' 13. A Father's Prayer.

"Stories From The Silver Moon Cafe" was Mick's first studio album of new songs in nearly five years. The label's appended moniker, adding "LongHall," was his idea after the same from King Arthur. And as Newbury's singles and albums had been released by a dozen different labels, he was making a statement about the desired long haul. "Stories" was produced and engineered by the incomparable Paula Wolak, who traveled from Nashville to capture the sessions on a hard drive pro recorder.

"I did the vocal work, Mick said, "out of Marty Hall's house (in Eugene)... That's where the studio is... when I was gone that six weeks... He's got a home studio back there... That's where I did all the mastering and all the interludes." Referred to as Longhall Studio in the liner notes, Marty explained, "In my home I had a studio connected to a separate apartment. Mickey liked the feel of the unit, which was quite separate from the rest of the house, probably because its walls were lined with rough cedar and there were lots of skylights. These were features of the studio he had built in his home in Vida some years before."

"Marty's studio was on the back of his house," Rosemurgy elaborated, "accessible through a bedroom where Mickey stayed when he was 'in residence.' It was narrow (maybe 12' wide) and long (20'), with Marty's mixing board and recording gear to the left at the end of the room. Mickey sat in a comfy chair with the mic in front of him facing the board. Sometimes he played his guitar, often the Susie Guitar. (Dave Plummer of Iowa had handcrafted the instrument of Brazilian rosewood; and on its back, artist Keith Nelson airbrushed a portrait of Susan taken from a picture, Mick explained, "the day we got married.") Recording often occurred at night when Marty was home from working. Mickey liked working then. He was very comfortable and loved being with Marty... a most gracious host who added a great deal of support and input into those sessions."

Mick also loved the view of the backyard from the den. Marty had created a beautifully landscaped setting of flora, fountains, waterfalls, birdhouses, a Japanese garden and tall Oregon pine. The men enjoyed taking their morning coffee at the picture window, as God's creatures gathered in the garden: bluebirds, robins, rabbits, raccoons, squirrels, chipmunks, hummingbirds... "It looked like a Disney scene," Mick said, "like the cast from Bambi." He was very comfortable in Marty's home. Incidentally, frog sounds on the album are authentic... During the sessions, Mick asked son Chris to guard the backyard - to quiet the croaking creatures. Perhaps the critters had continued hopping west from Texas, where, Mick claimed, he had introduced them at age 10.

Whether or not karma can be established, Marty recalled when, "He and Chris arrived with lots of respiratory-aid equipment and musical trappings, including a new golden microphone and his guitars, one of which was his special and beloved Susie Guitar. R.B. Lindsay, the world-class mouth-harpist from Texas who has played with the likes of Hank Williams, Jr., also became a regular at my home most days during Mickey's stay."

"I would leave for work and Mickey would get about his writing and editing. When he stayed with me, he wrote in his bed, which would be literally covered with many yellow ruled legal-size tablets and separate sheets of paper with verses, ideas, song fragments and other ideas Mickey considered valuable enough to write down. When I would return home about five o'clock or so, he would show me what he had done during the day, thumping out a rhythm on his chest while singing acappella. It was show-and-tell time, and Mickey demanded on-the-spot feedback about the quality of his work. Around 10 PM, Mickey was ready to do some singing. He and I would have a sip or two, he of tequila and I of rum, and then we would record."

"After several weeks of this routine, Bob Rosemurgy and Paula came to Oregon to get some serious recording done. Paula brought her wonderful Neve microphone preamplifier and Roland 1680 digital recorder. Together with Mickey's new microphone, Paula's gear made it possible to get a respectable recording quality, especially given her engineering talents. The day before Paula had to return to Nashville, Mickey found himself feeling strong and in good voice. He and Paula hit the 'record' button and worked for about eight solid hours. Some of what appears on 'Stories From The Silver Moon Cafe' and virtually all of what appears on 'A Long Road Home' was recorded during Mick's stay at my home. There are twenty-some unreleased tunes in various stages of completion," such as *Tilde*, *Mississippi Moon, Help Me Son, Little Blue Robin, Road To Damascus* and *The Two Step Goes On.*

Marty helped design the CD cover, saying, "Mickey would want to examine and reexamine each hue and textural change, then go back and forth until he came upon exactly the image and visual feel he was after. This visual editing was similar to his lyrical editing with respect to its intensity."

Several songs on "Stories" are exceptional. Marty's *Twenty Years And Sweet Dreams Ago* is a brilliant ballad, with a moving verse: "I saw myself in the mirror just the other day / I saw the lines of age and the signs of rage in my face." Mick sings it magnificently, respectfully making it a Newbury song. The interlude following *Twenty Years* features Bob Rosemurgy's high school "badass bluegrass band."

Classical themes abound on the album, melodically and poetically. First, Newbury laments with "a solitary whippoorwill," evocative of John Keats; and then, "in a solitary moment," he prophesizes, reminiscent of The Beats. What a brave soul he was to confront *Some Memories Are Better Left Alone*, and considering his physical condition at the time, it is amazing he was able to wing it. Though the sustained high notes would tax the best balladeer, Mickey sang the song beautifully, as if he willed it. Several levels of meaning are contained in the chorus, "Lying in the darkness / I am waiting for the dawn." The lyrics showcase Newbury The Poet and include an invented word:

> *A solitary whippoorwill is singing in the night*
> *I watch until he spreads his wings and he sails into the sky*
> *Somewhere in the distance I can hear his plainful song*
> *He said some memories are better left alone*

*Lie To Me Darlin* is a waltz that should be required listening for psychology grad students. On *Down N' Dirty* the way Newbury's laugh becomes the train is staggering. The final verse in *Oh Mama... brand New man*, is his clever way of paying homage to Randy Newman. "It's written in his style," said Newbury, "his piano chords... One of the best songs ever written is (Newman's) *I Think It's Going To Rain Today*... I always wanted to record that..."

When asked why he redid *Why You Been Gone So Long* so differently from the original '73 version, Mick replied, "I want people to know that songs can be done... in other words you can dress your children many different ways... dependin' on whether they're gonna go hikin' or dancin.'" He rewrote the final verse:

<u>1973</u>
*There ain't nothing I wanna do*
*Oh, I guess I could get stoned*
*And let the past paint pictures in my head*
*Kill a fifth of Thunderbird and try to write a sad song*
*Tell me baby, why you been gone so long*

<u>2000</u>
*Nothin' I wanna do*
*I guess I could go home*
*Let that honeysuckle wind blow through my hair*
*Jump in my ol' Chevy / Chase that freight train down*
*Goodbye Tenaha, Timpson, Bobo and Blair*

Getting stoned at thirty-something is replaced by just going home at sixty. Tenaha, Timpson, Bobo and Blair are four small east Texas towns in Shelby County that once were on the same passenger rail line. The popularity of the saying originated from a porter in Houston announcing the departure of a train on the Houston, East and West Texas line. The porter called out destinations along the way to Shreveport, and the alliteration of "Tenaha, Timpson, Bobo, and Blair" made it a favorite of passengers. The great Tex Ritter wrote and recorded a song by that title. Mr. Ritter was a man that Mickey and his mother knew and revered, and Mick pays homage to him here.

*Dancing Shadows* presents an intoxicating repetition of swirling motifs, a nocturnal piece with just one set of lyrics at the midway point: "Dancing shadows on the wall / Reaching out for one another / I look into your eyes / And fall so endlessly I can see forever..." And that cello just breaks your heart... *A Storm Is Comin* is pure folk gospel, perhaps an apocalyptic reference. Ray Charles should cut the song immediately. Finally, no ending or beginning could be more proper than *A Father's Prayer.*

*Bless this day*
*That it might be*
*Free from all uncertainty*
*Free from tears and fears and doubt*
*Peace is all that matters*

Incidentally, Mick decided not to use the original concluding stanza in *A Father's Prayer*, reserving it for a future song, *Brother Peter.*

*Bless this bread that we now break*
*Bless this food that we partake*
*That we remember one who died*
*That we could see through loving eyes*
*Oh, faith, faith is all that matters*


Nashville continued to prosper in 2000. Replacing the Opryland theme park, the new 200-store Opry Mills celebrated its grand opening on May 11th. The 1.1 million-square-foot retail complex, dubbed Shop-ryland by locals, boasted 15 anchor stores, including the 125,000-square-foot Nashville Bass Pro Shop outdoor emporium. Located within steps of the Grand Ole Opry House are the Opryland Hotel and Convention Center, and The General Jackson Showboat. Fifteen million visits were projected during its first year.

Concurrently, Mick transferred the website to his proprietary domain name, mickeynewbury.com, explaining he left songs.com due to "a conflict of interest with the Nashville based Gaylord Corporation." Though not as crowded as Shop-ryland, the new website would soon average hundreds of "unique" visitors per day. Guests were made to feel at home on the Porch and were greeted by a Tiffany lamp, which clicked ON and OFF. Tupper Saussy remembered, "The lampshade theme of his website reminded me of his enthusiasm over the first Tiffany lampshade he'd ever seen (around 1968), the one that hung in the sunroom just off our library."

Mick loved communicating with Front Porch Friends and did his best to reply to questions and salutations. Besides posting under his name, he also used Poe and ~*~. Confined to bed in his Springfield home, the conversations provided him with a much-needed focus beyond. Discussions ran the gamut from birthday wishes to grandchildren to Monet to music to prayer requests. Soon ~*~ would have an opportunity to meet a few of the new cyber-voices.

On August 18, the Second Gathering of the Newburys and Front Porch Friends took place in the Cascadia Room, at the Village Green Resort in Cottage Grove, Oregon. (Susan's senior prom had been held in this room 35 years earlier.) Jeff Stave tirelessly organized logistics and technical details of the event, and Ron Lyons served as master of ceremonies. Oregon Public Broadcasting videotaped the special event for future broadcast as a documentary.

Ron wrote, "He walked to the middle of the big room with his back facing the courtyard windows and told everybody to gather around, and it became a look at Newbury in the creative raw. Surrounded by scattered legal pad sheets of handwritten lyrics, he sang (half unfinished songs, such as) *I Don't Love You*, and for the first time in my life, I really understood the meaning of the word 'breath-taking.' He borrowed Shirley Lindsay's bifocals as he sang *Down 'N Dirty* and a little bit of a song about a mockingbird, an old man, and the rain. My most abiding memory from Gathering 2: The best example of serenity I have ever seen is Mickey Newbury singing with his eyes closed."

"Susan showed up and watching her take care of Mickey says more about their relationship than any words could. Laura Shayne and Stephen were also there. Porch Friends started coming back in, and Mickey hung out answering questions until Miss Susie said it was naptime..."

Susie appreciated her husband's new friends. "I've been very, very grateful," she explained, "for the chatboard and for his fans... I mean friends... fans is not the right word... because as he's been ill and in a situation where most people would be very isolated and very homebound... he has not been. He has felt the wonderful love and support of these people, and it has been an encouragement to him to go ahead and write. On this last album that he finished, he probably wrote enough material in two to three weeks to do three more albums. Well, he wouldn't have done that if he had been isolated, you know if he had been totally cut off. He's still communicating with people. That's what songwriting is all about."

During the Gathering, Mickey stated, "All these people basically have the same personalities... A psychologist would have a ball with the friends of mine on that chatboard... And it's meant a lot to me because since I've been inactive you know... It's more of a support group... It's not like a fan club... We have become friends."

It was easy to become his friend. "Mickey was always freely accessible to everyone," Marty Hall explained. "He built no fences, no walls. His telephone number (541-726-4173 - now disconnected) and name were in the phone book. He did not have a firewall separating him from his fans, or from those who sought to take him to task. This is a huge statement given the dimension of Mickey's professional accomplishments and sheer number of people who desired access to him on a daily basis. It also demonstrates a huge and shared commitment by Susan and the children, to whom the extended family of Newbury fans and I owe a huge debt of gratitude."

**ALBUM # 23** 'Frisco Mabel Joy (Mountain Retreat MR 1269-2) is a remastered, reissue of the 1970 album, and includes one bonus song: *San Francisco Mabel Joy*, which did not appear on the original release.

252

**ALBUM** 'Frisco Mabel Joy Revisited (Appleseed Recordings) contains the following songs: 1. Prologue - Bill Frisell 2. An American Trilogy - Midnight Choir 3. How Many Times Must The Piper Be Paid For His Song - Walkabouts 4. Interlude - Bill Frisell 5. The Future's Not What It Used To Be - Gary Heffern 6. Mobile Blue - Dave Alvin & The Guilty Men 7. Frisco Depot - Meredith Miller Band 8. You're Not My Same Sweet Baby - Chuck Prophet 9. Interlude - Bill Frisell with Robin Holcomb 10. Remember the Good - Michael Fracass 11. Swiss Cottage Place - David Halley 12. How I Love Them Old Songs - The Hole Dozen 13. San Francisco Mabel Joy - Kris Kristofferson.

Peter Blackstock and Chris Eckman, editors of the top-drawer <u>No Depression</u> magazine, produced the first tribute to Mickey, titled "Frisco Mabel Joy Revisited." As an alternative country ensemble, contemporary versions are performed of songs from Newbury's classic 1970 LP. The CD ends on a surprise as Kristofferson performs *San Francisco Mabel Joy*. He said he didn't want to do the song, though, as the way Mickey did it originally was "perfect." Blackstock coordinated the project as a labor of love, and Mickey appreciated the noble gesture.

Moreover, Mickey treasured Earl Wynn's selfless efforts to gather and issue compilations of Mickey's songs recorded by other artists. Earl released 110 covers over five CD volumes, showcasing the diversity of interpretation of Newbury's music. From Carol Channing's *How I Love Them Old Songs* to Ronnie Milsap's *The Future's Not What It Used To Be*, these are remarkable collections, which Earl expertly packaged and gave away free of charge. Yes, the hard work was complimentary, and Mickey loved it.

Mickey loved hearing new songs that were well written, too, and Marty Hall spoke of a prominent example. "Over the years I found several (well-written new songs) to share with him, and his reactions were always insightful and valuable to me as a songwriter. One day I brought Mickey a song I believed to be particularly affecting. It is *Flow Gently, Sweet Afton* and was performed by Nickel Creek. The music was written by one of the members of the group, and the words were written by Robert Burns. I had no idea who Robert Burns was, but I was sure of one thing: he was a great wordsmith."

"When I sent the tune to Mickey, he really enjoyed all aspects of if. This song was quite an artistic achievement, as it was elegantly simple in its production and performance as it was in its composition. Mickey explained to me that Burns was a very, very famous 18th Century Scottish poet. Then Mickey confided in me that once many years ago in Nashville, Kris Kristofferson had told Mickey that he was 'an American Robert Burns.'

Mickey had to do some quick research to understand the dimension of Kris' compliment. But not until Mickey heard this beautiful Burns poem put to music did the full impact of Kris' compliment hit home. Mickey told me he wanted to make sure to tell Kris this story, but I never heard of him doing so."

Mickey was still writing songs... even in his weakened physical state. Addressing her father's struggles, Laura Shayne wrote, "What made Dad feel alive? Poetry. What kept him breathing on nights when he thought, and hoped, he would be dead by morning? Poetry... the simple thought in the back of his mind that maybe, just maybe, he would write a brilliant song that night. And many times, he did..."

Mickey had so much to say. When asked during an <u>Omaha Rainbow</u> interview if he ever had a problem of the well drying up, he replied, "Not really, because if the well dries up, I'll write about the well drying up." It never came to that however, as Laura Shayne explained: "His well was not only full, but overflowing."

In another interview, Mickey told Jodi Krangle, "Here I am at 60, I still love to write. I love words... wrapped in music. It's funny; I detest letter writing and yet, I so dearly love songwriting. So, I will continue to write songs, I suppose until my last breath. I will record until I cannot hear... phrase a line... or... no longer love this most selfish mistress." John D. Loudermilk might have summed up suitably when he stated, "Mickey Newbury aptly reflected the pathos of the dedicated songwriter."

"A songwriter writes because he has to," Newbury explained to Dorothy Hamm a few weeks later. "There are some people who write for the money; and that's okay. But if there wasn't a penny in it, I'd still write." But Mick knew the other side of the coin, too, advising Ron Lyons, "It just kills me that I can't just stay in the studio... I would stay in the studio from now until I sucked my last breath... I still would not get done everything I would like to get done... I just don't have the money to do it... It's real frustrating." Nevertheless and incredibly, Mickey would release one more masterpiece during 2001.

The year began as George W. Bush was inaugurated as the 43rd President of the United States. A "compassionate conservative," Bush had grown up in Midland and Houston, where his father - the 41st President - worked in the oil industry before turning to a life in politics. During the time of Mickey's life, 12 men served as President... four were Texans, and one was a red dirt Georgia farmer.

One prominent Texan, Willie Nelson - who allegedly smoked a stogie on the White House roof - telephoned Mick on March 10 with great news. He had recorded *Just Dropped In* and *33rd of August*, and the songs would be included on his next CD, "Rainbow Connection." "Willie called me at 3 AM to play them to me on the phone," Mick explained. He especially liked the way Willie interpreted *Just Dropped In*, as slow R&B. Willie would tell the "Dallas Music Guide" in 2002, "*33rd of August*, Mickey Newbury's song, is a little piece of literature that is really good." Mick appreciated the gesture as did the CMA. Willie would receive CMA and Grammy nominations for the album.

Mickey was hospitalized in early May with congestive pneumonia. Before going to the hospital - feeling ill - he fell out of bed and crawled to the bathroom. "I can't die on the toilet," he told Susan. "Elvis died on the toilet. Damn it! This is the *American Trilogy* curse!" Laughing hysterically, he finally allowed Susan to call for an ambulance. "We've been married for 32 years, she explained, "and I still can't get him to do what I want him to do... There's not an agent alive who would have had the patience, but we love him like he is."

The ambulance quickly delivered Mick to the hospital, and while there, he flat-lined twice. He later remarked to buddy Phil Weedon that during one of the episodes, he "met with Roy Orbison." When the author spoke with Mick about the hospital experience, he would say, "It wasn't so bad. I met some new people."

The author visited Mickey in his Springfield home on May 16. We discussed kids, friends, Texas, music, movies, computers, past lives, artistic drawings, how prayer works, Leonardo da Vinci, the Old Testament, the relation of Genesis to Darwin's Theory of Evolution and his inventions - such as a device that keeps a guitar in tune. He was well versed on the topic of human evolution, considering the subject was not taught in his Houston schools. For his 61st birthday, the author gave him a 1000-page picture book, titled Millennium In Pictures. Randomly thumbing through the volume, Mick explained dozens of pictures - in extraordinary detail - without reading the captions.

During the visit, Laura Shayne brought home a stray dog, a big brown one. While she did her best to persuade Dad to let her keep the animal, he jokingly said, "Seems like I've been takin' care of kids and dogs all my life." Verses from *That Lucky Old Sun* came to mind... By the way, Newburys oft feasted on "Laura-raised beef." The first two, Susan said, "were Texas Longhorns named Sam and Bill, and the last two were two very mean Black

Angus named Cookie and Cream. They tried to run the girl down several times... I guess they saw that (hungry) look in her eye."

After resolving the canine question ("No!"), Mick attempted to play the piano and sing a new song. He was unable to do so, as he needed to return to bed for an immediate breathing treatment. Few people realize how ill Mick was during the final years. Refusing to broadcast his physical demise for empathy, sympathy or monetary gain, he continued to express concern over the well being of others. Sidestepping his situation, he demanded reports on the author's daughter and mutual friends. Following the visit, Mick wrote, "It is rough... this ole life, and I suppose it was supposed to be, for how else could we appreciate what is to come. A man who cannot see is never blinded by the lights, but he also lives his life in the darkness." The similarity is striking between this comment and Reverend Newbury's speech in the 1994 movie, "Skins."

Sad news arrived on June 30 when Mickey's friend, Chet Atkins died. He was 77 and had been in frail condition for some time. The funeral was held at Nashville's Ryman Auditorium, former home of the Grand Ole Opry. Atkins recorded more than 75 albums of guitar instrumentals and sold more than 75 million albums. He played on hundreds of hit records, including those of Elvis - *Heartbreak Hotel*, Hank Williams Sr. - *Your Cheatin' Heart* and The Everly Brothers - *Wake Up Little Susie*. As an executive with RCA Records for nearly two decades beginning in 1957, Atkins played a part in the careers of Jim Reeves, Charley Pride, Jerry Reed, Dolly Parton, Waylon Jennings, Eddy Arnold, Roy Orbison and many others. His guitar style influenced a generation of rock musicians even as he helped develop an easygoing country style to compete with it. And as a senior RCA executive, he always gave Mickey a fair shake. "Chet," Mick eulogized, "would always come in and play on at least one song on my albums, and never turn in a time card. God bless him."

# Chapter XVIII: *Long Road Home*
## July 2001 - October 2002

**A**LBUM (August) The Mickey Newbury Collection (Box Set) - as above 1998 info - *digitally remastered.*

**ALBUM # 24 (**November) A Long Road Home (LongHall / Mountain Retreat MR 1017-2) contains the following songs: 1. In '59 2. I Don't Love You 3. The Last Question (In the Dead of the Night) 4. Here Comes The Rain, Baby 5. One More Song Of Hearts And Flowers 6. A Moment With Heather 7. Where Are You Darlin¹ Tonight? 8. So Sad 9. Maybe 10. A Long Road Home 11. 116 Westfield Street.

When asked if he had considered writing his life's story," Mickey replied, "I did... It was called *A Long Road Home.*" Coloring the reply as only Newbury the songwriter could, he added, "The book is written. The title is <u>Gnashville The Real Deal</u>. The cover is two men sitting at a card table slipping one another aces of spades. In small type at the very right... corner are the words... 'Dead men have no reason to lie.' The deal has been made with a major publisher... It is your guess when it will be released... heh... he."

But who could imagine in his sixth decade as a songwriter-singer, the ailing Newbury would deliver his pièce de résistance? In conversation with Jack Williams, Mickey confided that *A Long Road Home* might well be his swan song. Though Jack did his best to mock the comment, sadly Mickey would be proved right. The album would become the final movement of a symphony; incredibly, he saved the magnum opus for last. Mickey had prepared his entire life for the session, and he was totally focused on the subject at hand.

Classically Newbury, melody and lyrics are fused into single emotional statements - but in the vein of "Looks Like Rain" - he fused the whole album. Originally to be titled, "Long Road Home, Blue To This Day," each song adds a chapter to his memoirs, profoundly personal statements about regrets, yearnings, rigged games, earthly trials, fleeting fortunes and voyages through Dante's Rings. Newbury speaks to us as if we're seated comfortably next to him, sippin' brandy by a roarin' fire. He confides in us as if we've known each other for ages, and one gets the distinct impression he has until mornin' to tell the story. Intimacy and immediacy are conveyed sincerely, and sage advice from an old soul follows. "Listen closely," he whispers, "I want you to know this." And then as track one begins against a backdrop of strumming guitars, he gets right to it:

**IN '59**

*I was born in a shotgun shack that leaned against a railroad track.*
*I could hear a whistle blow all the way to Del Rio.*
*I was turnin' seventeen when I packed up my hopes and dreams,*
*Loaded up my old beat up car, turned the key and burned the tar...*

*I burned that highway down in '59.*
*Yes, I burned that two-lane highway down in 1959.*
*I never did look back; I did not see that railroad track,*
*But I burned that highway down in '59.*

*Winter came to '65; I fought the cold to stay alive.*
*And when I tried to light a fire, I was burned by my desire.*
*There I was at 24, faded dreams and nothin' more.*
*So, I hit the road again, but, oh, that road hits back my friends.*

*I burned that highway down in '69.*
*Yes, I burned that four-lane highway down in 1969.*
*I never do look back.  I do not see that railroad track.*
*Burned that highway down in '69.*

*The Seventies were kind to me; I was young... I was free.*
*Had it all, and then some more.  I could walk through any door.*
*Then a storm in '83 caught me too far out to sea.*
*I hit a reef, and I ran aground on the streets of guitar town.*

*I burned that highway down in '89.*
*Yes, I burned that four-lane highway down in 1989.*
*And I never did look back.  I could not see those railroad tracks.*
*In '89 I burned that highway down.*

*I can hear my Mama pray... prayin' for a better day.*
*I can hear my daddy say, 'Honey, I will find a way.'*
*He worked his fingers to the bone to make that shotgun shack a home.*
*He kept his sadness deep inside; Had that dream the day he died.*

*I burned that highway down in '59.*
*Burned that dirt road highway down in 1959*
*I never will look back that I won't see that railroad track.*
*I burned that highway down in '59.*

*So, Que Paso? to the Hotel California.*
*Adios to the Mason-Dixon Line.*
*I've a rendezvous with the Lady, East of Eden.*
*I burned that highway down in '89.*
*Yes, I burned that highway down in '89.*

Tracks one and ten are heavy bookends, weighing in at 11:20 and 10:02. Between the epic sagas, Newbury fills in a few details, beginning on track 2: "I don't love you anymore" was all little darlin' had to say. Justifiably, he next asks her to explain (track 3), "Where did the truth lie in your eyes?" With such sadness about (track 4), the sensible forecast is for teary weather; and then understandably (track 5), he's "cruisin' down the avenue" doing his best to make sense of it all. Still, he can't help but wonder (track 7) where darlin' is tonight, and, he finally admits (track 8), "She left me so heartbroken... and so sad." But "maybe," he concludes with a twist (track 9)... "I never did love you."

As guitar and cello waltz together slowly and sweetly, Newbury continues:

### A LONG ROAD HOME

*How I long to feel the salty wind off Galveston Bay*
*in my face once again.*
*A warm southern wind on my weather-worn skin*
*Perhaps I would not feel so old.*
*Now I long to hold the golden sand, in the hollow of my hand.*
*Stand for a while there and fill in the hole*
*left in the heart of a wounded old soul.*

*Here's to tomorrow; here's to today.*
*Here's to whatever I never did say.*
*Here's to old friends who have gone separate ways.*
*Here's to the memories.*

*How I long to be in those East Texas woods.*
*I would be in those old piney woods if I could,*
*On a hot summer mornin' down Centerville Way*
*The windows rolled down in my old Chevrolet.*

*Cruisin' the backroads with nothin' but time...*
*three nickels short of having a dime...*
*Miles from the highway... no hill left to climb.*
*Me and the whisperin' pine...*

*Here's to tomorrow; here's to today.*
*Here's to whatever I never did say.*
*Here's to your love, you are happy, I pray...*

*Out on this long stretch of Interstate 10,*
*that ol' Del Rio station just keeps rollin' right in.*

259

*Many the night it was my only friend.*
*Just me and the radio…*

*The Silver Moon Cafe was once out this way.*
*Like Route 66, boys, it too had its day,*
*and this rusty old sign here is all that remains.*
*My, how the times have changed.*

*They tell me ol' Bud Rose hocked his guitar;*
*Bought a ticket to Nashville to become a big star.*
*Now he works on a bottle, and he lives in a car.*
*Do you still have your dreams?*

*You remember the old town here yesterday?*
*The walk from the Ryman to the Linebaugh Cafe?*
*We would stop in at Tootsie's and Tubb's on the way,*
*And slowly head East down to First and Broadway…*

*Hey look at that ol' river, Bud, how it keeps rollin on by.*
*If it was a clock I could stop, I would try…*
*I would let it roll down on about '65.*
*Perhaps I would not feel so old…*

*Hoist all the sails, Bud, to hell with the breeze.*
*Send me a wind that will bend every tree.*
*A storm that will bring every man to his knee.*
*Here's to the howlin' sea.*

*Here's to tomorrow; here's to today.*
*Here's to whatever I never could say.*
*Here's to the piper; the bastard's been paid*

*Down on this long stretch of Interstate 10,*
*El Paso, to Phoenix, to LA, and then, it is north to northwest,*
*I just follow the wind,*
*And by midnight tonight I will be home in Springfield again.*

In the end, Mick squared himself with the pernicious piper and followed the wind home to his family. He did however have another story to share, vis-à-vis the dwelling of his youth at *116 Westfield Street*. As Mick's final testimonial is delivered by what could pass for the slow movement of a Schubert piano trio, he implores, "Who would have thought it could ever come tumblin' down… That is my childhood." Returning to where he began, Mickey has taken us full circle; but still, he was not done. Realizing what survives the terrible test of time, he closes with a cognition, perhaps inspired by Matthew 6:19-21: "Nothing is certain and certainly nothing is sure. Only a dream so it seems will be sure to endure." Through it all... the man's spirit persevered. He still had his dreams.

A pretty song on "Long Road Home" is veiled in vagueness, evocative of The Beats. A clue to the significance of *Hearts And Flowers* may be found in early 1997 verses that failed to make the "LRH" album. The discarded lines - from an Augusta, Georgia concert - might have been too abrupt:

> *Dancin' diamonds, midnight cities, in the shadows all the pretties*
> *All the suckers and all the liars, all the truckin' shuckin' jivers*
> *Cruisin' down the avenue, suddenly I saw the truth*
> *I know what I never knew: All the neon lights are blue*
> *Wheels are hummin'*
>
> *And he said, 'All you need is love'*
> *Then, callously we shot the dove*
> *And we nailed it to a twisted tree*
> *We said, 'It cannot fly but it is free'*

In August of 2000, Mick told the author, the song was driving him nuts; he was still wrestling with the lyrics. Mick considered titling the "LRH" album, "All The Neon Lights Are Blue." Though enigmatic, an explanation may be found in his background. Across Europe, one will see establishments with soft blue neon lighting; these are places where you will find ladies of the evening. During his four-year stint in the Air Force, Mick would have noticed the continent's blue neon. Also, the first neon signs were dubbed "liquid fire," and the word "blue" suggests sadness. The lyric may reference temptation, sin, hell... And then... there is the apparent reference to the crucifixion...

> *Starin' at the flashin' neon lights lightly dancin' off down those Jackson City streets*
> *APPLES DIPPED IN CANDY*

Newbury The Poet shines on the album, quite brilliantly on *So Sad*:

> *Yes, I waited all that mornin' to hear her say, 'I love you.'*
> *In the mornin' light she glistened like a ruby in a stickpin.*
> *Then she whispered something into the wet, red-leaded window,*
> *But she said nothing; she left me so heartbroken*
> *I was SO SAD...*

Mick changed singing style and tempo to suit breathing requirements and vocal ability. He sang several songs softly, whispering a few words on *I*

261

*Don't Love You* and *So Sad*, while *Long Road Home* and *Hearts And Flowers* were slowed from 4/4 to 3/4 time. Mick explained the change to Ginny Gnadt, "I feel very well about the sessions. I cannot sing as well as I could when I was 30, but there is something about having to depend on interpretation as opposed to vocal gymnastics that has become very appealing to me. The important thing is to tell the story."

Also, Rosemurgy pointed out, "The pure tenor had aged and the emotions rang with more depth; the voice had grown and aged to the nature of the lyric; and it had an edge, but remained pure and compelling. It sounded like he had lived and felt and survived all of those sorrowful times. At his best, Mickey was one of the best vocalists... When he began to lose some of the range and power, he was still better than most."

"He brought an unequalled emotional level to his performance," Rosemurgy continued, "that made the listener internalize the song - listen 'from the inside' so to speak, rather than just hearing a song performed. He was the Absolute Best at that." Laura Shayne capped the point, "He didn't memorize his songs and sing them, he recreated them every time he picked up his guitar... He was a creator, not a writer."

Critics praised the album, starting with Peter Blackstock who called it a "masterpiece." Blackstock wrote, "Each (song) is arranged exquisitely and delivered with a melody so melancholy that Waylon and Willie should recut *Luckenback, Texas* and change the line to 'Newbury's pain songs,' all apologies to Hank Williams." Concluding the article, Blackstock stated, "Mickey Newbury still has his dreams." Writer Al Moir agreed. "A Long Road Home," tracing his life story in song since 1959, is Mickey Newbury's masterpiece, a fitting epitaph to his greatness." And Erik Hage of All Music Guide observed, "Newbury may be embattled physically, but the creative fires burn fiercer than ever. This is a remarkable album." Finally, Moshe Benarroch wrote, "By now I think I should compare Newbury's work to a Bach cantata or to Mozart's Requiem... This is the kind of CD that makes me forget I have a collection of 5,000 CDs and LPs."

Interesting commentary came from writer Nate Sparks: "Much like most Newbury's work, 'A Long Road Home' has arrangements resembling what the Nashville Sound would've been if Chet Atkins was the most forlorn man in America. With this backdrop, Newbury paints pictures of a past, both hurtful and yearned for."

"At times elegiac in feel and content," Peter O'Brien wrote, "this is a remarkable work by any standard from a man now virtually bedridden and in constant need of oxygen to relieve his condition. How he could sustain his distinctive singing style under these circumstances is almost beyond understanding." Marty Hall concurred. "Paula Wolak did such a wonderful job on 'Long Road Home.' It's a superbly produced piece of music. But in its basic, essential form... just Mickey and his guitar... given the fact that he was on the oxygen... it was still such a stunning piece of music. It's bigger than life."

Ted Cheavens, a senior animator who worked on the Disney movie "Aladdin," designed the cover artwork for "Long Road Home," depicting Mick in a cool '50 "Merc" convertible. He wrote, "Mickey is everything you think he is and MORE! He is a joy to know and one of the most talented men I've ever known!" Mick explained, "I played *Little Blue Robin* for him (Cheavens) and he loved it. Now, he wants to use the song to do an illustrated children's book and also to make an animated movie." The reply? "That's fine, as long as I have creative control..."

**ALBUM** "A Tribute To Mickey Newbury" consists of 23 tracks contributed by the Front Porch Friends. The collection was not offered commercially. Produced and edited by Mickey's friend and fellow Oregonian, Jeff Stave, the labor of love was given to Mick as a Christmas present. The author submitted a song he had written - pedestrian at best - titled, *I Remember When*, relevant because Mickey completed it by adding the final verse: "Without the good, without the bad / There would be no need my friend / To remember when." The two highlights, however, include a cover of *Just Dropped In* by Mickey's son, Joe, and *When I Heard Newbury Sing*, a moving accolade from Jonmark Stone. The songs came from friends in ten states and seven countries.

A dozen friends also came together to surprise Mick with a laptop for Christmas. (Evidently, a virus had wiped out the old machine, though it seemed "something" was always happening to his computer. He blamed Bill Gates... but... "Don't get me started!") Unwrapping the present, he found the Mac system he wanted, with familiar OS 6.1 and Netscape 4.5. Mick was happy with the present and grateful to Santa.

On the day after Christmas, he suffered a stroke, and another one followed on January 2. The second one was more serious, causing a loss of hand control and difficulty in speaking. Until Mick's facilities returned a few months later, he would be unable to use two key lifelines, telephone and computer. Adding to the mix and making matters worse, a serious problem shared by stroke victims is depression, an emotional state already familiar to Mickey. He'd been down before, but this time it was serious. He was disconnected.

**ALBUM # 25** A rerelease of the '99 "Moon," disc 1 features additional bass by Craig Nelson. Disc 2 is unchanged.

**ALBUM # 26** Winter Winds (LongHall / MR 3147-2) contains the following songs: 1. The 33$^{rd}$ Of August 2. <u>Ramblin' Blues</u> 3. <u>Lie To Me Darlin</u> 4. Nights When I Am Sane 5. Just Dropped In 6. Genevieve 7. <u>Jubie Lee's Revival</u> 8. Apples Dipped In Candy 9. <u>Angeline</u> 10. San Francisco Mabel Joy 11. <u>Poison Red Berries</u> 12. Heaven Help The Child 13. <u>Winter Winds Blow</u> 14. Saint Cecilia 15. You're My Lady Now 16. What Will I Do.

Released in February, "Winter Winds" is a post-production remake - a changed soundscape - of 1993's "Nights When I Am Sane." With four songs excluded and six songs added (underscored), it is a different album. Bob Rosemurgy explained, "Mickey loved it. It was the only one we did without Mickey's oversight, as he was doing 'Long Road Home' and I wanted to redo the 'Nights' CD using this method. Michael McDonald of Eugene did the mixing and mastering, and Paula Wolak did the violin, cello and bass overdubs. Mickey said it was his favorite CD, but I think that would change a bit depending on how he felt. It certainly was one of them. Mine too. It turned out great and confirmed what I had always thought: Mickey would be best produced with a string quartet (guitar, bass, violin and cello) plus his guitar and voice. Just enough for the different moods and textures without too much. Of course, what made it work was the work Paula and Michael did."

Marty Hall agreed. "'Winter Winds' is remarkable that it ever got to be. When Mickey did 'Nights,' he was not happy with it at all, and that was the hallmark of that period. There was a lot of icky stuff connected with Winter Harvest, and it just didn't work out the way he planned. Then, to have it come back to life in the form of 'Winter Winds' was amazing... In what was both an ironic and a very pleasant turn of events, Rosemurgy, Wolak and McDonald in 2001 conspired to rework the 'Nights' CD basic tracks into what was later released as 'Winter Winds,' and in the process produced what proved to please Mickey more than any of his later productions. Most Newbury fans have difficulty recognizing that 'Winter Winds' is, in fact, in large part the basic tracks found on 'Nights.'"

Prior to the album's release, the author sent Mickey copies of home-designed CDR album covers. Mick said he really liked a few, especially one showing him with silver hair, eyes closed, playing guitar. Mick selected this shot for the "Winter Winds" cover. The picture had been sent to the author by Steve Enfinger, who digitized it from original form. Steve then should have been credited for the album's cover, and that was Mick's written desire.

Bill Littleton favorably reviewed "Winds," writing, "Speaking of legends and characters, Mick has done it his way to an extent that defies comprehension, within music business perceptions. His songs have worked well for a large diversity of recording artists, yet his own recordings thumb their noses at cubbyholes, a sin Radio and too many consumers find unforgivable. Ah, but the rest of us... We get off on the fact that somebody keeps coming up with songs that go deeper than a hook line repeated 14 times and with recordings that dare you to listen to the words."

Cubbyholes continued to be fashionable in 2002, as country songwriters played follow the leader. From analysis of the 21 number ones during the year, statistician/writer Ralph Murphy advised the secret to commercial success: "Start by selecting love songs with an average length of three minutes to three minutes and thirty seconds, leaning toward mid to up-tempo, in 4/4 time... using conventional first-person... Throw in a thirteen-second intro, get your listener to the title in sixty seconds (or less) with the title repeating no more than seven times, and you're in the running!" This "analysis" would have sickened Newbury.

Come January, Mick was still fighting. "I've been almost dying all my life," he stated bluntly. "Whooping cough almost killed me at six. Encephalitis almost took me at eight. Broke my back when I was 23. Was in the hospital with pneumonia at 35. And now, doctors don't know how I'm able to breathe with advanced pulmonary fibrosis, which has led to pneumonia and congestive heart failure. My lungs are completely gone now. So any extra time here for me has been a real blessing."

"I have worried my poor wife and Mama to death. My religion will not let me end my own life... This has taught me that there is no tomorrow. You should do the things today that need to be done. Tomorrow is too late. I'm talkin' about playin' golf, makin' love to your wife, going on that trip... whatever... I would like to be around to see my kids grow up... Newbury men don't live very long. We're like comets... we burn brightly, but not for very long."

> *I awoke this morning and looked at my life*
> *It was filled with so much sorrow and grief*
> *And in my troubled mind, I could see thru all my strife*
> *That time is only a thief*

*Yes, TIME IS A THIEF that will steal your tomorrows*
*And leave you only yesterday*
*Yes, TIME IS A THIEF that will rob you of the years*
*Your youth the only ransom you can pay*

*So treasure each little moment*
*Don't let a single minute slip away*
*TIME IS A THIEF that will rob you of the years*
*And never return one yesterday*

"I am going to have my body cremated and then sell little urns of my ashes for profit," Mick said slowly. "Will spell it 'New Berry.' Everyone will want one! Can't you hear 'em advertisin' it on TV? Ha ha ha ha ha! Man, I know that's black humor..." Attempting to change the subject, the author asked, "Mick, do you remember when you and Kristofferson and the gang would get together and play songs?"

"Yes I do. That's when I was Mickey Newbury." Then he changed the subject back again. "I had a dream. Saw my new body from the waist up. It was a smooth, healthy body." He spoke of another dream. He was holding his Dad's hand; his Dad was holding his Dad's hand... and on... Mick was ready, and he tried to prepare his friends.

*I look into your eyes*
*And fall so endlessly I can see forever*
*DANCING SHADOWS*

*Sun come up*
*Sun go down*
*My last night on the town*
*I tell myself that every time*
*My word ain't worth one thin dime*
*I need a DOWN N' DIRTY honky tonkin' song*
*So won't you chill me out and haul my body home*

*I've a rendezvous with the Lady, East of Eden*
*IN '59*

*Oh TILDE can you see that mountain*
*There is a river on the other side*
*No trouble and no care will be waitin' for me there*
*It is just beyond the sky*

After suffering considerably, Mick's friend Waylon Jennings died of diabetes-related health problems on February 14 at age 64. A few weeks later,

266

Susan piloted a 1977 GMC RV from Oregon to Texas, so Mick could visit Mamie, Jerry, Joe, cousins, friends and fans.  The vehicle had been a thoughtful gift from Earl and Suzy Wynn and delivered by Ernie and Gail Bunch.  Mick wanted to make one last trip to the Lone Star state before he died.  Residing in Oregon for 30 years, he missed Texas and his side of the family.

His children did, too.  Daughter Leah, a Mormon missionary, wrote, "I would love to hear stories of Daddy from members of his family.  Living in Oregon, we were really close to my Mom's extended family, but aside from Granny (Mamie) and Uncle Jerry, I have never known his family or him from his family's point of view."

And so Mickey wished to visit Texas one last time before departing this earth.  Throughout the 8,000-mile round trip - a long road home - Susan navigated the land yacht, while her ailing husband convalesced in bed.  Laura Shayne accompanied them and attended to her Dad's needs.  She wrote, "Struggling at times, my dad loved being on the road!  And when we crossed the border into Texas, he yelled, 'I'm home!  I made it!  Hot damn!  I'm home.'"

They went to Mamie's place in New Caney, a timber town on the Southern Pacific rail line on the northern outskirts of Houston.  While Mick was there, several friends had the opportunity to visit with him.  On March 21, Bud Wilhite, Randy Brown and Magne Hellesjo drove from Canyon.  "We made it to Mamie's about 10 AM," Bud remembered, "just as Susie was coming out of the motor home.  Dave Franklin drove up with his grandbaby, Kalea.  Randy was playing the Susie guitar while Kalea and Mick played Pee Pie.  Mick gave Randy a page from the famous yellow song notebook for each of us.  Magne was on cloud nine.  He told us he 'would have made the trip from Norway just to shake Mickey's hand.'  Susie came in after four hours and said it was time for Mickey to rest.  We had a great time but were saddened to see our hero confined to bed and in such pain.  We will never know how he remained so upbeat and positive."

"The big memory for me that day," Randy wrote, "was when we were leaving.  I was the last out of the motor home and Mick called me back to his nest and grabbed my hand, looked me in the eye and said, 'I'd appreciate it if you wouldn't tell anybody how bad I am.'  I told him I hadn't planned to and his eyes welled up with tears; then my eyes welled up with tears.  We just sat there holding hands crying for several minutes and then the corners of his mouth turned up into a smile and we both started laughing."

On Memorial Day weekend, Mick telephoned Bud to advise him that he and Susie were passing through Wichita Falls (The Northern Gateway) on the way back to Oregon. At Bud's invitation, they agreed to spend the night but would need some assistance. "Bud called and asked me if I had a 20 amp plug in my studio," Randy explained, "that Mick and Susan needed a place to plug in that rickety beast of a motor home. The first night there, we just visited in the motor home and listened to the wind and the trains across the valley. I told Mick I was sorry for all the noise, and he laughed saying that it was music to his ears."

"Mick called Donna Barnes, Bud remembered, "and started singing *Oh Donna* to her. She promptly hung up on him. He called back and she was very embarrassed; Susie told us 'nobody had ever hung up on Mickey while he was singing.' Donna and Albert Mendoza drove up the following day. We cooked steaks and Albert and Randy did some pickin' and singin.' Mick played and sang and told wonderful stories. He was in great form and even sang a Billy Holiday version of *Mood Indigo*."

The evening was special to Randy, too, who wrote, "Mickey picked out some chords I'd never seen before and made them sound like magic. He rolled them into a progression that he repeated several times and then put some words on the end something like, 'She grew tired of me and now she's gone.' He looked up and said, 'that's the whole song... You don't need a bunch of useless words. Whew! Blew me away! He was stronger than I'd seen him and he sat in the garage and picked out a couple of songs and showed us some licks in 'E' tuning. He still looked good silhouetted against that full moon with a guitar in his hands. One of the last times I guess. Sweet Memories!"

"We said our goodbyes," Bud reminisced, "and I think we all knew it would be our last time to see each other in this life. How lucky we were to become friends with the man who had such an impact on our hearts." Mickey was westbound the following morning. With Susan again piloting the RV, they arrived home on May 31.

> *Down on this long stretch of Interstate 10*
> *El Paso, to Phoenix, to LA, and then, it is north to northwest*
> *I just follow the wind*
> *And by midnight tonight I will be home in Springfield again*
> *A LONG ROAD HOME*

The next day, an exhausted Susan was still unable to slow down, and she wrote, "Laura and I are gong to go fix the tractor now... The 'it' got it." Through the hard times, in dealing with the illness, Mickey was blessed to have Susan at his side and literally at the wheel.

*Bless this woman here at my side*
*When I need a place to hide*
*I crawl into her loving eyes*
*Where I find a place to sleep*
*Love is all that matters...*
*A FATHER'S PRAYER*

Son Chris perfectly expressed the sentiment during an August 2000 interview with Ron Lyons: "I know this interview is about Mickey Newbury, but it's definitely not just him. There's another half to that. The combination of him and my mother... I think they've done a pretty good job with the family. She's a Saint, in one word... If we're going to do a one-word description. She puts up with a lot from everybody... including me."

*Bless this child with trusting eyes*
*That he may grow to realize*
*Right from wrong and truth from lies*
*For the truth is all that matters*
*A FATHER'S PRAYER*

Additional announcements concerning Mick's alma mater came in May. First, Gaylord Entertainment Company advised they would "split-off" Acuff-Rose Music Publishing. Referring to Acuff-Rose as a "non-core asset," Gaylord said it would keep its stake in the Missouri-based Bass Pro Shops. Two months later it was announced that King of Pop Michael Jackson and Sony Music - the Sony/ATV venture - had agreed to pay $157 million for Acuff-Rose's 55,000-song library. Sony/ATV also owns copyrights to The Beatles and Dylan.

The Milwaukee Journal Sentinel then ran a sensational story on July 7 about the new co-owner of Newbury's catalog. "The recording companies really, really do conspire against the artists," Michael Jackson announced to the media. "They steal, they cheat, they do everything they can..." Jackson, Al Sharpton and attorney Johnnie Cochran recently had formed a coalition to investigate whether record labels are financially exploiting artists. As co-owner of Newbury's catalog, it remains to be seen if Jackson will practice as he preaches...

A variety of artists continued to record Newbury's material. "Warriors Of The World," an album by heavy metal band, Manowar, shot up the world's charts in June, entering the German chart at number two and the Austrian chart at number six. Why did a metal group grab the attention of Newbury fans? The album's sixth track is *An American Trilogy*. Mary Breon of the

Manowar organization explained, "Mr. Newbury is one of Joey DeMaio's heroes." (DeMaio is Manowar's bassist.) The group also released the song as a single and performed it live at the opening show of the world's biggest music fair, the Popkomm, in Cologne on August 14. Backed by choir and full string orchestra, the performance was broadcast on Sat1 during prime time viewing.

On the U.S. music scene, August and September were active months. Thirty-seven years after Dylan shocked folkies at the Newport Folk Festival by plugging in, he returned to the scene of his legendary crime on August 3, but this time he unplugged. Starting out acoustically, he alternated between electric and acoustic guitars. Mick's good friend Jack Williams also played at the festival.

On September 5, to honor American roots music, the U.S. Senate passed Resolution 316 commemorating 2003 as Year of the Blues. Then on September 13, Susan and daughter Laura Shayne sang the national anthem at a Springfield High School assembly. Laura is also a champion rodeo rider, and she whistles like her Daddy.

On September 29 - the date when the Great Depression began - Susan had lay down with Mickey, holding his hand. She dozed off for a few minutes and when she opened her eyes, Mickey had passed on. Susan was still holding his hand. It rained in Oregon for the first time in days.

> *I find myself seeking her hand as I drift off to sleep*
> *Had I never known her God only knows where I'd be*
> *SONG FOR SUSAN*

> *Lying in the darkness*
> *I am waiting for the dawn*
> *SOME MEMORIES ARE BETTER LEFT ALONE*

Bob Rosemurgy wrote, "Mickey died in his sleep and at peace last night (2:30 AM at his home in east Springfield). For these past years, he has fought with great courage against a relentless disease, and his body finally wore out last night. His spirit now soars free. He was always in good cheer, keeping the pain and struggle out of sight from us. Now he has no pain and sleeps in ease and peace. We share the sorrow of Susie, Chris, Leah, Stephen, Laura, Mamie, Jerry, Joe and all of his family. Mickey's family reaches around the world, and includes all whose lives he touched, enriched and healed. He will be missed by all."

Buell Chapel Funeral Home in Springfield handled the arrangements. In place of flowers, contributions in Mickey's memory could be made to the

Vietnam Veterans Assistance Fund. He did not want a formal ceremony, so on October 5, a few family members and close friends briefly made their way to the gravesite to pay their respects. It rained that morning and was a gray overcast day.

"Mickey was buried at the Pioneer (Greenwood) Cemetery between Springfield and Vida, just outside Leaburg on Greenwood Road," wrote Rosemurgy. "It is a quiet country cemetery in a beautiful location between beautiful green and wooded hills. Mickey had picked it out himself. It is close to the golf course he frequently played. An Air Force honor guard presented the flag to Mamie and *Taps* was played."

"A few of us spoke in vain attempt to capture the unfathomable dimension of this man," Marty Hall stated. "Jonmark Stone's song - *When I Heard Newbury Sing* - was played during the ceremony, as was *Blue Sky Shining*, *A Father's Prayer* and *His Eye Is On The Sparrow*. There was a momentary skip on one of the songs, proving to everyone's satisfaction that Mickey was, indeed, with us still..." At 2 PM PDT, Mickey's worldwide family of friends shared one minute of silence, and at 2:01, each played a Newbury song.

"He was a wonderful husband and father," Susan wrote. "He just took care of his family. We'd have kids, and he'd take the next year off to change diapers... Our family feels the love, and we are so grateful for it. Mickey believed in music, and friends and his Savior... He has always been thankful for all three, and never thought much of what the rest of the world put their trust in... I know that Mick is fishing with his dad. He told me that was the first thing he wanted to do. Then he wanted to find out where all those Newburys come from... He only had one fault... He always wanted to be the first to try something. I'm gong to have to talk to him about that when I catch him..."

> *The dancing stops but the music goes on*
> *Doggone my soul HOW I LOVE THEM OLD SONGS*

# Reprise

Staged at the Opry House on November 7, 2002, the 36th Annual CMA Awards show appeared on CBS, and Newbury's name and passing went unmentioned. Willie Nelson was nominated for the album, "Rainbow Connection," containing two Newbury songs. Anyway, Alan Jackson swept the awards, walking away with five trophies, due primarily to the song *Where Were You (When The World Stopped Turning)*. Jackson's lament of the September 11 tragedies proved a huge success commercially, and perhaps it did bring healing to many.

The scenario brought to mind a conversation. After the 9/11 terrorists attacks on America, record companies raced to market to release patriotic songs, and emotional buyers stampeded stores to snatch them up. As Mickey was deeply concerned over the family's finances following his imminent departure, the author offered a suggestion.

"Hey Mick, why don't ya rerelease *An American Trilogy* backed with *America The Beautiful*? I think it'd be a killer right now."

"I can't do that. I won't plan my success based on people's suffering."

**ALBUM # 27** On February 4, 2003, Raven - a reissue label of Australia - released a CD titled "Harlequin Melodies, The Complete RCA Recordings... Plus." The 22-track CD contains Mickey's RCA material from "Harlequin Melodies" and "Sings His Own" plus seven "bonus tracks" from the MCA LP, "Sweet Memories." Though the album provides collectors with 15 cuts on CD for the first time (licensed from BMG-RCA), these productions are a terrible representation of Newbury's catalog. Snake-oil advertisements bemoaned, "This release is a fitting and timely tribute to an extraordinary artist gone before his time." In so much as Mickey loathed the RCA productions and his estate was not consulted beforehand, the release is improper and disrespectful as a "tribute." In the interest of making money for the record company, the release may prove "timely."

**ALBUM # 28** Camden / BMG - a reissue budget UK label - was next to jump on the bandwagon a mere two months later, releasing in April a CD titled, "Harlequin Melodies." The effort packages 14 songs from Mickey's RCA recordings... also included on the Australian Raven issue.

Mickey's comment would probably be, "And the two-step goes on..."

# Epilogue: *Whistle-Stops*

T.S. Eliot understood the relationship of the forest to the trees, writing, "We must know all of Shakespeare's work in order to know any of it." Similarly, Mickey Newbury's art - the words, verses, songs and albums - are all links to the chain. "Every Newbury line," wrote one of his friends, "was carefully thought out so that it would go with his work as a whole. Everything ties together at the end. I believe he could see the end from the beginning."

Common references and metaphors with parallel focus permeate Newbury's work. In *The Silver Moon Cafe*, for instance, he paints a picture of Guthrie, a town originally addressed in his classic, *Cortelia Clark*. Why did he choose this one twice? And by the way, where in the world is Guthrie?

First, Guthrie is the perfect word; it sounds Southern, plus it sounds familiar. The poet in Mickey paid great attention to the way words worked or sounded together. Sonically, the word phrases well within the songs. Then there's also Woody Guthrie, which contributes to the word's instant familiarity.

Newbury initially raised Guthrie in *Cortelia Clark*, the beautiful ballad recorded in 1972 in Nashville, where he and Cortelia lived. As the story goes, Mickey and the blind old black man "went to Guthrie just to see the trains." Note that Nashville is a mere 50 miles south of a Guthrie, Kentucky, a tiny town on the Tennessee-Kentucky border. A large train depot operated there at the time; it was demolished in the late seventies. Could this be the place?

Mickey left an obvious and immediate marker in the song's opening: "I was just a boy the year / The Blue Bird Special came through here / On its first run south to New Orleans." If a train had originated in Guthrie, Kentucky and headed straight south, it would have indeed passed through Nashville en route to The Big Easy. So Guthrie, Kentucky does make sense as the earthly point of reference; and moreover, Susan Newbury confirmed this to be true. "He wrote the song on the way to Kentucky," she said, "and after we got back. There was a noticeable train depot and switching yard in Guthrie that we went past every time we drove to Kentucky."

In the song's moving finale, Cortelia departed Nashville, ascending to heaven; and then at last, his dreams were no longer "chained to a depot down in Guthrie." Nashville, though unmentioned in the song, and Guthrie are left... at best as purgatorial references... at worst as whistle-stops farther south. Now we're ridin' on the Newbury Train.

275

Twenty-eight years later, Mick would continue the conversation. Raising the town again, he offered a peek at its truck stop, *The Silver Moon Cafe*. In truth, on the west side of Guthrie, where highways 11, 41, 79, 181 and 848 converge, a rest stop called Tiny Town once stood. It was "out on the highway," he sang in *The Silver Moon Cafe*, where truckers spent time "pouring coffee down…"

Mick empathized with the waitress working there. "As busy as she can be," he disclosed, the only way she could "hold on to her sanity." In the end, she escaped with her better half, as he delivered the family from the predicament, while singing, "There's a blue moon in Kentucky / I'm on this two-lane out of town / Just one stop to pick up my lady / Population three more down." This could be Mick, Susan and Baby Chris pullin' out of Nashville, forever leavin' the glow of blue neon.

Two more Newbury songs visit the leavin' theme, but for rhyme, rhythm and meter, a three-syllable place was required, so Kentucky was used. In the 1975 song, *Leaving Kentucky*, Mickey explained the deal, "The road down to Nashville's / Like crystal and stone / A place where a man / Sells his soul for a song." As crystal is clear and stone is hard, he was eloquently admitting that it was clearly hard - spiritually destructive - to barter with the southerly piper. Continuing, "God knows I loved her too much I can see / Much more than she could have ever loved me…" For good reason then, he confessed on the record, he was "Leavin' Kentucky and going back home."

Finally, in the 1994 song, *East Kentucky*, Mickey owned up to the past: "In the shadow of the tall pines / I did love her with no shame." Again, he was speaking of the Glittertown whore, Miss Gnashville. And so for good reason and with 20/20 vision, he concluded the sermon with: "Dusty highway, take me to Denver. I will not be coming back." Mick wrote the song in the early seventies, when he and Susie checked out of Guitar Town for higher latitude.

These tales of Guthrie… Kentucky and East Kentucky sketch an outline of Mickey Newbury's Gnashville. He left it to us to connect the dots. Talk about dancin' with the devil… The man's ingenious imagery could even hide hell in a gorgeous melody. In more embraceable terms, however, the stories present the God-awful places we frequent and the painful mistakes we make, while doing our best to survive. Ultimately, he did not write about coordinates on a map. Newbury wrote about places of the heart… and at the end of the day… when the train leaves the station… the enlightened spirit.

# Last Words
## (in alphabetical order)

*I never met Mick except by email and telephone, but I knew him for thirty years with my ears and my heart. One of the proudest days of my life was when Mick called me to tell me he was putting one of my reviews of his CD on his website. He was a sweet, loving man that was wonderful to my lady Barb who was and is terminally ill. He would talk to her on the phone like they were dear, old friends... but you know Mick made everybody feel special... Artistically, Musically and otherwise we will never see his like again... God Bless Mickey Newbury.*
**Hank Beukema**

*Mickey Newbury and his music have been my invisible, but constant companions for thirty years or more. In those final years he became my very dear friend as well. Few have had such an impact on my life. He is missed. He cannot be replaced. Farewell My Friend.*
**Meeks Booker**

*I love ya, pal! just says it all...*
**Keith Bowman**

*Mickey had the wisdom of the ages and the talent of the gods. His voice will forever echo in the hearts and minds of all those who are privileged to listen. He was loyal to listeners, his loved ones, his friends and to himself. He was a songwriter's songwriter, a singer's singer and most of all a friend's friend. I will always miss him.*
**Rick Brashear**

*Mickey Newbury is forever. Like anything overwhelmingly beautiful in nature, Mickey defies words but is felt, mostly in the heart. His music is simply everything I ever want to hear. His loving friendship, to one so everyday as myself, is a gift that I carry with me, one of my most precious possessions. Mickey is a music genius with the voice of an angel and the truth of God above. I love him.*
**Karen Warne-Bull**

*For many, emotions are the most difficult thing to put a pen to. It's not that we don't feel... We're just incapable of reaching the depths with tangible words. Mickey Newbury had a gift of expression rivaled by none. His music and lyrics will, if you allow yourself to go, take you places you've never been. They open doors formerly unknown and make self-awareness a much simpler task. His music has done so much for me, making me better*

277

*understand myself. No self-help book will ever reveal as much as the music.*
**Ernie Bunch**

*I played Mickey's music while painting his portrait* (used on the front cover of this book). *I had the undeniable sense of his presence there with me in my studio! Hearing his CD's for the first time, I fell under the spell of his deeply moving and soulful lyrics and his gentle, appealing voice as he sang them. I never had the pleasure of meeting him, but while doing his portrait, I came to feel I knew him. It was a deeply moving experience. Now, he and his music will forever be a part of my life.*
**Mary Shelton Burson**

*As in the lyric of Mickey's 'American Trilogy': 'All my trials Lord, will soon be over'… His trials are over, but his music will be alive forever as, 'Sweet Memories.' We have lost a legend; I have lost a friend…*
**Larry Butler**

*Hey Old Man, how're you feelin'? Good for the 1st time in a while, hey? You dreamed about writing the perfect song. One where each note led inexorably to the next in the melody, each word, when sung, told singer/listener what the next word had to be. You can sing it for me soon, Old Man. Man, we had good times at the first and great times at the last. I 'wish we hadn't let the middle get away. It would have been fun to watch each other's kids grow up and to see Barbara and Susie get to know each other as girls. Susie and the kids are doing fine, me too, but you know that. You know, I didn't mind being a gatekeeper when you needed me to, watching your back, I guess. We watched each other's often enough in Biloxi. I miss talking to you. I love you old son.*
**Keith "Chaz" Chastain**

*When you get to your destination I'm sure you'll be amongst friends. I was pleased to have known you here and to call you friend. I will never forget you, your smile and your appreciation for life.*
**Paul Colby**

*Mickey left us all with 'Sweet Memories.' God, he was so good! We will never see another one like him coming down the road. 'Sail Away' in peace Mickey.*
**Mike Considine**

*Since the early seventies, we are great fans of Mick and play his music over and over. In good and bad times, his music gives us satisfaction and peace of mind. Mickey, we will always remember the good.*
**Wim and Thea Danielse**

*I was seventeen years old when Mick touched my life with his words and music. Whether the song is one of sorrow or celebration I've always thought each of Mick's songs is a prayer, and that for thirty-seven-plus years now both Mick and God have allowed me to listen in on their most private conversations. I loved Mick. Mick loved me. I miss him terribly, but I take great comfort in knowing we'll see each other again.*
**Randy Dodds**

*During my nearly 40-year career in radio and television, I've interviewed many musicians and writers. Most said it was about the art, not the money. Mickey Newbury was the only one who lived up to that statement every day.*
**Jeff Douglas** (Founder KINK radio & Oregon Art Beat)

*Kathy and I felt Mick with us on our trip many times... coming out of Utah into Idaho 'bout 6:00 AM (early start to make Washington before night); I had just come out of a stretch of road covered with fresh snow... front was passing west to east... to my left there was a break in the clouds and there was a big ol' moon setting right over Oregon... I just said, 'Good morning Mick... you told me you'd guide my way when we came west.' I sure miss him.*
**Steve & Kathy Enfinger**

*Mickey - My introduction to you was hearing "Looks Like Rain" for the first time. I was stationed in Fairbanks, Alaska in 1970. It was much more than just a breath of fresh air in a dark, dismal place. You reached within the confines of my soul and spoke only to me. In 1978, I had the honor of being in the presence of you singing and playing guitar in Globe, Arizona. You treated me like I was an old friend. It was sublime. You are sorely missed.*
**Mary Frank**

*When I first met Mickey in 1977, I knew nothing of his legendary status as a songwriter. I was aware of his recording of 'American Trilogy,' and thought it was incredible, but knew nothing of the rest of his career. He was my friend before I came to hear the music. I think we were closer over the last six or seven years of his life than during the earlier part of our friendship. I will always be grateful for those last years and for what I learned from him.*
**Dave Franklin**

*In 1971, Dottie West told me I looked enough like Mickey Newbury that I had to be able to write songs. I might have looked like him, but I sure couldn't write like him. He was one of a kind and I miss him.*
**Larry Gatlin**

*If it weren't for Mickey and his music none of this would be the same - neither the Flora-Bama nor the Frank Brown International Songwriters' Festival.*
**Joe Gilchrist**

*Stumbling upon Mickey's website by a strange twist of fate opened my life to a stunningly beautiful type of music I'd never heard before. But even more important to me was the opportunity to interact with a down-to-earth man of such genius and compassion. He welcomed me into his 'family of friends' on his website and shared them with me - a treasure I would not trade for anything. I suspect he taught us more about love, courage and kindness than anyone would ever imagine.*
**Ginny Gnadt**

*As for changing my life as a songwriter, I would have never written 'Alone In Love' or 'Heaven On Earth' or 'The Fool In Me' - had it not been for Mickey. Those songs are attempts at capturing what he did and somehow incorporating it into what I do... Mickey knew about my attempts to transfer some of his craft into my own and encouraged it. He would sing new songs to me over the phone (some of which I recorded... ) He was a hero of mine.*
**David Grossman**

*Because I just know you are reading this, Mickey... Here's to the songs that got away... here's to your love you let stay... Miss your sweet-sly-smiling voice and wink more than could ever be rightly said, Mick. Thank you for your touch upon our lives. Go Easy and with my love, dear friend.*
**Marty Hall**

*A lifelong love of Mickey's music brought Deborah and I together in 1998. We were married in October 1999 and owe our happiness to Mickey. How we miss him!*
**Dale & Deborah Hamilton**

*I admired Mickey's writing... his voice... his humor... his stories... his riddles... his brilliant, quirky, intelligent mind, which could skip and jump from subject to subject 'cross cities, fields, continents and time. If good conversation is one of life's treasures (and it is), then Mickey Newbury was a gold mine. I admired his courage and the way he refused to let circumstances defeat him. I loved him.*
**Dorothy Hamm**

*I was lucky to meet and know Mickey. 'Love is all that matters,' he sang. Beyond the technical wizardry of an accomplished wordsmith there is the true and simple message told with grace and style. Thank you, Mickey, for the hours of conversation. Thank you for the music. Thank you for the*

*songs that capture the myriad moments that are the seconds, minutes and years of all our lives; past, present and future…*
**Brian Highley**

*I am so thankful that I found The Front Porch where I have been given so much and asked for so little in return. Rest easy Mickey.*
**Gerry Howell**

*An Incredible Man… An Incredible Friend… Damn, I Miss Ya Mick.*
**Ed Heffelfinger**

*He was a modest man who just wanted to be known as a songwriter. He will go down in my memory as a dear friend and an extremely gifted and warm human being whose loss will be greatly felt by all those who simply listened to his beautiful songs.*
**Frank Ifield**

*He put an entire emotional lifetime into every song he played and sang. He made us laugh and cry, but mostly we sat there transfixed in his presence, sharing the extremes and feelings of a life many of us will never have any other way to know. One of the few true musical artists of our time, there will never be another like my friend, Mickey.*
**Casey Kelley**

*His Spirit has gone where there's Goodness and music. So, what I say is move over Gant, another great tenor has arrived and God wants him to sing in the choir. See you later, Mick.*
**Rock Killough**

*I spoke to Mickey last June, and I told him I loved him, and Mickey said, 'I love you too honey.' I really miss him. I suppose we all do.*
**Una Kinsella**

*Mickey Newbury is one of our greatest songwriters, right up there with Stephen Foster. I learned more about songwriting from him than any other writer, watching him put simple words and music together in a way that breaks your heart. He fought a lifelong battle to get our kind of music the respect it deserves, and I will always be grateful for our friendship.*
**Kris Kristofferson**

*When you write a song, what you leave out shows the depth of your respect for the feelings and imaginations of your listeners. It's about allowing people to enter your song and feel welcome. Mickey Newbury's music invites you in and makes you feel at home.*
**Doug Lang**

*Thank you Mickey for your sweet and generous spirit. You have given me gifts that I will cherish for all time. So long for now old friend.*
**Ken Lambert**

*Last May, I lost my father... His burden's lifted, his pain now gone... Doors closed, bridges burned... I did not cry. Thirty-three years ago a man lifted me to hear and see a world of sweet memories, rain, broken diamond necklaces, laboring winters... and Waycross boys; of hearts and doors to open, of bridges to build, of souls in pain cleansed and thus, redeemed... I came to hear his music, to know his music, and to love this man... Then in September, I learned of Mickey's passing... The nights went still, the darkness stayed... Where was the rain? I cried.*
**Joey Latunski**

*September 23, 2002, around 2:30 pm as I was leaving his home: Ron: 'Mickey, thank you for being my friend.' Mick: 'No, Ron, thank you for being MY friend.' The last magic in person moment.*
**Ron Lyons**

*Time*
*Somehow I thought that I controlled time / God made it just for my pleasure*
*Now I know it belongs to no one / It's something that all men should treasure*
*I thought you'd be here everyday / I thought you'd be here forever*
*Took for granted I'd see you again / I now know the meaning of never*
*I thought I'd say I love you / But that's not what real men should do*
*Real men are weak I never did speak / I'm hoping to God that you knew*
*Somehow I thought that I controlled time / I'd tell you my feelings some day*
*Now all the words I wanted to speak / Are words that I never can say*
**Larry Moore**

*Although Mickey is classified as a songwriter/singer, his primary role was that of teacher. His teaching of the 'Giving' of ourselves to one another is central to the body of his work. He wrote it, sang it, but most importantly, lived it. Few, like Mick, have or will come this way again. We have suffered a mighty loss, but have gained mightily in the knowledge of this man and his labors.*
**Jim Moreillon**

*I fell in love with Mickey's music in 1971 and I had the privilege of meeting the great man in England on his last tour some 6 years back I think. He was on the Don Williams tour and my musical buddy's and I spent the night talking to Mickey about music and influences. The highlight of my life, never forgotten, always there. Nobody came close to Mickey's voice and never will, and his songs are the greatest backdrop of American Country Music. God bless you Mickey for all those years of stunning music.*
**Peter Morrison**

*I will love you for all eternity.*
**Lana Nelson**

*He was one of the best writers we've ever had and one of the best friends I've ever had.*
**Willie Nelson**

*I was in Gulfport, Mississippi, in 1993 listening to a friend at the piano. He asked if I had ever heard of Mickey Newbury. He proceeded to play 'She Even Woke Me Up' and 'American Trilogy.' I knew the songs well but not the writer. Two weeks later at a Songwriters Festival in Gulf Shores, Alabama, I got to meet and hear Mickey. The first song he sang was 'San Francisco Mabel Joy.' I was hooked! I soon found Mickey was not only a gifted singer/songwriter but also a man who loved people. It was a privilege to have known him.*
**Bili Pahlman**

*Our lives will be forever changed, not because he left us, but because he touched us… I love you Mickey. See you in the New Jerusalem.*
**Andrew W. Polk**

*For almost thirty-five years I have tried to adequately describe to those who ask what Mickey Newbury and his music has meant to me on a daily basis. I have come to the conclusion that I truly cannot. Words are so inadequate. All I can say is that I love Mickey Newbury as a songwriter, as a singer, as a brother, as a friend. His passing has left a void in my life that will never be filled. The likes of Mickey Newbury will never come our way again. With his passing, I have come to realize how very special he was and how very special his music was and is.*
**Mary Anne Potter**

*We all expected this day would come, but that doesn't lessen the pain of losing him, or how much we're going to miss him. If all the pickers meet and jam in heaven, you know Mickey is there. I bet the first one he seeks out is Steven Foster.*
**Drew Reid**

*I always felt as if I were sitting next to a giant when we performed together on stage and as if I were finally at home. There was never any other place on earth I'd rather have been than on stage touring with Mickey. I think he was an angel in a songwriter suit and I never saw a single demon around us, not ever. He was a humble, gentle man, and full of mischief.*
**Marie Rhines**

*It was the year that I died, when I first heard the music of Mickey Newbury. That was back in 1973... I was 21... I was all alone, but then, I guess... I was born alone. 'When you're alone there's nothin' as slow as passin' time. When you're afoot there's nothin' as fast as a train.' His music heavily impacted upon my heart. It reached out through all my confusion and isolation and touched my soul... deep into my soul. It lifted me up and carried me into the clouds... I am still there today... just Mickey and me. God bless you Dear Heart.*
**David Riddell (Aussiedave)**

*Mickey was a friend and a colleague, and I regret more than I can say having not been in touch with him these last few years. His wife and family are in my prayers.*
**Kenny Rogers**

*We had a long visit that day (July of 2002), and he was getting tired... so... I told him goodbye... then I hugged him and told him that the Front Porch loved him, and he meant so much to all of us.*
**Karen Runk**

*In my life, as with so many others, Mickey Newbury was providential.*
**Tupper Saussy**

*I met Mickey in 1969 at our music publisher (Acuff-Rose) offices in Nashville. I was the new guy there and he was well established as a premier songwriter and artist of extraordinary passion... When I recorded his song 'Mobile Blue,' he was there and just smiled as if I were Roy Orbison or something and our friendship never wavered from that moment... Lately he asked me for Autoharp lessons, and I so looked forward to some time alone with this dear and gentle person. Sadly, C'est la vie... No one, then or now, will ever possess his way with words and melody and our heartstrings are stronger now from his gentle tug... Shine On Mickey, Shine On.*
**Gove Scrivenor**

*Mick's music will forever be my favorite form of entertainment.*
**Archie Shepherd**

*In 1997 I ran across Mickey's phone number and called him. I had been listening to and loving his music for more than 20 years. We talked for three hours and became instant friends. We talked for hours on end from then on for more years, and I got to meet him and hug him finally, at his Mom's house last summer. I always separated in my mind the friend I talked to on the phone and the inestimable artist, singer and songwriter that I was listening to on my CD player. I think Mickey did too. I think he had not the*

*slightest idea how great and beautiful his music was, he always downplayed it. He was the best. I still have the music, the CDs, the art, the lyrics, the beauty. I would give it all up to talk to by buddy one more time. I'm sure he's playing piano with Stephen Foster. Love you, Pal.*
**Bill Smith**

*Mickey was one of the kindest persons I ever met. I miss him.*
**Connie Smith**

*If you only knew, when I first came to Nashville about '68, I knew what I wanted to do but I was searching for a song in my heart that no one else was singing. It was so elusive, but so perfect. Then comes this beauty in his house-car carrying all of his pills in an old gray sock. You started the music, you started the joy and you started my heart.*
**Sammi Smith**

*We became Mickey Newbury fans when we heard 'Frisco Mabel Joy.' Since then we have spent many happy hours listening to him. Mickey's lyrics read like poetry. We have introduced Mickey's music to all of our extended family. Our family now boasts three generations of Mickey Newbury fans.*
**Lois and Chet Spencer**

*Over a lifetime, how many people have you met that really made a change in your life... whose words and actions made a difference? Mickey was such a person... a great singer and songwriter, but also a great teacher of life. I've lost a friend, but music and the world has lost a master. Love ya Pal.*
**Roy Stamps**

*'Drop by for a cup of coffee Jeff,' Mickey's Email suggested. I did! That cup of coffee lasted seven hours! With my little gut string Martin he sang 'In '59.' 'Your guitar has great tone. The neck is perfect!' Then he played my big one; 'Has Jack (Williams) played this?' Next he coaxed me to play; 'Chris,' he shouted, 'come listen to this!' Finally, I shared a recording of a student singing 'Shenandoah.' 'Yep, I wish I'd sung it that way.' He was like that to everyone. He made us feel as important to him as he was to us. Three bells, Mick.*
**Jeff Stave**

*Mickey was one of a kind and I miss him everyday.*
**Jonmark Stone**

*What a wonderful gift God gave us in such a talented man that had so much affect on many people in many ways.*
**Tex Toler**

*We wrote songs, Mickey wrote poetry. I was a songwriter; Mickey was a poet who wrote better songs than I did.*
**Sonny Throckmorton**

*Mick has finally gone over that long road home. I still have a lot of traveling to do, but I am grateful for the ride he gave me. Thanks.*
**Joop van den Bosch**

*When I remember Nashville in years to come, the two men I'll remember and feel blessed to have shared some music with are Chet (Atkins) and Mickey - as different as they can be, but both giants and visionaries.*
**Roy Vogt**

*Knowing Mickey Newbury and his music has raised the standard of everything I try to do. I am a better photographer because of him.*
**Phil Weedon**

*I'm no Saint, but I have heard the voice of an angel.*
**Val Weedon**

*Mickey Newbury phenomenally gave so much of himself to so many people. He was real to everyone who reached out to him, and I consider myself so very fortunate to have been his friend. He tried to prepare me for his departure when the end was near, and out of honor, I am seeking everyday, something new to be happy about in this beautiful world he loved so much.*
**Susan Williamson**

*I can best memorialize him in 2 ways, by continuing to perform his songs, and by never settling for an adequate line.*
**Larry Jon Wilson**

*The day I was born my mother was listening to Mickey. I have grown up on Mickey and got to meet him several times. He always had the time to teach me, help me and he still does to this day through his music. Mickey Newbury was a teacher and my hero.*
**Amber Wirths**

*There are givers and there are takers in this world, Mickey Newbury was a giver. For a big part of my life, I thought of his music, his words as a storybook about pain and wonder, and people he loved who loved him. Then I somehow came to think of it as a rulebook telling me the do's and dont's of how to live. Mickey has been many things to me. And so, at last I hear it as I think he intended; it's heart, soul, where you reveal yourself, where he and I can come together. I love and miss him.*
**Judy Wirths**

286

*The world has lost a true legend, and I've lost the best friend I ever had. I never knew anybody who gave of himself more. He helped out tons of singers who are major right now, and he never took any credit.*
**Ron Woolman** (Mickey's former manager)

*There are so many people across this great planet whose lives were touched by this man and his music... Sing with those angels my friend. Your voice was angelic and your songs so divine.*
**Claude Wooley**

*Mickey's music was an experience of a lifetime... knowing Mickey and his family is a lifetime experience.*
**Earl Wynn**

*Mickey Newbury's albums are to American music what Mark Twain's books are to American literature. Still, his friendship means more to me than all that. 'Save a street in Glory Lord...'*
**Joe Ziemer**

# Interviews

*The Newbury Family:*
Mickey Newbury, Susan Newbury, Mamie Newbury, Doug Byrd
*Others:*
Mary Frank Andrews, Bill Barnett, Detta Beach, Pat Boone, Talmage Bell, Keith (Chaz) Chastain, Mike Considine, Dave Franklin, Chuck (CAG) Gengler, Martin (Marty) Hall, Mike Henley, Jac Holzman, Doyle Jones, Peggy Lamb (of Acuff-Rose), Ron Lyons (plus Ron's outstanding interviews of Mickey and Kris Kristofferson), Jim Moreillon, Marie Rhines, Sammi Smith, Roy Stamps, Jeff Stave, Jonmark Stone, Tess Turner, Phil Weedon, Bud Wilhite, Earl Wynn

# Front Cover

The wonderful front cover portrait of Mickey was painted by Mary Shelton Burson, an exceptional artist from Alabama. Thanks, Mary!

# Photos

Thanks to Mamie Newbury for 11 pictures from her scrapbook:
(12) Mickey at four months
(13) Mickey at six with brother Jerry at four
(14) Mickey at six
(31) Mickey – 8th grade
(32) School Days
(33) The Embers Postcard
(34) The Embers with Julian Barnett
(52) On leave with brother Jerry
(106) Working on a song
(118) Relaxing on Old Hickory Lake
(118) Milton, Mamie, Mickey and Susan

(78) Mickey circa 1968: Thanks to an unknown source
(148) Concert poster – At UCLA: Thanks to Charlene Gordon
(164) At a benefit concert: Thanks to Mary Frank Andrews

Thanks to Connie Smith for three wonderful pictures:
(182) Too Tall Mick with Guy Clark at the Birchmere
(211) Jesse Winchester and Mickey
(212) Mickey at the Birchmere

*Photos*

(228) Micks handwritten lyrics: Author's personal collection
(229) At Flora-Bama: Thanks Phil Weedon (English not British)
(230) Immediately following...Thanks to Mary Anne Potter
(246) Mamie, Mick & the author: Thanks to Earl & Suzi Wynn

Thanks Chagares Photography for professional image scanning.
Thanks 1st Books, especially Catherine Carver & Anne Clemmer.

# Bibliography

"Elvis Defends Low-Down Style," Kays Gary, <u>Charlotte Observer</u>, June 27, 1956 *Summary:* Elvis talks about "colored folks" singing his music long before he did.

"Songwriter Mickey Newbury," <u>Billboard</u>, May 4, 1968 *Summary:* Following contract signing, MN poses w/ RCA & Acuff-Rose execs and Jay Boyette, his manager.

"Inside The Grand Ole Opry," Larry King, <u>Harper's Magazine</u> (reprinted <u>Life Magazine</u> & Oct <u>Reader's Digest),</u> 7/68 *Summary:* First nationwide MN article, history of country music, Opry's popularity, Nashville's importance, MN's arrival

"Are My Thoughts With You," <u>Billboard</u>, July 20, 1968 *Summary:* Song review

"Harlequin Melodies," <u>Billboard</u>, August 17, 1968 *Summary:* LP review

<u>GO</u> magazine (WMCA edition), # 132, September 27,1968 *Summary:* Cover features 9" x 9" color picture/ad of "Harlequin Melodies" LP. Also includes article on the tragic death of Roy Orbison's two sons. (<u>GO</u> promoted itself as "world's largest circulation of any pop weekly.")

"Mickey Newbury - Country Music Roots," Bill Grine, <u>Country Song Roundup</u>, March 1969 *Summary:* Interview - first hit with Don Gibson (FFFF), The Embers, country roots, writing songs

"New Stars On The Horizon - Mickey Newbury," <u>Hit Parader</u>, June 1969 *Summary:* MN brief bio and signing with RCA. Paul McCartney and Jimi Hendrix are featured on the cover.

"A New Generation Of Country Music - Mickey Newbury," (as told to) Jim Delehant, <u>Hit Parader</u>, October 1969 *Summary:* Autobiographical narration, Jimmy Rodgers, The Embers, Mexican kids, Elvis, Dylan...

"Nashville Sound Spreads To The Village's Bitter End," <u>The Tennessean</u>, May 3, 1970 *Summary:* How Nashville music is changing, Paris in the 20's

"Mickey Newbury / Roxy - Bitter End, New York," Nancy Erlich, <u>Billboard</u>, ~ May, 1970 *Summary:* Brief write-up of Newbury's April 22 show at the Bitter End East

*Bibliography*

Skip Weshner Show (KRHM-Los Angeles), Audio Interview, ~ June 1970 *Summary:* Houseboat, marriage, MN sings 5 songs (special thanks to Frank Blau, executor of Mr. Weshner's estate)

"Country Star Of The Month - Mickey Newbury," Staff Editors, <u>Song Hits</u>, October 1970 *Summary:* Brief bio and overview

"Mickey Newbury Doin' His Thing," Bill Anderson, Editor, <u>Country Song Roundup</u>, November 1970 *Summary:* Country music trends, why MN won't write commercial songs, why he won't tour, Fillmore West, The Bitter End, Funny Familiar Forgotten Feelings; MN is "really happy," future goals, disappointing LP sales

"Superstars, Poets, Pickers, Prophets," William Hedgepeth, <u>Look Magazine</u>, July 13, 1971 *Summary:* Brief overview of MN

"Mickey Newbury Doin' His Thing," Interview by Bill Anderson, Editor, <u>Country Song Roundup</u>, Annual, Fall 1971 (Reprinted from the November 1970 issue, summarized above.)

"Frisco Mabel Joy," Karin Berg, <u>Rolling Stone</u> # 96, November 25, 1971 *Summary:* Very positive review of the LP

"MN: Funny, Familiar and Remembered," Albert Hall, <u>Country Song Roundup</u>, December 1971 *Summary:* Discusses diversity of MN's songs, country stars going to LA, signing with Elektra

"Emerging Genius," Staff Editors, <u>Hit Parader</u>, April 1972 *Summary:* Excerpts from Dec 1971 article in <u>Country Song Roundup</u>, "MN: Funny, Familiar & Remembered"

<u>Disco 45 </u>(a UK magazine), No. 21, July 1972 *Summary:* Lyrics to MN's song, "An American Trilogy"

"MN Sings His Own," Editors, <u>Billboard</u>, 1972 *Summary:* "Sings His Own" is selected as "A <u>Billboard</u> Pick" album.

"Newbury, Country Boy," <u>Melody Maker</u> (UK pub), October 28, 1972 <u>Summary</u>: MN interview during visit to England

"Mickey Talking," Martin Neil, <u>Disc</u> (UK publication), November 25, 1972 *Summary:* Good interview (Houston childhood to 1972)

## Bibliography

"Playbill, 2nd Annual Elektra Records WEA Distributors Convention," Phoenix, Arizona, January 4-6, 1973 *Summary:* 20 pages on Elektra artists (MN, Judy Collins, New Seekers, Bread) who attended this gig

"Mickey Newbury," Del Porter, Folk Scene, Vol. 2, No. 2, April 1974 *Summary:* Review of "Live At Montezuma/Looks Like Rain"

"Mickey Newbury - I Came To Hear The Music," Robert Adels, Country Music, Vol. 2, No. 10, June 1974 *Summary:* Very positive review of the album

"MN Sings The Eternal Blues," Rice Wiseman, Rolling Stone, May 8, 1975 *Summary:* MN's disdain for the road and the music business, spending 2 years in his room, brief bio

"UK Ninth International Festival of Country Music Program," April 1977 *Summary:* Brief overview / bio of MN

"The Mickey Newbury Interview," Peter O'Brien (April 10 in UK), Omaha Rainbow, Issue 13, June 1977 *Summary:* Excellent long interview which focuses on MN's biography, 1962 - 1977

"Mickey Newbury - Rusty Tracks Review," Lola Scobey, Country Music, June 1977 *Summary:* Self-explanatory

"MN's Thoughts On Songwriting," Russell Shaw, Country Song Roundup, June 1977 *Summary:* Interview with MN on songwriting philosophy and tools of the trade

"Mickey Newbury's Root Music," Staff Editors, Country Music People, December 1977 *Summary:* Brief bio, review of Looks Like Rain, An American Trilogy and Rusty Tracks

"Mickey Newbury," Editor - Pembroke Picker, The Pedal Steel Guitarist, Vol. 2, No. 1, 1978 *Summary:* Wonderful MN interview with emphasis on his influence on music and writing

"Mickey Newbury - His Eye Is On The Sparror," Mitch Cohen, Country Music, Vol. 6, No. 9, June 1978 *Summary:* Review of the album

"NSAI Elects Four Hall of Fame Members," Editors, Country Music, Jan/Feb 1981 *Summary:* MN's 1980 induction into the Songwriter's Hall of Fame

*Bibliography*

"Tootsie's Shines in Tarnish of Lower Broadway," Bob Campbell, <u>Country Music</u>, Jan/Feb 1981 *Summary:* Brief history of Tootsie's Orchid Lounge in Nashville

"Songwriter Brings Golden Hits To New Age," Thomas Goldsmith, <u>Nashville Tennessean Showcase</u>, 6/12/88 *Summary:* Brief, complimentary history of MN and story of "In A New Age"

"Newbury - An Affecting, Gentle Return," Robert Hilburn, <u>Los Angeles Times</u>, July 14, 1988 *Summary:* Brief overview of MN and a positive review of his performance at the Roxy in L.A.

"Dancing With Your Demons - Mickey Newbury (Re)visited," Don Negri, <u>Dirty Linen</u> #26, Summer 1989 *Summary:* Excellent review of MN's songwriting mastery, analysis of his lyrics, review of "In A New Age"

"Jack Bernhardt Collection," Audio Interview, February 19, 1990 *Summary:* Kristofferson & songwriting in the sixties

"Mickey Newbury - An Outlaw Tale," Allen Harbinson, <u>Goldmine Magazine</u>, April 6, 1990 *Summary:* Well written MN biography and LP review

"A Songwriter's Seminar" (VHS video tape), 1992 *Summary:* Five legendary songwriters (including MN) discuss their craft

"Faces - Places: One From The Heartland," Deborah Evans Price, <u>Us</u> magazine, Issue 186, July 1993 *Summary:* Report of 1993 Farm Aid VI concert with picture of MN giving Lyle Lovett a kiss

"Frank Brown International Songwriters Festival," Ross Jaburg, <u>Performing Songwriter</u>, Issue 8, Sep 8, 1994 *Summary:* History of the festival and the Flora-Bama lounge and the interaction of participating songwriters

"Not For The Money - An Uncommon Songwriter," Michael McCall, <u>Nashville Scene</u>, September 15, 1994 *Summary:* MN's integrity will not allow him to compromise his artistic vision.

"Newbury's Pain Songs - Terrifying Beauty," Travis Corder, <u>Music Row</u>, Vol. 14, October 14, 1994 *Summary:* Postulates that MN ranks perhaps as America's most terrifying songwriter

"Shrimp Boats: A Galveston Dolphin's Smorgasbord," Dagmar Fertl and Bernd Wursig, October 30 1995 *Summary:* On-board conditions for a shrimper

294

## Bibliography

"Mickey Newbury Remembers," Kurt Wolff, <u>No Depression</u>, March 1997 *Summary:* Emphasizes MN's influence on Nashville and other artists plus the beauty of his music

<u>Songwriters On Songwriting: The Expanded Version</u>, Paul Zollo, September 1997 *Summary:* Thirty-one songwriters discuss their methods and the way their songs came to be

"Crystal and Stone: The Mickey Newbury Collection," George H Lewis, <u>Popular Music and Society</u>, 1998 *Summary:* Very well written review of the MN Box Set

"Mickey Newbury - Bluebird Cafe," <u>No Depression</u>, January-February 1998 *Summary:* Favorable review of Mick's performance

"The Amazing Tupper Saussy," John Branston, <u>Memphis Flyer</u>, May 18, 1998 *Summary:* Bio of Mr. Saussy

<u>Careless Love</u>, Peter Guralnick, 1999 *Summary:* Volume two of perhaps the best Elvis Presley biography

"Rhythm & Views: Mickey Newbury," Dave Mc Elfresh, <u>Tucson Weekly</u>, January 25, 1999 *Summary:* Short review of Box Set

Article (untitled), Tom Geddie, <u>Buddy</u> (Dallas) magazine, 1999 *Summary:* Positive review of "It Might As Well Be The Moon"

"Quicksilver Daydreams," Peter Blackstock, <u>No Depression</u>, March 1999 *Summary:* Excellent review of the Box Set with emphasis on the first four albums

"Nashville Songwriters Hall of Fame," Edward Morris, <u>Music City News</u>, May 1999 *Summary:* Overview of writers who have made the NSHF. Brief bio of MN

"MN - Just Droppin In" with Album Discography, Joe Ziemer, <u>Goldmine</u>, June 2, 2000 *Summary:* Recap of MN's career; what he is like as a person

"A Muse's Muse Interview With Mickey Newbury," Jodi Krangle, <u>musesmuse. com</u>, 2000 *Summary:* MN as a songwriter

<u>Country Roads</u>, Brian Hinton, August 1, 2000 *Summary:* Influences on today's country music

*Bibliography*

Follow the Music, Jac Holzman & Gavan Daws, August 30, 2000 *Summary:* The life and high times of Elektra Records in the great years of American pop culture

"MN Is The Song Poet," Dorothy Hamm, American Songwriter, September 2001 *Summary:* Brief overview of MN with emphasis on how he writes songs

"An Interview With Wayne Moss," Derek Halsey, February 2002 *Summary:* Moss discusses Cinderella Studio

"Mickey Newbury - A Long Road Home," Peter Blackstock, No Depression # 38, March 2002 *Summary:* Review of the album

"America's Music," (special issue) U.S. News & World Report, July 8-15, 2002 *Summary:* Review of American music, from Yankee Doodle to Hip-Hop

"Mickey Newbury," Al Moir, Country Music People (UK pub), November, 2002 *Summary:* Heartfelt tribute, 3-page article

"Sweet Memories - Mickey Newbury Remembered," Alan Cackett, Maverick (UK pub), November 2002 *Summary:* Two-page well-written tribute

"Farther Along: Mickey Newbury, 1940-2002," Peter Blackstock, No Depression, November 2002 *Summary:* Very well-written (perhaps the best) tribute to MN

"18th Annual Frank Brown International Songwriters Festival," November 2002 *Summary:* Program for the festival includes MN tribute with comments from songwriters & celebrities

"Remembering Mickey Newbury - A Songwroter's Poet," Jim Nash, Nashville Music Guide, Nov 2002 *Summary:* Terribly written MN tribute. Also features MN on cover. (Name is spelled "Newberry" throughout.)

"33 Things You Should Know About Willie Nelson," Phil Sutcliffe, Blender, 2002 *Summary:* Self-explanatory

"Mickey Newbury Dies At 62," Michael McCall, Country Music, December/January 2003 *Summary:* Brief tribute

Sweet Memories, LaVyrle Spencer, C 1984, Released 2003 *Summary:* Romance novel, pp 327-8 contains MN lyric: "My world is like a river / As dark as it is deep"

"Mickey Newbury - Harlequin Melodies," Album (CD) Liner Notes, Peter O'Brien, January 2003 *Summary:* Review of "Harlequin Melodies" and synopsis of MN's career

"Harlequin Melodies - The Complete RCA Recordings Plus," Mark Brend, Record Collector, June 2003 *Summary:* Well-written review of the CD

"Folks, Shut-up And Listen," Larry Schwartz, August 20, 2003 *Summary:* Article onTroubadour folk club in Melbourne, Australia

"My Memories of Michael and Mickey," Claude Wooley, East Texas Today, August/September 2003 *Summary:* Heartfelt tribute to MN and Michael Hargraves

"A Look At The #1 Country Songs of 2002," Ralph Murphy, American Songwriter, November/December 2003 *Summary:* Statistical analysis of "successful" formula ingredients of 21 top songs

"The Silver Seal," Charles A. Johnson *Summary:* Realistic account of life aboard a shrimp boat

Mickey Newbury: An American Treasure (2-CD set on the Mountain Retreat label), Ron Lyons, 2004 *Summary:* Highly recommended audio biography. May be ordered at www.mickeynewbury.com

# Mickey Newbury Album Discography

## (1968-1988 REF # IS USA LP... 1991-2003 REF # IS USA CD)

**1968** Harlequin Melodies (RCA LSP-4043); released in the UK as Funny Familiar Forgotten Feelings RCA LSA3157

**1969** *Looks Like Rain (Mercury SR-61236)

**1971** *Frisco Mabel Joy (Elektra EKS-74107. Released in the UK as Elektra K42105); Quad as Elektra EQ-4107; 8-track as ET8-4107; 8-track quad as 8Q-4107; Cassette as TC 54107

**1972** Sings His Own (RCA LSP4675). Released in the UK as SF 8268; in Australia as APRS-2001

**1973** *Heaven Help The Child (Elektra EKS-75055). Released in the UK as K 42137. Issued as 8-track as Elektra ET-85055; Cassette as TC 55055

**1973** Mickey Newbury - Recorded Live At Montezuma Hall, San Diego State University, March 6, 1973 (Promo with blue cover) Single LP. (Elektra EK-PROMO 20)

**1973** *Live At Montezuma Hall / Looks Like Rain (2LP Elektra 7E-2007; cassette C2-2007; 8-track T-82007) LLR was rerelease.

**1974** *I Came To Hear The Music (Elektra EKS-7E-1007). Released in the UK as K 42162. Issued as 8-track as Elektra ET-81007; Cassette as TC 51007

**1975** *Lovers (Elektra 7E-1030). Released in the UK as K 52017. Issued as 8-track as Elektra ET-81030; Cassette as TC-51030

**1977** *Rusty Tracks (ABC Hickory AH-44002) *See 1979+*. Released in the UK as ABCL 5215. Issued as cassette and 8-track as ABC Hickory HA 44002 H

**1978** *His Eye Is On The Sparrow (ABC Hickory HA-44011) *See 1979+*; issued as cassette & 8-track as ABC Hickory HA44011H

**1979** *The Sailor (ABC Hickory HB 44017) *See 1979+*; released in Canada as ABC Hickory 9311-44017. Issued as cassette as ABC Hickory HB 44017 H.

**1979+** MCA acquired ABC Hickory and rereleased three MN LPs: Rusty Tracks (MCA-802), His Eye Is On The Sparrow (MCA-803) and The Sailor (MCA-804). The albums have the original ABC Hickory number plus the hot-stamped MCA number.

**1981** *After All These Years (Mercury / Polygram SRM-1-4024); cassette as Mercury / Polygram MCR-4-1-4024

**1985** Sweet Memories (MCA-945); cassette as MCA-945

**1988** In A New Age (Airborne ACD-101) This was the first Newbury album released on CD and was issued in a "longbox." Was also issued as an LP under Airborne AB-101, cassette as R:3765-50101. These were American releases.

**1988** In A New Age (LP - Airborne ABL-61000; CrO2 cassette as ABT-61000) Canadian releases with totally different sound; was immediately recalled.

**1991** Best of Mickey Newbury (Curb D2-77455)

**1994** Nights When I Am Sane (Winter Harvest WH 3301-2); issued as cassette as Winter Harvest WH 3301-4

**1996** Lulled By The Moonlight (Mountain Retreat) limited, numbered edition to 2000, autographed by MN.

> **1999** Lulled By The Moonlight (Mountain Retreat MR 0238 4) "Unlimited" reissue of 1996 album, not autographed

> **2003** Lulled By The Moonlight (MR 1683-2) Reissue of 1999 album. As back cover could not be duplicated, it was redone; face close-up is taken from back cover of Heaven Help The Child; eyes are not as blue and track list print is fainter.

**1998** Live In England (Mountain Retreat MR 0519 2)

**1998*** The Mickey Newbury Collection (Mountain Retreat) Includes 10 albums indicated with *. Released as 8-CD box set.

> **2001** As above but CDs are remastered - with "Digitally Remastered" sticker on front of box.

**2003** Includes new booklet cover and page on MN's passing. *Digitally Remastered* <u>printed</u> on cover & spine.

**1999** It Might As Well Be The Moon (Mountain Retreat MR7488-2) Double CD set featuring (Disc 1) rerelease of 1988's In A New Age (American) with added instrumentation (Mike Elliott), plus (Disc 2) a live 1988 concert. Front spine of the '99 jewel case has "2 CD" in same black tone as spine color. CDs have blue covers of the front and back of the moon.

> **2002** It Might As Well Be The Moon (Mountain Retreat MR7488-2) Rerelease of the 1999 CD, featuring a newly revised Disc 1; Mike Elliott is removed & Craig Nelson (additional bass) is included. Disc 2 is unchanged. Front spine of the '02 jewel case, has "2 CD" in white. CDs have computer revisions of the front cover painting.

**2000** Stories From The Silver Moon Café (LongHall / Mountain Retreat MR 8160-2)

**2000** 'Frisco Mabel Joy (Mountain Retreat MR 1269-2) Reissue of 1971 album w/ bonus material

**2001** A Long Road Home (LongHall / Mountain Retreat MR 1017-2)

**2002** Winter Winds (Nights When I Am Sane with <u>changed soundscape; 4 songs excluded, 6 added</u>) (LongHall/MR 3147-2)

**2003** Harlequin Melodies - The Complete RCA Recordings... Plus (Raven RVCD-158, Australian label) Consists of RCA '68 LP Harlequin Melodies, RCA single Organized Noise, RCA '72 Sings His Own; plus seven "bonus tracks" from MCA '85 LP Sweet Memories.

**2003** Harlequin Melodies (Camden/BMG 82876511532, UK Release) Consists of RCA '68 LP Harlequin Melodies plus RCA '72 Sings His Own

# Mickey Newbury Singles (45's) Discography

## Hickory (recording arm of Acuff-Rose), '65 - '67
Who's Gonna Cry When I'm Gone / Eastham Prison Farm *(45-1298)*
Lonely Place / Well I Did (Last Night) *(45-1312)*
There is a Time to Die / Travelin' Man *(45-1344)*
Anyway You Want Me / (It Might Not Take) Too Much *(45-1370)*
Baby Just Said Goodbye / After The Rains *(45-P-1419)*
Dreaming In The Rain / Leavin Makes The Rain Come Down *(45-P-1463)*

America The Beautiful / Same M/S (dated 1979) *(45-K-1673)*

*Acuff-Rose issued many 1-sided, 10", 45rpm demo acetates.*

## RCA Victor, 1968
Are My Thoughts With You / Weeping Annaleah (pic sleeve) *(47-9570)*
Are My Thoughts With You / Weeping Annaleah *(47-9570)*
Sweet Memories / Got Down On Saturday (Sunday In The Rain) *(47-9632)*
*Organized Noise / The Queen *(47-9690)*

## Mercury, 1969
San Francisco "Mable" Joy / T. Total Tommy *(72975)*
Sunshine / Sad Satin Rhyme *(73036)*
Sunshine / Sunshine M/S *(DJ-198)*

## Elektra - An American Trilogy, '70 - '73
An American Trilogy / Sunshine *(EK-45064-A "Spun Gold")*
An American Trilogy / An American Trilogy Stereo *(E-45329A)*
An American Trilogy / San Francisco Mabel Joy *(EKS-45750)*
ditto / ditto (UK release) *(K 12047 "Treasured Tracks")*
An American Trilogy / Mobile Blue (French: "Glory Halleluiah") *(12 090)*
ditto / Remember The Good (pic sleeve; Kinney, German) *(ELK12063)*
ditto / Frisco Depot (Australian release) *(EKM 46005)*

## TRAV, Remember The Good, Program #132 (18388) ~ 72
Over Remember The Good, MN is interviewed by host, Bill Huie, and MN explains the basis for An American Trilogy. This ultra-rare 4:03 mono 45 recoding was produced by TRAV: Television, Radio, Audio-Visuals, Presbyterian Church, Atlanta. The religious program was titled, "What's It All About?" The backside features a Stephen Stills program.

## Elektra - All Other Releases, '70 - '75
Baby's Not Home / You Only Live Once In A While *(E-45206-A)*
Baby's Not Home / Baby's Not Home M/S *(E-45206-A)*
Lovers / Lovers M/S *(E-45238-A)*
Sail Away / Sail Away M/S *(E-45256-A)*
Mobile Blue / Mobile Blue M/S *(EK-45771-X)*
Mobile Blue / Frisco Depot *(EK-45771-X Y)*
Remember The Good / Remenber The Good M/S *(EK-45789-A)*
How I Love Them Old Songs / Remember The Good *(EK-45789-B)*
Heaven Help The Child / Heaven Help The Child M/S *(EK-45840-A)*
Sunshine / Sunshine M/S *(EK-45853-A)*
Sunshine / Song For Susan *(EK-45853-A / EK-45853-B)*
Love Look At Us Now / Love Look At Us Now M/S *(EK-45889-A)*

## ABC Hickory, '77 - '79
Hand Me Another Of Those / Leavin' Kentucky *(AH-54006)*
Makes Me Wonder If I Ever Said Goodbye / Shenandoah *(AH-54015)*
Gone To Alabama / Westphalia Texas Waltz *(AH-54025)*
It Don't Matter Anymore / Wish I Was *(AH-54034)*
Looking For The Sunshine / A Weed Is A Weed *(AH-54042)*

## MCA Records / Hickory, 1980
Blue Sky Shinin' / Darlin' Take Care Of Yourself *(MCA-41032)*

## Polygram Mercury, 1981
Country Boy Saturday Night / Same M/S *(57061DJ)*

## **RCA Victor - Paris (French issue), 1982
Blue Sky Shinin / I Don't Know What They Wanted Me To Say *(PB 8879)*

## Airborne Records, 1988
An American Trilogy / San Francisco Mabel Joy *(ABS-10005)*

*Mick did not recall recording *Organized Noise* at RCA, but at Elektra. "Produced by Felton Jarvis" is stated on the RCA 45, and this perplexed MN. The versions are quite different; RCA's is softer and simpler.

**Not sure why RCA-France released this rare record in 1982. *MN left RCA in 1968.* The two songs were released by ABC Hickory in 1978 and 1979. After acquiring ABC Hickory in late '79, MCA rereleased the songs. Perhaps, then, MCA licensed RCA-France in 1982... but why? The record had limited market. The songs are the same versions as the 78/79 issues. Is not a bootleg as the packaging is too professional. Is in a pic sleeve.

# Mickey Newbury Music Releases By Label

| Label | Year | 45 | LP | CD | Comments |
|---|---|---|---|---|---|
| Herald | 1956 | 1 | | | The Embers |
| Mercury | 1957-8 | 2 | | | The Embers |
| Acuff-Rose | 1965-7 | | | | Many demos |
| Hickory | 1965-7 | 6 | | | |
| RCA Victor | 1968 | 3 | 1 | | |
| Mercury | 1969 | 2 | 1 | | |
| Elektra | 1971-5 | 11 | 6 | | |
| RCA Victor | 1972 | | 1 | | |
| ABC Hickory | 1977-9 | 6 | 3 | | |
| MCA/ABC Hickory | 1979-80 | 1 | 3* | | *Reissue |
| Mercury/Polygram | 1981 | 1 | 1 | | |
| RCA Victor (Paris) | 1982 | 1 | | | |
| MCA | 1985 | | 1 | | |
| Airborne | 1988 | 1 | 2 | 1 | |
| Curb | 1991 | | | 1 | |
| Winter Harvest | 1994 | | | 1 | |
| Mountain Retreat (M.R.) | 1996-9 | | | 13 | Incl 8-CD set |
| M.R. / Longhall | 2000-3 | | | 3 | To present |
| Raven (Australia) | 2003 | | | 1 | Reissue label |
| Camden (UK) | 2003 | | | 1 | Reissue label |

*Note:* One 45 contains two songs.

# Compilations, Festivals & PSAs

**Zig Zag Festival (Mercury Records Presents), SRD-2-29, double LP, Studio Release, ~ 1970:** MN performs San Francisco "Mable" Joy. Other performances by Sir Douglas Quintet, Jerry Lee Lewis, Big Mama Thorton, Mother Earth, Joe Cocker, Young Bloods, Screamin' Jay Hawkins, Tracy Nelson, Kenny Rankin, Rod Stewart, Blue Cheer, David Bowie…

**Elektra Records, October Releases, Promotional (non-commercial) LP, E-PROMO-7, Sept 1971:** MN performs How Many Times (Must The Piper Be Paid) and Mobile Blue. Other performances by Crabby Appleton, Cyrus, Incredible String Band and Bridget St John.

**Big Sur Festival (One Hand Clapping), Columbia, LP-KC31138 (Reel-CR31138, Canada LP-KC31138) Concert, 1972:** MN performs San Francisco Mabel Joy (duet with Joan Baez) and 33$^{rd}$ of August (solo). Other performances by Joan Baez, Kris Kristofferson, Taj Mahal and Blood, Sweat & Tears. Includes poster featuring MN with above performers.

**New Magic In A Dusty World, LP, Elektra K22002, Studio Releases, 1972:** MN performs An American Trilogy. Other performances by The Doors, Judy Collins, Harry Chapin, Carly Simon, Bread, The Ship, Goodhunter, Curt Boetcher, Plainsong, Casey Kelly, Veronique Sanson, Aztec Two-step

**Promo EP, MN's Remember The Good, Elektra SAM 8, England Performance, 1972:** Also includes a performance by Plainsong and Harry Chapin. Is in a cream-colored, fold out tri sleeve with short bios on each performer by John Tobler (Zig Zag). Back cover states: "Queen Elizabeth Hall 7.45pm 20th October."

**Mellow Memories (later rereleased as The Video Late-Show: Rock And Roll Call), VHS & BETA, ~ 1972:** This is a video compilation of hit songs from the sixties and early seventies. While playing guitar, MN sings (lip-synchs) An American Trilogy, the version from 'Frisco Mabel Joy. Mick's performance is the last one; he closes the video. Other performances by Neil Diamond, John Denver, Helen Reddy, The Association, Bobby Sherman, Jerry Reed, Tommy James and the Shondells, Diana Ross & the Supremes, Nitty Gritty Dirt Band, Wayne Newton, Shirley Bassey, Billy Joe Royal, The Osmonds, Brian Hyland, Loggins and Messina, Harpers Bizarre, David Cassidy, Dionne Warwick and Sonny and Cher.

**Something Out of the Ordinary, LP, Elektra EK-PROMO-18, Studio Releases, January 1973:** MN performs Heaven Help The Child. Other performances by New Seekers, Billy Mernit, Veronique Sanson, Dana Cooper, Curt Boetcher, Carly Simon, Bread, Judy Collins and Don Agrati.

**Elektra Records, Fall Releases, Promotional (non-commercial) LP, EK PROMO 22, 1973:** MN performs Bugger Red Rap and Bugger Red Blues. Other performances by Casey Kelly, Atomic Rooster, Jobriath, Skymonters, Jo Jo Gunne, Harry Chapin, Joni Mitchell & Painter.

**Elektra-Asylum Records, Summer Sampler, Promotional (non-commercial) LP, PROMO 23, 1974:** MN performs If I Could Be. Other performances by Bob Dylan & The Band, Queen, Harry Chapin, Souther-Hillman-Furay Band, Eagles, Chris Jagger, Jobriath, Rod Taylor, Dick Feller, Melba Montgomery, Eddie Rabbit and Jimmy Webb.

**Get Off II, Produced by Nat'l Assoc of Progressive Radio Announcers, LP, NAPRA-2, Stereo, 1975:** Distributed only to radio programmers in 1975, this is a rare LP collection of 30 and 60 second public service announcements (PSAs), featuring ~ 4 dozen rock / pop / folk artists, delivering anti-drug messages. Produced by Richard Perry. Artists speaking these unique PSAs (typically over a bed of their music): Gregg Allman, America, Beach Boys, Chuck Berry, Mel Blanc (as voice of 5 Looney Tune characters), Jackson Browne, George Carlin, Chambers Bros., Deep Purple, E.L.O., Jose Feliciano, Fleetwood Mac, Genesis, Al Green, Herbie Hancock, James Gang, Gladys Knight, Dave Mason, Curtis Mayfield, Steve Miller, Persuasions, Poco, Pointer Sisters, Linda Ronstadt, Seals & Crofts, Carly Simon, James Taylor, Three Dog Night, Mary Travers, Robin Trower, Paul Williams, Jackie Wilson, Johnny Winter, Bill Withers, Peter Yarrow, Yes and Jesse Colin Young. MN speaks his 30 second anti-drug piece over his 1 x 1 Ain't 2.

**AFRTS (American Forces Radio & Television Services), LP, P-15364 / RL 52-5, ~ 1975:** MN performs Sail Away. Other performances by Steppenwolf, Kraftwerk, Helen Reddy, Nancy Sinatra, South Shore Commission, Shirley Caesar, Barry White, The Brecker Brothers, Lettermen, The Jackson 5, Pablo Cruise

**20 United Stars Of America, LP, WEA Musik GMBH 65 872, 1976:** MN performs An American Trilogy. Other performances by Trini Lopez, Beach Boys, Linda Ronstadt; Crosby, Stills, Nash & Young; Carly Simon, Eagles, Emmylou Harris, Gordon Lightfoot, Esther Philips, The Doors, Manhattan Transfer, Bette Middler, Tony Orlando & Dawn, Ella Fitzgerald, Frank & Nancy Sinatra, Roberta Flack, Ike & Tina Turner, Aretha Franklin and Peggy Lee.

**Ride This Train, 3 LP Set, Watermark C774-5, American Country Countdown, October 29, 1977:** Distributed to select country radio programmers, the set contains "Top 45" train songs. MN's Cortelia Clark (studio version) is included. Other performances by Johnny Cash, Glenn Campbell, Marty Robbins, Vernon Dalhart, Hank Snow, The Easy Riders, Roy Acuff, Dick Curless, Doc Watson, Delmore Bros., Merle Travis, Jimmie Rodgers, Merle Haggard, Jim Reeves, Josh White, The Homesteaders, Sheb Wooley, Hank Williams, Everly Bros., Charlie Pride, Lefty Frezzell, Hank Thompson, Earl Scruggs, Arlo Guthrie, Rusty Draper, Kingston Trio, The Eagles, Don Gibson and Dick Feller.

**Bread & Roses Festival of Acoustic Music, LP, Fantasy F-79009, Concert, October 1977:** Recorded live at the Greek Theater, UC Berkeley, California. MN performs San Francisco Mabel Joy. Other performances by Jesse Colin Young, Pete Seeger, Ramblin' Jack Elliott, The Persuasions, Richie Havens, Buffy Sainte-Marie, Country Joe McDonald, Joan Baez, Hoyt Axton, Arlo Guthrie, Boys of the Lough, Dan Hicks, Tom Paxton, Jackson Brown, David Lindley, and a finale.

**Seventy Five Great Country Hits, Four LP Box Set, Innovative Music Productions IMP 98, ~ 1978:** MN performs Funny Familiar Forgotten Feelings. Other performances by Jim Reeves, Waylon Jennings, Don Gibson, Bobby Bare & Skeeter Davis, John Stewart, Hank Locklin, Faron Young, Roger Miller, George Hamilton IV, Willie Nelson, Dottie West, Dallas Frazier, Jerry Reed, Charlie Pride, Alabama, Eddy Arnold, Chet Atkins, John D. Loudermilk, Don Gibson, Dolly Parton & Porter Waggoner, Jim Ed Brown & Helen Cornelius, Tom T. Hall, Jerry Lee Lewis and Hank Snow.

**Blowin' In The Wind, Reader's Digest RB6-183-1/2 / RDK-5568/F, Cassette 2 (also issued as a 7-record set), 1985:** MN performs An American Trilogy. Other performances by The Mamas and The Papas, Kenny Rogers and T.F.E., Gale Garnett, Merrilee Rush and The Turnabouts, Bobby Goldsboro, Sammi Smith, The Nitty Gritty Dirt Band, Glen Campbell & Bobby Gentry, Bread, James Taylor, Gordon Lightfoot, Matthews' Southern Comfort, Joan Baez, Carly Simon, Lobo, Sailcat, The New Seekers, Danny O'Keefe, America and Judy Collins.

**Texas A Musical Celebration, 150 Years, CD - Tomato 2696562, (Double LP - Tomato 2696561), Concert, 1986:** Recorded live at the Austin Opera House. MN performs Wish I Was (Willow Tree), backed up by the "First Take" band. Other performances by Asleep At The Wheel, Johnny Gimble, Ray Wylie Hubbard, Roy Head & Alex Harvey.

**Classic Country, Vol. 6, CD, Pulse PLS CD 506 (KAZ Music UK), 1989:** MN performs Funny Familiar Forgotten feelings. Other performances by Porter Waggoner, Connie Smith, Ronnie Milsap, Willie Nelson, Jim Ed Brown/ Helen Cornelius, Dottie West, Dolly Parton, John Hartford, Michael Nesmith, Norma Jean, Pee Wee King, Danny Davis & The Nashville Brass, Bill Monroe & The Bluegrass Boys

**Country - Soft 'N' Mellow, Reader's Digest Music # 200, 1989:** MN performs She Even Woke Me Up To Say Goodbye. Other performances by George Strait, Elvis Presley, Barbara Mandrell, Jerry Reed, Charley Pride, Roy Orbison, Willie Nelson, Eddie Rabbit & Juice Newton, Bill Anderson, Floyd Cramer, Chet Atkins, Patsy Cline, Eddy Arnold, Dolly Parton, Alabama, Jim Reeves, Ray Price, Kenny Rogers & TFE, KT Oslin, Linda Ronstadt, Sonny James, Bobby Bare & Skeeter Davis, Ronnie Milsap, Don Williams, Jim Ed Brown, Glen Campbell & Bobbie Gentry, Ed Bruce, Dottie Wes, The Browns, Steve Wariner, Waylon Jennings & Jessi Colter, Crystal Gayle, Johnny Cash, The Everly Brothers...

**Country Pikink, Katalognr SX 2865, Polish LP, 1990:** Accompanied by Marie Rhines at a Polish festival, MN performs *Shenandoah* and *She Even Woke Me Up To Say Goodbye.* Marie plays solo on *Big Rock Candy Mountain.*

**Anniversary Collection, Opryland Music Group, Double CD, 1991:** Issued to commemorate Acuff-Rose's half century in business (on Oct 30, 1992), the 51-song set includes three MN songs: An American Trilogy (performed by Elvis), Just Dropped In (performed by T.F.E.) and Sweet Memories (performed by MN - from his '68 RCA Harlequin Melodies). Also included are Willie Nelson, Everly Brothers, Roy Orbison, Don Gibson, Marty Robbins, Patsy Cline, Patti Page, Ricky Nelson, Fats Domino and several others.

**Frank Brown Songwriters Festival, Cassette Vol I-III, Concerts at the Flora-Bama, 1992:** MN performs Genevieve, Gone To Alabama, Birmingham Jail and Ramblin' Blues. Other performances by Hank Cochran, Red Lane, Alan Rhody, Billy Joe Shaver, Jack Williams, Gove Scrivenor, Rock Kilough, Larry Jon Wilson, Larry Butle, Jay Hawkins...

**John Laws Country Collection CD 2, Columbia 474947 2, 1993:** John Laws is a famous / notorious Australian DJ and a Newbury friend/fan. He also covered one of MN's songs: How I Love Them Old Songs (not on this CD). MN performs Let's Say Goodbye One More Time. Other performances by: Freiheit, John Williamson, Aaron Tippen, Oak Ridge Boys, Joe Diffie, Jimmy Buffett, Marty Robbins, Don Mclean, John Denver, Glen Campbell,

Gatlin Bros, Merle Haggard, Highwaymen, Mel McDaniel, Tom T. Hall, Willie Nelson, B.J. Thomas, Larry Gatlin and Chas'n Dave.

**Classic Country - Lonesome Number One, Vol 4, CD, BMG/Castle Australasia, PCD 10038, 1994:** MN performs Funny Familiar Forgotten Feelings. Other performances by: Dolly Parton, John Hartford, Jim Ed Brown & Helen Cornelius, Michael Nesmith, Dottie West, Willie Nelson, Danny Davis, Pee Wee King, Norma Jean, Don Gibson, Chet Atkins, Hank Locklin, Bobby Bare & Skeeter Davis, Connie Smith, Dave & Sugar, Porter Waggoner, Bill Monroe

**Those Were The Days: 30 Years Of Great Folk Hits, 4-CD Set, Reader's Digest Music #220C, 1996:** This is a 4-CD box set containing 84 songs. Also contains a 48-page booklet, detailing the artists and history of each song. MN performs An American Trilogy and San Francisco Mabel Joy. Other performances by Lovin' Spoonful, Bobbie Gentry, Mamas & Papas, Kingston Trio, Seekers, Melanie, Harry Belafonte, Billy Grammer, Kenny Rogers & TFE, Jimmie Rodgers, Harry Chapin, Brothers Four, Bobby Bare & James Taylor, Jim Croce, Judy Collins, Don McLean, Arlo Guthrie, Phoebe Snow, Joan Baez, Terry Jacks, Bellamy Brothers, Ocean, Carly Simon, Nitty Gritty Dirt Band, America, Seals and Crofts, Mary MacGregor, Matthews' Southern Comfort, Brewer and Shipley, Melanie, Nilsson, Dion, Peter & Gordon, Linda Rondstadt, The Byrds, Cher, Arlo Guthrie, New Christy Minstrels, The Youngbloods, Donovan...

**Folk Favorites of the 60s & 70s, Readers Digest - Warner Special Products Canada CPCD-8504, 1997:** This is a 4-CD box set containing 80 songs. Also contains a 56-page booklet, detailing the artists and history of each song. MN performs Sweet Memories ('73 version). Other performances by Harry Chapin, Jim Croce, Carly Simon, Melanie, Linda Rondstadt, Fleetwood Mac, James Taylor, New Seekers, Kenny Rogers & TFE, Donovan, Kingston Trio, Glen Campbell, Trini Lopez, Lovin' Spoonful, Sonny and Cher, Everly Brothers, Association, Jimmie Rodgers, Mamas and the Papas, Judy Collins, Mason Williams, Spanky and Our Gang, Chad Mitchell Trio with John Denver, Byrds, Arlo Guthrie, Crosby, Stills & Nash, Lobo, Jonathan Edwards, America, Nitty Gritty Dirt Band, Bread, Bobbie Gentry, Delaney & Bonnie, Steve Goodman, John Sebastian, Emmylou Harris...

**Stars and Stripes Forever, Vol II, CD, Volcano 32040-2, 1998:** MN performs An American Trilogy. Other performances by The Killer Cadet Band, Kate Smith, The Classic Cohan, The American Philharmonic Orchestra & Chorus, Glenn Miller, The Limeliters, Lee Greenwood, The Spirit of Freedom Singers and Sandi Patty.

**Don't Fight It: Original Versions of Songs That Inspired Tom Jones, CD, Connoisseur, 2000:** MN performs FFFF. Other performances by Brook Benton, Jerry Lee Lewis, Bobby Bare, Chuck Jackson, Lonnie Donegan, Wilson Pickett, Clyde McPhatter, Ben E. King, 5th Dimension, David Houston & Tammy Wynette, Bill Withers, Jerry Reed, Gladys Knight…

**The Spotlite Series: Spotlite On Ember Records, Vol 1, CD, COL-CD-5653:** This is a collection of 25 Doo-Wop songs, mostly from the fifties, on the Ember label. Includes Paradise Hill by The Embers and several songs from The Five Satins, and others (distributed by Collectables Records).

**Mercury Records Doo-Wop, Vol 1, CD, CD5001:** This is a collection of 26 Doo-Wop songs, mostly from the fifties. Track # 14 is I'm Sorry Dear by Don Angelo, lead singer of MN's Doo-Wop group, The Embers. In late '58, the group released it as a Mercury single (# 71580X45) under the name "Don Angelo." The other Embers: MN, James Walker and Chuck "CAG" Gengler sing back up. Guest artist Kenny Rogers plays stand-up bass.

## Newbury Videography (commercial releases)

Mellow Memories (The Video Late-Show: Rock And Roll Call), VHS/BETA, 1972

Swim Team, VHS Movie, Directed by James Polakof, Prism 7502, 1979

A Songwriter's Seminar, 1992

Skins/Gang Boys, Movie, Directed by Wings Hauser, Spectrum SP0808, 1994

Nights When I Am Sane, Winter Harvest WH 3301-3, 1994

# Albums By Other Artists Named After A Newbury Song

After All These Years - Tompall & Glaser Brothers (Elektra 60148)

A Grain Of Sand - Cowboy Johnson (CD w/ 12 Newbury songs: Moon House)

American Trilogy - Elvis Presley (Imperial Records, DR 1124 - three LP box set)

American Trilogy - Vic Willis Trio (Phonorama PR5559)

An American Trilogy - J.D. Sumner (LP: Skylite SLP-6347) (Cassette: SSC 6347)

Cortelia Clark - Josh White Jr. (CD: Silverwolf SWCD 1028)

Frisco Mabel Joy Revisited (Tribute CD w/ 13 Newbury songs: Appleseed)

Funny Familiar Forgotten Feelings - Tom Jones (Parrot PAS 71011)

Funny Familiar Forgotten Feelings - Van Trevor (Royal American RA 2800)

Gonna Plant Me Some Seeds – Jeannie Hoffman & David Friesen (GR 003)

How I Love Them Ol' Songs - Danny Davis & Nashville Brass (RCA APL1-2721)

How I Love Them Old Songs - Johnny Bond (Lamblion 4002)

How I Love Them Old Songs - R. Van Denboom Family (CD: Briarhill FT99-101)

If You Ever Get To Houston Look Me Down - Don Gibson (ABC 9311-44007)

Looking For The Sunshine - Kingston Trio (Xeres Records SCH 1-10006)

Organized Noise - Bill Woody (MCA-3095)

She Even Woke Me Up To Say Goodbye - Jerry Lee Lewis (Mercury SRS67128)

*Albums By Other Artists Named After A Newbury Song*

Sweet Memories - Jack Blanchard & Misty Morgan (Chalice CR 92544, 2-LP set)

Sweet Memories - Ray Charles (London 31C 064 61109)

Sweet Memories - Curt Ramsey's Champagne Quintet (Ranwood 8038)

Sweet Memories - Everly Brothers (CD: Ariola Express 295728-201)

Sweet Memories - Con Hunley (CD: IMMI Records CDSM001)

Sweet Memories - Willie Nelson (RCA AHL1-3243, also as AYL1-4300)

Sweet Memories - Willie Nelson (BMG/Timeless Music - three CD box set)

Sweet Memories - Sue Thompson (Hickory H3F-4511)

Sweet Memories - Sue Thompson (Sundown SDLP 024) (UK issue)

Sweet Memories - Tumbleweeds (BASF 19 25755 6)

The Future's Not What It Used To Be - Waddington Family (Ripchord SLP1065)

You've Always Got The Blues - K. Ceberano, W. Matthews, CD: ABC836055-2

Why You Been Gone So Long - Johnny Darrell (UAS 6707)

Wish I Was - Mabel Joy (Mabel Joy is the band) (CD: Bam Caruso KIRI111CD)


*Albums contain title song or lyric written by MN.*
*Album is LP unless stated otherwise.*

# Mickey Newbury Songs Covered By Others - Alphabetical By Song

## NUMBER

33rd of August - Joan Baez
33rd of August - David Allan Coe
33rd of August - Waylon Jennings
33rd of August - Gordon Lightfoot (unreleased)
33rd of August - Scotty McKay
33rd of August - Al Murphy
33rd of August - Willie Nelson
33rd of August - The Chocolate Covered Dump Truck

## A

Al - Glenn Barber
A Man Can Never Go Back Home - Eddie Albert
A Man Can Only Stand So Much Pain - Tony Joe White
An American Trilogy - 101 Strings
An American Trilogy - Stephen Ackles
An American Trilogy - Alain Morisod & Sweet People
An American Trilogy - Jeff Allen
An American Trilogy - Alshire Singers
An American Trilogy - American Choirs
An American Trilogy - Pawel Baczkowski
An American Trilogy - Barbary Coast
An American Trilogy - Bill Carson Band
An American Trilogy - Juanita Booker
An American Trilogy - Brendan Boyer
An American Trilogy - Bob Brolly
An American Trilogy - Bron's Tones
An American Trilogy - Floyd Brown
An American Trilogy - Sandy Burnett
An American Trilogy - Butch Butler
An American Trilogy - Glen Campbell
An American Trilogy - Canadian Orpheus Male Choir
An American Trilogy - Trent Carlini
An American Trilogy - Johnny Cash (w/ the Goodpasture Christian School)
An American Trilogy - Dean Chance
An American Trilogy -Tony Chance
An American Trilogy - Enrique Chia
An American Trilogy - City of Cork Male Voice Choir
An American Trilogy - William Stanley Coleman
An American Trilogy - John Conlee
An American Trilogy - Johnny Cook
An American Trilogy - Billy Crash Craddock
An American Trilogy - Cumberland Quartet
An American Trilogy - Cwmbach Male Choir
An American Trilogy - Kenny Dale
An American Trilogy - Dealer's Choice
An American Trilogy - DeGlasblazers
An American Trilogy - Sydney Devine
An American Trilogy - Ral Donner (w/ Scotty Moore, DJ Fontana, Jordanaires)

An American Trilogy - Skip Dowers
An American Trilogy - Dread Zeppelin
An American Trilogy - Dreamer
An American Trilogy - Dublinaires
An American Trilogy - Dunvant Male Choir
An American Trilogy - Johnny Earle (titled it, "Glory, Glory America")
An American Trilogy - Freeway
An American Trilogy - John Gary
An American Trilogy - Mickey Gilley
An American Trilogy - Grant & Forsyth
An American Trilogy - David Grayson
An American Trilogy - Jack Greene and Jeannie Seely
An American Trilogy - Sammy Hall
An American Trilogy - Hallmark of Harmony
An American Trilogy - George Hamilton IV
An American Trilogy - Jet Harris/Tony Meehan (of British band, The Shadows)
An American Trilogy - Hi-Marks
An American Trilogy - Stan Hitchcock
An American Trilogy - Ron & Haven Howard
An American Trilogy - T.K. Hulin
An American Trilogy - Indiana University Marching Hundred
An American Trilogy - Ellis James (with the Jordanaires)
An American Trilogy - James J. Johnson & The James Boys
An American Trilogy - Tom Jones
An American Trilogy - Jordanaires
An American Trilogy - Keel & Sullivan
An American Trilogy - Stan Kenton
An American Trilogy - Kimo
An American Trilogy - LA Motion Picture Orch.  ("American Trilogy Medley")
An American Trilogy - Land of Lakes Choirboys
An American Trilogy - Leland Four
An American Trilogy - Les Poppy's
An American Trilogy - Greg London (w/ LA Motion Picture Orch)
An American Trilogy - London Symphony Orchestra
An American Trilogy - London Unity Orchestra
An American Trilogy - Joe Longthorne
An American Trilogy - Charlie Louvin
An American Trilogy - Ray Loverock
An American Trilogy - Keith Manifold
An American Trilogy - Manowar
An American Trilogy - Lena Martell
An American Trilogy - Mike Maxfield
An American Trilogy - Meat Loaf
>An American Trilogy - Midnight Choir
An American Trilogy - Mike Sammes Singers
An American Trilogy - Jody Miller
An American Trilogy - Jerry Morris
An American Trilogy - Morriston Orpheus Choir
An American Trilogy - Motherlode
An American Trilogy - Al Murphy
An American Trilogy - Sam Neely
An American Trilogy - Wayne Newton
An American Trilogy - Joe Paul Nichols
An American Trilogy - Oakridge Boys
An American Trilogy - Nigel Ogden (with Nigel on organ and 14 choirs)
An American Trilogy - Roy Orbison (unreleased)

An American Trilogy - Orion (Jimmy Ellis)
An American Trilogy - Osmond Brothers
An American Trilogy - Osmonds
An American Trilogy - Patriots
An American Trilogy - Pete's Black Art
An American Trilogy - Poynton Commodores
An American Trilogy - Billy Pratt
An American Trilogy - Elvis Presley
An American Trilogy - PJ Proby
An American Trilogy - Ricky D. Randolph
An American Trilogy - Gary Raye
An American Trilogy - Ronnie Reno & The Reno Tradition
An American Trilogy - Rhodes Brothers
An American Trilogy - Rhonda
An American Trilogy - Roy Ridenour
An American Trilogy - Ray Romano
An American Trilogy - Sax Machine
An American Trilogy - Shelfield Male Voice Choir
An American Trilogy - Dale Shelnut
An American Trilogy - Showboat
An American Trilogy - Steve Sifford
An American Trilogy - Singing Cadets (Texas A & M) (arranged by Lojeski)
An American Trilogy - Christer Sjögren (titled it "Glory, Glory, Halleluja")
An American Trilogy - David Solo
An American Trilogy - Spruce Street Singers
An American Trilogy - Ron Stein
An American Trilogy - Stu Stevens
An American Trilogy – Doug Stevenson
An American Trilogy - JD Sumner & The Stamps
An American Trilogy - Tanzorchester Klaus Hallen
An American Trilogy - The Belknaps
An American Trilogy - The Branson Brothers
An American Trilogy - The Carolina Opry Singers
An American Trilogy - The Dallas Boys
An American Trilogy - The Dixie Echoes
An American Trilogy - The Fantastic Puzzle
An American Trilogy - The Goads
An American Trilogy - The Gravel Pit
An American Trilogy - The Jack d'Johns
An American Trilogy - The Journeymen
An American Trilogy - The Lang Brothers
An American Trilogy - The Lettermen
An American Trilogy - The London Welsh Male Voice Choir
An American Trilogy - The Notre Dames
An American Trilogy - The Rankins
An American Trilogy - The Rockin' Royle's
An American Trilogy - The Serendipity Singers
An American Trilogy - The Way Choir (Victor Paul Wierwille production)
An American Trilogy - Kendy Toms
An American Trilogy - Lee Towers
An American Trilogy - Randy Travis
An American Trilogy - Two's Company
An American Trilogy - US Armed Forces Symphony
An American Trilogy - US Naval Academy Drum & Bugle Corps
An American Trilogy - US Navy Band
An American Trilogy - Ricky Valance

## Mickey Newbury Songs Covered By Others - Alphabetical By Song

An American Trilogy - Vocal Majority
An American Trilogy - Lou Vuto
An American Trilogy - Dottie West
An American Trilogy - Westchester Brassmen
An American Trilogy - Danny White
An American Trilogy - Andy Williams
An American Trilogy - Vic Willis Trio
An American Trilogy - Wright Brothers
Angeline - Joan Baez
Angeline - Alex Harvey
Angeline - J. David Sloan
Anyway You Want Me - Gene & Debbe (MN wrote Hear & Now LP notes)
Are My Thoughts With You – Jeannie Hoffman & David Friesen
Are My Thoughts With You - Etta James
Are My Thoughts With You - Mayf Nutter
Are My Thoughts With You - Linda Ronstadt
Are My Thoughts With You - Kenny Rogers & T.F.E.
Are My Thoughts With You - Earl Scruggs

## B

Baby Just Said Goodby - Roy Acuff Jr.
Baby's Not Home - Don Gibson
Baby's Not Home - Roy Head
Baby's Not Home - Diane McCall
Baby's Not Home - Sue Thompson
Beer Drinking, Honky Tonkin' Blues – Billy Mize
Blue Sky Shinin - Glen Campbell & The Nelson Riddle Orchestra
Blue Sky Shinin - Janie Fricke
Blue Sky Shinin - Marie Osmond
Buttercup - Neal Ford & The Fanatics

## C

Come Back Baby - Rogue Show
Come Back Baby - The Sound Investment (with Neal Ford)
Cortelia Clark - Kingston Trio
Cortelia Clark - Lorence Hud
Cortelia Clark - Josh White Jr.
Country Boy Saturday Night - Cowboy Johnson
Cowboys Don't Cry - Waylon Jennings
Cowboys Don't Cry - World Standard

## D

Darlin Take Care of Yourself - BC Craddock
Darlin Take Care of Yourself - R.E. Hardaway
Darlin Take Care of Yourself - Tammy Wynette
Dizzy Lizzy - Roy Orbison (unreleased)
Dizzy Lizzy - Bill Woody
Don't Wanna Rock - Sammi Smith
Dreamin' In The Rain - Glass Bubble (aka The Birdwatchers)

## E

East Kentucky - Toni Jolene (unreleased)

# F

Five Miles From Home - Pat Boone
Five Miles From Home - Jerry Jaye
Five Miles From Home - Tom Jones
Five Miles From Home - Bob Luman
Frisco Depot - Robert Forster
Frisco Depot - Thom Fricker
Frisco Depot - Waylon Jennings
Frisco Depot - Cowboy Johnson
>Frisco Depot - Meredith Miller Band
Frisco Depot - Pat Newbury
Frisco Depot - Rab Noakes
Frisco Depot - Scott Walker
Funny Familiar Forgotten Feelings - Stephen Ackles
Funny Familiar Forgotten Feelings - Bobby Angel
Funny Familiar Forgotten Feelings - Joan Baez
Funny Familiar Forgotten Feelings - Mandy Barnett
Funny Familiar Forgotten Feelings - Larry Butler
Funny Familiar Forgotten Feelings - Calhoun Twins
Funny Familiar Forgotten Feelings - Vicki Carr
Funny Familiar Forgotten Feelings - Tony Christie
Funny Familiar Forgotten Feelings - Floyd Cramer
Funny Familiar Forgotten Feelings - Tony Crane & His Band
Funny Familiar Forgotten Feelings - Roly Daniels
Funny Familiar Forgotten Feelings - Jackie Edwards
Funny Familiar Forgotten Feelings - Gron Eini
Funny Familiar Forgotten Feelings - Liebkind Johnny Eljon
(translated to Finnish by Reponen Pertti, "Kauniit Kuolleet Tunteet")
Funny Familiar Forgotten Feelings - Brian Evans
Funny Familiar Forgotten Feelings - Thom Fricker
Funny Familiar Forgotten Feelings - Don Gibson
Funny Familiar Forgotten Feelings - Craig Giles
Funny Familiar Forgotten Feelings - Arlene Harden
Funny Familiar Forgotten Feelings - Anita Harris (w/ Mike Margolis Orch.)
Funny Familiar Forgotten Feelings - Corey Hart
Funny Familiar Forgotten Feelings - Freddie Hart
Funny Familiar Forgotten Feelings - Helmut Jensen Orchestra
Funny Familiar Forgotten Feelings - Englebert Humperdinck
Funny Familiar Forgotten Feelings - Toni Jolene
Funny Familiar Forgotten Feelings - Tom Jones
Funny Familiar Forgotten Feelings - Pat Kelly
Funny Familiar Forgotten Feelings - Dominic Kirwan
Funny Familiar Forgotten Feelings - Peter Lees
Funny Familiar Forgotten Feelings - Roy Orbison (unreleased)
Funny Familiar Forgotten Feelings - Tony Osborne
Funny Familiar Forgotten Feelings - Kiyohiko Ozaki
Funny Familiar Forgotten Feelings - Jack Rogers
Funny Familiar Forgotten Feelings - Sanchez (reggae arrangement)
Funny Familiar Forgotten Feelings - Neil Scott
Funny Familiar Forgotten Feelings - Ossie Scott
Funny Familiar Forgotten Feelings - Tommy Scott
Funny Familiar Forgotten Feelings - Statler Brothers
Funny Familiar Forgotten Feelings - Geoff StJohn
Funny Familiar Forgotten Feelings - Buffy St. Marie
Funny Familiar Forgotten Feelings - Sue Thompson
Funny Familiar Forgotten Feelings - Van Trevor

*Mickey Newbury Songs Covered By Others -*
*Alphabetical By Song*

Funny Familiar Forgotten Feelings - Ricky Valance
Funny Familiar Forgotten Feelings - Dottie West
Funny Familiar Forgotten Feelings - Ann Williamson


# G
Gallup Ain't Goin' Nowhere - Clay Hart
Gone To Alabama - Swampwater
Good Morning Dear - Pat Boone
Good Morning Dear - Box Tops
Good Morning Dear - Ray Charles
Good Morning Dear - Jim Chesnut
Good Morning Dear - Don Cherry
Good Morning Dear - Tennessee Ernie Ford
Good Morning Dear - Thom Fricker
Good Morning Dear - Don Gibson
Good Morning Dear - Frank Ifield
Good Morning Dear - Lois Johnson
Good Morning Dear - Deanna Marie
Good Morning Dear - Wayne Newton
Good Morning Dear - Roy Orbison
Goodnight - Susan Jacobson
Goodnight - Bill Mullis
Got Down On Saturday (Sunday In The Rain) - Roy Head
Got Down On Saturday (Sunday In The Rain) - Tom Jones
Got Down On Saturday (Sunday In The Rain) - Sonny and Doug
Got Down On Saturday (Sunday In The Rain) - Soul Survivors
Got Down On Saturday (Sunday In The Rain) - Sum Pear


# H
Hand Me Another - Johnny Rodriguez (titled it "Hand Me Another Of Those")
Hand Me Another - Gary Stewart
Harlequin Melodies - Jim Ed Brown
Heaven Help The Child - Chris Fraser
**Here Comes The Rain Baby - Eddy Arnold (Country)
Here Comes The Rain Baby - Don Cherry (titled it "Here Comes The Rain")
Here Comes The Rain Baby - Don Gibson
Here Comes The Rain Baby - Roy Orbison
Here Comes The Rain Baby - Sammi Smith
Here Comes The Rain Baby - Jimmy Soldridge (and the Happy Yanks)
Here Comes The Rain Baby - Jerry Wallace
Here Comes The Rain Baby - J.A. Woolery
Here's To Forever - Jim Ed Brown
Here's To Forever - Margaret Elliot
Here's To Forever - Sammi Smith
Here's To Forever - Sue Thompson
How I Love Them Old Songs - Susan Alcorn
How I Love Them Old Songs - Johnny Bond
How I Love Them Old Songs - Jim Ed Brown
How I Love Them Old Songs - Eugene Chadbourne & Susan Alcorn
How I Love Them Old Songs - Carol Channing
How I Love Them Old Songs - Dakota Night (titled it "Doggone My Soul...")
How I Love Them Old Songs - Danny Davis & Nashville Brass
How I Love Them Old Songs - Don Gibson
How I Love Them Old Songs - Mickey Gilley
How I Love Them Old Songs - Tompall Glaser

How I Love Them Old Songs - Group Contry Road
How I Love Them Old Songs - Cowboy Johnson
How I Love Them Old Songs - Daliah Lavi (German, "Die Songs von Gestern")
How I Love Them Old Songs - John Laws
How I Love Them Old Songs - Eddy Mitchell
How I Love Them Old Songs - Bill Monroe
How I Love Them Old Songs - New Seekers (titled it "Doggone My Soul...")
How I Love Them Old Songs - Carl Smith
>How I Love Them Old Songs - The Hole Dozen
How I Love Them Old Songs - Sue Thompson
How I Love Them Old Songs - Ron Van Denboom
How I Love Them Old Songs - Gene Vincent
How I Love Them Old Songs - Mike & Bernie Winters
>How Many Times (Must The Piper Be Paid For His Song) - Walkabouts
How's The Weather - Toni Jolene (duet with Mickey Newbury) (unreleased)
How's The Weather - Pat Newbury & Danny Tice


# I

I Don't Think About Her No More - Bill Anderson (titled it "Poison Red Berries")
I Don't Think About Her No More - Eddy Arnold (titled it "Poison Red Berries")
I Don't Think About Her No More - Glenn Barber (titled it "Poison Red Berries")
I Don't Think About Her No More - Bobby Bare (titled it "Poison Red Berries")
I Don't Think About Her No More - Anita Carter (titled it "Poison Red Berries")
I Don't Think About Her No More - Eddie Y. Eldon ("Poison Red Berries")
I Don't Think About Her No More - George Hamilton IV
I Don't Think About Her No More - Jan Howard (titled it "Poison Red Berries")
I Don't Think About Her No More - Johnny Rodriguez ("Poison Red Berries")
I Don't Think About Her No More - Wynn Stewart ("Poison Red Berries")
I Don't Think About Her No More - Don Williams
I Don't Think About Her No More - Tammy Wynette (... Him... )
If You Don't Love Me (Why Don't You Leave Me Alone) - Bob Luman
If You Ever Get To Houston (Look Me Down) - Don Gibson
If You Ever Get To Houston (Look Me Down) - Cowboy Johnson
If You See Her - Waylon Jennings
If You See Her - Mabel Joy
If You See Her - Al Murphy
If You See Her - Pat Newbury
If You See Her - Johnny Rodriguez
If You See Her - Petr Spaleny (in Czech, "Kdyz Ji Potkas")
If You Want Me To I'll Go - Don Gibson
If You Want Me To I'll Go – Del Reeves
If You Want Me To I'll Go - Bobby Wright
In Christiansted (Higgins / Newbury) - Bertie Higgins
I Still Love You (After All These Years) - Tompall And The Glasser Brothers
I Still Love You (After All These Years) - Stu Stevens
I Sure Feel More (Like I Do Than I Did When I Got Here) - Joe Stampley
I Sure Feel More (Like I Do Than I Did When I Got Here) - The Uniques
It Don't Matter Anymore - Johnny Darrell ("It Just Don't Matter Anymore")
I Wish I Could Say No To You - Mickey Gilley (titled it "Say No To You")
I Wish I Could Say No To You - Tom Jones
I Wish I Could Say No To You - Ray Peterson (titled it "Wish I...")
I Wish I Could Say No To You - Carl Smith

## Mickey Newbury Songs Covered By Others -
### *Alphabetical By Song*

**J**

Just As Long As That Someone Is You - Jimmy Ellege
Just Between Us - Silver & Degazio
Just Between Us - Bill Woody
Just Dropped In... Rosen Alex
Just Dropped In... Nick Cave
Just Dropped In... Duck's Breath Mystery Theatre w/ Randee of the Redwoods
Just Dropped In... Tinsley Ellis
Just Dropped In... Free
Just Dropped In... Urbie Green
Just Dropped In... Die Haut
Just Dropped In... Betty LaVette
**Just Dropped In... Kenny Rogers & T.F.E. (Pop / Rock)
Just Dropped In... Jerry Lee Lewis
Just Dropped In... Willie Nelson (2001 version)
Just Dropped In... Willie Nelson (2002 version)
Just Dropped In... Mojo Nixon and the Second Edition
Just Dropped In... Wayne Perkins
Just Dropped In... Reef
Just Dropped In... Slim Chance And The Convicts
Just Dropped In... Styvar Manor
Just Dropped In... Supergrass
Just Dropped In... The Turn Ups


**L**

Lead On - Joe Atkinson
Lead On - Cowboy Johnson
Leave Me Tomorrow But Love Me Tonight - Johnny Rodriguez
Let Me Stay Awhile - John Davidson
Let Me Stay Awhile - Waylon Jennings
Let Me Stay Awhile - Al Martino
Let Me Stay Awhile - Smithsonian Institute
Let Me Stay Awhile - Bergen White
Let's Have A Party - David Frizzell
Looking For The Sunshine - Arne Benoni
Looking For The Sunshine - George Grove
Looking For The Sunshine - Frank Ifield
Looking For The Sunshine - Kingston Trio
Looks Like Baby's Gone - Roy Acuff Jr
Looks Like Baby's Gone - The Stonemans
Looks Like Baby's Gone - Larry Jon Wilson
Love Look At Us Now - Johnny Rodriguez
Love Look At Us Now - Joe Simon
Love Look At Us Now - Edward Woodward
Love Look At Us Now - Bobby Wright
Lovers - Kingston Trio
Lovers - Pat Newbury & Danny Tice
Lovers - Olivia Newton-John
Lovers - Charlie Rich
Lovers - Cliff Richard
Lovers - Walker Brothers
Lovers - Kim Wells

322

# M

Make Me Believe - Mickey Gilley
Make Me Believe - Johnny Tillotson
Makes Me Wonder If I Ever Said Goodbye - Cowboy Johnson
Makes Me Wonder If I Ever Said Goodbye - Toni Jolene (unreleased)
Makes Me Wonder If I Ever Said Goodbye - Johnny Rodriguez
Makes Me Wonder If I Ever Said Goodbye - Kenny Rogers
Makes Me Wonder If I Ever Said Goodbye - Kin Vassy
Mary Wanna Marry Me - Neal Ford & The Fanatics
Maurie - Frank Ifield
Maurie - Swinging Gentrys
Mister Can't You See - Bamses Venner (in Danish, "I en lille bad der gynger")
Mister Can't You See - Buffy St. Marie
Mister Can't You See - Glenn Yarbrough
Mobile Blue - Crow / David Wagner
>Mobile Blue - Dave Alvin & the Guilty Men
Mobile Blue - Clay Hart (titled "Mobile Blues")
Mobile Blue - Waylon Jennings
Mobile Blue - Cowboy Johnson
Mobile Blue - Iain Matthews (formerly of Plainsong)
Mobile Blue - Brian Maxine (with Fairport Convention) (titled "Mobile Blues")
Mobile Blue - Jerry Metcalf (titled "Mobile Blues")
Mobile Blue - Ted Roddy and the King Conjure Orchestra
Mobile Blue - Gove Scrivenor
Mobile Blue - Staton Brothers Band

# O

One Times One Ain't Two - Steve Alaimo
One Times One Ain't Two - Neal Ford & The Fanatics
Only You Forever - Gary Buck
Organized Noise - Bill Woody

# P

Pictures From The Past - J.A. Woolery
Poison Red Berries (aka "I Don't Think About Her No More") - Bill Anderson
Poison Red Berries (aka "I Don't Think About Her No More") - Eddy Arnold
Poison Red Berries (aka "I Don't Think About Her No More") - Glenn Barber
Poison Red Berries (aka "I Don't Think About Her No More") - Bobby Bare
Poison Red Berries (aka "I Don't Think About Her No More") - Anita Carter
Poison Red Berries (aka "I Don't Think About Her No More") - Johnny Cash
Poison Red Berries (aka "I Don't Think About Her No More") - Eddy Y. Eldon
Poison Red Berries (aka "I Don't Think About Her No More") - Jan Howard
Poison Red Berries (aka "I Don't Think About Her No More") - Johnny Rodriguez
Poison Red Berries (aka "I Don't Think About Her No More") - Wynn Stewart

# R

Remember The Good - Eddy Arnold
Remember The Good - Brook Benton
Remember The Good - Vickie Britton
Remember The Good - Roy Clayborne
Remember The Good - Harley Cummins (titled it "I Remember The Good")
>Remember The Good - Michael Fracasso
Remember The Good - Thom Fricker
Remember The Good - Randy Holland (titled it, "I'll...")

Remember The Good - Jan Howard
Remember The Good - Claudine Longet
Remember The Good - Wayne Newton
Remember The Good - Roy Orbison
Remember The Good - Ray Romano
Remember The Good - Johnny Tillitson
Remember The Good - Glenn Yarbrough

# S

Sail Away - Charlie Pride
San Francisco Mabel Joy - Joan Baez
San Francisco Mabel Joy - Joan Baez & Mickey Newbury
San Francisco Mabel Joy - Box Tops (titled "Georgia Farm Boy")
San Francisco Mabel Joy - David Allan Coe
San Francisco Mabel Joy - John Denver
San Francisco Mabel Joy - Doug Geeting
San Francisco Mabel Joy - Waylon Jennings
>San Francisco Mabel Joy - Kris Kristofferson
San Francisco Mabel Joy - John Laws
San Francisco Mabel Joy - Kenny Price
San Francisco Mabel Joy - Earl Richards (aka Earl Sinks)
San Francisco Mabel Joy - Kenny Rogers
San Francisco Mabel Joy - Jonmark Stone
She Even Woke Me Up To Say Goodbye - Lynn Anderson (He... )
She Even Woke Me Up To Say Goodbye - Brook Benton
She Even Woke Me Up To Say Goodbye - Randy Brown (Windmill)
She Even Woke Me Up To Say Goodbye - Ed Bruce
She Even Woke Me Up To Say Goodbye - Bob Duncan
She Even Woke Me Up To Say Goodbye - Jerry Garcia (of Grateful Dead)
She Even Woke Me Up To Say Goodbye - Larry Gatlin
She Even Woke Me Up To Say Goodbye - Don Gibson
She Even Woke Me Up To Say Goodbye - Jack Greene
She Even Woke Me Up To Say Goodbye - Stan Hitchcock
She Even Woke Me Up To Say Goodbye - Jericho Harp
She Even Woke Me Up To Say Goodbye - Cowboy Johnson
She Even Woke Me Up To Say Goodbye - Jerry Kennedy & Friends
She Even Woke Me Up To Say Goodbye - Kenny Rogers & T.F.E.
She Even Woke Me Up To Say Goodbye - Diverse Kunstnere
She Even Woke Me Up To Say Goodbye - Jerry Lee Lewis
She Even Woke Me Up To Say Goodbye - Charlie Louvin
She Even Woke Me Up To Say Goodbye - Lonnie Mack
She Even Woke Me Up To Say Goodbye - Jimmy McCoy
She Even Woke Me Up To Say Goodbye - Ronnie Milsap
She Even Woke Me Up To Say Goodbye - Roy Orbison (unreleased)
She Even Woke Me Up To Say Goodbye - Perry Sisters (He... )
She Even Woke Me Up To Say Goodbye - Keith Richards
She Even Woke Me Up To Say Goodbye - Troy Seals
She Even Woke Me UP To Say Goodbye - Roberta Sherwood (He... )
She Even Woke Me Up To Say Goodbye - J. David Sloan
She Even Woke Me Up To Say Goodbye - Hank Snow
She Even Woke Me Up To Say Goodbye - Swamp Dogg
She Even Woke Me Up To Say Goodbye - Johnny Tillitson
She Even Woke Me Up To Say Goodbye – Honey West ("He...")
She Even Woke Me Up To Say Goodbye - Don Williams
Sunshine - Ray Charles
Sunshine - Don Gibson

Sunshine - Sherwin Linton
Sunshine - Juice Newton
Sunshine - Earl Richards (aka Earl Sinks)
Sunshine - Kenny Rogers & T.F.E.
Sunshine - Ray Stevens
Sunshine - Gene Vincent
Sunshine - Scott Walker
Sunshine - Bill Woody
Sweet Memories - Arranmore
Sweet Memories - Nora Aunor
Sweet Memories - Joan Baez
Sweet Memories - Brook Benton
Sweet Memories - Jack Blanchard and Misty Morgan
Sweet Memories - Vicki Carr
Sweet Memories - Anita Carter
Sweet Memories - Ray Charles
Sweet Memories - Don Cherry
Sweet Memories - Brian Collins
Sweet Memories - Floyd Cramer
Sweet Memories - Curt Ramsey's Champagne Quintet (w/ Steve Smith)
Sweet Memories - Jimmy Day
Sweet Memories - Lenny Dee
Sweet Memories - Daniel Donnell
Sweet Memories - Everly Brothers
Sweet Memories - Don Gibson & Dottie West (Duet)
Sweet Memories - Hank Haller
Sweet Memories - Con Hunley
Sweet Memories - Frank Ifield
Sweet Memories - Etta James
Sweet Memories - Waylon Jennings and Jessi Colter (unreleased)
Sweet Memories - Cowboy Johnson
Sweet Memories - B B King
Sweet Memories - Brenda Lee
Sweet Memories - Brenda Lee & Ricky VanShelton (Duet)
Sweet Memories - Hank Locklin
Sweet Memories - Lulu
Sweet Memories - Charlie McCoy
Sweet Memories - Willie Nelson
Sweet Memories - Roy Orbison (unreleased)
Sweet Memories - Ray Price
Sweet Memories - Buck Reed
Sweet Memories - Jerry Reed
Sweet Memories - John L. Riley
Sweet Memories - Buffy St. Marie
Sweet Memories - Joe Simon
Sweet Memories - Lisa Stansfield
Sweet Memories - Lucille Starr
Sweet Memories - Sue Thompson
Sweet Memories - Tumbleweeds
Sweet Memories - Ricky VanShelton
Sweet Memories - Steve Wariner & Dottie West (Duet)
Sweet Memories - Rudy Wesley
**Sweet Memories - Andy Williams (Easy Listening)
Sweet Memories - Johnny Williams
Sweet Memories - Bill Woody
Swiss Cottage Place - Thom Fricker

>Swiss Cottage Place - David Halley
Swiss Cottage Place - Roger Miller
Swiss Cottage Place - Oystein Sunde (in Norwegian, "I Oslo et sted")
Swiss Cottage Place - Sue Thompson


# T
Tell Me A Story - Perry Como
Tempted - Johnny Williams
That Was The Way It Was Then - John Allan Cameron
That Was The Way It Was Then - Brenda Lee
That Was The Way It Was Then - Jerry Lee Lewis
That Was The Way It Was Then - Egbert Meyers (Drents, Nooit meer as toen)
The Future's Not What It Used To Be - Walter Craft
The Future's Not What It Used To Be - Ronnie Dove
>The Future's Not What It Used To Be - Gary Heffern
The Future's Not What It Used To Be - Ronnie Milsap
The Future's Not What It Used To Be - Waddington Family
**Time Is A Thief - Solomon Burke (Rhythm & Blues)
Time Is A Thief - Cate Brothers
Time Is A Thief - Jimmy Elledge
Time Is A Thief - B B King
Time Is A Thief - Pink Industry
Time Is A Thief - Vincent Rocco
Turn That Frown Upside Down - Roy Acuff Jr.
Truly Truly True - Gene & Debbe (MN wrote Hear & Now LP cover notes.)
Truly Truly True - Roy Orbison


# W
Weeping Annaleah - Peter Belli & Four Roses (in Danish, "Hold jer fra Lone")
Weeping Annaleah - Box Tops
Weeping Annaleah - Nick Cave (titled it "Sleeping Annaleah")
Weeping Annaleah - Sammy Hall (with The Birdwatchers)
Weeping Annaleah - Tom Jones
Weeping Annaleah - Bob Shane
Weeping Annaleah - Gordon Waller
When Do We Stop Starting Over - Don Gibson
When The Baby In My Lady Gets The Blues - Colin Scot ("Baby In My Lady")
Why You Been Gone So Long - Roy Acuff Jr.
Why You Been Gone So Long - Bill Anderson
Why You Been Gone So Long - Bobby Bare & Mickey Newbury (Duet)
Why You Been Gone So Long - Big Smith
Why You Been Gone So Long - Stacy Dean Campbell
Why You Been Gone So Long - Anita Carter (of the Carter Family)
Why You Been Gone So Long - Tommy Cash
Why You Been Gone So Long - Coastline
Why You Been Gone So Long - David Allan Coe
Why You Been Gone So Long - Jessi Colter
Why You Been Gone So Long - Lee Conway
Why You Been Gone So Long - Country Gazette
Why You Been Gone So Long - Johnny Darrell
Why You Been Gone So Long - Family Tree (w/ ex-Byrds Skip Battin/John York)
Why You Been Gone So Long - David Frizzell
Why You Been Gone So Long - Don Gibson
Why You Been Gone So Long - Tim Graves
Why You Been Gone So Long - Clay Hart

*Mickey Newbury Songs Covered By Others -*
*Alphabetical By Song*

Why You Been Gone So Long - Kelvin Henderson
Why You Been Gone So Long - Hickory Hill
Why You Been Gone So Long - Hill Mellis & Co.
Why You Been Gone So Long - Chris Hillman
Why You Been Gone So Long - Insane Pony
Why You Been Gone So Long - Cowboy Johnson
Why You Been Gone So Long - Pete Krebs / Danny Barnes
Why You Been Gone So Long - Andy Lee
Why You Been Gone So Long - Brenda Lee
Why You Been Gone So Long - Mylon Le Fevre
Why You Been Gone So Long - Jerry Lee Lewis
Why You Been Gone So Long - Jerry Lee Lewis & Dolly Parton (Duet)
Why You Been Gone So Long - Teddy Morgan & The Pistolas
Why You Been Gone So Long - Bill Oliver
Why You Been Gone So Long - Parker Hill Road
Why You Been Gone So Long - Gene Parsons
Why You Been Gone So Long - Carl Perkins
Why You Been Gone So Long - Phish (with Dick Solberg on fiddle)
Why You Been Gone So Long - Poutnici
Why You Been Gone So Long - Redwing (titled it "Tell Me Baby Now Why...")
Why You Been Gone So Long - Ricochet
Why You Been Gone So Long - Tony Rice
Why You Been Gone So Long - Jeannie C. Riley
Why You Been Gone So Long - Zeke Sheppard
Why You Been Gone So Long - Sammi Smith (unreleased)
Why You Been Gone So Long - Billy & Terry Smith
Why You Been Gone So Long - Smithsonian Institute
Why You Been Gone So Long - Buffy St. Marie
Why You Been Gone So Long - Stained Glass Window
Why You Been Gone So Long - Station (titled it "Tell Me Baby Now Why...")
Why You Been Gone So Long - Ric Steinke & Linda Hausler
Why You Been Gone So Long - Nat Stuckey (titled it "Tell Me Baby Why...")
Why You Been Gone So Long - Joe Sun
Why You Been Gone So Long - Sue Thompson
Why You Been Gone So Long - Uncle Sam
Why You Been Gone So Long - Lorraine Walden & Friends
Why You Been Gone So Long - White Brothers (formerly Kentucky Colonels)
Why You Been Gone So Long - Clarence White w/ Ry Cooder (of Byrds fame)
Why You Been Gone So Long - Jack Williams
Why You Been Gone So Long - Larry Jon Wilson
Why You Been Gone So Long - Jim Wise
Wish I Was - Paal Flaata
Wish I Was - Gamma
Wish I Was - Cowboy Johnson
Wish I Was - Mabel Joy
Wish I Was - Sammi Smith (unreleased)
Wish I Was - Jonmark Stone
Wish I Was - Bill Woody ("I...")

# Y

Yesterday's Gone - Johnny Van Zant Band
You Only Live Once In A While - Glenn Barber
You Only Live Once In A While - Gary Buck
You Only Live Once In A While - Frank Ifield
You're Not My Same Sweet Baby - Thom Fricker
You're Not My Same Sweet Baby - Waylon Jennings

## Mickey Newbury Songs Covered By Others -
## Alphabetical By Song

>You're Not My Same Sweet Baby - Chuck Prophet
You've Always Got The Blues - Bobby "Blue" Bland
You've Always Got The Blues - Debra Byrne and Kate Ceberano
You've Always Got The Blues - Kate Ceberano
You've Always Got The Blues - Cowboy Johnson
You've Always Got The Blues - B B King
***You've Always Got The Blues - Kate Ceberano & Wendy Matthews (Duet)

# Mickey Newbury Songs Covered By Others - Alphabetical By Artist Last Name & Band First Name

## NUMBER
101 Strings - An American Trilogy

## A
Stephen Ackles - An American Trilogy
Roy Acuff Jr. - Baby Just Said Goodby
Roy Acuff Jr. - Looks Like Baby's Gone
Roy Acuff Jr - Turn That Frown Upside Down
Roy Acuff Jr - Why You Been Gone So Long
Steve Alaimo - One Times One Ain't Two
Alain Morisod & Sweet People - An American Trilogy
Eddie Albert - A Man Can Never Go Back Home
Susan Alcorn - How I Love Them Old Songs
Rosen Alex - Just Dropped In...
Jeff Allen - An American Trilogy
Alshire Singers - An American Trilogy
American Choirs - An American Trilogy
Bill Anderson - Poison Red Berries (aka "I Don't Think About Her No More")
Bill Anderson - Why You Been Gone So Long
Lynn Anderson - She Even Woke Me Up To Say Goodbye (He... )
Bobby Angel - Funny Familiar Forgotten Feelings
Arranmore - Sweet Memories
**Eddy Arnold - Here Comes The Rain Baby (Country)
Eddy Arnold - Poison Red Berries (aka "I Don't Think About Her No More")
Eddy Arnold - Remember The Good
Joe Atkinson - Lead On
Nora Aunor - Sweet Memories

## B
Pawel Baczkowski - An American Trilogy
Joan Baez - 33rd of August
Joan Baez - Angeline
Joan Baez - Funny Familiar Forgotten Feelings
Joan Baez - San Francisco Mabel Joy
Joan Baez - Sweet Memories
Joan Baez & Mickey Newbury - San Francisco Mabel Joy
Bamses Venner - Mister Can't You See (Danish, "I en lille bad der gynger")
Barbary Coast - An American Trilogy
Danny Barnes / Pete Krebs - Why You Been Gone So Long
Glenn Barber - Al
Glenn Barber - Poison Red Berries (aka "I Don't Think About Her No More")
Glenn Barber - You Only Live Once In A While
Bobby Bare - Poison Red Berries (aka "I Don't Think About Her No More")
Bobby Bare & Mickey Newbury (Duet) - Why You Been Gone So Long
Mandy Barnett - Funny Familiar Forgotten Feelings
Peter Belli & Four Roses - Weeping Annaleah (Danish, "Hold jer fra Lone")
Arne Benoni - Looking For The Sunshine
Brook Benton - Remember The Good

# Mickey Newbury Songs Covered By Others -
## *Alphabetical By Artist Last Name & Band First Name*

Brook Benton - She Even Woke Me Up To Say Goodbye
Brook Benton - Sweet Memories
Big Smith - Why You Been Gone So Long
Bill Carson Band - An American Trilogy
Jack Blanchard and Misty Morgan - Sweet Memories
Bobby "Blue" Bland - You've Always Got The Blues
Johnny Bond - How I Love Them Old Songs
Juanita Booker - An American Trilogy
Pat Boone - Five Miles From Home
Pat Boone - Good Morning Dear
Box Tops - Good Morning Dear
Box Tops - San Francisco Mabel Joy (titled "Georgia Farm Boy")
Box Tops - Weeping Annaleah
Brendan Boyer - An American Trilogy
Vickie Britton - Remember The Good
Bob Brolly - An American Trilogy
Bron's Tones - An American Trilogy
Floyd Brown - An American Trilogy
Jim Ed Brown - Harlequin Melodies
Jim Ed Brown - Here's To Forever
Jim Ed Brown - How I Love Them Old Songs
Randy Brown (Windmill) - She Even Woke Me Up To Say Goodbye
Ed Bruce - She Even Woke Me Up To Say Goodbye
Gary Buck - Only You Forever
Gary Buck - You Only Live Once In A While
**Solomon Burke - Time Is A Thief (Rhythm & Blues)
Sandy Burnett - An American Trilogy
Butch Butler - An American Trilogy
Larry Butler - Funny Familiar Forgotten Feelings
Debra Byrne and Kate Ceberano - You've Always Got The Blues


# C

Calhoun Twins - Funny Familiar Forgotten Feelings
John Allan Cameron - That Was The Way It Was Then
Glen Campbell - An American Trilogy
Glen Campbell & The Nelson Riddle Orchestra - Blue Sky Shinin
Stacy Dean Campbell - Why You Been Gone So Long
Canadian Orpheus Male Choir - An American Trilogy
Trent Carlini - An American Trilogy
Vicki Carr - Funny Familiar Forgotten Feelings
Vicki Carr - Sweet Memories
Anita Carter - I Don't Think About Her No More (titled it, "Poison Red Berries")
Anita Carter - Sweet Memories
Anita Carter - Why You Been Gone So Long
Johnny Cash (w/ the Goodpasture Christian School) - An American Trilogy
Johnny Cash - Poison Red Berries (aka "I Don't Think About Her No More")
Tommy Cash - Why You Been Gone So Long
Cate Brothers - Time Is A Thief
Nick Cave - Just Dropped In...
Nick Cave - Weeping Annaleah (titled it "Sleeping Annaleah")
Kate Ceberano and Debra Byrne - You've Always Got The Blues
***Kate Ceberano & Wendy Matthews (Duet) - You've Always Got The Blues
Eugene Chadbourne & Susan Alcorn - How I Love Them Old Songs
Dean Chance - An American Trilogy
Tony Chance - An American Trilogy
Carol Channing - How I Love Them Old Songs

## Mickey Newbury Songs Covered By Others -
### Alphabetical By Artist Last Name & Band First Name

Ray Charles - Good Morning Dear
Ray Charles - Sunshine
Ray Charles - Sweet Memories
Don Cherry - Good Morning Dear
Don Cherry - Here Comes The Rain Baby (titled it "Here Comes The Rain")
Don Cherry - Sweet Memories
Jim Chesnut - Good Morning Dear
Enrique Chia - An American Trilogy
Tony Christie - Funny Familiar Forgotten Feelings
City of Cork Male Voice Choir - An American Trilogy
Roy Clayborne - Remember The Good
Coastline - Why You Been Gone So Long
David Allan Coe - 33rd of August
David Allan Coe - San Francisco Mabel Joy
David Allan Coe - Why You Been Gone So Long
William Stanley Coleman - An American Trilogy
Brian Collins - Sweet Memories
Jessi Colter and Waylon Jennings - Sweet Memories (unreleased)
Jessi Colter - Why You Been Gone So Long
Perry Como - Tell Me A Story
John Conlee - An American Trilogy
Lee Conway - Why You Been Gone So Long
Johnny Cook - An American Trilogy
Country Gazette - Why You Been Gone So Long
BC Craddock - Darlin Take Care of Yourself
Billy Crash Craddock - An American Trilogy
Tony Crane & His Band - Funny Familiar Forgotten Feelings
Walter Craft - The Future's Not What It Used To Be
Floyd Cramer - Sweet Memories
Floyd Cramer - Funny, Familiar Forgotten Feelings
Crow / David Wagner - Mobile Blue
Cumberland Quartet - An American Trilogy
Harley Cummins - Remember The Good (titled it "I Remember The Good")
Curt Ramsey's Champagne Quintet (w/ Steve Smith) - Sweet Memories
Cwmbach Male Choir - An American Trilogy

# D
Dakota Night - How I Love Them Old Songs (titled it "Doggone My Soul...")
Kenny Dale - An American Trilogy
Roly Daniels - Funny Familiar Forgotten Feelings
Johnny Darrell - It Don't Matter Anymore (titled it "It Just Don't Matter Anymore")
Johnny Darrell - Why You Been Gone So Long
>Dave Alvin & the Guilty Men - Mobile Blue
John Davidson - Let Me Stay Awhile
Danny Davis & Nashville Brass - How I Love Them Old Songs
Jimmy Day - Sweet Memories
Dealer's Choice - An American Trilogy
Lenny Dee - Sweet Memories
DeGlasblazers - An American Trilogy
John Denver - San Francisco Mabel Joy
Sydney Devine - An American Trilogy
Die Haut - Just Dropped In...
Diverse Kunstnere - She Even Woke Me Up To Say Goodbye
Daniel Donnell - Sweet Memories
Rai Donner (w/ Scotty Moore, DJ Fontana, Jordanaires) - An American Trilogy
Ronnie Dove - The Future's Not What It Used To Be

Skip Dowers - An American Trilogy
Dread Zeppelin - An American Trilogy
Dreamer - An American Trilogy
Dublinaires - An American Trilogy
Duck's Breath Mystery Theatre w/ Randee of the Redwoods - Just Dropped In
Bob Duncan - She Even Woke Me Up To Say Goodbye
Dunvant Male Choir - An American Trilogy


**E**

Johnny Earle - An American Trilogy (titled it, Glory, Glory America)
Jackie Edwards - Funny Familiar Forgotten Feelings
+Gron Eini - Funny Familiar Forgotten Feelings
+Liebkind Johnny Eljon - Funny Familiar Forgotten Feelings
+(translated to Finnish by Reponen Pertti, titled, "Kauniit Kuolleet Tunteet")
Eddie Y. Eldon - Poison Red Berries (aka "I Don't Think About Her No More")
Jimmy Elledge - Just as Long As That Someone Is You
Jimmy Elledge - Time Is A Thief
Margaret Elliot - Here's To Forever
Tinsley Ellis - Just Dropped In...
Brian Evans - Funny Familiar Forgotten Feelings
Everly Brothers - Sweet Memories


**F**

Family Tree - Why You Been Gone So Long (w/ ex-Byrds Skip Battin/John York)
Paal Flaata - Wish I Was
Tennessee Ernie Ford - Good Morning Dear
Robert Forster - Frisco Depot
>Michael Fracasso - Remember The Good
Chris Fraser - Heaven Help The Child
Free - Just Dropped In...
Freeway - An American Trilogy
Janie Fricke - Blue Sky Shinin
Thom Fricker - Frisco Depot
Thom Fricker - Funny Familiar Forgotten Feelings
Thom Fricker - Good Morning Dear
Thom Fricker - Remember The Good
Thom Fricker - Swiss Cottage Place
Thom Fricker - You're Not My Same Sweet Baby
David Frizzell - Let's Have A Party
David Frizzell - Why You Been Gone So Long


**G**

Gamma - Wish I Was
Jerry Garcia (of Grateful Dead) - She Even Woke Me Up To Say Goodbye
John Gary - An American Trilogy
Larry Gatlin - She Even Woke Me Up To Say Goodbye
Doug Geeting - San Francisco Mabel Joy
Gene & Debbe - Anyway You Want Me (MN wrote Hear & Now LP notes.)
Gene & Debbe - Truly Truly True (MN wrote Hear & Now LP notes.)
Don Gibson - Baby's Not Home
Don Gibson - Funny Familiar Forgotten Feelings
Don Gibson - Good Morning Dear
Don Gibson - Here Comes The Rain Baby
Don Gibson - How I Love Them Old Songs
Don Gibson - If You Ever Get To Houston (Look Me Down)

Don Gibson - If You Want Me To I'll Go
Don Gibson - She Even Woke Me Up To Say Goodbye
Don Gibson - Sunshine
Don Gibson & Dottie West (Duet) - Sweet Memories
Don Gibson - When Do We Stop Starting Over
Don Gibson - Why You Been Gone So Long
Craig Giles - Funny Familiar Forgotten Feelings
Mickey Gilley - An American Trilogy
Mickey Gilley - How I Love Them Old Songs
Mickey Gilley - I Wish I Could Say No To You (titled it "Say No To You")
Mickey Gilley - Make Me Believe
Tompall Glaser - How I Love Them Old Songs
Tompall And The Glasser Brothers - I Still Love You (After All These Years)
Glass Bubble (aka The Birdwatchers) - Dreamin' In The Rain
Tim Graves - Why You Been Gone So Long
David Grayson - An American Trilogy
Urbie Green - Just Dropped In...
Jack Greene - She Even Woke Me Up To Say Goodbye
Jack Greene and Jeannie Seely - An American Trilogy
Grant & Forsyth - An American Trilogy
Group Contry Road - How I Love Them Old Songs
George Grove - Looking For The Sunshine


# H

Sammy Hall - An American Trilogy
Sammy Hall (with The Birdwatchers) - Weeping Annaleah
Hank Haller - Sweet Memories
>David Halley - Swiss Cottage Place
Hallmark of Harmony - An American Trilogy
George Hamilton IV - An American Trilogy
George Hamilton IV - I Don't Think About Her No More
R.E. Hardaway - Darlin' Take Care Of Yourself
Arlene Harden - Funny Familiar Forgotten Feelings
Jericho Harp - She Even Woke Me Up To Say Goodbye
Jet Harris/Tony Meehan (of British band, The Shadows) - An American Trilogy
Anita Harris w/ Mike Margolis Orchestra - Funny Familiar Forgotten Feelings
Clay Hart - Gallup Ain't Goin' Nowhere
Clay Hart - Mobile Blue (titled "Mobile Blues")
Clay Hart - Why You Been Gone So Long
Corey Hart - Funny Familiar Forgotten Feelings
Freddie Hart - Funny Familiar Forgotten Feelings
Alex Harvey - Angeline
Roy Head - Baby's Not Home
Roy Head - Got Down On Saturday (Sunday In The Rain)
>Gary Heffern - The Future's Not What It Used To Be
Helmut Jensen Orchestra - Funny Familiar Forgotten Feelings
Kelvin Henderson - Why You Been Gone So Long
Hickory Hill - Why You Been Gone So Long
Bertie Higgins- In Christiansted (Higgins / Newbury)
Chris Hillman - Why You Been Gone So Long
Hill Mellis & Co. - Why You Been Gone So Long
Hi-Marks - An American Trilogy
Stan Hitchcock - An American Trilogy
Stan Hitchcock - She Even Woke Me Up To Say Goodbye
Jeannie Hoffman & David Friesen - Are My Thoughts With You
Randy Holland - Remember The Good (titled it, "I'll...")

Jan Howard - Poison Red Berries (aka "I Don't Think About Her No More")
Jan Howard - Remember The Good
Ron & Haven Howard - An American Trilogy
Lorence Hud - Cortelia Clark
T.K. Hulin - An American Trilogy
Englebert Humperdinck - Funny Familiar Forgotten Feelings
Con Hunley - Sweet Memories


# I

Frank Ifield - Good Morning Dear
Frank Ifield - Looking For The Sunshine
Frank Ifield - Maurie
Frank Ifield - Sweet Memories
Frank Ifield - You Only Live Once In A While
Indiana University Marching Hundred - An American Trilogy
Insane Pony - Why You Been Gone So Long


# J

Susan Jacobson - Goodnight
Ellis James with the Jordanaires - An American Trilogy
Etta James - Are My Thoughts With You
Etta James - Sweet Memories
Jerry Jaye - Five Miles From Home
Waylon Jennings - 33rd of August
Waylon Jennings - Cowboys Don't Cry
Waylon Jennings - Frisco Depot
Waylon Jennings - If You See Her
Waylon Jennings - Let Me Stay Awhile
Waylon Jennings - Mobile Blue
Waylon Jennings - San Francisco Mabel Joy
Waylon Jennings and Jessi Colter - Sweet Memories (unreleased)
Waylon Jennings - You're Not My Same Sweet Baby
Cowboy Johnson - Country Boy Saturday Night
Cowboy Johnson - Frisco Depot
Cowboy Johnson - How I Love Them Old Songs
Cowboy Johnson - If You Ever Get To Houston (Look Me Down)
Cowboy Johnson - Lead On
Cowboy Johnson - Makes Me Wonder If I Ever Said Goodbye
Cowboy Johnson - Mobile Blue
Cowboy Johnson - She Even Woke Me Up To Say Goodbye
Cowboy Johnson - Sweet Memories
Cowboy Johnson - Why You Been Gone So Long
Cowboy Johnson - Wish I Was
Cowboy Johnson - You've Always Got The Blues
James J. Johnson & The James Boys - An American Trilogy
Lois Johnson - Good Morning Dear
Toni Jolene - East Kentucky (unreleased)
Toni Jolene - Funny Familiar Forgotten Feelings
Toni Jolene - How's The Weather (duet with Mickey Newbury) (unreleased)
Toni Jolene - Makes Me Wonder If I Ever Said Goodbye (unreleased)
Tom Jones - An American Trilogy
Tom Jones - Five Miles From Home
Tom Jones - Funny Familiar Forgotten Feelings
Tom Jones - Got Down On Saturday (Sunday In The Rain)
Tom Jones - I Wish I Could Say No To You

## Mickey Newbury Songs Covered By Others -
### Alphabetical By Artist Last Name & Band First Name

Tom Jones - Weeping Annaleah
Jordanaires - An American Trilogy

## K

Keel & Sullivan - An American Trilogy
Pat Kelly - Funny Familiar Forgotten Feelings
Jerry Kennedy & Friends - She Even Woke Me Up To Say Goodbye
Kimo - An American Trilogy
B B King - Sweet Memories
B B King - Time Is A Thief
B B King - You've Always Got The Blues
Kingston Trio - Cortelia Clark
Kingston Trio - Looking For The Sunshine
Kingston Trio - Lovers
Stan Kenton - An American Trilogy
Dominic Kirwan - Funny Familiar Forgotten Feelings
Pete Krebs / Danny Barnes - Why You Been Gone So Long
>Kris Kristofferson - San Francisco Mabel Joy

## L

LA Motion Picture Orch.  - An American Trilogy ("American Trilogy Medley")
Land of Lakes Choirboys - An American Trilogy
Betty LaVette - Just Dropped In...
Daliah Lavi - How I Love Them Old Songs (German, "Die Songs von Gestern")
John Laws - How I Love Them Old Songs
John Laws - San Francisco Mabel Joy
Andy Lee - Why You Been Gone So Long
Brenda Lee - Why You Been Gone So Long
Brenda Lee - Sweet Memories
Brenda Lee - That Was The Way It Was Then
Brenda Lee & Ricky VanShelton (Duet) - Sweet Memories
Peter Lees - Funny Familiar Forgotten Feelings
Leland Four - An American Trilogy
Les Poppys - An American Trilogy
Mylon Le Fevre - Why You Been Gone So Long
Jerry Lee Lewis - Just Dropped In...
Jerry Lee Lewis - She Even Woke Me Up To Say Goodbye
Jerry Lee Lewis - That Was The Way It Was Then
Jerry Lee Lewis - Why You Been Gone So Long
Jerry Lee Lewis & Dolly Parton (Duet) - Why You Been Gone So Long
Gordon Lightfoot - 33rd of August (unreleased)
Sherwin Linton - Sunshine
Hank Locklin - Sweet Memories
Greg London (w/ LA Motion Picture Orch) - An American Trilogy
London Symphony Orchestra - An American Trilogy
London Unity Orchestra - An American Trilogy
Claudine Longet - Remember The Good
Joe Longthorne - An American Trilogy
Charlie Louvin - An American Trilogy
Charlie Louvin - She Even Woke Me Up To Say Goodbye
Ray Loverock - An American Trilogy
Lulu - Sweet Memories
Bob Luman - Five Miles From Home
Bob Luman - If You Don't Love Me (Why Don't You Leave Me Alone)

# M

Mabel Joy - If You See Her
Mabel Joy - Wish I Was
Lonnie Mack - She Even Woke Me Up To Say Goodbye
Keith Manifold - An American Trilogy
Manowar - An American Trilogy
Deanna Marie - Good Morning Dear
Lena Martell - An American Trilogy
Al Martino - Let Me Stay Awhile
Iain Matthews (formerly of Plainsong) - Mobile Blue
***Wendy Matthews & Kate Ceberano (Duet) - You've Always Got The Blues
Mike Maxfield - An American Trilogy
Brian Maxine (with Fairport Convention) - Mobile Blue (titled "Mobile Blues")
Diane McCall - Baby's Not Home
Charlie McCoy - Sweet Memories
Jimmy McCoy - She Even Woke Me Up To Say Goodbye
Scotty McKay - 33rd of August
Meat Loaf - An American Trilogy
>Meredith Miller Band - Frisco Depot
Jerry Metcalf - Mobile Blue (titled "Mobile Blues")
Egbert Meyers - That Was The Way It Was Then (Drents, Nooit meer as toen)
>Midnight Choir - An American Trilogy
Mike Sammes Singers - An American Trilogy
Jody Miller - An American Trilogy
Roger Miller - Swiss Cottage Place
Ronnie Milsap - She Even Woke Me Up To Say Goodbye
Ronnie Milsap - The Future's Not What It Used To Be
Eddy Mitchell - How I Love Them Old Songs
Billy Mize – Beer Drinking, Honky Tonkin' Blues
Mojo Nixon and the Second Edition - Just Dropped In...
Bill Monroe - How I Love Them Old Songs
Teddy Morgan & The Pistolas - Why You Been Gone So Long
Jerry Morris - An American Trilogy
Morriston Orpheus Choir - An American Trilogy
Motherlode - An American Trilogy
Bill Mullis - Goodnight
Al Murphy - 33rd of August
Al Murphy - An American Trilogy
Al Murphy - If You See Her


# N

Neal Ford & The Fanatics - Buttercup
Neal Ford & The Fanatics - Mary Wanna Marry Me
Neal Ford & The Fanatics - One Times One Ain't Two
Sam Neely - An American Trilogy
Willie Nelson - 33rd of August
Willie Nelson - Just Dropped In... (2001 version)
Willie Nelson - Just Dropped In... (2002 version)
Willie Nelson - Sweet Memories
Pat Newbury - Frisco Depot
Pat Newbury - If You See Her
Pat Newbury & Danny Tice - Lovers
Pat Newbury & Danny Tice - How's The Weather
New Seekers - How I Love Them Old Songs (titled it, "Doggone My Soul...")
Juice Newton - Sunshine

## Mickey Newbury Songs Covered By Others -
### Alphabetical By Artist Last Name & Band First Name

Wayne Newton - An American Trilogy
Wayne Newton - Good Morning Dear
Wayne Newton - Remember The Good
Olivia Newton-John - Lovers
Joe Paul Nichols - An American Trilogy
Rab Noakes - Frisco Depot
Mayf Nutter - Are My Thoughts With You

# O

Oakridge Boys - An American Trilogy
Nigel Ogden - An American Trilogy (with Nigel on organ and 14 choirs)
Bill Oliver - Why You Been Gone So Long
Roy Orbison - An American Trilogy (unreleased)
Roy Orbison - Dizzy Lizzy (unreleased)
Roy Orbison - Funny Familiar Forgotten Feelings (unreleased)
Roy Orbison - Good Morning Dear
Roy Orbison - Here Comes The Rain Baby
Roy Orbison - Remember The Good
Roy Orbison - She Even Woke Me Up To Say Goodbye (unreleased)
Roy Orbison - Sweet Memories (unreleased)
Roy Orbison - Truly Truly True
Orion (Jimmy Ellis) - An American Trilogy
Tony Osborne - Funny Familiar Forgotten Feelings
Marie Osmond - Blue Sky Shinin
Osmond Brothers - An American Trilogy
Osmonds - An American Trilogy
Kiyohiko Ozaki - Funny Familiar Forgotten Feelings

# P

Parke Hill Road - Why You Been Gone So Long
Gene Parsons - Why You Been Gone So Long
Dolly Parton & Jerry Lee Lewis (Duet) - Why You Been Gone So Long
Patriots - An American Trilogy
Carl Perkins - Why You Been Gone So Long
Wayne Perkins - Just Dropped In...
Perry Sisters - She Even Woke Me Up To Say Goodbye (He... )
Ray Peterson - I Wish I Could Say No To You (titled it "Wish I...")
Pete's Black Art - An American Trilogy
Phish - Why You Been Gone So Long (with Dick Solberg on fiddle)
Pink Industry - Time Is A Thief
Poutnici - Why You Been Gone So Long
Poynton Commodores - An American Trilogy
Billy Pratt - An American Trilogy
Elvis Presley - An American Trilogy
Kenny Price - San Francisco Mabel Joy
Ray Price - Sweet Memories
Charlie Pride - Sail Away
PJ Proby - An American Trilogy
>Chuck Prophet - You're Not My Same Sweet Baby

# R

Ricky D. Randolph - An American Trilogy
Gary Raye - An American Trilogy
Redwing - Why You Been Gone So Long (titled it "Tell Me Baby Now Why...")
Buck Reed - Sweet Memories

## Mickey Newbury Songs Covered By Others -
### Alphabetical By Artist Last Name & Band First Name

Jerry Reed - Sweet Memories
Reef - Just Dropped In...
Del Reeves - If You Want Me To I'll Go
Ronnie Reno & The Reno Tradition - An American Trilogy
Rhodes Brothers - An American Trilogy
Rhonda - An American Trilogy
Tony Rice - Why You Been Gone So Long
Charlie Rich - Lovers
Cliff Richard - Lovers
Earl Richards (aka Earl Sinks) - San Francisco Mabel Joy
Earl Richards (aka Earl Sinks) - Sunshine
Keith Richards - She Even Woke Me Up To Say Goodbye
Ricochet - Why You Been Gone So Long
Roy Ridenour - An American Trilogy
Jeannie C. Riley - Why You Been Gone So Long
John L. Riley - Sweet Memories
Vincent Rocco - Time Is A Thief
Ted Roddy and the King Conjure Orchestra - Mobile Blue
Johnny Rodriguez - Hand Me Another (titled it "Hand Me Another Of Those")
Johnny Rodriguez - If You See Her
Johnny Rodriguez - Leave Me Tomorrow But Love Me Tonight
Johnny Rodriguez - Love Look At Us Now
Johnny Rodriguez - Makes Me Wonder If I Ever Said Goodbye
Johnny Rodriguez - Poison Red Berries (aka "I Don't Think About Her No More")
Jack Rogers - Funny Familiar Forgotten Feelings
Kenny Rogers - Makes Me Wonder If I Ever Said Goodbye
Kenny Rogers - San Francisco Mabel Joy
Kenny Rogers & T.F.E. - Are My Thoughts With You
**Kenny Rogers & T.F.E. - Just Dropped In... (Pop / Rock)
Kenny Rogers & T.F.E. - She Even Woke Me Up To Say Goodbye
Kenny Rogers & T.F.E. - Sunshine
Rogue Show - Come Back Baby
Ray Romano - An American Trilogy
Ray Romano - Remember The Good
Linda Ronstadt - Are My Thoughts With You


## S

Buffy St. Marie - Funny Familiar Forgotten Feelings
Buffy St. Marie - Mister Can't You See
Buffy St. Marie - Why You Been Gone So Long
Buffy St. Marie - Sweet Memories
Sanchez - Funny Familiar Forgotten Feelings (reggae arrangement)
Sax Machine - An American Trilogy
Colin Scot - When The Baby In My Lady Gets The Blues ("Baby In My Lady")
Neil Scott - Funny Familiar Forgotten Feelings
Ossie Scott - Funny Familiar Forgotten Feelings
Tommy Scott - Funny Familiar Forgotten Feelings
Gove Scrivenor - Mobile Blue
Earl Scruggs - Are My Thoughts With You
Troy Seals - She Even Woke Me Up To Say Goodbye
Bob Shane - Weeping Annaleah
Shelfield Male Voice Choir - An American Trilogy
Dale Shelnut - An American Trilogy
Zeke Sheppard - Why You Been Gone So Long
Roberta Sherwood - She Even Woke Me UP To Say Goodbye (He... )
Showboat - An American Trilogy

## Mickey Newbury Songs Covered By Others -
## Alphabetical By Artist Last Name & Band First Name

Steve Sifford - An American Trilogy
Silver & Degazio - Just Between Us
Joe Simon - Love Look At Us Now
Joe Simon - Sweet Memories
Singing Cadets (Texas A & M) - An American Trilogy (arranged by Lojeski)
Christer Sjögren - An American Trilogy (titled it "Glory, Glory, Halleluja")
Slim Chance And The Convicts - Just Dropped In…
J. David Sloan – Angeline
J. David Sloan - She Even Woke Me Up To Say Goodbye
Billy & Terry Smith - Why You Been Gone So Long
Carl Smith - How I Love Them Old Songs
Carl Smith - I Wish I Could Say No To You
Sammi Smith - Don't Wanna Rock
Sammi Smith - Here Comes The Rain Baby
Sammi Smith - Here's To Forever
Sammi Smith - Why You Been Gone So Long (unreleased)
Sammi Smith - Wish I Was (unreleased)
Smithsonian Institute - Let Me Stay Awhile
Smithsonian Institute - Why You Been Gone So Long
Jimmy Soldridge (and the Happy Yanks) - Here Comes The Rain Baby
Sonny and Doug - Got Down On Saturday (Sunday In The Rain)
Hank Snow - She Even Woke Me Up To Say Goodbye
David Solo - An American Trilogy
Soul Survivors - Got Down On Saturday (Sunday In The Rain)
Petr Spaleny - If You See Her (in Czech, "Kdyz Ji Potkas")
Spruce Street Singers - An American Trilogy
Stained Glass Window - Why You Been Gone So Long
Joe Stampley - I Sure Feel More (Like I Do Than I Did When I Got Here)
Lisa Stansfield - Sweet Memories
Lucille Starr - Sweet Memories
Staton Brothers Band - Mobile Blue
Station - Why You Been Gone So Long (titled it "Tell Me Baby Now Why…")
Statler Brothers - Funny Familiar Forgotten Feelings
Ron Stein - An American Trilogy
Ric Steinke & Linda Hausler - Why You Been Gone So Long
Ray Stevens - Sunshine
Stu Stevens - (I Still Love You) After All These Years
Stu Stevens - An American Trilogy
Doug Stevenson - An American Trilogy
Gary Stewart - Hand Me Another
Wynn Stewart - I Don't Think About Her No More (titled it, "Poison Red Berries")
Geoff StJohn - Funny Familiar Forgotten Feelings
Jonmark Stone - San Francisco Mabel Joy
Jonmark Stone - Wish I Was
Nat Stuckey - Why You Been Gone So Long (titled it "Tell Me Baby Why…")
Styvar Manor - Just Dropped In…
JD Sumner & The Stamps - An American Trilogy
Sum Pear - Got Down On Saturday (Sunday In The Rain)
Joe Sun - Why You Been Gone So Long
Oystein Sunde - Swiss Cottage Place (in Norwegian, "I Oslo et sted")
Supergrass - Just Dropped In…
Swamp Dogg - She Even Woke Me Up To Say Goodbye
Swampwater - Gone To Alabama
Swinging Gentrys – Maurie

# T

Tanzorchester Klaus Hallen - An American Trilogy
The Belknaps - An American Trilogy
The Branson Brothers - An American Trilogy
The Carolina Opry Singers - An American Trilogy
The Chocolate Covered Dump Truck - 33rd of August
The Dallas Boys - An American Trilogy
The Dixie Echoes - An American Trilogy
The Fantastic Puzzle - An American Trilogy
The Goads - An American Trilogy
The Gravel Pit - An American Trilogy
>The Hole Dozen - How I Love Them Old Songs
The Jack d'Johns - An American Trilogy
The Journeymen - An American Trilogy
The Lang Brothers - An American Trilogy
The Lettermen - An American Trilogy
The London Welsh Male Voice Choir - An American Trilogy
The Notre Dames - An American Trilogy
The Rankins - An American Trilogy
The Serendipity Singers - An American Trilogy
The Sound Investment (with Neal Ford) - Come Back Baby
The Stonemans - Looks Like Baby's Gone
The Rockin' Royle's - An American Trilogy
The Turn Ups - Just Dropped In…
The Uniques - I Sure Feel More (Like I Do Than I Did When I Got Here)
The Way Choir - An American Trilogy (Victor Paul Wierwille production)
Sue Thompson - Baby's Not Home
Sue Thompson - Funny Familiar Forgotten Feelings
Sue Thompson - Here's To Forever
Sue Thompson - How I Love Them Old Songs
Sue Thompson - Sweet Memories
Sue Thompson - Swiss Cottage Place
Sue Thompson - Why You Been Gone So Long
Johnny Tillitson - Make Me Believe
Johnny Tillitson - Remember The Good
Johnny Tillitson - She Even Woke Me Up To Say Goodbye
Kendy Toms - An American Trilogy
Lee Towers - An American Trilogy
Randy Travis - An American Trilogy
Van Trevor - Funny Familiar Forgotten Feelings
Tumbleweeds - Sweet Memories
Two's Company - An American Trilogy

# U

Uncle Sam - Why You Been Gone So Long
US Armed Forces Symphony - An American Trilogy
US Naval Academy Drum & Bugle Corps - An American Trilogy
US Navy Band - An American Trilogy

# V

Ricky Valance - An American Trilogy
Ricky Valance - Funny Familiar Forgotten Feelings
Ron Van Denboom - How I Love Them Old Songs
Ricky VanShelton - Sweet Memories
Ricky VanShelton & Brenda Lee (Duet) - Sweet Memories

## Mickey Newbury Songs Covered By Others - Alphabetical By Artist Last Name & Band First Name

Johnny Van Zant Band - Yesterday's Gone
Kin Vassy - Makes Me Wonder If I Ever Said Goodbye
Vic Willis Trio - An American Trilogy

# W

Waddington Family - The Future's Not What It Used To Be
Honey West - She Even Woke Me Up To Say Goodbye ("He Even...")
Danny White - An American Trilogy
Larry Jon Wilson - Looks Like Baby's Gone
Larry Jon Wilson - Why You Been Gone So Long
Bobby Wright - If You Want Me To I'll Go
Bobby Wright - Love Look At Us Now
Gene Vincent - Sunshine
Gene Vincent - How I Love Them Old Songs
Vocal Majority - An American Trilogy
Lou Vuto - An American Trilogy
Lorraine Walden & Friends - Why You Been Gone So Long
>Walkabouts - How Many Times (Must The Piper Be Paid For His Song)
Walker Brothers - Lovers
Scott Walker - Frisco Depot
Scott Walker - Sunshine
Jerry Wallace - Here Comes The Rain Baby
Gordon Waller - Weeping Annaleah
Kim Wells - Lovers
Rudy Wesley - Sweet Memories
Dottie West - An American Trilogy
Dottie West - Funny Familiar Forgotten Feelings
Dottie West & Don Gibson (Duet) - Sweet Memories
Dottie West & Steve Wariner (Duet) - Sweet Memories
Westchester Brassmen - An American Trilogy
Bergen White - Let Me Stay Awhile
White Brothers (formerly Kentucky Colonels) - Why You Been Gone So Long
Clarence White w/ Ry Cooder (of Byrds' fame) - Why You Been Gone So Long
Tony Joe White - A Man Can Only Stand So Much Pain
Josh White Jr. - Cortelia Clark
Andy Williams - An American Trilogy
**Andy Williams - Sweet Memories (Easy Listening)
Don Williams - I Don't Think About Her No More
Don Williams - She Even Woke Me Up To Say Goodbye
Jack Williams - Why You Been Gone So Long
Johnny Williams - Sweet Memories
Johnny Williams - Tempted
Ann Williamson - Funny Familiar Forgotten Feelings
Mike & Bernie Winters - How I Love Them Old Songs
Jim Wise - Why You Been Gone So Long
Edward Woodward - Love Look At Us Now
Bill Woody - Dizzy Lizzy
Bill Woody - Wish I Was ("I...")
Bill Woody - Just Between Us
Bill Woody - Organized Noise
Bill Woody - Sunshine
Bill Woody - Sweet Memories
J.A. Woolery - Here Comes The Rain Baby
J.A. Woolery - Pictures From The Past
World Standard - Cowboys Don't Cry
Wright Brothers - An American Trilogy

Tammy Wynette - Darlin Take Care of Yourself
Tammy Wynette - I Don't Think About Her No More (… Him… )

# Y

Glenn Yarbrough - Mister Can't You See
Glenn Yarbrough - Remember The Good


** In the late sixties, Mickey had major hits on four different charts:
Here Comes The Rain Baby - Eddy Arnold *(Country #1)*
Just Dropped In… - Kenny Rogers & T.F.E. *(Pop / Rock # 5)*
Sweet Memories - Andy Williams *(Easy Listening #1)*
Time Is A Thief - Solomon Burke *(Rhythm and Blues #1)*

*** Soundtrack Australian Broad.  Commission's 8-part TV series "Stringer"

>13 covers from tribute album "Frisco Mabel Joy Revisited"

Cowboy Johnson's 12 covers on 2004 MN tribute, "A Grain of Sand"

The list is current as of April 1, 2004.

# INDEX

# INDEX

# MICKEY NEWBURY ALBUM INDEX

# About The Author

Following the Second World War, Joe Ziemer's parents left Oklahoma for the sandy pastures of Southern California. Joe spent his early years in Bakersfield, a tough oil town. When he turned 12, the family moved south, way south to an even tougher oil town; to Maracaibo, Venezuela, where Joe and his sister Paulette were the only blondes in the country.

Upon graduating from a Georgia military academy as Superior Cadet, he joined a rock and roll band in Maracaibo. The US Army lassoed Ziemer in '68, ultimately assigning him to the top-secret Courier Service in Washington D.C.

After completing his military obligation, Joe enrolled in College of the Redwoods, where he was elected Student Body President. Additional studies at the University of California brought a B.A. in Social Psychology and appointment as a full Regents Scholar.

Ziemer has served broadcasters for 25 years, supplying audio, video and transmission equipment to worldwide radio and TV stations. The profession has taken him to over 100 countries. In 1996, his Indiana company won a prestigious Exporter of the Year award.

Passionate about free speech, Joe was Editor of Radio World International Newspaper from 1984 to 1989. He has written several journal articles.

Joe is happily married to Roxanne and proud to be the father of five children.

Printed in the United States
46438LVS00004B/37